Hubert Eichheim
Monika Bovermann
Lea Tesařová
Marion Hollerung

BLAUE BLUME

Deutsch als Fremdsprache

Kursbuch
Englische Ausgabe

Übersetzung
John Stevens

Max Hueber Verlag

Beratung:
Petra Byll, Nigora Mirzoeva, Miluše Krajčovičová

Dieses Werk folgt der seit dem 1. August 1998 gültigen Rechtschreibreform. Ausnahmen bilden Texte, bei denen künstlerische, philologische oder lizenzrechtliche Gründe einer Änderung entgegenstehen.

€ 3. 2. 1. | Die letzten Ziffern
2006 05 04 03 02 | bezeichnen Zahl und Jahr des Druckes.
Alle Drucke dieser Auflage können, da unverändert,
nebeneinander benutzt werden.
1. Auflage

Redaktion: Andreas Tomaszewski, Andrea Mackensen
Umschlaggestaltung: independent Medien-Design, München
Zeichnungen: Sepp Buchegger
Layout: Cultural Communication, Marlene Kern, München
Satz: TextMedia, Erdmannhausen
Druck und Bindung: Ludwig Auer GmbH, Donauwörth
Printed in Germany
ISBN 3-19-101620-1

Inhalt

Introduction

The **Blaue Blume** (**Blue Flower**), a concept that originated in the period of German romanticism, is a symbol of humanity's constant search for perfection and happiness. To achieve this goal and find the Blaue Blume, a person must set off on a sometimes arduous journey of discovery to foreign lands. Learning the German language is a similar kind of adventure. The student opens him or herself up to a new, unfamiliar world, and enters the lives and thoughts of the people who speak the German language.

Blaue Blume is a German-as-a-foreign-language course covering the whole area from elementary up to the Certificate in German. It is aimed at adult learners.
All the texts are original, and the aim is not just to whet learners' appetite for German, but also tell them something about the people who speak the language. As texts with a rhyme are easier to remember and are a good way of introducing learners to the sound and rhythm of German, the book contains a large number of songs and poems.

Blaue Blume will also enable students to catch up on any lessons missed, or even to learn the language without a teacher.
Thus all instructions and rules are in English. In each of the 54 units, there is also a whole page in English where the texts and their contents are introduced, and information is given on features of language and essential learning strategies. Students are given a whole range of tips on how to access texts, while learning grammar at the same time. They acquire the skills and techniques they need to cope with any situation in which they are exposed to German.

Blaue Blume consists of a *coursebook* with CDs and cassettes, and also a *Handbuch*. This is intended for both teachers and students, and offers the following learning aids: a glossary in which the meaning of new words is explained in English, a key to all the exercises in the coursebook, and the transcript of all the texts recorded on the CDs. The *Handbuch* also contains an overview of all the grammatical structures, and exercises on vocabulary.

Das Gespräch

Cultural information

In this first unit you'll find several short conversations in German. One of them is an excerpt from a phone conversation with the well-known German satirist, Gerhard Polt. The unit revolves round the first contact we make with another person, how to greet them. The form of greeting varies from one German-speaking country to another, and one region to another. Actually, it's only about fifty years ago that standard German, the variety of German you'll be learning in this course, was spoken only in very educated circles and the big cities. Ordinary people spoke a dialect. With the exception of Switzerland, dialect use is becoming less and less common, although it is still to be heard in all areas.

One thing common to greetings in all regions is that people keep them short. In the working world in particular, people tend to say a quick word of greeting and then get straight down to business. That can come as something of a shock to foreigners, who often find it impolite, although it in fact isn't. Like many other languages, German differentiates between a polite form of address *Sie* ("you") and a more intimate one, *du, ihr* ("you" singular, and "you" plural). As you work your way through the book, watch out for when *du* is used and when *Sie,* and see what relationship the people have.

Learning strategies

The sentences in the texts are not broken down into their individual components and explained in detail. Get into the habit of learning sections of conversation as a whole without going into a grammatical analysis. The sentence *Kannst du mir helfen?* (Can you help me?) contains four words and a number of features of grammar that are not explained at this point. But you can still understand the sentence and use it correctly. Some grammar features appear quite a few times before their formal structure is explained.

Pronunciation

This first unit focusses on spoken language and the sound of it. Before you start concentrating on the correct formation of individual sounds, you should have a look at the melody and rhythm of the German language. Intonation, the stressing of words in a sentence, and emotional expression in combination with gestures and facial expressions also affect the meaning of an utterance. These elements can already tell you a lot about the meaning of the actual message.

German differentiates between falling ↘, rising ↗ and level → intonation. This determines whether an utterance appears complete, has a questioning tone, or whether a continuation is to be expected. If you listen intently to the intonation and the way individual words and whole sentences are accentuated, if you hum the melody and repeat the sentences on the cassette, you'll get a feeling for the sound of German and gradually develop a pronunciation with which you'll be able to make yourself understood.

Das Gespräch

1 a Listen to the conversation.

Das Gespräch

Hmmm
Was?
Hmmm
Hä?
Hmmm
Ha, ha, ha,
Hmmm

Norbert Höchtlen

b Try to imagine a possible situation: Who is talking to whom and where?
What might *Hmmm* mean?

2 **a** Listen to two conversations and look at the drawings below.
Which conversation goes with picture A, which with picture B? Enter the numbers in the boxes.

b Listen and read.

conversation 1

Das finde ich toll!
Was?
Genial ist das!
Hä?
Ein Meisterwerk!
Ha, ha, ha.
Du hast ja keine Ahnung!

conversation 2

Kannst du mir helfen?
Was?
Ich brauche Geld.
Hä?
2000 Euro.
Ha, ha, ha.
Bitte, du musst mir helfen!

c Listen to the conversations again and repeat: First just hum the intonation of the sentence, then repeat it.

Ja der Erwin!

3 **a** Listen to the conversation and answer the questions: Where are we? Who is talking to whom?

b Which words and expressions did you understand?

4 Listen and read.

greeting someone

Hallo! – Guten Tag! – Grüß Gott!
Grüezi! – Servus!

asking how someone is

Wie geht es Ihnen? – Wie geht es dir?
Wie geht's?

saying how you feel

Danke, gut. – Sehr gut, danke.
Es geht. – Schlecht.

reacting to it

Schön! – Gut! – Tut mir Leid.

asking someone to repeat the question

Wie bitte? – Was? – Warum?

reacting to the reply

Ach so. – Ja so. – Schade!

replying to a question positively

Klar! – O.K. – Natürlich!

ending a conversation

Ja, also ... – Also dann ... – O.K. dann ...

taking one's leave

Auf Wiedersehen! – Auf Wiederhören!
Ciao! – Tschüs! – Servus!

5 Please listen to the telephone conversation again. Underline in section 4 which words/expressions you hear.

Intonation: Satzmelodie, Satzakzent

Intonation

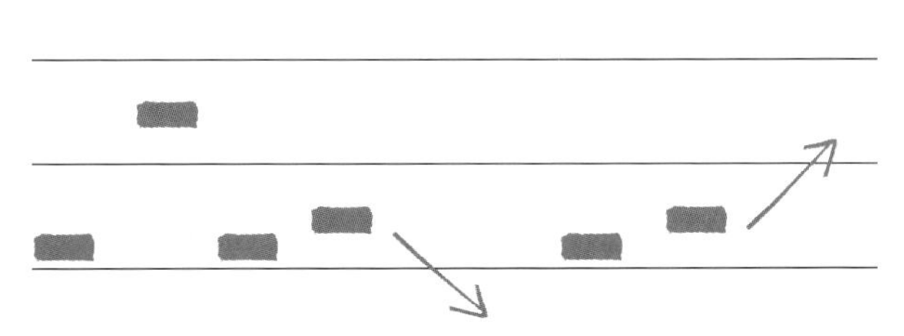

Wie geht es Ihnen? Wie bitte?

Sentence stress

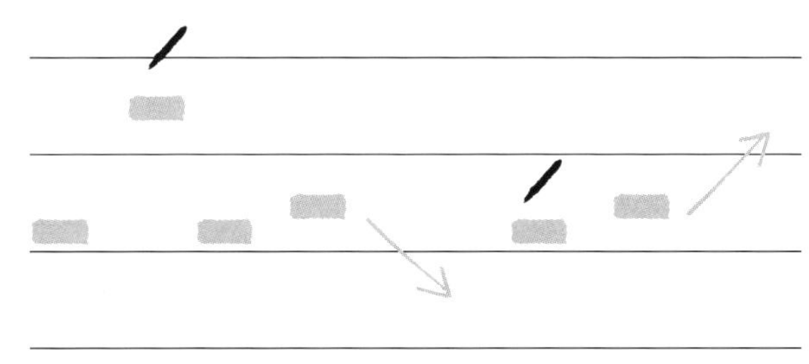

Wie geht es Ihnen? Wie bitte?

6 **a** Listen and repeat. Pay attention to intonation and stress.

Intonation falls ↘ or rises ↗ at the end of the sentence. The word with a stress mark has a higher or lower pitch and you speak more loudly.

b Listen again and read.

Hallo! ↘ – Guten Tag! ↘ Wie geht es Ihnen? ↘ – Wie geht es dir? ↘ Danke gut. ↘ – Es geht. ↘ Wie bitte? ↗ – Warum? ↗ Ach so. ↘ – Natürlich! ↘ Auf Wiedersehen! ↘ – Auf Wiederhören! ↘

7 **a** Write a telephone conversation in German and English. One person speaks German using expressions from section 4, the other asks and replies in English.

b Act out the telephone conversation.

Hallo, Sie!

8 The title of the cartoon is:
"A secret remains a secret!"
What kind of secret do you think it is?
Underline the words and expressions you understand in the speech bubbles.

9 Which of the texts below go with speech bubble A, B, or C of the cartoon?
Enter the letters in the boxes.

1 And you? Do you know my name?

2 I thought so.

3 Do you know my name?

A

B

C

10 Read, then translate into English.

Hallo, Sie! ....

more polite: Entschuldigung! ....

Entschuldigen Sie! ....

Hallo, du! ....

more polite: Entschuldigung! Entschuldige! ....

Wie heißen Sie? ....

Wie heißt du? ....

Wie ist Ihr Name? ....

Wie ist dein Name? ....

Mein Name ist ... .

Ich heiße ... .

Intonation: Satzmelodie, Satzakzent

11 a Listen and read.

Entschuldigung. ↘ – Entschuldigen Sie. ↘ Wie heißen Sie? ↘ – Wie ist Ihr Name? ↘

- Entschuldigung. ↘ Wie heißen Sie? ↘
- Mein Name ist Becker. ↘
  Und wie heißen Sie? ↗

- Entschuldigung! ↗
- Ja, bitte? ↗
- Wie ist Ihr Name? ↘
- Ich heiße Petra. ↘ Und Sie? ↗

b Listen again and repeat.

12 Listen and indicate the intonation ↘ ↗ and stress ´.

- Entschuldigung. Wie heißt du?
- Ich heiße Inga. Und du?

- Entschuldige.
- Ja, bitte?
- Wie heißt du?
- Martin. Und du?

13 Make short dialogues with the expressions from sections 10 and 4.

14 Read form 1 and enter your particulars in form 2.

1

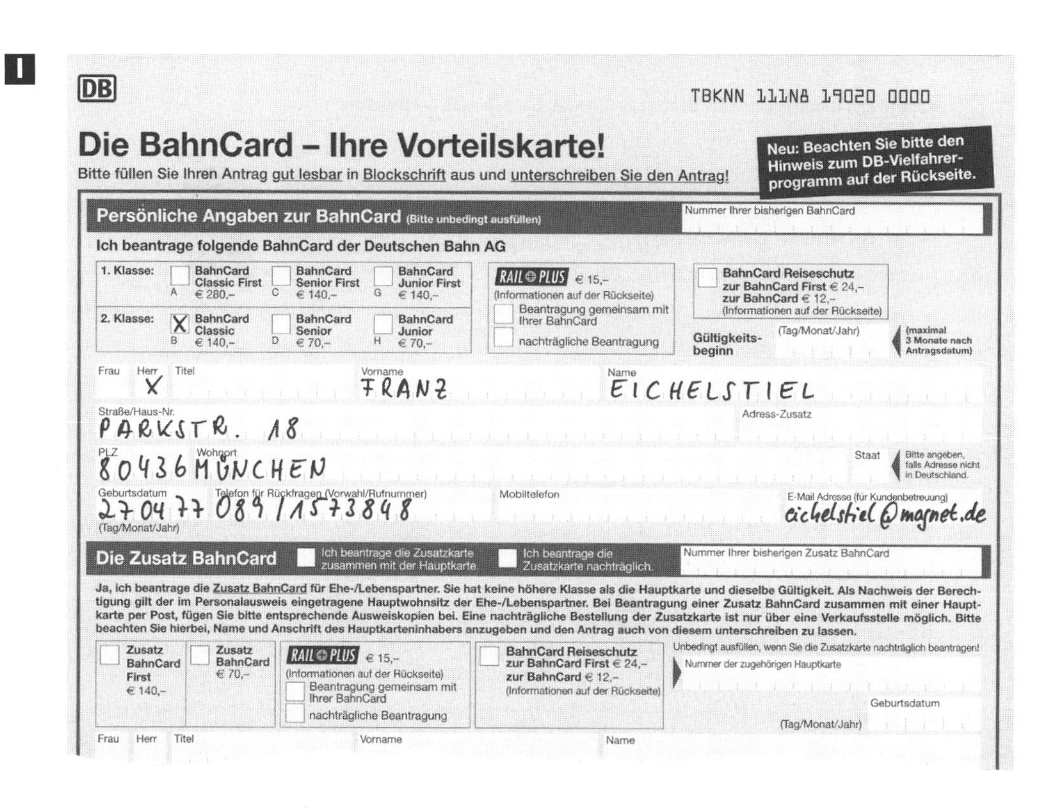

DB TBKNN 111N8 19020 0000

Die BahnCard – Ihre Vorteilskarte!

Bitte füllen Sie Ihren Antrag gut lesbar in Blockschrift aus und unterschreiben Sie den Antrag!

Neu: Beachten Sie bitte den Hinweis zum DB-Vielfahrerprogramm auf der Rückseite.

Persönliche Angaben zur BahnCard (Bitte unbedingt ausfüllen) — Nummer Ihrer bisherigen BahnCard

Ich beantrage folgende BahnCard der Deutschen Bahn AG

1. Klasse:	A ☐ BahnCard Classic First € 280,–	C ☐ BahnCard Senior First € 140,–	G ☐ BahnCard Junior First € 140,–
2. Klasse:	B ☒ BahnCard Classic € 140,–	D ☐ BahnCard Senior € 70,–	H ☐ BahnCard Junior € 70,–

RAIL PLUS € 15,– (Informationen auf der Rückseite)
☐ Beantragung gemeinsam mit Ihrer BahnCard
☐ nachträgliche Beantragung

☐ BahnCard Reiseschutz zur BahnCard First € 24,– zur BahnCard € 12,– (Informationen auf der Rückseite)

Gültigkeitsbeginn (Tag/Monat/Jahr) (maximal 3 Monate nach Antragsdatum)

Frau | Herr: X | Titel | Vorname: FRANZ | Name: EICHELSTIEL

Straße/Haus-Nr.: PARKSTR. 18 | Adress-Zusatz

PLZ: 80436 | Wohnort: MÜNCHEN | Staat (Bitte angeben, falls Adresse nicht in Deutschland)

Geburtsdatum (Tag/Monat/Jahr): 27 04 77 | Telefon für Rückfragen (Vorwahl/Rufnummer): 089/1573848 | Mobiltelefon | E-Mail Adresse (für Kundenbetreuung): eichelstiel@magnet.de

Die Zusatz BahnCard ☐ Ich beantrage die Zusatzkarte zusammen mit der Hauptkarte. ☐ Ich beantrage die Zusatzkarte nachträglich. — Nummer Ihrer bisherigen Zusatz BahnCard

Ja, ich beantrage die Zusatz BahnCard für Ehe-/Lebenspartner. Sie hat keine höhere Klasse als die Hauptkarte und dieselbe Gültigkeit. Als Nachweis der Berechtigung gilt der im Personalausweis eingetragene Hauptwohnsitz der Ehe-/Lebenspartner. Bei Beantragung einer Zusatz BahnCard zusammen mit einer Hauptkarte per Post, fügen Sie bitte entsprechende Ausweiskopien bei. Eine nachträgliche Bestellung der Zusatzkarte ist nur über eine Verkaufsstelle möglich. Bitte beachten Sie hierbei, Name und Anschrift des Hauptkarteninhabers anzugeben und den Antrag auch von diesem unterschreiben zu lassen.

☐ Zusatz BahnCard First € 140,– | ☐ Zusatz BahnCard € 70,– | RAIL PLUS € 15,– (Informationen auf der Rückseite) ☐ Beantragung gemeinsam mit Ihrer BahnCard ☐ nachträgliche Beantragung | ☐ BahnCard Reiseschutz zur BahnCard First € 24,– zur BahnCard € 12,– (Informationen auf der Rückseite)

Unbedingt ausfüllen, wenn Sie die Zusatzkarte nachträglich beantragen! Nummer der zugehörigen Hauptkarte — Geburtsdatum (Tag/Monat/Jahr)

Frau | Herr | Titel | Vorname | Name

2

DB TBKNN 111N8 19020 0000

Die BahnCard – Ihre Vorteilskarte!

Bitte füllen Sie Ihren Antrag gut lesbar in Blockschrift aus und unterschreiben Sie den Antrag!

Neu: Beachten Sie bitte den Hinweis zum DB-Vielfahrerprogramm auf der Rückseite.

Persönliche Angaben zur BahnCard (Bitte unbedingt ausfüllen) — Nummer Ihrer bisherigen BahnCard

Ich beantrage folgende BahnCard der Deutschen Bahn AG

1. Klasse:	A ☐ BahnCard Classic First € 280,–	C ☐ BahnCard Senior First € 140,–	G ☐ BahnCard Junior First € 140,–
2. Klasse:	B ☐ BahnCard Classic € 140,–	D ☐ BahnCard Senior € 70,–	H ☐ BahnCard Junior € 70,–

RAIL PLUS € 15,– (Informationen auf der Rückseite)
☐ Beantragung gemeinsam mit Ihrer BahnCard
☐ nachträgliche Beantragung

☐ BahnCard Reiseschutz zur BahnCard First € 24,– zur BahnCard € 12,– (Informationen auf der Rückseite)

Gültigkeitsbeginn (Tag/Monat/Jahr) (maximal 3 Monate nach Antragsdatum)

Frau | Herr | Titel | Vorname | Name

Straße/Haus-Nr. | Adress-Zusatz

PLZ | Wohnort | Staat (Bitte angeben, falls Adresse nicht in Deutschland)

Geburtsdatum (Tag/Monat/Jahr) | Telefon für Rückfragen (Vorwahl/Rufnummer) | Mobiltelefon | E-Mail Adresse (für Kundenbetreuung)

Die Zusatz BahnCard ☐ Ich beantrage die Zusatzkarte zusammen mit der Hauptkarte. ☐ Ich beantrage die Zusatzkarte nachträglich. — Nummer Ihrer bisherigen Zusatz BahnCard

Ja, ich beantrage die Zusatz BahnCard für Ehe-/Lebenspartner. Sie hat keine höhere Klasse als die Hauptkarte und dieselbe Gültigkeit. Als Nachweis der Berechtigung gilt der im Personalausweis eingetragene Hauptwohnsitz der Ehe-/Lebenspartner. Bei Beantragung einer Zusatz BahnCard zusammen mit einer Hauptkarte per Post, fügen Sie bitte entsprechende Ausweiskopien bei. Eine nachträgliche Bestellung der Zusatzkarte ist nur über eine Verkaufsstelle möglich. Bitte beachten Sie hierbei, Name und Anschrift des Hauptkarteninhabers anzugeben und den Antrag auch von diesem unterschreiben zu lassen.

☐ Zusatz BahnCard First € 140,– | ☐ Zusatz BahnCard € 70,– | RAIL PLUS € 15,– (Informationen auf der Rückseite) ☐ Beantragung gemeinsam mit Ihrer BahnCard ☐ nachträgliche Beantragung | ☐ BahnCard Reiseschutz zur BahnCard First € 24,– zur BahnCard € 12,– (Informationen auf der Rückseite)

Unbedingt ausfüllen, wenn Sie die Zusatzkarte nachträglich beantragen! Nummer der zugehörigen Hauptkarte — Geburtsdatum (Tag/Monat/Jahr)

Frau | Herr | Titel | Vorname | Name

Dualismus

The texts

Your introduction to written German makes use of two texts from different periods. The first is a contemporary poem about the contrasts we find in the world. The other is an excerpt from the oldest German-Latin picture dictionary, dating back to the 16th century. "Orbis sensualium pictus" (The visible world) was the name the educationalist Johann Amos Comenius gave his dictionary, an invaluable aid when learning a foreign language. The entry "Himmel" (sky) will give you a taste of what it contains.

JOH. AMOS COMMENII,
ORBIS SEN-
SUALIUM PICTUS.
Hoc est,
Omnium fundamentalium in Mundo Re-
rum & in Vitâ Actionum
Pictura & Nomenclatura.
Die sichtbare Welt /
Das ist /
Aller vornemsten Welt-Dinge und Le-
bens-Verrichtungen
Vorbildung und Benahmung.
REBUS · OMNIA SPONTE FLUANT ABSIT VIOLENTIA
NORIBERGÆ,
Typis & Sumptibus MICHAELIS ENDTERI.
Anno Salutis cIↄ Iↄc LVIII.

Learning strategies

Don't be put off when you come across words you don't understand when reading a text. The main thing is to learn quickly how to work out the meaning of texts and sentences that include language that is unfamiliar to you. Strategies include:

- recognizing the word class, its form and function
- working out the meanings from the context and other factors
- accessing any missing information in a dictionary.

There is little sense in approaching this on a theoretical level, without any concrete context, so you can try the techniques out on the texts "Dualismus" and "Der Himmel". You should use the third text about Comenius' biography to try working out meaning and content without recourse to a dictionary.

Language

Mein Name ist Becker.

As in most other languages, there are two word classes that play a major role in German sentences: the noun (das Nomen), used to denote living beings, objects, events and abstract concepts, and the verb (das Verb), whose main role is to express what these living beings do or what happens to objects or concepts. Unlike in nearly all other languages, German nouns are spelt with a capital letter. They also have an article (der Artikel). If you look up a noun in a dictionary, information about the article will indicate what gender the noun has (*der* = masculine, *die* = feminine, *das* = neuter) and often what the plural form is. The best thing is to learn every noun with its article and plural form.

Capital letters are also used in German at the beginning of a sentence or when a word from another word class is used as a noun. In the poem "Dualismus" you'll find nominalized verbs, e.g. *stehen* – *Stehen* (stand, standing) and adverbs, e.g. *oben* – *Oben* (above).

Dualismus

1 The world consists of contrasts and opposites. Which pairs of contrasts and opposites can you think of? Take notes in English.

2 a Listen to the poem and read. Did you recognise any of the contrasts? If so, make notes in English.

b What could be the function and the meaning of the word *und*?

c Now look up the words on the left (in front of *und*) which you have not understood in a dictionary and write down their meaning in English.

d Which do you think is the corresponding contrast? Guess first, then check in the dictionary.

Dualismus

Himmel und Hölle,
Meer und Strand,
Ebbe und Flut,
Tag und Nacht,
Oben und Unten,
Links und Rechts,
Stehen und Liegen,
Dienen und Beherrschen,
Liebe und Tod,
Krieg und Frieden,
Gott und Teufel,
Hass und Vergebung.

Der Kompromiss
heißt
Mensch.

Hans Jürgen Schumacher

3 This is how Comenius presented the entry in *Der Mensch* in "Orbis Pictus". Which of the terms from the poem can you also find in the wood engraving? Make notes.

Homo.

Der Mensch.

Wortarten

4 You can find five different parts of speech in the poem: noun, adverb, conjunction, verb and article.

a Which extract from the dictionary represents which part of speech? Write the term above the extract.

b Find the different parts of speech in the poem and write them below the extract.

Tag *der;* -*(e)s,* -*e;* **1** der Zeitraum von 24 Stunden (zwischen 0⁰⁰ u. 24⁰⁰ Uhr): *Die Woche hat sieben Tage; „Welchen Tag haben wir heute?/Was ist heu-*

Himmel, ...

hei·ßen; *hieß, hat geheißen;* [Vi] **1** *(Name +)* ***h.*** e-n bestimmten Namen haben: *„Wie heißen Sie?" – „Ich heiße Helga Huber"; Wie heißt er denn mit*

der[1], *die, das; bestimmter Artikel;* **1** verwendet vor Substantiven, die etw. einmalig Vorhandenes bezeichnen: *die Erde, der Mond, die UNO usw* **2** ver-

adverb

und *Konjunktion;* **1** verwendet, um (in e-r Art Aufzählung) einzelne Wörter, Satzteile od. Sätze miteinander zu verbinden: *Susanne und Monika; ein*

un·ten *Adv;* **1** an e-r Stelle, die *(mst* vom Sprecher od. vom Handelnden aus gesehen) tiefer als e-e andere Stelle liegt: *Auf den Bergen liegt noch viel Schnee,*

5 These are further examples from two different dictionaries. Note how they present the individual parts of speech.

Der Artikel

word stress / long *e* — part of speech

der, bestimmter Artikel

pronunciation — part of speech

der [deːɐ] **I.** art **1.** Nom sg

Das Nomen

article — plural

Nacht die; -, Näch-te

word stress / short *a*

word stress — pronunciation — plural — gender

Nacht [ˈnaxt, pl. ˈnɛçtə] < -, Nächte >f

Das Verb

infinitive

hei·ßen; hieß, hat geheißen; [Vi]

division

present — past — perfect — part of speech

heißen [ˈhaisn] <heißt, hieß, geheißen> I. vi

Die Konjunktion

part of speech

und Konjunktion

pronunciation — part of speech

und [ˈʊnt] konj

Das Adverb

division — part of speech

un-ten adv

6 Make a list of the nouns which you have come across so far, with articles and plurals.

7 a Try to find words you already know in the text "Der Himmel".
Then compare picture and text. Note the numbering.

Der **Himmel** 1

Dreht sich
und geht
um die **Erde** 2
die in der Mitte steht
Die **Sonne** 3
wo sie ist
scheint immer
auch wenn
die **Wolken** (das Gewölk) 4
sie uns nehmen
und macht mit ihren **Strahlen** 5
das **Licht**
das Licht, den **Tag**.
Gegenüber
ist die **Finsternis** 6
daher die **Nacht**.
Bei Nacht
scheint der **Mond** 7
und die **Sterne** 8
schimmern / blinken.
Abends 9
ist die **Dämmerung**:
Morgens
die **Morgenröte** 10
und das Tagen.

Cœlum.

Der Himmel.

Comenius

(11)

Cœlum 1	Der Himmel 1
rotatur,	drehet ſich/
& ambit	und gehet
Terram, 2	um die Erde/ 2
ſtantem in medio.	die in der Mitten ſtehet.
Sol, 3	Die Sonne/ 3
ubiubi eſt,	ſie ſey wo ſie ſey/
fulget perpetuò:	ſcheinet immer:
utut	ob ſchon
Nubila 4	das Gewülcke 4
eum nobis eripiant;	ſie uns raubet;
facitq;	und machet
ſuis *Radiis* 5	mit ihren Strahlen 5
Lucem;	das Liecht;
Lux, *Diem*.	das Liecht / den Tag.
Ex oppoſito,	Gegen über
ſunt *Tenebræ* 6	iſt die Finſternis 6
inde *Nox*.	daher die Nacht.
Noćte,	Bey Nacht/
ſplendet *Luna*, 7	ſcheinet der Mond/ 7
& *Stellæ* 8	und die Sternen 8
micant, ſcintillant.	ſchimmern / blincken.
Veſperi 9	Des Abends/ 9
eſt *Crepuſculum*:	iſt die Demmerung:
Manè,	Des Morgens/
Aurora 10	die Morgenröte 10
& *Diluculum*.	und das Tagen.

(***)

IV. Ignis.

Comenius

b What is it in German?
Fill in the nouns with their article.

the light	das Licht
the sun	....
the sky	....
the moon	....
the clouds	....
the stars	....
the earth	....

8 Underline every word which you think is a verb:

Der Himmel – Dreht sich – und geht ...

Aussprache: Vokale (lang, kurz)

9 Listen and pay attention to the stressed vowel. Is it long or short?
Mark the length of the vowel: _ long or • short.
Himmel Liebe

liegen • dienen • links • Krieg • bitte • Frieden • Ebbe • Meer • rechts •
stehen • Mensch • Tag • Nacht • Hass • Name • Strand • oben • Gott •
Tod • unten • gut • Flut

Aussprache und Orthographie

10 Write down further examples.

pronounce	write	
i, e, a, o, u kurz	i, e, a, o, u	links, ...
	i, e, a, o, u + Doppelkonsonant (mm, tt,..., ck)	Himmel, ...
i, e, a, o, u lang	i, e, a, o, u	oben, ...
	ie, ieh, ee, eh aa, ah oo, oh uh	liegen, stehen, ...

11 The following text is a concise biography of Comenius. It consists almost entirely of key words in note form, often abbreviated, e.g. *dt.* for *deutsch*.
Answer the following questions without the help of a dictionary. A number of visual clues and other aids (asterisk *, cross †, quotation marks "...", lists ..., ..., ... etc.) will help you work out the information.

1 What nationality is Comenius?
2 When was Comenius born?
3 Which were his three professions?
4 What are the titles of his best known books?
5 What was Comenius' name in Czech?

Comenius, Johann Amos,

eigtl. Jan Amos Komenský

* 28.03.1592, † 15.11.1670, tschech. Theologe und Pädagoge; Bischof der Böhm. Brüder, seit 1656 in Amsterdam; begründete den systematischen Unterricht, forderte für das Schulwesen die Aufeinanderfolge von häuslicher Erziehung, Volksschule (Ausbildung in dt. Sprache), Lateinschule, Universität. Werke: „Orbis sensualium pictus" (Bilderfibel), „Didactica magna" (Große Unterrichtslehre) u. a.

aus: *Das neue Duden-Lexikon*

Das Alphabet

12 How to spell in German. Read and listen.

A	**I**	e **R**	**Ä**, a Umlaut
B e	**J** ot	e **S**	**Ö**, o Umlaut
C e	**K** a	**T** e	**Ü**, u Umlaut
D e	e **L**	**U**	**ß** es**Z**ett
E	e **M**	**V**au	
e **F**	e **N**	**W**e	
G e	**O**	i **X**	klein **a, b, c, d, …**
H a	**P** e	**Y**psilon	groß **A, B, C, D, …**
	Q u	**Z**ett	

The umlauts *ä, ö, ü* are a special feature of the German language. As each of them resembles a certain vowel they are called *Umlaut* + vowel when spelling words.

13 Ask how to spell a word and spell it yourself.

Wie schreibt man das? Bitte buchstabieren Sie.

Mensch • Gott • Teufel • dienen • beherrschen • stehen • liegen • Meer • Himmel • Hölle • heißen • Licht

Wo ist das?

14 a Listen and repeat.

Wo ist	der Himmel?	Der Himmel ist	**oben.**
	die Hölle?	Adam und Eva sind	**unten.**
	der Strand?		**rechts.**
	der Mensch?		**in der Mitte.**
Wo sind	Adam und Eva?		**im Bild.**
Wo steht	das Nomen?	Das Nomen steht	**im Text.**
	„Liebe und Tod"?		**in Übung 2.**
	„Das Gespräch"?		**auf Seite 8.**

b Where are the sun, the earth, the moon in the drawing "Der Himmel"? Where are the stars, the clouds?

Wo ist die Sonne? – Die Sonne ist ...

Wo sind die Sterne? – Die Sterne sind ...

zu Hause sein ...

Cultural information

The text "Being at home" was written by a student learning German at the University of Zurich in Switzerland. As a starting point, the teacher just gave students the sentence *Zu Hause sein heißt eine Sprache haben* (Being at home means having a language). The foreign students wrote impromptu texts on the topic in German.

In Switzerland languages are something of special relevance as the country has four official languages: French, Italian, Rhaeto-Romanic (a Romance language only spoken by a minority of 0.6% of the population) and German. Swiss German, however, is only identical with the German you are learning in this course in its written form. In most situations of everyday communication the Swiss speak Swiss German, an Alemannic dialect, which Austrians and Germans find somewhat difficult to understand. Feature films from Switzerland are therefore always subtitled.

Language

German has words which are similar or identical in many languages, such as *Hotel, Universität, diskutieren*. These are called internationalisms. During the course of the centuries, German has repeatedly adopted linguistic elements from other languages. Latin, as the language of the church, also played quite a role, as it did all over Europe. Internationalisms are easy to spot once you know what changes they underwent when they entered German. And of course they help you find your way into a lot of texts more easily.

Names of countries, too, sound similar in most languages. As in English, they usually have no article, with a few exceptions. Some of these are: *die Schweiz, die Türkei, die Niederlande, die USA, die Ukraine, die Slowakei.*

Learning strategies

If you want to understand a text in a foreign language, knowing something about the external form and layout is a good thing because this is linked to the text variety. If you see a text on the front page of a newspaper, then you know that it probably contains information about important current affairs. A graphic design with just visual elements, as in advertising texts, also tells us something about the text variety. If we see someone, their gestures, facial expression, and maybe even their clothes will give us similar information. When you're listening to the radio, background sounds, the speaker's voice and mood are useful aids to understanding. So you should always start off by asking yourself questions like: what external features can help me understand this text? What kind of text is it? Who is trying to say what to whom?

Zu Hause sein

Chen Zhaohui

1 The statement *Zu Hause sein heißt eine Sprache haben* prompts the author to ask questions and try to find answers.

Wo ist man zu Hause?	Wo: asking for the place man: general, all human/living beings
Ein Wurm, ein Vogel … A worm, a bird	specific living beings
tief in der Erde, hoch in der Luft deep in the ground, high in the air	a specific place
Aber ich? Wo bin ich zu Hause? …	ich: oneself

Why is the author hesitant about giving an answer for himself?

2 Listen to the text.

Eine gemeinsame Sprache – internationale Wörter

German has many words derived from other languages, e.g. from Latin, Greek, English, French. Some are probably words in your own language.

3 Which of these words do you recognise because they are similar in spelling or in sound when you read them out loud? Put the words you recognise in a table.
What do they mean in your own language?

Hotel Diskussion diskutieren Distanz Kino

Qualität Politik Musikfestival Konzert Foto

Information fotografieren informieren Konferenz Restaurant

Fitnesscenter Zentrum Film

Sport filmen Bus Physik

Museum Optimist Musikant Natur

Klima Idealismus Ingenieur Psychologe Maschine

Orthographie Grammatik Melodie

Biographie Student

4 Do you know any other internationalisms in your own language? What could their German equivalents be? Experiment using endings from this list and check your result against a dictionary.

Foreign words can have different endings in German.

Nouns e. g.:

-(t)ion	-anz	-ik	-ine	-um	-ist	-ie
-ur	-ismus	-enz	-eur	-ologe	-ant/-ent	-ität

Verbs:

-ieren

Intonation: Wortakzent

5 Listen and indicate the main stress within the word.

Radio ● Taxi ● Musik ● Musikant ● Telefon / Telefon ● Zentrum ● Information ● Literatur ● Museum ● Problem ● Hotel ● Diskussion ● Ingenieur ● Konzert ● Politik ● Politiker ● Maschine ● Apparat ● Fotoapparat ● Biographie ● Melodie ● Psychologe ● Optimist ● international / international

6 Which syllable carries the main stress?
Read the words in section 5 out loud and enter them in the table.

1st syllable	2nd/3rd syllable	final syllable
Rádio, ...	....	....
....	....	....
....	....	....
....	....	....
....	....	....

Eine gemeinsame Sprache – die Optik

7 The format of a text can help you understand some words.
Compare the two texts with similar texts in your own language.
What could the highlighted words mean?
Translate them into your own language.

Susanna Schreiner

* 14.3.1921 † 18.5.2000

In Liebe und Dankbarkeit
Maria Schreiner-König
im Namen aller Angehörigen

Trauergottesdienst am Freitag, um 14.00 Uhr
in der Kirche St. Martin in Niederweiler.
Beerdigung am Freitag, dem 24. Mai 2000, anschließend
auf dem Waldfriedhof.

Inhalt

3

Land – Sprache – Nationalität – Person

8 a Supply the missing words.

Land	Sprache	Nationalität	Person m/f
....	Deutsch	deutsch	Deutscher / Deutsche
....	Schweizerdeutsch Italienisch, Französisch	schweizerisch	Schweizer / Schweizerin
....	Deutsch	österreichisch	Österreicher / Österreicherin
....	Französisch	....	Franzose / Französin
....	Türkisch	....	Türke / Türkin
....	Italienisch	....	Italiener / ....
....	Englisch	britisch	Brite / Britin
....	Schwedisch	....	Schwede / Schwedin
....	....	....	....

b Supply the words for your own country, your own language ...

c Make a list for the countries you are interested in.

Ich bin ..., Ich heiße ...

9 Listen and read.

Wie heißt du?	Agata.
Woher kommst du?	Aus Polen.
Welche Sprache sprichst du?	Polnisch und Deutsch.
Wo wohnst du?	In Wien.
Bist du Österreicherin?	Nein, ich bin Polin.

Wie heißen Sie?	Jean Lacroix.
Woher sind Sie?	Aus der Schweiz.
Welche Sprache sprechen Sie?	Französisch.
Sind Sie Franzose?	Nein, ich bin Schweizer.
Wo wohnen Sie?	In Genf.

10 Das ist Semra. Sie lebt auch in Wien.

Complete the questions and give the answers.

1 Wie .... du?
....

2 Woher .... du?
....
....

3 Welche Sprache .... du?
....

4 Wo .... du?
....

11 Supply the interrogative pronoun, the verb ending, the subject.

1 .... heißen Sie?
2 .... wohnst du?
3 .... kommen Sie?
4 Semra leb....... in Wien.
5 Ich heiß....... Agata.
6 Wo wohn....... du?
7 .... heiße Semra.
8 Wo wohnst .... ?
9 Sind .... Franzose?

Verb und Subjekt

	Agata	komm **t**	aus Polen.
	Sie	leb **t**	in Wien.
Wo wohn **st**	**du**?		

The **subject** determines the verb **ending**.

Das Verb: Präsens Singular

12 Supply the forms of *sein* and the missing verb endings.

Personalpronomen	sein	heißen	kommen	sprechen
ich	....	heiß........	komm........	sprech........
du	**bist**	heiß........	komm........	sprich........
Sie	....	heiß........	komm........	sprech........
er/sie/es/man	**ist**	heiß **t**	komm **t**	sprich **t**

13 a Write about yourself.
Wie heißen Sie? Woher kommen Sie? Wo wohnen Sie? Welche Sprache sprechen Sie?

b Take another person's text and introduce them.
Das ist ... Er/Sie kommt ...

Der Satz: Aussage, Wortfrage, Satzfrage

Ich spreche Deutsch und Englisch.	**statement**
Woher kommst du?	**questions with interrogative pronoun** (Wie? Woher? Wo? Welche?)
Kommen Sie aus Deutschland?	**yes/no-question** (Antwort: Ja/Nein)

14 a Fill in examples from section 11.

	1	2	
statement	....	....	....
quest. with int. pronoun	....	....	....
yes/no-question	Sind	Sie	....

b Initial or second position? Complete the rule.

statement, question with interrogative pronoun:
verb takes .... position.
yes/no-question: verb takes .... position.

15 What are the questions? Write them using the *du*-form (a) and the *Sie*-form (b).

1 a .... ? Ich heiße Anna.
b .... ?

2 a .... ? Ich wohne in Frankfurt.
b .... ?

3 a .... ? Ich spreche Italienisch und Deutsch.
b .... ?

4 a .... ? Ich komme aus Italien.
b .... ?

16 Make questions.

1 aus Schweden – sein – Sie
2 Sie – in Stockholm – wohnen
3 Italienerin – du – sein
4 Sie – auch Englisch – sprechen
5 in Hamburg – leben – du
6 Deutsch – sprechen – du

Intonation: Frage, Aussage

17 Listen and indicate the intonation: ↘ or ↗.

■ Wie heißen Sie?
▲ Ich heiße Andreas.
■ Sind Sie Deutscher?
▲ Nein, ich bin Schweizer.
■ Wo wohnen Sie?
▲ In Basel. Und wie heißen Sie?

In a statement the intonation falls at the end of the sentence ↘.
Questions with interrogative pronouns can have falling ↘ or rising ↗ intonation:
↘ Information is important.
↗ Making contact with and interest in the partner is important.
Yes/no-questions mainly have rising intonation ↗.

18 Read the questions in section 15 with different intonation.

Verstehen Sie?

19 Listen and repeat.

Das verstehe ich nicht. Sprechen Sie bitte langsam. Wiederholen Sie bitte.
Wie heißt das auf Englisch/Deutsch? Erklären Sie das bitte.

Farben hören – Töne schmecken

The text

The texts are from a review of the book "Farben hören, Töne schmecken" (Hearing colours, tasting sounds) by the American neurophysiologist Cytowic. They are about people who have unusually strong links between two or more senses. A picture triggers a sensation of smell, they associate a sound with colours, or have a musical image of events or objects. These people are called synaesthetes – derived from the ancient Greek words *syn* (simultaneous) and *aesthesis* (perception) – as they experience one stimulus with several senses at once. Synaesthetes are often very creative people, and include many artists. Their memory also works far better than other people's. The phenomenon is the subject of research in both the USA and Germany. The results may one day help us to learn foreign languages better and faster.

Learning strategies

We have all found at one time or another that we remember things far better when we create a link between them and something else. This experience can be utilised in learning. This unit deals with learning new words. When you do this, make sure you always establish connections to words you already know:

- Connect words belonging to the same topic, just as Comenius did several hundred years ago.

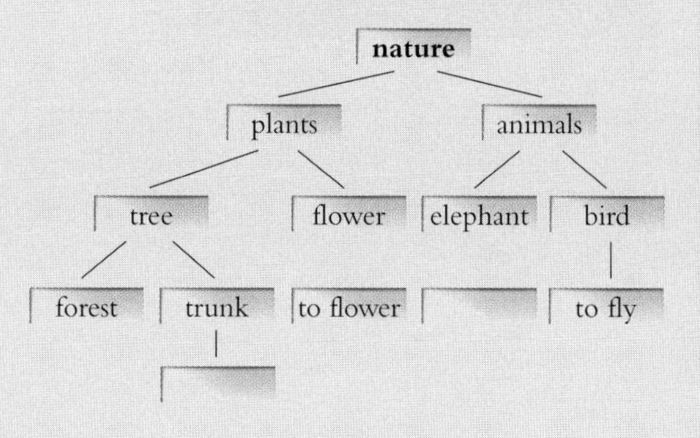

- Note down nouns with their matching verbs or adjectives.

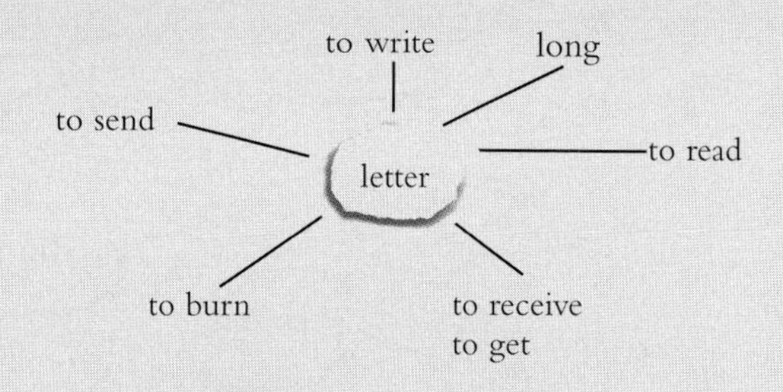

- Make associations for a word.
  red: warm, flower, sunset, correcting a mistake
- Rank words and put them in order on a scale.

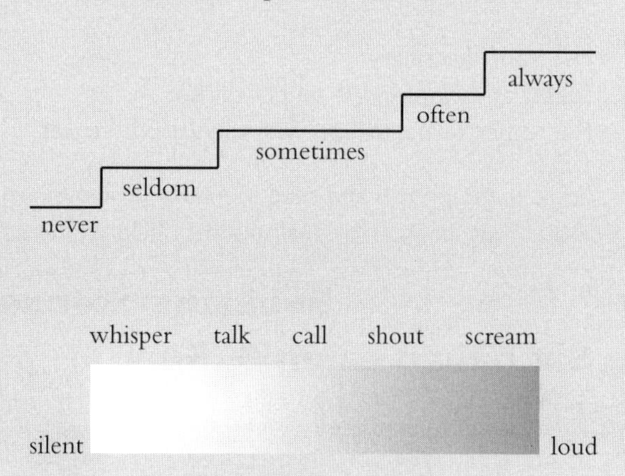

When you establish associations or a sequence, choose your own individual criteria, and give your notes an appropriate format using graphics and colour.

In this textbook you only find original texts and these are mostly unabridged. However, every text consists of parts which contain important information and other parts which expand and offer explanations. In this unit, the important parts of the reading texts are in normal print and you only need to work on these. The other parts of the texts appear in lighter print. This will make the texts easier for you to understand.

Farben hören – Töne schmecken

1 Read the web of words.

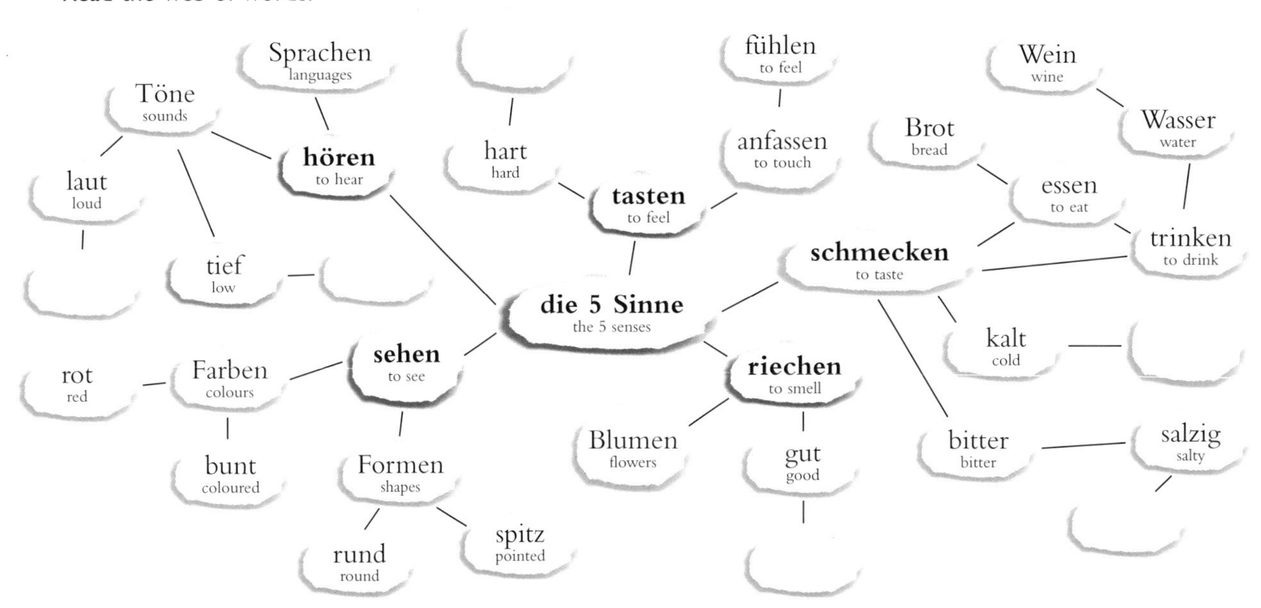

2 Use your dictionary.

a Supply antonyms in the empty circles.

b Find other terms that go with the various senses.

3 Look at the photos and read the texts (just the highlighted sections).
Watch out for internationalisms, they help you understand the texts.

Synästhetiker sehen mehr als andere: Sie haben einen 6. Sinn.

A

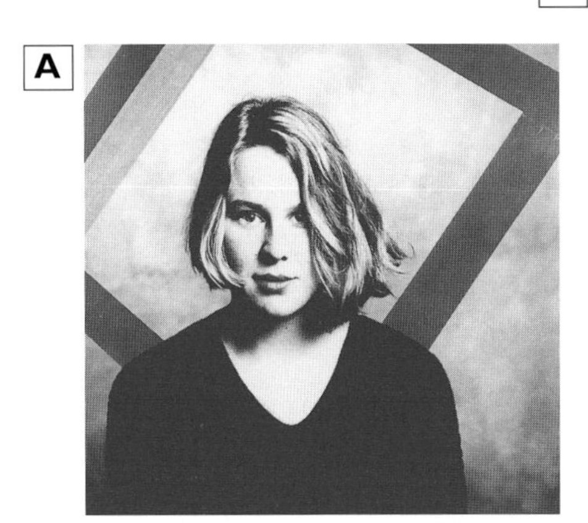

Insa Schultz schmeckt in Formen und Farben. Wenn sie etwas isst, sieht sie bunte, geometrische Figuren. Alles Bittere empfindet sie wie eine schwarze Fläche mit orangefarbenen Zylindern. Bei Salzigem denkt sie automatisch an reflektierende Glaskugeln.

denken an: to think of

B

Svea von Zitzewitz assoziiert Vokale mit Rot, Blau und Gelb. Seit frühester Kindheit verbinden sich für die Geschichtslehrerin bestimmte Buchstaben mit bestimmten Farben. Diese Fähigkeit nutzt sie als Eselsbrücke, um sich Daten farblich zu merken.

C

Margret Jadamowitz – Heute blau, morgen grün und übermorgen taubengrau – für die 76-Jährige hat jeder Wochentag eine spezielle Farbe. Auch ihr Geschmacks-, Geruchs- und Tastsinn sind koloriert: Am besten schmeckt ihr grünoranger Wein, bei Muskelkater hat sie gelbe Schmerzen.

aus: *DIE ZEITmagazin*

D

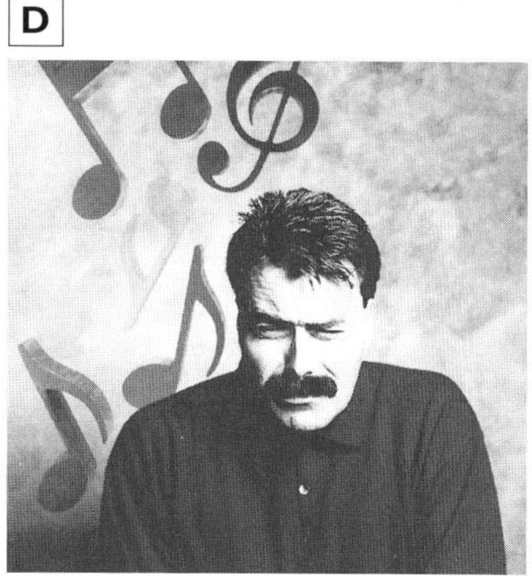

Matthias Waldeck hört Musik nicht nur, er sieht sie auch. Bei jedem Ton läuft in seinem Kopf ein Film aus bunten, manchmal sehr komplizierten Formen ab.

4 Which link goes with person A, B, D? Enter the letters in the boxes.

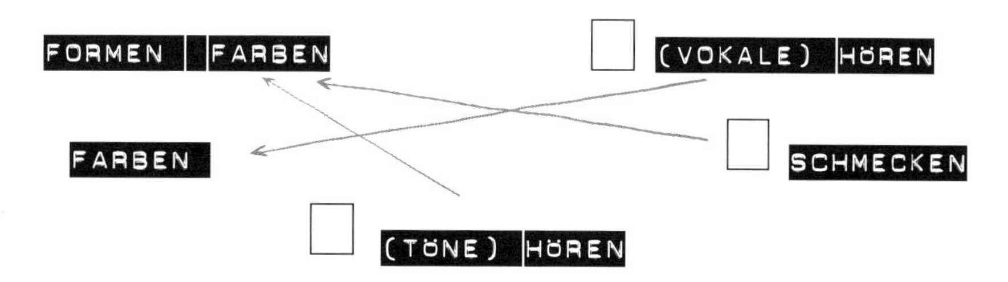

5 Enter the letter that fits.

1 Person .... sieht einen Film aus bunten Formen, wenn sie Musik hört.

2 Person .... hört Vokale und sieht Farben.

3 Person .... sieht Figuren und Farben, wenn sie etwas isst.

4 Person .... lebt in Farben.

6 Are you a synaesthete yourself?

Ich assoziiere ... mit ...
Bei ... sehe ich / höre ich / fühle ich / denke ich an ...

7 What do you associate with these words?

blau **Blume** **blaue Blume**

Textzusammenhang verstehen

People and objects are mentioned again and again in a text. Once they've been introduced at the beginning, they are referred to by means of personal pronouns and other circumlocutions.

Insa Schultz schmeckt in Formen und Farben.

Wenn sie etwas isst, sieht sie bunte, geometrische Figuren.

Matthias Waldeck hört Musik nicht nur,

er sieht sie auch.

Margret Jadamowitz – Heute blau, morgen grün und übermorgen taubengrau – für die 76-Jährige hat jeder Wochentag eine spezielle Farbe.

8 Draw arrows as in the example above.

Synästhetiker sehen mehr als andere. Sie haben einen 6. Sinn. Z. B. hören sie Töne nicht nur, sie sehen sie auch, sie assoziieren sie mit Farben und Formen.

nouns	personal pronouns
Insa Schultz / die Sprache	sie
Matthias / der Tag	er
das Restaurant	es
die Synästhetiker / die Töne (Plural)	sie

9 Substitute personal pronouns or other circumlocutions for the underlined nouns.

Mario kommt aus Italien. Mario hört Musik nicht nur, Mario riecht die Musik auch. Wenn Mario italienische Popmusik hört, riecht Mario das Meer.

Jana lebt in Berlin. Jana kommt aus Tschechien. Jana spricht Tschechisch und Deutsch. Wenn Jana das deutsche Wort Gott hört, denkt sie an den tschechischen Sänger Karel Gott.

Das Verb: Präsens Singular und Plural

10 Supply the missing verb forms.

Personalpronomen	hören	sehen	haben	sein
ich	....	seh **e**	hab **e**	....
du	....	sieh **st**	ha **st**	....
Sie	....	seh **en**	hab **en**	....
er/sie/es/man	....	....	ha **t**	....
wir	hör **en**	seh **en**	hab **en**	**sind**
ihr	hör **t**	seh **t**	hab **t**	**seid**
Sie	hör **en**	seh **en**	hab **en**	**sind**
sie	hör **en**	seh **en**	hab **en**	**sind**

The verb ending is a signal for:

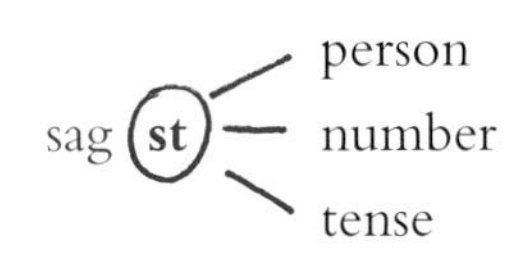

Some verbs change the vowel of the stem in the *du*-form and in the *er/sie/es/man*-Form.
e → i/ie: sprechen (to speak), du sprichst, er spricht
a → ä: fahren (to drive), du fährst, er fährt
They are called irregular verbs.

11 Supply the infinitive form.

1 Jean spricht Französisch. ....

2 Matthias hört Musik nicht nur, er sieht sie auch. ....hören,..............................

3 Wenn Insa etwas Salziges isst, denkt sie an Glaskugeln. ....

12 Supply the correct form of the verbs given in brackets.

1 Synästhetiker .... einen 6. Sinn. Sie .... mehr als andere. (haben, sehen)

2 Insa Schultz .... in Formen und Farben. (schmecken)

3 Wenn sie etwas ...., ... sie bunte, geometrische Figuren. (essen, sehen)

4 Frau von Zitzewitz .... Vokale mit Farben. (assoziieren)

5 Für Margret Jadamowitz .... jeder Wochentag eine spezielle Farbe. (haben)

6 Matthias Waldeck .... Musik und .... sie auch. (hören, sehen)

7 Ich.......................... Töne. (riechen)

8 .... du /.......................... Sie Farben? (hören)

9 .... du / .... Sie Vokale mit Farben? (assoziieren)

10 Wenn ich etwas Salziges ...., ... ich an Glaskugeln. (essen, denken)

11 .... du /.......................... Sie Synästhetiker? (sein)

12 .... du / .... Sie einen 6. Sinn? (haben)

Aussprache: Vokale (lang, kurz)

13 Listen and watch out for the stressed vowel. What can you hear: long _ or short • ? Tick the boxes.

	a (lang)	a (kurz)		e (lang)	e (kurz)		i (lang)	i (kurz)		o (lang)	o (kurz)		u (lang)	u (kurz)
1	☐	☐	1	☐	☐	1	☐	☐	1	☐	☐	1	☐	☐
2	☐	☐	2	☐	☐	2	☐	☐	2	☐	☐	2	☐	☐
3	☐	☐	3	☐	☐	3	☐	☐	3	☐	☐	3	☐	☐
4	☐	☐	4	☐	☐	4	☐	☐	4	☐	☐	4	☐	☐

14 Listen and write.

1 Die Bl..........me r..........cht g..........t.

2 Oh, das schm.......... b..........er.

3 Er hört Mus..........k und s..........t F..........rmen.

4 J......der T......g h......t eine spezi..........e Farbe.

5 N..........me, V..........rname, Telefonn..................er, Str.......ße – warum fr........gen S..........?

Wörter lernen

15 a Read the words quickly (30 seconds). Close your book and write down the words you remember.

Himmel Farbe hören Musik leise Nacht Frieden zu Hause Natur Vogel

b Repeat the exercise with these words.

Deutschland stehen grün Diskussion Maschine Orthographie rund
Auf Wiederhören gut rechts

c From which list did you remember more words? Why?

16 a Read the words. Look them up in a dictionary if you don't remember the meaning.

anfassen • Apparat • Auf Wiedersehen! • bitter • Blume • bunt • Deutsch • Gott • grün • Film • diskutieren • Entschuldigung! • Erde • blau • essen • Farbe • Form • gelb • Gespräch • grau • gut • Guten Tag! • hören • hart • heute • Himmel • Ingenieur • international • Italien • kalt • Kino • kommen • Konferenz • Konzert • Kopf • Krieg • laut • leben • leise • Liebe • Luft • Maschine • Meer • Mensch • morgen • Musik • Nacht • Natur • Qualität • Radio • Restaurant • riechen • rot • rund • süß • schön • Schade! • schlecht • schmecken • Sprache • sehen • sprechen • Tag • trinken • Tut mir Leid. • warm • Tod • wohnen • Wie bitte? • Wie geht's? • weich

b Make various webs of words with these words and expressions. Make selections that either all relate to a particular topic or allow you to associate them with a picture/story.
Write one word in a circle in the centre that acts as a summary for all the words in the web.

17 Nouns in German are masculine, feminine or neuter. This is not always logical. Compare.

der Krieg	war	**die Liebe**	love	**das Wort**	word
	French: la guerre (f)		l'amour (m)		le mot (m)
	Latin: bellum (n)		amor (m)		verbum (n)

a Enter the nouns from section 16a in the table below.

maskulin (m) der	**neutral (n) das**	**feminin (f) die**
....	....	....
....	....	....
....	....	....
....		....
		....

b Try whenever possible to make an association between the noun and its article, e.g.

Das Haus   der Mann / die Frau   ist für beide.

You can also choose different colours for the articles and write down the nouns in these colours.

Zeit

Cultural information

This unit teaches you the numbers and the time in German. But first, a short note about the importance of time for Germans. First and foremost comes punctuality of course. As long ago as the Middle Ages, the divisions in the day were determined by the ringing of bells in towers. Bureaucrats and the military eventually enshrined the importance of punctuality, and especially accurate timekeeping by the clockmakers in Switzerland, with the result that it plays a more major role than anywhere else in the world. There are, however, two sides to this. People say: *Er ist pünktlich wie die Eisenbahn* (as punctual as the railways), which means, "He'll be dead on time". However, when people say: *Er ist pünktlich wie ein Maurer* (as punctual as a bricklayer), they mean that he won't work a minute longer than he absolutely has to.

Although the punctuality cult is no longer adhered to quite so rigidly in Germany nowadays, there are two situations when you should always make sure you're on time: when you have a business appointment and when you've been invited as a guest. When someone in Germany gives a dinner party for 10 people, then more often than not they all appear outside the front door at the same time, and the hostess gets into a panic because she has to cope with 5 bunches of flowers and 10 coats to hang up all at the same time.

Language

When people used to go out and buy eggs in Germany, they got 12. So they used to say, "Can I have *ein Dutzend* (a dozen) eggs" and not *zwölf* (twelve). There are historical reasons for this. The old system of counting based on the number 12, which still determines the way we count the hours and months, was used in commerce up to modern times. As a result we count up to twelve and beyond twelve in a different way. So we say *zehn, elf, zwölf*, but *dreizehn, vierzehn* etc. One peculiarity about German is that two-digit numbers are spoken with the units first, and then the tens. But then with hundreds, the unit is again spoken first: *einhundert* (one hundred).

Learning strategies

When you are learning the numbers, it is a good idea to underline the figure which is said first: 13 (drei-zehn), 23 (drei-und-zwanzig), 98 (acht-und-neunzig), 224 (zwei-hundert-vier-und-zwanzig).

When you're telling the time, it probably sounds rather strange to say *halb acht* (half past seven) when you mean 7:30. *Halb* always refers to the following hour. You won't have this problem if you use the formal way of telling the time: *sieben Uhr dreißig* (seven thirty). But the people you talk to won't always do this, so you at least have to understand the form with *halb*. If you don't, you might not be punctual the next time you get an invitation. And that would be dreadful, wouldn't it?

Zeit

A

Zeit die; -, -en; **1.** nur Sg; das Vorübergehen der Augenblicke, Stunden, Tage, Wochen, Monate, Jahre; die Zeit vergeht schnell, langsam; viel, wenig, keine Zeit haben

B

Zeitwörter

Arbeitszeit
Freizeit
Unterrichtszeit
Urlaubszeit
Jahreszeit
Tageszeit
Uhrzeit
Jugendzeit
Schulzeit
Weltrekordzeit
Zeit haben
keine Zeit haben
die Zeit vergeht

C

Stechuhr. Zeitschriftenwerbung um 1920

D

Kirche St. Peter in Zürich mit größtem Zifferblatt Europas

Schon um 2055 v. Ch. sind bei den Ägyptern Sonnenuhren als Kalender gebräuchlich.

Sonnenuhr des mittelalterlichen Bauern: die fünf Finger und ein Strohhalm.

E

F

Inhaltsverzeichnis
Das Verb

1. Die Tempora
A. Präsens
   Formen
   Der Gebrauch des Präsens
B. Perfekt
   Formen
   haben oder sein
C. Präteritum
   Formen
   Gebrauch der Vergangenheitsformen (Perfekt und Präteritum)
D. Das Plusquamperfekt
   Formen
   Der Gebrauch des Plusquamperfekts
E. Das Futur I und II
   Formen

G

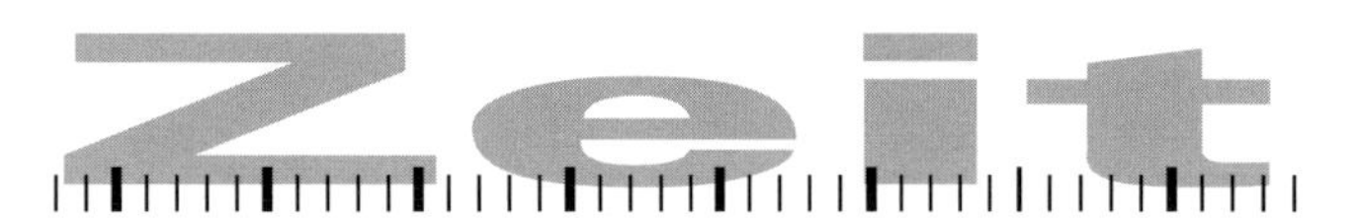

Vergangenheit - Gegenwart - Zukunft

1 Which text, which picture goes with which of the sentences below? Enter the letters.

1 ☐ explains the word *Zeit*.
2 ☐ refers to the form and the function of time in language.
3 ☐ shows word combinations with *Zeit*.
4 ☐ shows the monitoring of time in the workplace.
5 ☐ shows the passage of time.
6 ☐ shows the early methods of timekeeping.
7 ☐ shows a clock from a country famous for clocks.

Wortbildung: Komposita

The nouns in text B (→ page 28) are compounds made up of the root word *Zeit* and a modifier (or several modifiers), e.g. *Arbeit*.

2 Split the compounds up into their components: *Arbeit/s/zeit, Welt/rekord/zeit*, ... and put them in a table along with their articles. Look up any parts you don't know in a dictionary.

noun + noun modifier		root word			adjective + noun modifier		root word		
der Tag	+	die Zeit	=	die Tageszeit	frei	+	die Zeit	=	die Freizeit

Wortakzent

3 a Listen and mark the main stress: Árbeitszeit.

Freizeit • Urlaubszeit • Uhrzeit • Tageszeit • Jahreszeit • Weltrekordzeit

b Modifier or root word? Fill in the gaps in the rule.

Compounds consisting of noun + noun
The .... determines the article.
Sometimes *s* or *es* are inserted between the nouns: Arbeit**s**zeit, Tag**es**zeit.
The stress is on ....

4 Form compounds with the root words *Sprache* and *Land*.

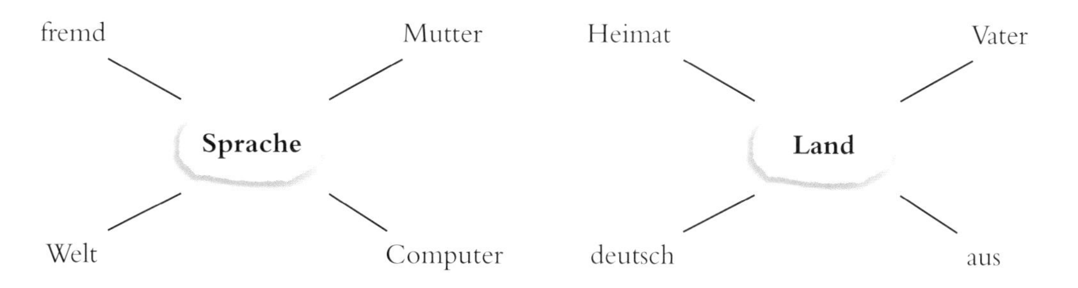

Zahlen: Kardinalzahlen

5 Listen and read. Then read the text out aloud.

Nacht in der Wildnis

Zwei Augen funkeln.
Ein Tiger im Dunkeln!

Vier Augen:
Zwei!

Sechs Augen:
Drei!

Sie zwinkern uns zu:
Macht's gut, ihr dort!
Und gehen
auf leisen Sohlen fort.

Josef Guggenmos

6 Listen and read. Then repeat.

0 null	1 eins	11 **elf**	21 einundzwanzig	40 vierzig
	2 zwei	12 **zwölf**	22 zweiundzwanzig	50 fünfzig
	3 drei	13 dreizehn	23 dreiundzwanzig	60 **sech**zig
	4 vier	14 vierzehn	24 vierundzwanzig	70 **sieb**zig
	5 fünf	15 fünfzehn	25 fünfundzwanzig	80 achtzig
	6 sechs	16 **sech**zehn	26 sechsundzwanzig	90 neunzig
	7 sieben	17 **sieb**zehn	27 siebenundzwanzig	100 (ein)hundert
	8 acht	18 achtzehn	28 achtundzwanzig	200 zweihundert
	9 neun	19 neunzehn	29 neunundzwanzig	
	10 zehn	20 **zwanzig**	30 dreißig	1000 (ein)tausend

7 a Listen and mark the main stress: dreizehn

fünfzehn ● fünfzig ● sieben ● siebzehn ● siebzig ● zwanzig ● sechsundzwanzig ● dreißig ● dreiunddreißig ● sechzig ● sechsundsechzig ● hundert ● einhundert ● zweihundert

b Listen again and repeat.

c Tick the words you hear.

1	6	16	2	3	7	10
2	9	19	17	70	13	30

3	23	32	15	50	75	57
4	18	80	41	40	38	83

8 Which numbers are missing? Fill them in.

1 eins .... drei ....

2 neun ....

3 sechs .... acht ....

4 zwei .... vier ....

9 Listen and write down the telephone numbers.

Die Uhrzeit

zwölf Uhr
vierundzwanzig Uhr / null Uhr

neun Uhr
einundzwanzig Uhr

drei Uhr
fünfzehn Uhr

sechs Uhr
achtzehn Uhr

Viertel vor — Viertel nach

halb

formal:		informal:
18:30	achtzehn Uhr dreißig	**halb** sieben
06:15	sechs Uhr fünfzehn	**Viertel nach** sechs
15:45	fünfzehn Uhr fünfundvierzig	**Viertel vor** vier

10 Read the times of day and fill them in.

Viertel nach eins
ein Uhr fünfzehn
dreizehn Uhr fünfzehn

....
....
vierzehn Uhr dreißig

zehn nach sechs
sechs Uhr zehn
....

halb vier
drei Uhr dreißig
fünfzehn Uhr dreißig

....
vier Uhr fünfundvierzig
sechzehn Uhr fünfundvierzig

....
....
....

What do you say when?
From 1 am until midday: ein Uhr, drei Uhr, acht Uhr, zwölf Uhr.
From 1 pm until midnight you have two options e.g.:
ein Uhr/dreizehn Uhr, sechs Uhr/achtzehn Uhr, zwölf Uhr/vierundzwanzig Uhr/null Uhr.

11 In which order do you hear the times of day? Fill in the numbers.

☐	8 : 30	☐	3 : 30	☐	11 : 00	☐	14 : 15	☐	9 : 45
☐	2 : 40	☐	7 : 55	☐	10 : 15	☐	4 : 15	☐	5 : 10

Nach der Zeit fragen

Wie viel Uhr ist es? **Wie spät** ist es?

Wann / Um wie viel Uhr öffnet die Bibliothek / beginnt der Unterricht / kommst du?
Von wann bis wann ist die Bibliothek geöffnet?
Von wann bis wann dauert der Unterricht?
Wie lange ist ... geöffnet? / **Wie lange** dauert ...?/
Wie lange bleiben Sie?

Die Zeit angeben

(Es ist) elf (Uhr). (Es ist) zehn nach elf.
(Es ist) zwei Uhr dreißig / vierzehn Uhr dreißig / halb drei.

Um neun (Uhr).
Von neun **bis** achtzehn Uhr.
Von neun **bis** elf Uhr dreißig.
Von neun **bis** elf (Uhr). **Bis** elf (Uhr).
Fünf Stunden/Minuten/Sekunden.
Eine Viertelstunde. (15 Minuten)
Eine halbe Stunde. (30 Minuten)
Eine Dreiviertelstunde. (45 Minuten)
Eineinhalb Stunden. (1,5 Stunden)

12 Ask and answer.

Von wann bis wann ist die Bibliothek, die Bäckerei, ... geöffnet? Wie lange ist ... geöffnet?

Bibliothek
Mo – Fr
9.00 – 18.00

Puppen-Museum
täglich, außer Sonntag
10.00 – 12.00
15.00 – 17.00

Bäckerei Kaiser
Auch am Sonntag
frische Brötchen
9.00 – 11.00

Informationszentrum
Mo – Fr 8.00 – 20.00

Von wann bis wann haben Sie Unterricht? Wie lange dauert der Unterricht? Wie lange ist die Pause?

13 How do you ask?

Wie viel Uhr / Wie spät ist es? Wann? Um wie viel Uhr? Wie lange?

1 Der Unterricht beginnt um 10 Uhr.
2 18 Uhr.
3 Der Workshop ist von 14 bis 16 Uhr.
4 Wir bleiben eine Stunde.
5 Ich komme um halb acht.
6 Eine Unterrichtsstunde dauert 45 Minuten.
7 Um 3 Uhr.
8 Halb neun.

Die Zahl 7

14 **a** What do you associate with the number 7?

Die 7 Todsünden

Je 7 Paare von den „reinen" Tieren kommen auf die Arche Noah.

In der Antike gab es 7 Weltwunder.

Im Märchen gibt es die 7 Raben, die 7 Zwerge, die Siebenmeilenstiefel, die Prinzessin Siebenschön.

In der Bibel macht Gott die Welt in 6 Tagen und am 7. Tag ruht er sich aus.

7 Töne hat die Tonleiter. (westliche Musik)

Rom liegt auf 7 Hügeln.

Pharao träumt von 7 fetten und 7 mageren Kühen.

b Germans say:

seine sieben Sachen packen   im siebten Himmel sein   das verflixte 7. Jahr

What could that mean?

Irrtümer

The texts

An argument resulted in an interesting book. The issue was whether smoking and smokers are responsible for higher costs in the health service, as most people believe. Two professors did some research and found that health spending in the country would be much higher if it weren't for smokers.

The reason: regular smokers die sooner and are less of a burden to the health service than people who lead a seemingly healthy life.

The outcome prompted the two professors to have a close look at similar issues to see if they could uncover other errors of judgement. They published their results in a book called "Lexikon der populären Irrtümer – 500 kapitale Missverständnisse, Vorurteile & Denkfehler von Abendrot bis Zeppelin" (Encyclopedia of popular errors – an A-Z of 500 major misunderstandings, prejudices & misconceptions).

People today have more information at their disposal than ever before. But this doesn't mean there is less ignorance and prejudice (das Vorurteil) than before. The fact is that people make judgements (das Urteil) without informing themselves properly first.

The various nationalities in the Alpine region also have prejudices about one another. The Ötzi joke is a classic example: when scientists found *Ötzi,* a mummified corpse, over 3000 years old, in a glacier in the Ötztaler Alpen, they had to decide what nationality this human being might have belonged to. He couldn't be Austrian, they said, as brain tissue had been found. He couldn't be Italian either, because he had tools with him. Maybe he was Swiss because he'd been overtaken by a glacier. Oh probably he was German, after all nobody else goes off into the mountains with sandals on. So now you work out for yourself what prejudices there are doing the rounds in these four countries.

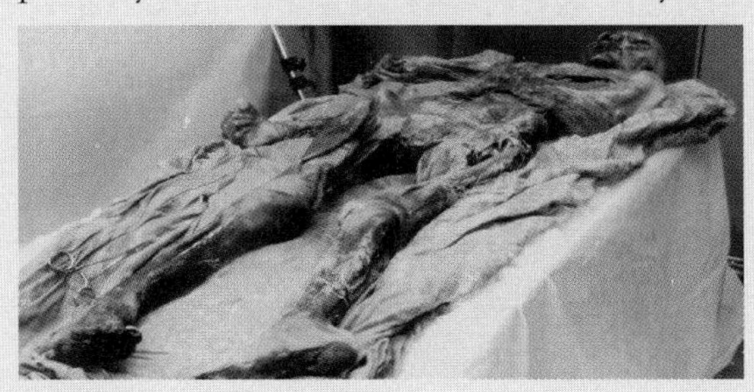

Der „Ötzi"

When you learn a foreign language you automatically have a close look at the culture and civilisation which shaped the language. In the process you will always find out that you have misconceptions, in other words prejudices. Learning a foreign language is one way to dissolve such prejudices, as the language helps you communicate and develop understanding.

Language

Ich verstehe **den** Text. **Der** Text ist interessant. The verb determines which case the noun takes. You have so far only learnt the noun in the nominative case (der Nominativ). German, however, has four cases: nominative, accusative (der Akkusativ), dative (der Dativ) and genitive (der Genitiv). As you can see from the example, the case (Nominativ, Akkusativ) is marked by the article (der, den). The noun itself stays mostly unchanged. This is why you need to learn every noun with its article.

Learning strategies

You can understand most texts if you know the meaning of the key words in them. These words give a text its specific meaning. So it's important to recognise which are the key words in a text. They often already appear in the heading. You can spot them, too, by their frequency in the text (sometimes changed and in a different form). Numbers can also be key words or can make them precise. So you should pay special attention to numbers. Once you have mastered this strategy, you can do without a dictionary most of the time. When you have guessed the meaning of a word, it's worth considering what helped you get there.

Irrtümer

1 Reconstruct the headings from the book "Lexikon der populären Irrtümer".

a Underline the words you already know.

b Then match up the two parts.

1 h	2 ☐	3 ☐	4 ☐	5 ☐	6 ☐
7 ☐	8 ☐	9 ☐	10 ☐	11 ☐	12 ☐

1	Frankenstein	**a**	hatte Kolonien.
2	Religion	**b**	macht dünn.
3	Chinesen	**c**	ist Opium für das Volk.
4	Einstein	**d**	ist schlecht für die Zähne.
5	In England	**e**	haben gelbe Haut.
6	Fast Food	**f**	war ein armer Schlucker[1].
7	Alkohol	**g**	regnet es mehr als in Italien.
8	Diät	**h**	ist ein Monster.
9	Kanada	**i**	war ein schlechter Schüler.
10	Nur Europa	**j**	wärmt.
11	Mozart	**k**	ist ungesund.
12	Schokolade	**l**	liegt nördlicher als Deutschland.

[1] armer Schlucker: poor devil

2 Read the following text.

a First try to grasp the meaning of the numbers:
bis zu 100 Jahre, 70 bzw. 76 Jahre alt, keine 50.

b Which word do these numbers refer to?

c Then look for key words, i.e. for expressions that appear frequently, also in a modified form.

Elefanten werden bis zu 100 Jahre alt

Die ältesten Elefanten, deren Alter nachgewiesen werden konnte, wurden bisher laut Guiness Book of Records 70 bzw. 76 Jahre alt. Die meisten werden aber keine 50.

aus: *Lexikon der populären Irrtümer*

Der Artikel: unbestimmter/bestimmter Artikel, Nullartikel

3 Some nouns in the headings of section 1 have an indefinite article (ein, eine), others have a definite article (der, die, das) and yet others have a zero article (Nullartikel). Make a list.

indefinite article ein armer Schlucker ....

definite article das Volk ....

zero article (no article) Frankenstein ....

....

....

indefinite article	Im Zoo ist **ein Elefant**.	nouns which appear for the first time in the text and are not defined more precisely
definite article	Das ist **der Elefant** Hugo. Das sind **die Elefanten** Willi und Hugo.	nouns defined more precisely
	Der Elefant ist 70 Jahre alt.	reference to a noun which is known to the speaker or listener
	Religion ist Opium für **das Volk**.	generally known and unique terms
zero article	Im Zoo sind **Elefanten**.	plural form of the indefinite article
	Schokolade ist schlecht für die Zähne.	general items, food, drink – not defined more precisely
	Einstein kommt aus **Ulm**.	names of people, cities, nationalities and countries
	Sport machen, **Zeit** haben	some fixed combinations of noun and verb

4 Definite, indefinite or zero article? Make sentences.

Das ist Adam.

2 Er heißt – Comenius.

3 Das ist – Sonne.

1 Das ist – Adam.

5 Das ist – Mensch.

4 Das ist – Tasse Tee.

6 Das ist – Italien.

7 Das ist – Mond.

8 Das sind – Blumen.

10 Das ist – Schulbus.

9 Das ist – Kaffee.

11 Das ist – Verb.

12 Das ist – Nomen.

5 Definite, indefinite or zero article?

.... (1) Elefant steht auf der Straße. .... (2) Mann kommt. .... (3) Elefant fragt: „Ist das .... (4) Bibliothek?" „Ja", sagt........................ (5) Mann, „das ist .... (6) Universitätsbibliothek. Sie öffnet um neun Uhr." „Ich habe keine Zeit", sagt .... (7) Elefant. „Um 9 Uhr beginnt .... (8) Arbeit im Zoo. Was machen Sie heute?" „Ich mache ....(9) Musik in .... (10) London. Ich bin .... (11) Engländer." „Interessant!", sagt .... (12) Elefant.

Das Nomen: Nominativ, Akkusativ

6 **a** Listen and repeat.
b Write the sentences in English and learn them by heart.

Hören Sie den Dialog. ....

Wie schreibt man das Wort? ....

Buchstabieren Sie das Wort. ....

Lesen Sie den Text. ....

Markieren Sie den Akzent. ....

Ergänzen Sie die Verbformen. ....

Wiederholen Sie den Satz. ....

Machen Sie eine Liste. ....

Schreiben Sie einen Dialog. ....

7 Compare the articles in the nominative and accusative case. Mark the differences.

	Singular			**Plural**
	maskulin	**neutral**	**feminin**	**m, n, f**
Nominativ	**der** Satz **ein**	**das** Wort **ein**	**die** Liste **eine**	**die** Sätze, Wörter, Listen **—**
Akkusativ	**den** Satz **einen**	**das** Wort **ein**	**die** Liste **eine**	**die** Sätze, Wörter, Listen **—**

Nominativergänzung (N), Akkusativergänzung (A)

	Verb	
Nur Europa (N)	hatte	Kolonien (A).
Frankenstein (N)	ist	ein Monster (N).
Wie	schreibt	man (N) das Wort (A)?
Mozart (N)	war	kein armer Schlucker (N).
Diät (N)	macht	die Menschen (A) dünn.
Das (N)	sind	Verbformen im Präsens (N).

8 Underline the verbs in the following sentences and fill in the gaps in the rule.

Frankenstein ist ein Monster.
Hören Sie den Dialog.
Wie schreibt man das Wort?
Ich verstehe den Schweizer nicht.
Chinesen haben gelbe Haut.

The verb .... has a **nominative supplement**:
Wer? (people), **Was?** (objects).

The verbs .... , ... ,

.... , ... ,

have an **accusative supplement**:
Wen? (people), **Was?** (objects).

Further verbs with accusative supplement:
anfassen, buchstabieren, ergänzen, erklären, essen, fotografieren, fühlen, informieren, lesen, machen, markieren, riechen, sehen, trinken, verstehen, wiederholen

9 Who does what? Combine person, verb and noun and make sentences.
z. B. Er buchstabiert das Wort. Petra hört einen Ton.

Andreas ● Petra ● Herr Kunkel ● ich ● du ● Sie ● er ● sie ● wir

buchstabieren ● erklären ● essen ● heißen ● hören ● lesen ● riechen ● schreiben ● sein ● trinken ● wiederholen ● verstehen ● lernen

die Blumen ● das Brot ● der Dialog ● die Grammatik ● der Kaffee ● Comenius ● der Satz ● die Fremdsprache ● der Text ● der Ton ● das Wort ● der Italiener

Zustimmen und widersprechen

10 Listen to the sentences and repeat.

\+ Das stimmt. Das ist richtig. Du hast Recht. Sie haben Recht.
\- Das stimmt nicht. Das ist falsch. Das ist nicht richtig.
+- Ich weiß nicht.

11 State your opinion about these claims using the sentences from section 10.

1 Elefanten leben in Afrika.
2 Einstein kommt aus Italien.
3 Mozart ist Österreicher.
4 Schokolade ist ungesund.
5 Comenius kommt aus Deutschland.
6 Der Louvre ist in Rom.
7 Religion ist gut für die Menschen.
8 Deutsch ist eine schöne Sprache.
9 Kompromisse sind schlecht.
10 Tee ist gesund.

Aussprache: *sch, s*

12 a Listen and repeat.

Wie schreibt man das? Schnell, bitte! der Schüler sie stehen die Stunde schlecht die Straße Sprechen Sie bitte langsam! Ich verstehe das nicht. Entschuldigung!

b Mark the *sch*-sounds in a.

Wie schreibt man das? Sprechen Sie bitte langsam.

st, sp are pronounced *scht* and *schp* at the beginning of a word (*stehen*) or a syllable (das *Ge-spräch, ver-stehen*).

13 *sch* or *s*? Fill in the gaps.

1 Wir ....prechen und ....reiben.

2 ....okolade ist ....lecht für die Zähne. ....ade!

3 Ein.........tein kommt aus ....panien? Das ....timmt nicht.

4 Hören Sie das Ge.........präch.

5 Wie ....pät ist es?

6 Buch.........tabieren Sie bitte das Wort.

14 Is the *s* voiceless or voiced? Please tick.

		voiceless	voiced			voiceless	voiced
1	der Satz	☐	☐	8	Und Sie?	☐	☐
2	die Liste	☐	☐	9	Wo ist das?	☐	☐
3	die Sonne	☐	☐	10	Wo sind sie?	☐	☐
4	die Musik	☐	☐	11	die Straße	☐	☐
5	das Wasser	☐	☐	12	das Haus	☐	☐
6	sehr gut	☐	☐	13	zu Hause	☐	☐
7	Ich heiße Anna.	☐	☐	14	langsam	☐	☐

The *s* is voiced at the beginning of a word or a syllable:
die **S**onne, die Mu-**s**ik.

The *s* is voiceless at the end of a word or a syllable:
das Hau**s** (aber: die Häu-**s**er, zu Hau-**s**e), die Li**s**-te.

ss and *ß* are always voiceless.

Ich hab's geschafft!

Cultural information

Although the German-speaking countries do not have many natural resources, and the geography is not always suitable for establishing industry, almost every village nowadays seems to have its own business. After the Second World War when everything seemed lost, everybody in Germany and Austria tried to make a new living for themselves as best they could. Many a small craftsman finished up a wealthy industrialist. But the man in the street also benefited from the *Wirtschaftswunder* (economic miracle) and after decades of hard work were finally able to say, "Ich hab's geschafft!"

The situation has become quite different for young people entering employment since the nineteen nineties. They either live off the accumulated wealth of their parents, or pursue career goals with a great sense of discipline and purpose, or else they join the great mass of the unemployed.

Anyone wanting to make a successful career for themselves in industry in Germany has a number of options open to them. Most work their way up from inside a company. Many top executives used to be apprentices in the same company and have never worked anywhere else. Nowadays, however, with flexibility being the order of the day, many try to achieve the same goal by changing jobs and companies several times. They apply for every job that's advertised. There is no harm in having connections, but many make it on their own merit. Good training naturally plays a not insignificant role. This can be done within a company or at the appropriate colleges. Large companies such as Siemens or Telekom have been offering their own academic training in-house for decades. These days they are specialising more and more in preparing their top managers for specific new tasks. Lifelong learning of new information and processes has become the watchword in all the German-speaking countries.

Language

Karl hat eine Schwester.
Das ist **seine** Schwester.
(Karl has a sister.
This is his sister.)

The possessive article (der Possessivartikel) *mein, dein, sein* etc. shows the relationship between two terms. They can be people, objects or abstract concepts.

Karl → seine Schwester

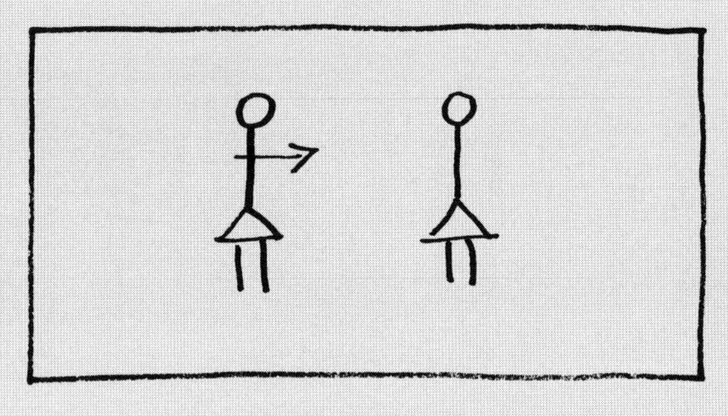

Anna → ihre Schwester

In terms of content, the possessive article relates to its word of reference (Karl → seine, Anna → ihre). *Sein* stands for Karl, *ihr* for Anna.

di**e** Schwester → sein**e** Schwester
der Chef → sein Chef
Er versteht sein**en** Chef.

The ending of the possessive article is determined by the gender, case and number of the noun that follows.

Ich hab's geschafft!

1

Read the picture story. What does *Ich hab's geschafft!*, mean, leaving out the last two pictures? Please tick.

1 I work a lot. ☐

2 I have achieved my aim. ☐

3 I have finished my work. ☐

2

Write the gender (*m*, *n* or *f*) next to the nouns and underline the possessive article *mein*.

Possessivartikel im Nominativ, Akkusativ

3 Put the possessive articles from the picture story in the table below.

	Singular maskulin		neutral	feminin	Plural m, n, f
	Nom.	Akk.	Nom. / Akk.	Nom. / Akk.	Nom. / Akk.
ich	....	mein**en**	....	....	mein**e**
du	....	....	....	....	....
Sie	Ihr	....	Ihr	....	....
er/es/man	sein	sein**en**	sein	....	sein**e**
sie	ihr	....	....	ihr**e**	....
wir	unser	....	....	unser**e**	....
ihr	euer	**euren**	euer	**eure**	**eure**
Sie	....	....	....	....	....
sie	ihr	....	ihr	....	ihr**e**

4 a Read the texts and underline the possessive articles and the nouns belonging to them.

Euro Markt

Unser Sonderangebot heute

Unsere Preise – Ihre Chance!

Atlantis Reisen

Reservieren Sie jetzt Ihren Urlaub!

Mallorca 7 Tage

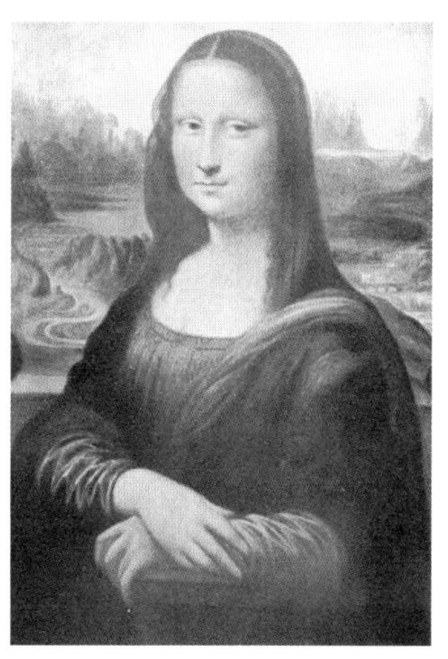

Mona Lisa und ihr weltberühmtes Lächeln

Hallo Juliane!
Heute ist dein 18. Geburtstag.
Alles Liebe und Gute
deine Franziska

der Chef und seine Sekretärin

b Write *m*, *n* or *f*, *Singular* (*Sg*) or *Plural* (*Pl*) and *Nominativ* (*N*) or *Akkusativ* (*A*) next to the nouns with possessive articles. Then enter the possessive articles in the table in section 3.

c Complete the table with all the missing possessive articles in their correct forms.

5 **a** Finish the sentences in the speech bubbles.

das Buch
die Zeitung
der Fotoapparat
das Auto
das Heft
der Kugelschreiber
die Tasche

b Repeat the exercise in the plural.
die Bücher ⦁ die Zeitungen ⦁ die Handschuhe ⦁
Sind das ...?

6 Finish the question with the nouns given below.

die Brille
der Schlüssel
der Ausweis
der Schirm
der Geldbeutel
die Handschuhe

Guten Tag!

Cultural information
In the German-speaking countries the day begins rather early. Food shops, newsagents and bakeries open at 7 am as most schools begin at about 8 am and most companies start work between 7 and 8 am. Up till 1st November 1996, all shops in Germany had to close by 6.30 pm, as early as 2 pm on Saturdays, and on Sundays nobody was allowed to sell anything at all. This meant the streets were dreary and deserted after the shops shut. There was a long drawn-out political quarrel about the issue. Many people wanted to be able do their shopping after work at their leisure. The trade unions and also many small shop owners, however, were strictly opposed to any changes. But the law did change, and shops can finally stay open until 8 pm and bakers are allowed to sell their rolls on a Sunday.

Language
In this unit you will learn about the verbal bracket (die Satzklammer), a defining grammatical feature of German. The American author Mark Twain, who took quite some interest in the German language, describes it in a satirical way as follows, "The Germans have another kind of parenthesis, which they make by splitting a verb into two and putting half of it at the beginning of an exciting chapter and the other half at the end of it. Can any one conceive of anything more confusing than that? These things are called 'separable verbs'. ... and the wider the two portions of one of them are spread apart, the better the author of the crime is pleased with his performance."
It is important to be aware of this special feature of German. When listening, you have to always bear in mind that a second part of the verb may follow at the end.

N. Gruner **steht** normalerweise, wenn er Unterricht hat, um 7 Uhr morgens **auf**. (N. Gruner normally gets up at seven when he has lessons.) The verb *aufstehen* is split into the two parts *stehen* and *auf*, and the others bits of the sentence are placed in between. It is a good idea to note down some typical examples of this sentence pattern and learn them by heart. It's also useful to make your own list of separable verbs (trennbare Verben) as you go along; putting them in simple example sentences will help you remember them.

Learning strategies
When you listen to a spoken text or a song on cassette, you have to make do without seeing the person and the setting, and this of course makes comprehension more difficult. So in this unit, the actual listening to the song is preceded by exercises which familiarise you with the non-linguistic setting. They focus on identifying background noises, recognizing the situation with the help of photos, and making guesses about who is talking to whom.

Guten Tag!

 **1** **a** Please listen. Which words, statements can you hear? What do the background noises mean? Make notes.

b Listen again and match the noises and statements to the photos. Write the numbers in the boxes next to the photos.

 **2** **a** Listen to the song and look at the photos at the same time.

b Listen to the song one more time and read the text.

Guten Tag!

Die Bäckerin macht den Laden auf.
Da stehen schon drei Kunden.
Der Direktor macht 'nen[1] Dauerlauf,
aber nur vier kurze Runden.

5 Die Leute von der Nachtschicht dürfen jetzt nach Hause geh'n[2].
Sie müssen den Tag von der falschen Seite seh'n.
Der Lehrer steigt ins Kabrio
und denkt an Karl den Großen.
Seine Frau hat schon den Koffer zu[3],
10 bügelt nie mehr seine Hosen.

Der Dichter deckt behutsam seine Schreibmaschine zu.
In seinem Kopf da spricht es immerzu:
Guten Tag! Guten Tag!
Es gibt[4] so viele Menschen, die man alle gerne mag[5].
15 Guten Tag!
So viele Menschen!

Thommie Bayer

1 'nen = einen
2 geh'n, seh'n = gehen, sehen
3 ... hat ... zu = short form of *hat ... zugemacht* = past tense of *zumachen*
4 Es gibt: there is
5 gerne mag: likes a lot

3 Write down the people from the text next to the photos in section 2: *die Bäckerin, die Kunden, ...*

4 Once again the text contains words which refer back to people/objects already mentioned (→ S. 24).

Die Bäckerin macht den Laden auf.

Da stehen schon drei Kunden. (Da = in front of the shop)

What do the following words refer to? *Sie* (line 6), *Seine* (line 9), *seine* (line 10), *seine* (line 11), *seinem* (line 12)? Use arrows to indicate your references.

5 **a** Underline the verbs in the text.

Die Bäckerin macht den Laden auf. ...

b Add the infinitives to the people in the photos in section 2.

einen Dauerlauf machen ◉ stehen ◉ nach Hause gehen ◉ bügeln ◉ in die Schule fahren ◉ den Laden aufmachen ◉ denken an ◉ den Koffer zumachen ◉ die Schreibmaschine zudecken

6 a Read the text.

Norbert Gruner ist Lehrer für Deutsch und Geschichte am Sophie-Scholl-Gymnasium. Er steht gern früh auf, frühstückt gemütlich und liest lange die Zeitung. Um halb acht fährt er in die Schule.
Der Unterricht fängt dort um Viertel vor acht an. Mittags kommt Norbert Gruner meist nach Hause. Nach dem Essen macht er einen Mittagsschlaf, dann korrigiert er Schülerarbeiten und bereitet den Unterricht für den nächsten Tag vor. Das Thema in der zwölften Klasse ist gerade Karl der Große. Das macht viel Arbeit. Abends geht er manchmal aus, dann trifft er Freunde und spielt vielleicht eine Partie Billard. Zwischen 11 und 12 Uhr geht er schlafen.

b Underline the verb forms of the following infinitives in the text.

aufstehen • frühstücken • lesen • fahren • anfangen • vorbereiten • ausgehen • treffen

Das Verb: trennbare Verben, Satzklammer

7 Complete the sentences from the song and from the text in section 6.

	Präfix/Verb		Verb		Präfix
1	auf/machen	Die Bäckerin	macht	....	auf
2	zu/decken	Der Dichter	....	....	....
3	auf/stehen	Norbert Gruner	....	....	....
4	an/fangen	Der Unterricht	....	....	....
5	vor/bereiten	Er	....	....	....
6	aus/gehen	Abends	....	....	....

Satzklammer (Verb … Präfix)

Intonation: Wortakzent

8 Listen and mark the main stress.

machen • aufmachen • zumachen • stehen • aufstehen • gehen • ausgehen • vorbereiten • vergessen • verstehen • zudecken • erklären • anfangen • besuchen • ergänzen

The verb is separable if the prefix is stressed:
áufstehen – Er steht um 8:00 Uhr auf.

The verb is inseparable if the stem of the verb is stressed:
verstéhen – Ich verstehe alles.

Sätze/Satzteile verbinden: *aber, und*

9 a Fill in the subjects and accusative objects from the song.

		1	2		
1		Die Bäckerin	macht		den Laden ..... auf.
2		Da	stehen	schon	.....
3		.....	macht		.....
4	**aber**	(.....)	(.....)	nur	.....,
5		.....	steigt		ins Kabrio
6	**und**	(.....)	denkt		an Karl den Großen.
7		.....	hat	schon	..... zu,
8		(.....)	bügelt	nie mehr	.....

The conjunctions *und*, *aber* or a comma connect two main clauses.

b What could be in the brackets? Put in the personal pronouns and the verb *macht*.

c Now have a closer look at the sentences. Why can the parts in brackets be left out?

10 Connect the sentences with *und* or *aber* or a comma. Put the parts that can be left out in brackets.

1 Der Lehrer denkt an Karl den Großen. Er denkt nicht an seine Frau.
2 Ich komme um 14:00 Uhr. Ich bleibe eine Stunde.
3 Jean ist Schweizer. Er spricht Französisch und Deutsch. Er spricht auch Englisch und Italienisch.
4 Wir machen einen Dauerlauf. Wir machen nur 2 Runden.

Tageszeiten

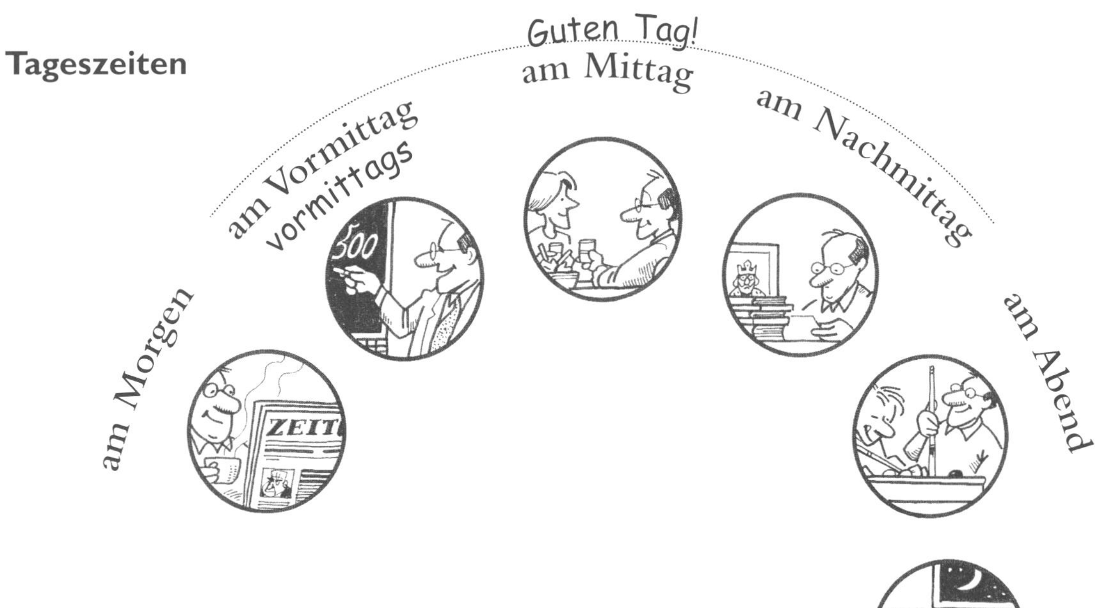

11 Add the following words to the drawing:

Guten Morgen! ◆ Guten Tag! ◆ Guten Abend! ◆ Gute Nacht! ◆ vormittags ◆ abends ◆ morgens ◆ nachmittags ◆ mittags ◆ nachts

12 **a** Read what people do during the course of a day.

b Write down some ideas of your own.

13 **a** Choose one of the two people and imagine what he/she does during the day.
Tick the activities in section 12.

b Make sentences.

Er (Sie) steht spät auf. Er (Sie) liest lange die Zeitung. ...

Der Satz: Hinweise zur Zeit

14 Underline all references to time in the text in section 6: time of day, clock times, *dann, manchmal.*

1	2		
Er	arbeitet		**morgens** nicht.
Er	liest		**morgens** lange die Zeitung.
Nachmittags	geht	er	oft ins Kino.
Dann/Danach	arbeitet	er	bis Mitternacht.

[References to time are often in initial position in a statement or come straight after the verb.]

15 Make a text out of your sentences in section 13 b. Add time references and possibly *manchmal* (sometimes), *immer* (always), *oft* (often). Connect the sentences with *und, aber.*

Am Montag fängt die Woche an.

- Was für ein Tag ist heute?
- Na, Montag!
- Noch vier Tage, dann ist Wochenende!

Montags sechs Seiten Sport in der Zeitung

Manche Leute arbeiten montags nicht. Sie machen blau. Blauer Montag!

Warum heißen manche Autos Montagsautos?

Friseur
Haar Art
Di–Fr 9.00–18.00
Sa 8.00–12.00
Montags geschlossen

Modimidofreisaso. Eine Woche in einem Wort.

16 In which situations and idioms in English does Monday play a special role?

17 a Listen and number the days of the week from 1–7.

Dienstag ☐ Freitag ☐ Montag ☐
Samstag ☐ Mittwoch ☐ Sonntag ☐
Donnerstag ☐

b Read out the days of the week in the correct order.

Die Zeit angeben: Wann?

	Wochentage		Tageszeiten		
gestern	am Montag	montags	am Morgen	morgens	gestern Morgen
heute	...	...	am Vormittag	vormittags	heute Morgen
morgen			am Nachmittag	nachmittags	morgen Vormittag, ...
	am Samstag/	samstags/	am Abend	abends	
	am Sonnabend[1]	sonnabends	in der Nacht	nachts	

am Montagmorgen, am Dienstagnachmittag, ...
montags, dienstags, ... = immer am Montag, Dienstag, ...; jeden Montag, Dienstag, ...

[1] *Am Sonnabend, sonnabends* is predominantly used in North Germany.

Wann sind Sie gut gelaunt?

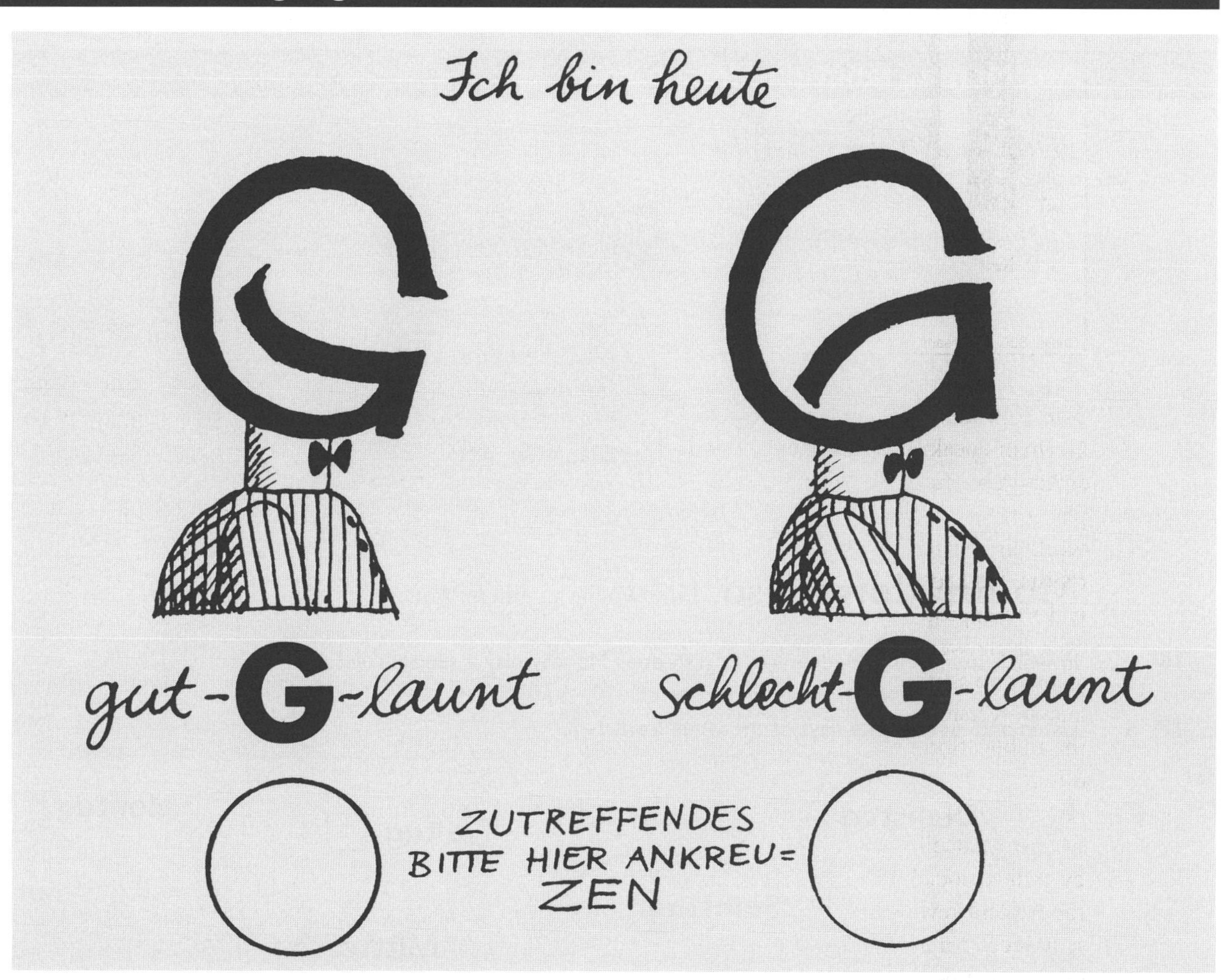

- Montags bin ich immer gut gelaunt.
- Was? Ich bin am Montag immer schlecht gelaunt!

18 And you? When are you in a good/bad mood? Why?

Maloche

Cultural information

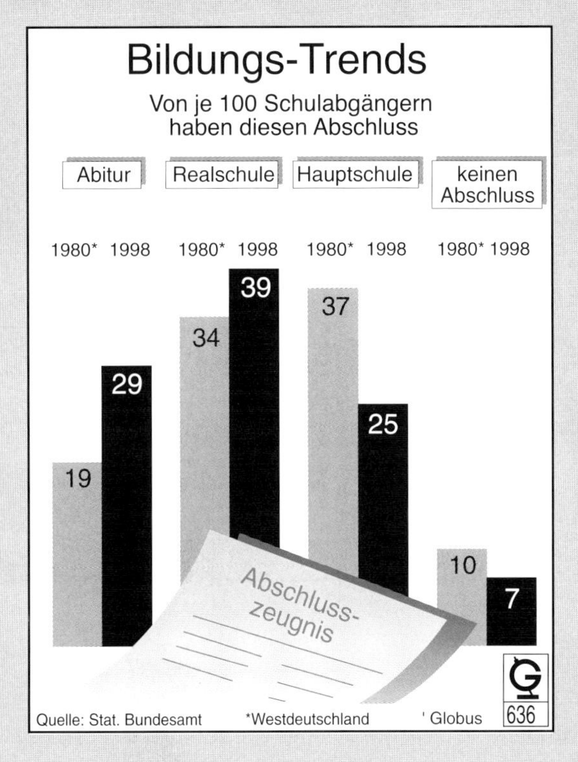

The seventies saw great social changes in the German-speaking countries. In industry and agriculture more and more workers were replaced by machines. Instead, people found work in the service industries (as bus drivers, typists, bank clerks and office workers) if they had the appropriate qualifications. Often, however, these were lacking. Academics and politicians were against opening up grammar schools and universities to the lower classes. But after the publication of the book "Die deutsche Bildungskatastrophe" (The disaster in German education) in 1965, reform of the school system gradually got under way, accompanied by radical social changes which culminated in the student revolt of 1968. What were the consequences for the education system? Equality of opportunity was the catchword that dominated the educational debate. However positive the subsequent developments may have been, there is no denying that they have also had a negative effect on family life, being the source of some quite major psychological problems. The text "Maloche" gives voice to the generation gap that developed and in fact still affects many families today.

The word *Maloche* is derived from the Yiddish word *melocho* and means hard work. It is still used today, especially in the Rhine-Ruhr region, the largest heavy industry and coal mining area in Europe, a region that is also home to big football clubs (Schalke, Dortmund, Bayer Leverkusen, Vfl Bochum). The reason may be that there has always been a long tradition of economic migration into the region. The large number of Polish names is an indication of where most of them originally came from.

Language

If you do not notice a negation (die Negation) you misunderstand a statement. Negation signals in German are the words *nicht* or *kein*.

Frankenstein ist **kein** Monster.
Fast Food ist **nicht** ungesund.

Kein negates a noun, *nicht* negates a more comprehensive statement.

Statements are often modified and made more precise by so-called modal verbs (die Modalverben) such as *müssen* (must, have to) and *können* (can, be able to).

Ich **muss** heute nicht so viel arbeiten.
(I don't have to work that much today.)

Ich **kann** heute faulenzen.
(I can laze about today.)

The forms of the modal verbs are irregular and cannot be practised often enough because of the famous verbal bracket.

Maloche

1 Who are the people in the picture story? Where is it taking place? How can you tell?

da is man nu = da ist man nun

un dann muß ma noch = und dann muss man noch

muß (old spelling) = muss

2 Which word is not good German for work?

3 Which words does the teacher use to correct the student? Which words does the son use to correct his father? Write down.

Lehrer	Sohn (son)
....	....
....	....

4 Listen to the dialogue. Watch out for the intonation.

5 The father does not speak dialect but a regional form of colloquial German. Read the extract for the headwords *Maloche, malochen* from two dictionaries.

Maloche

Ma·lo·che *die; -; nur Sg, bes nordd gespr;* die Arbeit im Beruf ⟨in die / zur M. gehen⟩
ma·lo·chen; *malochte, hat malocht;* [Vi] *bes nordd gespr;* sehr viel u. körperlich anstrengend arbeiten

Plur. -s *u.* ...occhi [maˈlɔki] ⟨ital.⟩ (*ital. Bez. für* böser Blick)
Ma|lo|che [*auch* ...ˈlɔ...], die; - ⟨hebr.-jidd.⟩ (*ugs. für* schwere Arbeit); **ma|lo|chen** (*ugs. für* schwer arbeiten, schuften); **Ma|lo|cher** (*ugs. für* Arbeiter)

ugs. = umgangssprachlich: colloquial
bes nordd gespr = besonders norddeutsch gesprochen: mainly used in spoken language in North Germany

6 Transform what the father says in the third picture into high German.

7 What does the father intend by *Dir werd ich gutes Deutsch beibringen!* Please tick.

1 I only speak good German. ☐
2 Your father knows everything better. ☐
3 I'm not going to be criticized by you. ☐

Negation: *nicht, kein*

8 Try to find one sentence each containing *nicht* and *kein* and write them down.

nicht: .... **kein:** ....

nicht* or *kein

Das ist schön. → Das ist **nicht** schön.
Der Vater sagt immer Maloche. → Der Vater sagt **nicht** immer Maloche.
Kein always negates a noun with an indefinite or a zero article.
Der Mann ist **ein** Monster. → Nein, er ist **kein** Monster.
gutes Deutsch → **kein** gutes Deutsch

9 Make the following sentences negative.

1 Einstein war ein schlechter Schüler. Einstein war **kein** schlechter Schüler.
Mozart war ein armer Schlucker . ...

2 Das ist ein deutsches Wort. Das ist **kein** deutsches Wort.
Das ist ein gutes Buch. ....

3 Sie ist Französin. Sie ist **keine** Französin.
Sie ist Lehrerin. ....

4 Bernd liest einen Satz. Bernd liest **keinen** Satz.
Inge schreibt einen Brief. ....

5 Klaus macht eine Liste. Klaus macht **keine** Liste.
Paul hat eine Uhr. ....

6 Erwin schreibt Sätze. Erwin schreibt **keine** Sätze.
Doris bügelt Hosen. ....

kein im Nominativ, Akkusativ

10 Fill in the forms from section 9.

	Singular			Plural
	maskulin	neutral	feminin	m, n, f
Nominativ	kein			Sätze
	Satz	.... Monster	.... Liste	.... Monster
Akkusativ	....			Listen

11 *Kein* or *nicht*? Make the following sentences negative.

1 In England regnet es ......nicht......... mehr als in Italien.
2 Chinesen haben .... gelbe Haut.
3 Fast Food ist .... ungesund.
4 Alkohol wärmt ....
5 Die Bäckerin hat .... Laden.
6 Schokolade ist .... schlecht für die Zähne.
7 Der Direktor macht .... Dauerlauf.
8 Einstein war .... schlechter Schüler.
9 Diät macht .... dünn.
10 Die Frau bügelt heute .... Hosen.
11 Mozart war .... armer Schlucker.

Intonation: Satzakzent

There can be several stresses in longer sentences:
Und mórgens geht mein Váter immer zur Árbeit. Aber mein Váter sagt Malóche. Mein Váter sagt ímmer Malóche.
A sentence has a sentence stress and mostly one or more rhythmic stresses. The sentence stress is always on the most important information..

12 **a** Listen and mark the stresses.

■ Und morgens geht mein Vater auf die Maloche.
▲ Maloche? Warum sagst du Maloche? Das heißt nicht Maloche. Das heißt Arbeit! Maloche ist nicht schön. Das muss Arbeit heißen.
■ Mein Vater sagt immer Maloche.
▲ Das ist kein gutes Deutsch. In gutem Deutsch heißt das Arbeit.
■ Mein Vater sagt aber immer Maloche.

b Listen again and underline the word which carries the sentence stress.

Das Verb: Modalverben Präsens (1)

13 *Kann* or *muss*? Fill the gaps.

1 Maloche .... man nicht sagen.

2 Das .... Arbeit heißen.

3 Man .... auch Job sagen.

14 Fill in the verb forms.

	müssen	**können**
ich	m**u**ss	k**a**nn
du	m**u**ss **t**	k**a**nn **st**
Sie	müss **en**	könn **en**
er/sie/es/man	....	....
wir	müss **en**	könn **en**
ihr	müss **t**	könn **t**
Sie	müss **en**	könn **en**
sie	....	....

15 *Können* or *müssen*? Put in the correct forms.

1 Das .... man nicht sagen.

2 Das .... Arbeit heißen.

3 Man .... Vater oder Papa sagen.

4 Immer .... ich aufs Essen warten.

5 Ich .... jetzt nach Hause gehen. Ich habe viel Arbeit.

6 Wir .... nicht kommen. Wir haben keine Zeit.

Satzklammer

Ich	muss	viel	arbeiten.
Ich	muss	heute viel	arbeiten.
Ich	muss	heute nicht so viel	arbeiten.
	Modalverb		**Verb im Infinitiv**

Satzklammer

16 What do teachers and students have to do?

Die Schüler müssen viel Deutsch sprechen. Die Lehrer müssen ...

viel Deutsch sprechen • den Unterricht vorbereiten • viel lesen und schreiben • zu Hause lernen • die Wörter buchstabieren • die Grammatik wiederholen • Schülerarbeiten korrigieren • laut sprechen • Übungen machen • in die Schule kommen • viel fragen • die Grammatik erklären

17 a Read the advertisement and underline all the internationalisms.

ANZEIGEN — BADISCHE ZEITUNG

Gehen auch Sie neue Wege:

☐ ☐ **Wir setzen neue Maßstäbe in der Medizintechnik: Als Mitglied der TRUMPF Gruppe entwickeln und produzieren wir medizinische Geräte und Instrumente zur physikalischen Therapie und Chirurgie. Ein hochmotiviertes und einsatzfreudiges Team sowie aktive Forschung und Entwicklung sind die Basis unseres Erfolges.**

☐ **Reizt Sie diese Herausforderung**
Dann senden Sie uns Ihre vollständige Bewerbungsunterlagen zu. Bitte mit Gehaltswunsch und frühestem Eintrittstermin.

HÜTTINGER

H

[1] **Hüttinger Medizintechnik GmbH + Co. KG**

☐ Frau Elisabeth Tegethoff
Elsässer Str. 8 (Postfach 772)
71910 Freiburg
http://www.huetting.com

Wir suchen kreative Verstärkung:

☐ **Sekretär/in der Geschäftsleitung**

☐ Sie übernehmen selbständig die deutsch- und englischsprachige Korrespondenz für unseren Geschäftsführer und Entwicklungsleiter. Weiterhin unterstützen Sie den Bereich Technische Dokumentationen.

☐ Sie sind **Fremdsprachensekretär/in** und besitzen sehr gute Englisch- und evtl. Französischkenntnisse. Sie haben eine vergleichbare Position seit ca. 3 Jahren inne und stellen dort Ihr Durschsetzungsvermögen und Ihr echtes Organisationsgeschick unter Beweis. Alle gäungigen PC-Anwendungen beherrschen Sie sicher.

☐ Einarbeitung (auch in SAP) ist bei uns selbstverständlich. Wir bieten Ihnen einen modern ausgestatteten Arbeitsplatz in einem international operierenden HighTech Unternehmen.

b Match the questions to the sections above. Fill in the numbers in the boxes next to the text.

1 What is the name of the company?
2 What does the company manufacture?
3 What are the products for?
4 Where is the company based?
5 Who is the company looking for?
6 What will the person have to do?
7 Which requirements must the person fulfil?
8 What does the company offer?
9 What does the applicant have to do?

Heute hier, morgen dort

Cultural information

The writer of the song "Heute hier, morgen dort", Hannes Wader, is one of the musicians in Germany and Austria who think about society and have a political message. *Liedermacher* (singer-songwriters) are what people like that are called. At the beginning, their audience was mainly made up of educated young people who tended to be on the left of the political spectrum. Later on, rock musicians also became a part of the singer-songwriter culture, singing songs with texts about social issues. But otherwise the music scene is divided. A large part of it is taken up by unpretentious, light *Schlagermusik* (popular music), which often still contains elements of the folk music that has now almost disappeared.

This sort of music is consumer-oriented, produced for quick sale and is almost entirely under the control of business. No singer of this kind has ever managed to become well-known outside Germany. Many educated people despise this style of music and, instead, go to classical music concerts and the opera. Thus a cultural class society has developed with two poles, U-Musik (*Unterhaltungsmusik*: light music) and E-Musik (*ernste Musik:* serious music). Just occasionally music groups nudge their way in between them, with music appealing to all social classes. All this has led to a general impoverishment of musical life. This is the reason why there is little light music that is familiar to listeners outside Germany. The times when Marlene Dietrich's chansons or Brecht's "Macky Messer" were heard all over the world are long since past. The few German rock groups who have made a name for themselves on the international scene sing in English and usually have English names, too. Exceptions are groups like "BAP" or "Die Toten Hosen". Apart from that, young people listen to music that comes from America, Britain and also Italy.

Language

In German there are two past tenses, the perfect (das Perfekt) and the past (das Präteritum), which is sometimes referred to as the Imperfekt in dictionaries. The perfect, which is introduced in this unit, is relatively easy to form using *haben* or *sein* and the past participle (das Partizip II). A distinction is drawn between regular and irregular verbs (regelmäßige und unregelmäßige Verben). Some grammars use the terms *stark* (strong) and *schwach* (weak). Start a list of irregular verbs that you can add to as you go along. Leave the past column empty for now; you can fill in those forms when you get to Units 18 and 20, where the past is introduced.

Infinitiv	Präsens	Präteritum	Perfekt: hat/ist + Partizip II
sprechen	spricht		hat gesprochen

Heute hier, morgen dort

1 The title of the song is "Heute hier, morgen dort". What could the song be about? Jot down ideas in note form.

2 a Check the meaning of the following words.

heute ◆ morgen ◆ hier ◆ niemals ◆ nun ◆ gestern ◆ da (hier) ◆ manchmal ◆ dort

b Mark the time and place words in different colours.

3 Listen to the song and read it at the same time.

Heute hier, morgen dort
bin kaum da, muss ich fort,
hab' mich niemals deswegen beklagt;
hab' es selbst so gewählt,
nie die Jahre gezählt,
nie nach gestern und morgen gefragt.
Manchmal träume ich schwer
und dann denk' ich, es wär'
Zeit[1] zu bleiben und nun
was[2] ganz andres zu tun.

So vergeht Jahr um Jahr
und es ist mir längst klar[3],
dass nichts bleibt, dass nichts bleibt,
wie[4] es war.

Hannes Wader

1 es wär' Zeit: it's about time
2 was = etwas
3 es ist mir längst klar: I realized a long time ago
4 wie (comparison): as

4 Mark the words listed in section 2a in the text with the appropriate colour.

5 Check the meaning of these verbs.

sich beklagen ◆ träumen ◆ wählen ◆ denken ◆ fragen nach ◆
bleiben ◆ fortmüssen ◆ tun ◆ zählen ◆ vergehen

6 The song is written partially in the present, partially in the past. Underline the verbs in the present and the verbs with a past form.

bin   hab ... beklagt   war

7 Listen to the song again. Add to or correct your notes from section 1.

Das Verb: Perfekt

Gegenwart – Vergangenheit

Ich bin heute hier und morgen dort. Ich habe mich niemals beklagt, ich habe es selbst so gewählt. Ich habe nie die Jahre gezählt. Jetzt aber denke ich manchmal, es wäre Zeit, hier zu bleiben und etwas anderes zu tun. Aber so vergehen die Jahre.

Present, always (it used to be like this and it still is now): Präsens
Past time: Perfekt

Satzklammer

The perfect consists of 2 parts: *haben* or *sein* + past participle.

8 Complete some more sentences from the song.

Ich	habe	mich niemals	beklagt.
Ich	habe	es	....
Ich	habe	nie	....
Ich	bin	nicht oft nach Hause	gekommen.
Ich	bin	nie lange dort	geblieben.
	haben/sein		**Partizip II**

Satzklammer

Partizip II

regelmäßige Verben				**unregelmäßige Verben**			
☐ zählen	**ge**	zähl	**t**	☐ kommen	**ge**	komm	**en**
☐ arbeiten	**ge**	arbeit	**et**	☐ schreiben	**ge**	schri**e**b	**en**
☐ diskutieren	–	diskutier	**t**	☐ sprechen	**ge**	spr**o**ch	**en**
☐ einkaufen	ein**ge**	kauf	**t**	☐ ausgehen	aus**ge**	**gang**	**en**
☐ erklären	–	erklär	**t**	☐ verstehen	–	verst**and**	**en**
	–/ge		**t**		**–/ge**		**en**

Exception e. g.: denken – ge·dach·t

9 Write the numbers of the explanations next to the relevant verbs in the table.

1 Verbs with a separable prefix have *ge* between the prefix and the verb stem: aufmachen – auf**ge**macht, aufstehen – auf**ge**standen.
2 Verbs ending in *-ieren* form their past participle without *ge*: buchstabieren – buchstabier**t**.
3 If the verb stem ends in *t* or *d*, the participle ending is *-et*: warten – gewart**et**.
4 Verbs with an inseparable prefix (e.g. *be*, *ge*, *er*, *ver*) form their participle without *ge*: vergehen – vergangen, besuchen – besucht.

Perfekt mit *haben* oder *sein*

***haben* + past participle**
Was hast du gestern gemacht?
Ich habe gearbeitet.

***sein* + past participle**
Er ist schon nach Hause gekommen.
Er ist früh aufgestanden.

Most verbs form their perfect with *haben*.
Verbs expressing a change of place (e.g. *kommen, gehen*) or of state (e.g. *aufstehen*) form their perfect with *sein*.
Also *bleiben, sein, werden*:

Ich bin ... geblieben. Du bist ... gewesen.
Er ist ... geworden.

10 Fill in the past participle or the infinitive in the table. Mark (with a cross) whether the perfect is formed with *haben* or *sein*. Then write sentences with the verbs.

	Infinitiv	haben	sein	Partizip II	
1	bleiben	☐	☒	geblieben	Ich bin eine Stunde dort geblieben.
2	sprechen	☐	☐	....	....
3	trinken	☐	☐	....	....
4	warten	☐	☐	....	....
5	schreiben	☐	☐	....	....
6	hören	☐	☐	....	....
7	beginnen	☐	☐	....	....
8	verstehen	☐	☐	....	....
9	aufstehen	☐	☐	....	....
10	sein	☐	☐	....	....
11		☐	☐	gemacht	....
12		☐	☐	gegessen	....
13		☐	☐	angefangen	....
14		☐	☐	getroffen	....
15		☐	☐	gesagt	....
16		☐	☐	gelesen	....
17		☐	☐	gesehen	....
18		☐	☐	ausgegangen	....

Ich will nicht mehr!

11 Which statement goes with which picture? Write the letter from the picture in the box.

1 I don't want to any more. ☐
2 I'm not allowed to. ☐
3 I'm too small. ☐

12 Translate the speech bubbles.

....

....

....

A ☐

B ☐

C ☐

13 Modal verbs can also be used without another verb: Ich will nicht. The meaning is made clear by the context, e. g: Ich will nicht **bleiben**. Add appropriate verbs to the speech bubbles.

14 Which statement from the song matches the picture story?

Das Verb: Modalverben Präsens (2)

15 a Write down the infinitive that belongs to the examples and explanations.

A	Ich kann das (nicht) auf Deutsch sagen.	**ability (inability)**	(nicht) können
B	Ich kann (nicht) hier bleiben. Du kannst den Brief (nicht) lesen.	**(im)possibility/permission**	....
C	Sie dürfen nach Hause gehen.	**permission**	....
D	Du darfst den Brief nicht lesen.	**forbidding/no permission**	....
E	Kann ich Sie etwas fragen?	**polite question**	....
	Darf ich etwas sagen? Darf ich bleiben?		....
F	Ich muss (nicht) Deutsch lernen.	**(no) necessity**	(nicht)................
G	Ich will (nicht) hier bleiben.	**wish/decision/plan**	....
H	Er mag Ilona (nicht). Magst du (keine) Schokolade? (Isst du (nicht) gern ...?)	**(no) liking/preference**	(nicht) mögen
I	Spielen wir Billard? Nein, ich mag nicht.	**no desire**	nicht..................

b Make further example sentences to match the given meanings.

c What meaning do the modal verbs *können, wollen, dürfen* have in the picture story? Add the letters from the overview to the boxes under the pictures.

d What other modal verb can be used to express *Ich will nicht mehr!*?

16 Fill in the verb forms.

	können	**dürfen**	**wollen**	**müssen**	**mögen**
ich	....	darf	....	....	mag
du	....	darfst	....	musst	....
Sie	....	dürfen	....	....	....
er/sie/es/man	kann	darf	....	....	....
wir	....	dürfen	....	....	....
ihr	....	dürft	wollt	....	mögt
Sie	....	dürfen	....	....	....
sie	....	dürfen	....	....	....

17 Fill in *dürfen, können, mögen, müssen, wollen.*

1 Sonntag! Ich .... nicht so früh aufstehen!

2 ■ .... ich die Zeitung haben? ▲ Ja, bitte.

3 ■ Gehen wir heute Abend aus? ▲ Nein, ich .... nicht, ich .... zu Hause bleiben und arbeiten. ■ Ja, wie immer, du .... zu Hause bleiben und fernsehen.

4 ■ .... Sie den Tee? ▲ Sehr. Was für ein Tee ist das?

5 Sie .... sehr gut Spanisch. Sie hat 3 Jahre in Barcelona gelebt.

6 ■ .... wir Sie einen Moment sprechen? ▲ Ja, aber schnell, ich habe wenig Zeit.

7 ■ Besuchen wir Regina? ▲ Heute .... ich nicht. Geht es auch morgen?

18 a Write sentences with the items given. Be careful with the word order.

dürfen ✎ wollen ✎
können ✎ müssen

bleiben ✎ gehen ✎
essen ✎ lesen ✎ fernsehen ✎
schreiben ✎ warten (auf)

montags ✎ so viel ✎ morgen ✎ jetzt ✎
ins Kino ✎ immer ✎ manchmal ✎ schnell ✎
Andreas ✎ nicht ✎ einen Brief ✎
die Zeitung ✎ um 6 Uhr ✎ so lange ✎
zu Hause ✎ 2 Stunden ✎ Schokolade

Du musst schnell schreiben, ich will nicht so lange auf einen Brief warten.

b Fill in *wollen, müssen, können, dürfen, mögen.*

Morgens ... ✎ Abends ... ✎
Am Wochenende ...

ich nicht ... ✎ ich nie ... ✎ ich immer ... ✎

Kunkels Dias

Cultural information

Germans are great travellers. They travel more than any other nation in the world. In 1995 German households spent an average of almost 1500 euros on their holidays. They can afford to as well. Not only because they have enough money – as long as they're not unemployed – but also because of the generous holiday entitlements. Take an average middle-class family: Herr Horst Wesel (45) is shop-floor manager in an engineering company, his wife Trude (38) works part-time in a bank. They have a 12-year-old son who is at grammar school.

Herr Wesel has 30 working days' holiday a year, Frau Wesel's entitlement is 28 days. On top of that there are 104 Saturdays and Sundays and 14 public holidays per year. The boy has a total of 12 weeks school holidays. The Wesels spread their holiday over the whole year so they can go away on a long trip twice a year. The summer holiday is more for relaxation and pleasure – the boy mustn't miss out, after all – and is spent on one of the so-called *Teutonengrills* (der Teutonengrill) on the beaches of the Adriatic, Mallorca, Florida or the North Sea, where the family just bakes in the sun. The second holiday is supposed to have some educational value. It should take them as far away as possible to somewhere definitely exotic. So they head for Thailand, Kenya or Greenland. The Wesels are the proud owners of state-of-the art photographic equipment and a brand-new video, and they always come back with rich pickings. The neighbours and friends after all must see that the Wesels have made it and can afford such fantastic trips.

Learning strategies

Let's assume you have to tell your German friends about your holiday. It's a good idea to note down a scenario first: What will I be asked? What will I tell them? How will I express my pleasure or displeasure? What might my conversation partners want to say?

Make notes on each of these questions in English and then in German. You'll find the material you need in your coursebook. But reference should be made to a dictionary, too. Work through your notes carefully and learn the important expressions and phrases by heart. It may be that the conversation takes a quite unexpected turn. If it does, correct your notes afterwards and put them in a folder till your next trip.

Kunkels Dias

1 Check the meaning of the words in the suitcase.

reisen • fahren • eine Reise machen •
fliegen • nach Österreich • in die Schweiz •
nach Deutschland • in die Türkei •
nach Frankreich • nach Italien •
nach Amerika • nach Afrika

2 **a** Make dialogues.

Was machen Sie	im Urlaub?	Ich fahre ....
Was machst du		Wir fliegen ....
Was macht ihr		Ich ....
Wohin fährst du		Ich bleibe zu Hause.
		Wir bleiben ....

b Speak the dialogues.

3 Read the poem.

I.

Herr Kunkel, Mathias,
hat dreitausend Dias
mit allem Komfort.
Für jede Reise
5 **hat Kunkel Beweise**
in Agfacolor!

II.

Er war auf Mallorca,
er war auf Menorca,
er war auch auf Capri,
10 **in Rom und Athen,**
und alle Bekannten
und Onkel und Tanten
und armen Verwandten,
die sollen das sehn!

III.

15 **Kaum ist man bei Kunkel,**
da macht er schon dunkel
und bittet um Ruhe,
und dann legt er los.
Da sieht man im Bilde
20 **die Gattin Mathilde**
und Schwägerin Hilde
in lebensgroß.

IV.

Mal speisen sie Pizza
in Nizza, Ibiza,
25 **mal sind sie zu Wasser,**
mal sind sie zu Land,
und alle Bekannten
und alle Verwandten,
die rufen ganz neidisch:
30 **Hochinteressant!**

Roswitha Fröhlich

4 The poem consists of four verses.

1 Where do we find out what Herr Kunkel does on holiday? ....

2 Where do we find out what places Herr Kunkel has been to? ....

3 In which verse does Herr Kunkel prepare his slide show? ....

4 Where are Herr Kunkel's relatives talked about? ....

5 Where do we find out something about the number of slides? ....

5 The poem contains a number of words used internationally, the meaning of others can be guessed from the context. Complete the list without looking in a dictionary.

geographical terms	relatives	first names	food	photography
Mallorca				

6 Reconstruct the sentences from the text.

		auf Capri
	macht	Beweise in Agfacolor
Herr Kunkel	war	in Athen
Er	bittet	um Ruhe
	hat	dreitausend Dias
		dunkel

Intonation: rhythmisches Sprechen

7 **a** Listen and read.

Kaum ist man bei Kunkel, / →
da macht er schon dunkel →
und bittet um Ruhe, / →
und dann legt er los. / ↘
Da sieht man im Bilde →
die Gattin Mathilde / →
und Schwägerin Hilde / →
in lebensgroß. ↘

b Read and mark the accented parts.

Mal speisen Sie Pizza
in Nizza, Ibiza,
mal sind sie zu Wasser,
mal sind sie zu Land,
und alle Bekannten
und alle Verwandten,
die rufen ganz neidisch:
Hochinteressant!

c Mark the pauses (/) and the melody (→ ↘).
d Read the texts aloud.

In the sentence the melody remains constant (→), even when there is a pause (/) between word groups. It only falls at the end of the sentence. (↘).

Urlaub machen

8 **a** Here are some expressions to do with *Urlaub*. Continue the list.

in der Sonne liegen • Tennis spielen • schwimmen • wandern • ausgehen • viel schlafen • fernsehen • besichtigen • einen Ausflug machen • faulenzen • lesen • ...

b What did you do on your last holiday / last weekend? Say what you did.

Verwandtschaftsbezeichnungen

9 Fill in the English equivalents.

Mann	Frau (*formal* Gattin)	Ehepaar ....
Sohn	Tochter	Kinder ....
Junge	Mädchen	
Bruder	Schwester	Geschwister ....
Vater	Mutter	Eltern ....
Schwiegervater	Schwiegermutter	Schwiegereltern ....
Großvater	Großmutter	Großeltern ....
Enkel	Enkelin	Enkelkinder ....
Neffe	Nichte	
Cousin	Cousine (Kusine)	
verheiratet	ledig	geschieden ....

10 Describe your family as in the example.

Ich habe zwei Geschwister, mein Bruder heißt Karl und ist noch ledig, meine Schwester Else ist verheiratet und hat drei Kinder. Sie wohnt in Karlsruhe.

Das Verb: Präteritum (1)

11 The poem describes actions in the present and in the past. What verb form is used? Mark the past in blue and the present in red.

12 Fill in the verb forms.

Herr Kunkel war auf Mallorca. Er hatte Urlaub.

	sein	**haben**
ich	war	hat **te**
du	war **st**	hat **test**
Sie	war **en**	hat **ten**
er/sie/es/man	....	....
wir	....	hat **ten**
ihr	war **t**	hat **tet**
Sie	....	hat **ten**
sie	....	hat **ten**

In speech the perfect is normally used to express the past. But with *sein* and *haben* the past forms *war* and *hatte* are preferred:

Er **war** in Mallorca. Er **ist** nach Mallorca **geflogen**.
Herr Kunkel **hatte** Urlaub. Er **hat** Dias **gemacht**.

13 Complete the sentences. Use the verbs *sein, haben, kommen, machen, bleiben, sehen, rufen* in the perfect or past.

Im Urlaub .... (1) wir in Spanien. Wir .... (2) viel Zeit. Ich .... viele Dias .... (3). Alle Verwandten und Bekannten .... zu mir nach Hause .... (4). Sie .... vier Stunden .... (5) und .... 300 Dias .... (6). 300 Mal .... sie .... (7): „Hochinteressant!“ Es .... (8) sehr schön.

Das Verb: Modalverben Präsens (3)

Er war in Rom und Athen und alle Verwandten **sollen** das sehen.

sollen

Alle Verwandten sollen das sehen.	Herr K. wants all his relatives to see it. Wish (indirect)
■ Sollen wir kommen? ▲ Natürlich sollt ihr kommen.	Is it your wish that we should come?
Du sollst nicht immer Maloche sagen.	You've been told you're not allowed to say Maloche.

14 Fill in the verb forms (endings as with other modal verbs, → S. 62)

sollen			
ich	....	wir	....
du	....	ihr	....
Sie	....	Sie	....
er/sie/es/man	....	sie	....

15 Make sentences with *sollen*. Use the following expressions.

zu Hause bleiben und lernen ● um 7 Uhr aufstehen ● schwimmen gehen ● nach Hause gehen ● nicht so viel arbeiten ● einen Sprachkurs machen ● „Arbeit“ sagen ● nicht so viel trinken ● fragen

1 Er wartet schon 2 Stunden. Er soll nach Hause gehen.
2 Sie schläft immer bis 10 Uhr. Sie ....
3 Er trinkt sehr viel. Er ....
4 ■ Ich habe keine Zeit. ▲ Du ....
5 ■ Wir machen keinen Sport. ▲ Ihr ....
6 Er sagt immer Maloche. Er ....
7 Ihr geht in die Disko? Ihr ....
8 ■ Ich kann kein Englisch. ▲ Sie ....
9 ■ Ich verstehe nichts. ▲ Dann .... du ....

Wie finden Sie ...?

16 **a** Fill in.

Wie finden Sie ....? (Das ist) wunderschön.

Wie findest du ....? (Das finde ich) super.

Wie gefällt dir ....? (Das gefällt mir) super, sehr, ganz gut, gar nicht.

Wie gefällt Ihnen ....?

Was hältst du von ....? (Davon halte ich) viel, nicht viel, gar nichts.

Was halten Sie von ....?

--- -- - -/+ ++ +++

todlangweilig hochinteressant

sehr langweilig sehr interessant

ziemlich langweilig ganz interessant, spannend

nicht besonders interessant

nicht besonders schön

ziemlich hässlich ganz schön

hässlich toll, sehr schön

schrecklich super, wunderschön

b Talk about cities, countries, films, objects, books, people. Make little dialogues.

- Wie gefällt Ihnen das Buch?
- Ich finde es nicht besonders interessant.

- Was halten Sie von Kunkels Dias?
- Ich finde sie super.

Ein Farbiger

Cultural information

When a group of people forms a minority in the face of a large majority group, be it on account of their religion, race, origin, language or culture, a feeling of inferiority often arises on the one side, of arrogance on the other. Over the last 50 years, more and more foreigners have settled in Germany, thus creating more minorities. The figures are 8.2% in Germany and 6.6% in Austria. Most are economic migrants from southern European and north African countries who have come looking for work. Then there are refugees and asylum seekers from all corners of the world where wars, conflicts and dictatorships make it impossible for people to live freely. In Switzerland, however, a large proportion of foreign residents (18% of the population) are from the states of the European Union. There are 7.173 million foreigners in Germany. The largest group is made up of 1.8 million Turks.

Berlin-Kreuzberg is the fourth-largest Turkish city after Istanbul, Ankara and Izmir. The presence of so many foreigners is not without its problems of course. It's interesting to note, however, that in cities like Frankfurt, where almost 30% of the population is of foreign origin, there is less friction than in the former East Germany with a foreigner ratio of only 1.7%. But unemployment is at its highest there and thus also the fear that someone could take away your job.

Language

Below you can see how the American writer Mark Twain made fun of one of German's strangest features, the end-position of the verb in a subordinate clause (Nebensatz). This phenomenon is indeed unusual and requires students of the language to take special care.

In particular when reading or listening, you have to be aware that the verb often doesn't come till right at the end of the sentence. That's because the end of what is said is almost always dependent on what comes at the beginning. The reader or listener has to remember what was said at the beginning. In order to develop a feeling for this, it's a good idea to first of all mark all the verb parts in sentences that you read, e.g.: Du kannst alle meine 500 Dias sehen, wenn du heute Nachmittag mit deiner Freundin zu mir kommst. (You can see all my 500 slides when you come to see me this afternoon with your girlfriend.)

Ein Farbiger

1 **a** Read the definitions.

Farbige der/die; -n; j-d., der farbig ist; ein Nicht-Weißer, bes. Neger od. Mulatte; ein Farbiger

Weiße der/die; -n; ein Mensch mit der hellen Hautfarbe, die z. B. für Europäer typisch ist; ein Weißer

Schwarze der/die; -n; j-d. mit schwarzer Hautfarbe; ein Schwarzer

farbig <Adj.> a) verschiedene Farben haben; b) eine andere Farbe als Weiß oder Schwarz; c) eine braune oder schwarze (od. rote od. gelbe) Hautfarbe haben

bunt <Adj.> mit mehreren verschiedenen Farben = farbig

b What are the words in English?

2 Read the text and underline the words you know.

Wenn ich zur Welt komme, bin ich schwarz;
wenn ich aufwachse, bin ich schwarz;
wenn ich krank bin, bin ich schwarz;
wenn ich in der Sonne gehe, bin ich schwarz;
5 **wenn ich friere, bin ich schwarz;**
wenn ich sterbe, bin ich schwarz.
Aber du!

Wenn du zur Welt kommst, bist du rosa;
wenn du aufwächst, bist du weiß;
10 **wenn du krank bist, bist du grün;**
wenn du in der Sonne gehst, bist du rot;
wenn du frierst, bist du blau;
wenn du stirbst, bist du grau.
Und du wagst[1] es, verdammt noch mal[2],
15 **mich einen Farbigen zu nennen[3]?**

unbekannter Verfasser

1 etw. wagen: dare (sth.)
2 verdammt noch mal: damn it
3 jdn. etw. nennen: call s.o. sth.

3 Read the second part of the text again (from line 8 on). Try to get the meaning of the unknown words from the colours. In which situation can a person be, for example, *rosa, grün, ...*?

4 **a** Who is *ich*? Who is *du*?
b What term should be used, in the author's opinion, for a white person?

5 Underline the subjects and the verbs in the text. In what position is the verb in the *wenn*-clause? Where is the subject in the main clause? Check your findings against the following table about word order.

Sätze verbinden: Hauptsatz (HS) und Nebensatz (NS), *wenn*

	1	2		
HS	Ich	bin	schwarz.	
NS+HS	**Wenn** ich zur Welt **komme**,	bin	ich schwarz.	
HS+NS	Ich	bin	schwarz,	**wenn** ich zur Welt **komme**.

Use of *wenn*

temporal: *Wenn* indicates that events or actions happen simultaneously in the present and future
question: Wann?
Wenn Kunkel eine Stadt besichtigt, macht er immer viele Dias.

conditional: The *wenn*-clause states a condition, the main clause states the consequence:
Wenn du heute kommst, kannst du meine Dias sehen.

6 Change some sentences in the text by starting with the main clause.

Ich bin ..., wenn ... Aber du! Du bist ..., wenn ...

7 a Complete with the sentences given.

Alle Verwandten kommen. ✎ Du kannst mich immer fragen. ✎ Das ist kein gutes Deutsch. ✎ Ich mache einen Mittagsschlaf. ✎ Wir machen einen Ausflug.

1 Wenn du etwas nicht verstehst, ...

2 Wenn es nicht regnet, ...

3 Wenn ich Geburtstag habe, ...

4 Wenn er Maloche sagt, ...

5 Wenn ich gegessen habe, ...

b Complete with your own ideas.

Ein Tag ist schön, wenn ....

Ein Dia-Abend ist spannend, wenn ....

Der Deutschunterricht ist interessant, wenn ....

Spur im Sand

Ging da ein Weißer,

ein Schwarzer,

ein Roter?

Der Sand sagt:

Ein Mensch.

Hans Baumann

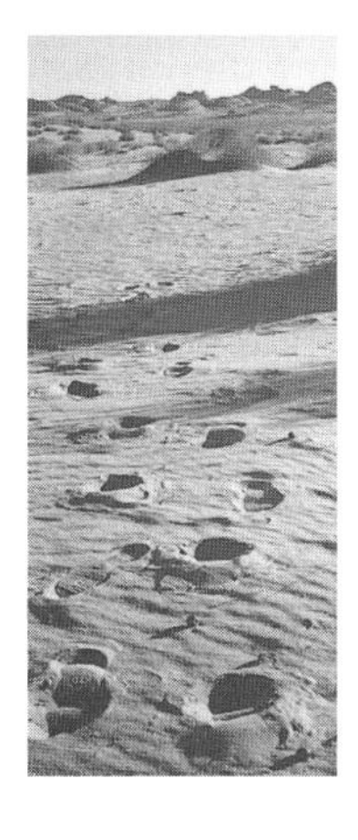

8 **a** Read the adjectives. You can work out the meaning of the unknown words from their opposites.

klein – groß ● dick – dünn ● arm – reich ● hässlich – schön ● intelligent – dumm ● alt – jung

b Rewrite the poem using the adjective pairs in a.

Ging da ein Kleiner, ein Großer? Der Sand sagt: ...

Aussprache: *er* und *e* am Wortende

9 Listen to the poem and repeat.

10 **a** Listen and read.

ein Deutscher ● eine Deutsche ● ein Weißer ● eine Farbige ● mein Name ● die deutsche Sprache ● ein Japaner ● dein Vater ● Entschuldige! ● bitter ● bitte ● die rote Farbe ● er ist Lehrer ● alle Schüler

b Listen again and repeat.

Wortbildung: Suffix *-er*

11 Read and fill in the nouns.

noun + *er*:	die Politik	der/ein Politiker	die Schule	der/ein Schüler
verb stem + *er*:	lesen	der/ein Leser	träumen	der/ein Träumer
	arbeiten	....	spielen	....
	sprechen	....	anfangen	.... (ä)
names of countries/ cities + *er*:	Japan	der/ein Japaner	Kanada	der/ein Kanadier (!)
	Berlin	der/ein Berliner		
	Österreich	....	Spanien	.... (!)
adjectives + *er*:	schwarz	ein Schwarzer[1]	links	ein Linker[2]
	rechts	ein Rechter[3]	grün	ein Grüner[4]
	reich	ein Reicher		

[1] with black skin; s.o. with very conservative ideas
[2, 3, 4] political terms

Der *Brief*

The texts

The good old love letter has now almost lost its raison d'être. Why write a letter when the telephone can transmit words a-plenty in no time at all? Well, Germans aren't the most prolific users of the telephone. *Fasse dich kurz!* (Keep it short!) used to be a notice to be found in phone boxes, and most people did. It costs money, and Germans tend to be thrifty. But since the arrival of the fax and e-mail, writing has experienced something of a revival.

Language

Foreigners often have some difficulty in deciphering German handwriting. Old people, like the writers of the letter to Hubert in this unit, learned the so-called *Sütterlinschrift* (Sütterlin script), based on old German writing and made compulsory in German schools between 1915 and 1941 as part of the wave of nationalism. The use of capital letters at the beginning of a sentence and for nouns and names means it is essential to distinguish between a capital letter, like P for example, and a small one like p, when writing by hand.
It's also important that the formal *Sie* and its possessive counterpart *Ihr* (as, for example, in: Ich habe Ihr Buch gelesen, Frau Wolf) are capitalized.
If a verb has two objects, one in the accusative and one in the dative, the basic word order is: dative object (die Dativergänzung D) before the accusative object (die Akkusativergänzung A).
Ich schreibe einer Freundin (D) einen Brief (A).

However, the accusative object often changes its position, depending on whether it's a noun or a pronoun, whether it provides a link to what has been said before, whether it contains information already mentioned or known to the reader, or whether information is to be stressed.

Learning strategies

German sentences can often be very long and encapsulated. Break sentences like this up into sections (following the punctuation) and write the sections down one underneath another. Work on each section separately, paying special attention to the meaning of the conjunctions. Work out the meaning of unknown words:

- from the word class: Die Ledersessel sind gelb, schwarz, weiß und **braun**. (e. g. adjectives)
- from associated words: Der **Zug** fährt langsam. (nouns from verbs)
  Meine Großmutter **starb** mit 88 Jahren. (verbs from nouns)
- from the context: Meine Großmuttter **starb** in hohem Alter. Sie wurde 88 Jahre alt. (Sometimes the following sentence is the key.)

Divide compounds up into their individual elements (you usually know one part).

Der Brief

1 The text is like a puzzle. Read it and note down.

1 Was ist *es* nicht? ....

2 Was ist *es*? ....

3 Was macht *es*? ....

Es kommt
von mir,
es geht zu dir.
Es ist kein Mensch,
es ist kein Tier.
Es ist nur dies:
ein Stück Papier.

Ein Stück Papier,
jedoch[1] *es spricht.*
Es bringt von mir
dir den Bericht[2]*:*
Ich hab' dich lieb,
vergiss mich nicht!

Josef Guggenmos

[1] jedoch = aber
[2] der Bericht: the report

2 Work out the meaning of the unknown nouns and verbs from the context or from words that you already know:
Ich **hab'** dich **lieb.** → Liebe.

Then check them in a dictionary.

3 Does the word *Bericht* fit this context? Suggest alternatives.

Personalpronomen: Nominativ, Akkusativ, Dativ

4 Fill in personal pronouns from the text.

Singular			Plural		
Nominativ	**Akkusativ**	**Dativ**	**Nominativ**	**Akkusativ**	**Dativ**
....	....	mir	wir	uns	uns
du	dich	....	ihr	euch	euch
Sie	Sie	Ihnen	Sie	Sie	Ihnen
er	ihn	ihm	sie	sie	ihnen
sie	sie	ihr			
....	es	ihm			

5 **a** Indicate for the personal pronouns in the text: N (Nominativ), A (Akkusativ), D (Dativ).
b Accusative or dative? Complete the rule.

After *von* and *zu*: the ....
After *lieb haben*, *vergessen*: the ....

Rätsel

> **Was ist das?**
> **Ich geb' es ihm**
> **ich geb' es ihr,**
> **ich geb' es oft,**
> **ich geb's auch dir**
> **und trotzdem bleibt es**
> **hier bei mir.**
>
> *Paul Maar*

6 Who is meant by the personal pronouns? Link with arrows.

ich	a female person
ihm	a male person
ihr	the person talking
dir	the person being spoken to
mir	

And what is *es*?

7 Fill in the personal pronouns in the correct form (A = Akkusativ, D = Dativ).

1 Er liebt .... und sie liebt .... (A) Er schreibt .... viele Briefe, aber sie schreibt .... nicht. (D)
2 Der Film gefällt .... (D), ich will .... noch einmal sehen. (A)
3 Wie geht es .... / .... ? (D) Danke, es geht .... sehr gut. (D)
4 Erklären Sie .... (D) bitte das Wort? Ich verstehe .... nicht. (A)
5 Ich bringe .... /.................. (D) das Buch, aber du musst / Sie müssen .... (A) auch lesen.

8 Fill in the personal pronouns in the right form.

This is how you can see in a dictionary what case the personal pronoun has to be in.

fragen, vt = Verb transitiv = Akkusativ	Ich frage .... (du)	Du hilfst .... (ich)
fragen, jdn. = jemanden = Akkusativ	Du fragst .... (ich)	Ich helfe .... (du)
antworten, vi = Verb intransitiv = Dativ	Ich antworte .... (du)	Sie hilft .... (er)
	Du antwortest .... (ich)	Er hilft .... (sie)
helfen, jdm. = jemandem = Dativ	Ist das ein Gespräch?	Wer hilft ....? (wir)

Liebe ... Lieber ...

9 **a** First look just at the external form of the text. What sort of text is it?
How can you tell?

Konstanz, 4. Juli 97

Lieber Hubert,

sicher bist du wieder vom Athos zurück, sicher war's wieder hochbefriedigend.
Dich zu treffen und wieder zu treffen war sehr schön. Das hat der Günter gut
gemacht, dass er uns zusammengebracht hat. Schön auch, dass ihr und meine
5 *neue Frau Marianne einander kennen gelernt habt. Dass du mit Margot auch*
befreundet gewesen bist, hat mich immer besonders gefreut. Du schreibst für
C. H. Beck ein Buch über Griechenland. Sehr gut und ich bin außerordentlich
gespannt darauf. Wie mir scheint, wirst du dabei das deutsch-griechische Ver-
hältnis anpeilen. Wenn ja, dann wird es bei dir sicher nicht um Platon und
10 *Winckelmann gehen, sondern um die Griechen, die heute in Griechenland rum-*
laufen.

Ich schicke dir eine längere Sache, die ich 1991–92 geschrieben
habe, einseitig, ich hatte damals einen Zorn, aber auf Seiten 107–127, die all-
gemeiner argumentieren, auch nicht ganz falsch.
15 *Ich habe damals dem Abakusverlag und meinem Freund Servatius ein Exemp-*
lar geschickt, aber nie eine Anwort bekommen. Möglicherweise regt es dich an,
vielleicht siehst du es ähnlich, vielleicht auch nicht. Jedenfalls: du verstehst.
Mach's gut, bleib gesund
und Auf Wiedersehen!

20 *Dein Gustav*

b Read the salutation and the complimentary close. What sort of a letter is it:
an official letter or a private letter?

c Skim through the letter. Who is it written to: an acquaintance or a good friend?

10 The letter covers several topics. Match the text sections to the summaries.

The writer	**Lines (from ... to ...)**
talks about the recipient's trip;	....
refers to a joint experience;	....
talks about what the recipient is doing;	....
reports something he himself did.	....

11 The sentence in lines 12–14 is very long. Work on it in sections as described on page 73.

Ich schicke Dir eine längere Sache,	What does *eine längere Sache* mean? The verb in the next section gives some information.
die ich 1991–92 geschrieben habe,	
einseitig,	Adjective: What is the thing like? *ein / Seite* Why is the thing one page?
ich hatte damals einen Zorn,	
aber auf Seiten 107–127,	*die Sache ist einseitig, aber*
die allgemeiner argumentieren,	
auch nicht ganz falsch.	*auch* ... What is it also like?

12 Underline the articles and nouns in the sentences.

Ich habe dem Abakusverlag und meinem Freund Servatius ein Exemplar geschickt.

- Du hast auch ein Buch geschrieben? Hast du es schon einem Verlag geschickt?
- Ja, aber das Thema gefällt dem Verlag nicht.
- Dann musst du das Buch schnell einem anderen Verlag schicken.
- Und wenn es dem auch nicht gefällt?
- Dann schickst du es einer Freundin.

Das Nomen: Dativ

13 Fill in the forms from the sentences in section 12.

	Singular			Plural
	maskulin	**neutral**	**feminin**	**m, n, f**
Dativ	d........... / .... Verlag	in **dem** / in ein**em** Buch	**der** / .... Freundin	**den** / — Freund**en**

ebenso: kein, mein, dein/Ihr, sein, ihr, unser, euer (**eurem, eurer**)/Ihr, ihr

Akkusativergänzung, Dativergänzung

In a sentence with a dative and an accusative object, the dative object is usually a person (Wem?), the accusative object a thing (Was?).

14 a Underline the accusative object and the dative object.
b Fill in the numbers of the explanations on page 78.

- Viele Menschen schreiben ihren Freunden keine Briefe mehr, aber ich. 1
- Hast du alle diese Briefe deiner Freundin geschrieben? ☐
- Klar!
- Und warum hast du ihr die Briefe nie geschickt? ☐
- Diese Briefe kann ich ihr nicht schicken. ☐
  Ich liebe Inge sehr, aber ich kann es ihr nicht schreiben. ☐
- Meiner Freundin schreibe ich nie einen Brief. ☐

Where is the dative object?

1 Dative before accusative: general rule.
2 Personal pronouns come before nouns.
3 Dative after accusative: both objects are unstressed personal pronouns.
4 The dative or accusative object can be at the beginning of the sentence: it then has special stress.
5 Dative after accusative: the accusative object refers to something known or previously mentioned

15 Complete the sentences with the sentence elements given.

a First underline the accusative object and the dative object.

b Then put the sentence elements in the right order.

1
- Was schreibst du da?
- meinem Freund Hannes / ich / einen Brief / schreibe.
- Darf ich ihn mal lesen? ... O je, den Brief kannst du ihm aber nicht schicken!

2
- Hast du kein Geld?
- habe / meinem Bruder / ich / gegeben / mein ganzes Geld.
- Was? / dein ganzes Geld / du / gegeben / ihm / hast ?

3
- Ich muss Ihnen etwas sagen.
- Tut mir Leid, ich habe keine Zeit.
  können / meinem Kollegen / Sie / erklären / Ihr Problem ?

4
- Du hast doch in Nizza viele Fotos gemacht.
  mir / kannst / du / geben / welche ?
- deinem Bruder / ich / habe / geschickt / alle Fotos .
- Gut, dann soll / mir / bringen / er / sie .

c Listen to the dialogues and repeat.

Anredeformen und Grußformen

16 Sort the salutations and complimentary closes into private and official ones. Then write down for each salutation the appropriate complimentary close(s).

Sehr geehrter Herr ..., Lieber Herr ..., Lieber Klaus,
Sehr geehrte Frau ..., Liebe Frau ..., Liebe Margret,
Sehr geehrte Damen und Herren,

Liebe Grüße Mit freundlichen Grüßen Herzliche Grüße
Alles Gute Mit freundlichem Gruß Mit herzlichen Grüßen
Viele Grüße Herzlichst Ihr/Ihre/dein/deine

Vergiss mich nicht!

17 Read the picture story. What could it say in the last picture?

Das Verb: Imperativ

18 a Fill in the forms from the picture story.

Question	**Command**
Stehst du auf?	....!
Ziehst du dich an?	....!
Steht ihr auf?	Steht auf!
Gehen wir jetzt?	Gehen wir jetzt!
Kommen Sie schnell?	Kommen Sie schnell!

b Compare the forms and complete the rule.

The imperative has four forms: *du*-form, *ihr*-form, *wir*-form and *Sie*-form.
The forms are generally derived from the question form.

du-form: the personal ending *-st* and the personal pronoun are omitted:
Kommst du?**!**

ihr-form: ....

wir-form / *Sie*-form: ....

special imperative forms

du-form:

Fahr nicht so schnell! — Verbs with a vowel change *a* → *ä* (fahren, du fährst).

Lies den Brief! **Iss** nicht so viel! **Putz** deine Schuhe! — If the verb stem ends in *s* or *z* (lesen, essen, putzen): only the *t* of the personal ending is omitted.

Hab doch mal Zeit für mich!

du/wir/Sie-form:

Sei doch mein Freund!
Seien wir / **Seien Sie** optimistisch!

19 a Listen and mark the intonation (↗ or ↘).

1 Bleiben Sie hier? ↗
2 Bleiben Sie hier!
3 Machen Sie schnell?
4 Machen Sie schnell!
5 Gehen wir!
6 Gehen wir?

b What do you hear: a question or a command? Write down ? or !

1 Kommen Sie zu mir
2 Sprechen wir Deutsch
3 Arbeiten wir jetzt
4 Sprechen Sie mit mir
5 Essen Sie noch etwas
6 Träumen Sie gut

20 Fill in the verbs in the imperative: *du*-form, *ihr*-form, *Sie*-form.

1 sein

....
.... pünktlich!
....

2 anrufen

....
.... doch mal ....!
....

3 sprechen

....
.... doch lauter bitte!
....

4 schreiben

....
.... doch mal wieder!
..Schreiben ...Sie..

Commands always have falling intonation.
doch in commands: reinforces a demand, a piece of advice
mal in commands: request (reinforced by *doch*)

21 You are sitting on the bus next to a woman reading a letter. Nosy as you are, you glance at the letter and see the following lines.

a Complete the letter. First jot down notes on these questions:

- Who wrote the letter?
- What sort of plan do they want to discuss?
- What points should Marianne think about?
- Why isn't the place a good one to meet in? What is better?

b From your notes write a text that would fit into the letter.

Liebe Marianne,
ich war sehr überrascht, als ein Brief von dir in meinem Briefkasten lag. Ich habe schon lange nichts mehr von dir gehört. Du schreibst, dass wir jetzt endlich unseren Plan besprechen müssen. Denkst du das wirklich? Ich finde ihn nicht mehr so gut. Aber wenn du unbedingt willst, dann mach dir schon mal Gedanken: Wie

Und frag auch

Hast du schon

Den Treffpunkt finde ich nicht gut. Dort

Also treffen wir uns

Sei bitte pünktlich!

*Weibs*bilder

Cultural information

School in the German-speaking countries is sometimes less strenuous than elsewhere. Nearly everywhere school is over at 1 o'clock. So children and teenagers have enough time to enjoy themselves and devote to their hobbies. But there is also a downside to this. There is usually no provision of food at school, and if both parents work full-time, a lot of children are left to their own devices and with nobody to keep an eye on them. But schoolchildren are also expected to spend part of the afternoon doing their homework (die Hausaufgabe, Hausaufgaben) or schoolwork (die Schularbeit). And for a lot of women, getting home after a day's work means the start of homework supervision. Because the next day the teacher is going to check up. Marks are awarded for homework, later added to the year's grade for oral work. And that's not the end of it either: in all subjects there are several tests a year (so-called Klassenarbeiten). Passing, and moving up to the next class is dependent on the average grade (der Notendurchschnitt) for all oral and written work through the course of the year. This system of continuous assessment has the advantage that every student – and hence the parents, too – are kept informed about how they are doing. So there is constant light pressure rather than a great fear preceding the once-a-year exams in other school systems.

Language

In this unit there is a picture story and an interview with the schoolgirl Stephie that has a lot of typical features of spoken speech. Specific listening comprehension techniques are practised. There are some photos with some information about what Stephie then says, and these therefore make comprehension easier.

Learning strategies

Words are best learned in a context. If learned in isolation, they just get blown away. But if you can link them to an experience or an insight, they lodge themselves faster and more firmly in your memory. Start a vocabulary card index. On the front of each card you note down just the word and its forms (wissen, weiß, hat gewusst) and write one or two example sentences. On the back you write the translation and your personal notes. Pop a fixed number of cards in your pocket every day, and get them out whenever you have a spare moment for learning.

Stufe				Alter
			Universität	23
		Fachhochschule		22
				21
				20
13	Ende der Schulpflicht		Abitur	19
12	**Berufsschule und**	**Berufsfachschule**	**Gymnasium**	18
11	**Betrieb** (Duales System)			17
10		mittlerer Abschluss nach 10 Jahren		16
09				15
08	**Hauptschule**	**Realschule**		14
07	(Gesamtschule)	(Gesamtschule)	(Gesamtschule)	13
06				12
05				11
04				10
03				09
02		**Grundschule**		08
01				07

Weibsbilder

1 First look at the pictures without reading the text, and think about what is meant by *Weibsbilder*

[1] Pflicht: duty [2] pauken = lernen

2 a Answer the questions in German or English.

Pictures 1 and 2

Who is the person on the right?

What has she got in her hand?

Who is on the left?

What's he doing?

What's on the sofa?

What's on the floor?

Pictures 3 and 4

What's the person on the left doing?

Picture 8

What's the person on the left doing now?

b What might a ninth and tenth picture be like? Draw them and describe them.

3 Read the text in the pictures, first silently, then out loud.

4 a Try to guess the meaning of the following expressions. Use the pictures and the context, too. Note down several possible solutions.

Zuerst kommt die Pflicht. ● Du weißt doch, dass ich heute ins Kino will. ● Da siehst du's. ● Vokabeln pauken. ● Du immer mit deinen Übertreibungen!

b After you've found the meanings and checked in a dictionary, note down the new words on cards, as in the example. You can add to the notes later.

wissen, weiß, hat gewusst Das weiß ich nicht. Ich habe das nicht gewusst. Du weißt doch / Sie wissen doch, dass ich heute ins Kino gehe.	know irregular difference from kennen

5 Read the text again and answer the questions.

1 Was soll die Tochter machen? Die Tochter soll ....

2 Was will die Tochter machen? Die Tochter will ins Kino, sich mit ihren Freundinnen treffen ....

....

....

3 Was will die Tochter nicht machen? ....

6 Complete with suitable verbs in the infinitive.

1 Ich will das nicht ... machen. ...

2 Du willst ins Kino ....

3 Ich will ins Schwimmbad ....

4 Du willst immer alles ....

Vorwürfe machen – auf Vorwürfe reagieren

7 a Listen to the dialogue from the picture story and read it at the same time. Which sentences do you find that express:

annoyance .... , reproach .... , arrogance .... ?

Fill in the numbers of the pictures.

b The following elements can be used to achieve the emotional result given. Mark them in the picture story.

Du weißt doch, dass ... /Du siehst doch, dass ... /Sie wissen doch, ...	reproach
Ja, ich weiß, aber ...	defending oneself
Wieso ...? /Warum ...?	contradicting
Du willst ins Kino, du willst Tennis spielen, du willst dich mit deinen Freundinnen treffen.	expressing annoyance through repetition
Da siehst du's. / Da hast du's.	showing that you're right

Die kleinen Wörter: *doch*

8 Listen to the picture story dialogue and repeat it sentence for sentence.
Try to find the right tone.

9 **a** Listen and mark the main stresses.

1 Du weíßt doch, dass ich keine Zéit habe.
2 Du weißt doch, dass ich gern fotografiere.
3 Du siehst doch, dass ich arbeite.
4 Du hast doch gehört, dass er nicht will.
5 Du weißt doch sehr gut, dass ich Diät mache.

b Repeat with the right tone and intonation.

c Make little dialogues with the following questions and the answers in a.

Gehst du mit in die Disko? — Du weißt doch, dass ich keine Zeit habe!

Warum hast du denn so viele Dias?
Gehst du mit ins Kino?
Hilfst du mir?
Willst du etwas essen?
Warum kommt er nicht?

Doch reinforces the emotion,
doch is unstressed.

10 Mutter: Du willst immer alles ... nur nicht Vokabeln pauken!
Tochter: Da siehst du's. Ich will doch nicht immer alles!

Listen and mark the main stress.

Ich will nícht immer alles.
Ich will dóch nicht immer alles. — The mother first told her daughter that she always wants everything.

Sie hat keine Zeit.
Sie hat doch keine Zeit. — First she said she had time.

Das Buch gefällt mir.
Das Buch gefällt mir doch. — At the beginning I didn't like the book.

Doch means contrary to expectation, contrary to an opinion;
doch is stressed.

11 Add *doch* and say the sentences.

1 Ich habe es nicht gemacht.
2 Wir waren nicht in Berlin.
3 Es regnet heute nicht.
4 Maria hat heute nicht Geburtstag.
5 Sie kommt nicht.
6 Ich trinke keinen Kaffee.

Das Verb *wissen*

Ich **weiß**, du willst immer alles.
Du **weißt** doch, dass ich heute ins Kino will.

12 Fill in the verb forms.

	wissen
ich	....
du	....
Sie	wiss **en**
er/sie/es/man	**weiß**
wir	wiss **en**
ihr	wiss **t**
Sie	....
sie	....

Sätze verbinden: *dass*

Du weißt doch, **dass ich ins Kino will.** Question about the subordinate clause: **Was** weiß ich?
Ich will ins Kino. Du weißt **das**.

	1	2	
HS+NS	Du	weißt,	**dass** ich ins Kino **will**.
NS+HS	**Dass** ich ins Kino **will**,	weißt	du.

Verbs like *wissen, finden, sagen, sehen, denken* have a *dass*-clause in answer to the question *Was*?

13 Form sentences with *dass*.

1 Ich bin krank. Sie wissen das.
2 Sie ist sehr intelligent. Du weißt das.
3 Wir haben kein Geld. Du weißt das.
4 Ich weiß nichts. Ich weiß das.

14 a Reply to the demands using the following expressions.

ins Kino ⬥ fernsehen ⬥ nicht zu Hause sein ⬥ nicht dick werden ⬥ in Italien sein ⬥ viel Arbeit haben ⬥ mich zuerst anziehen ⬥ keine Dias mögen

1 ■ Du musst noch Vokabeln lernen. ▲ Du weißt doch, dass ich ins Kino will.

2 ■ Du musst jetzt schlafen gehen. ▲ Du weißt doch, dass ich noch .....

3 ■ Du musst noch etwas essen. ▲ Du .....

4 ■ Du musst deine Mutter anrufen. ▲ .....

5 ■ Du musst dich rasieren. ▲ .....

6 ■ Sie müssen noch die Briefe schreiben. ▲ Sie .....

7 ■ Sie müssen Herrn Kunkel besuchen. ▲ .....

8 ■ Sie müssen unbedingt seine Dias sehen. ▲ .....

b Say these sentences. Give them an annoyed or strict tone.

15 Form sentences without *dass*.

1 Ich weiß, dass du immer alles willst. Ich weiß, du willst immer alles.
2 Sie hat gesagt, dass sie ins Schwimmbad gehen will.
3 Ich sehe, dass Sie viel Arbeit haben.
4 Er findet, dass sie wenig Zeit für ihn hat.
5 Ich habe gewusst, dass sie einen Ausflug machen wollen.
6 Ich habe gedacht, dass ich sie besuchen kann. Aber ich habe es nicht geschafft.

> *Dass* can also be omitted. If the main clause is negated, this is not possible.
>
> Ich habe gedacht, ich kann sie besuchen.
> But: Ich habe nicht gedacht, dass ich sie besuchen kann.

Aussprache: unbetontes e

16 a Listen and repeat.

geben ⬥ lernen ⬥ spielen ⬥ fahren ⬥ reisen ⬥ der Morgen ⬥ die Farben ⬥ ich gebe ⬥ ich lerne ⬥ ich spiele ⬥ die Farbe ⬥ die Erde ⬥ die Freude

> Unstressed *e* is spoken very weakly. In final syllables it can be dropped: e.g. der *Morg(e)n*, *reis(e)n*, but not after the consonants *m*, *n*, *l*, *r*: e. g. *fahren*, *kommen*.

b Repeat, keeping to the rhythm.

wiederholen – Wiederholen Sie! – Wiederholen Sie bitte!
fliegen – wir fliegen – Wir fliegen wie ein Vogel.

Stephie Betz

17 a What can you see in the photos?

A

B

C

b The photos show various aspects of Stephie's life. Which sentences go with which picture? Match.

1 Am Nachmittag fährt Stephie oft mit ihrem Fahrrad in den Park. [C]
2 Die Familie hat auch einen Hund. [ ]
3 Stephie war zuerst vier Jahre in der Grundschule. Jetzt ist sie am Gymnasium. [ ]
4 Die Wohnung hat zwei Zimmer, eine Küche und ein Bad. [ ]
5 Stephie muss die Küche und das Bad putzen. [ ]
6 Sie ist oft mit ihren Freunden und Freundinnen zusammen. [ ]
7 Sie erzählt ihrer Mutter von der Schule. [ ]
8 Stephie lernt Latein, Englisch und Spanisch an der Schule. [ ]
9 Am Nachmittag macht sie ihre Hausaufgaben. [ ]
10 Oft geht sie mit dem Hund spazieren. [ ]

18 Listen to the interview. In what order does Stephie talk about the following topics? Number them.

Schule [ ] Lernen zu Hause [ ] Freunde [ ] Hund [ ] Mutter [ ] Wohnung [ ]

19 Read the following excerpt from the interview.

Stephie, kannst du mir mal erzählen, wo du lebst, wie du lebst, mit wem?

In einer Wohnung in München, mit meiner Mutter zusammen. Sie hat ihr eigenes Schlafzimmer und ich habe mein eigenes Schlafzimmer. Wir teilen uns die Küche und das Bad. Eigentlich so eine ziemlich kleine Wohnung, aber es passt. Mein Hund gehört auch noch dazu, zur Family. Und mein Vater, der lebt mit seiner Frau eben 500 Meter weiter die Straße rauf mit meinem Halbbruder und das ist ganz o.k. Ich lebe ziemlich nah am Zentrum, das ist ganz praktisch: Ich kann mit meinem Hund immer mit dem Radl in den Englischen Garten oder sonst wohin fahren und das ist ganz praktisch. Ich brauche eigentlich kein Auto mehr.

20 The text contains a lot of elements of spoken language. Turn them into written language.

a Turn the incomplete sentences into complete ones.

In einer Wohnung in München, mit meiner Mutter zusammen.
Eigentlich so eine ziemlich kleine Wohnung.

b Underline the following expressions in the text.
es passt ● das ist ganz o.k. ● das ist ganz praktisch

Replace them with:
das gefällt mir ● das finde ich gut ● das ist schön ● sie ist groß genug

c The last three sentences begin with *Ich*. Avoid the repetitions. Link the sentences with conjunctions or start with a sentence element other than *ich*.

Die kleinen Wörter: *eigentlich*

21 Complete.

Eigentlich ist das eine kleine Wohnung. Aber sie ist groß genug für uns.
Ich brauche eigentlich kein Auto. Aber ...

- ■ Hast du keinen großen Stress? ▲ Eigentlich nicht. Aber ...
- ■ Hast du viel Freizeit? ▲ Ja, eigentlich schon. Aber ...

eigentlich is used to qualify a statement and indicate that there were originally other intentions or that expectations were not fulfilled.
Often a sentence with *aber* follows.

22 Add *eigentlich*.

1 ■ Du musst noch Vokabeln lernen. ▲ Ich will ..eigentlich............ heute Abend ins Kino.
2 ■ Können Sie bitte den Brief schreiben! ▲ Ich habe Urlaub.
3 ■ Sehen wir uns heute Abend? ▲ Ich habe keine Zeit.
4 ■ Hast du heute viel zu tun? ▲ Ja.

Stehkneipe

Cultural information

The journalist G. Aberle visited various stand-up bars (die Stehkneipe) and talked to the people there. The recording of one of the interviews in this unit is from the Ruhr, an area where coal-miners and steelworkers hot or dusty after work (called *Maloche* there) used to quench their thirst with one or more glasses of *Pils* (pilsener) in a bar of this kind, and maybe play a round of *Skat* (a popular card game).

Bars (die Kneipe) of this kind are to be found more in towns and cities than out in the country, and more in the north than in the south of Germany. They're mostly small or narrow rooms with a long bar and just a few tables. The customers – mostly locals – prefer to drink their beer standing up, exchanging a few words with the person next to them or with the landlord. Women are customers in this kind of bar too.

In the country it's still the old pub (das Wirtshaus) where the farmers go in the early evening to play a game of cards at the regulars' table (der Stammtisch) and talk over the events of the day over a glass of beer or wine. The local VIPs usually drop in too, often to do their political business. There's a cynical saying that whoever has control of the airspace above the regulars' table also has the say in local politics. In towns and villages today, a lot of pubs are run by Greeks, Asians and Italians.

The social function of pubs and inns has changed little over the past few years. People who are lonely can forget their troubles for a while at least, as it's customary in many pubs for a stranger to join a table and start up a conversation with the people sitting there.

Language

The people in the Ruhr like to keep things short and not use a lot of unnecessary words. Often an utterance consists of a single word, a half-sentence, an elliptic expression. "Weil ich Durst habe" (Because I'm thirsty) the man in the bar says in answer to the question why he's sitting there. Reasons are often given in a sub-clause with *weil*, or a simple statement. So the answer to the question "Warum sitzen Sie hier?" (Why are you sitting here?) could also be simply: "Ich habe Durst."

Stehkneipe

1 Listen and read the dialogue.
Gerhard Aberle (A) unterhält sich mit einem Gast (G) in einer Stehkneipe in Dortmund.

A Wie lange sitzen Sie schon hier?
G Wie lange ich hier sitze? Na, seit ungefähr, sagen wir, fünf Minuten vor sechs.
A Wie lange werden Sie noch hier sitzen?
5 **G** Ich würde sagen, so ungefähr bis Feierabend.
A Warum sitzen Sie hier?
G Weil ich Durst habe.
A Aus keinem anderen Grund?
G Nein, ich hatte meinen freien Tag, nicht, als Kellner, nicht,
10 und da sitze ich hier und trinke mein Glas Bier.
A Warum trinken Sie es nicht zu Hause?
G Ich trinke nicht zu Hause. Allein schmeckt mir das Bier nie. Es schmeckt nur in Gesellschaft 'n[1] Glas Bier.
A Wie alt sind Sie?
15 **G** Fuffzig[2].
A Verheiratet?
G Nie.
A Warum?
G Die Nase voll.

Gerhard Aberle

[1] 'n = ein
[2] fuffzig = fünfzig

2 In which line does the customer say something about

		Line
1	his age;	☐
2	his job;	☐
3	his marital status;	☐
4	why he drinks in the bar?	☐

3 Check the meaning of the following terms and expressions.
Feierabend • Ich hatte meinen freien Tag • in Gesellschaft • (Ich habe) die Nase voll.

4 The text contains several incomplete sentences, as is often the case in speech. Underline them.

5 **a** Find the questions for these answers in the text.
Seit ungefähr fünf Minuten vor sechs.
Weil ich Durst habe.
Fünfzig.
Nie.

b Turn the answers into complete sentences.
Ich sitze hier seit ...

6 **a** Listen to the dialogue again.
b What other questions might Gerhard Aberle ask? Note them down.

Intonation: Satzakzent

7 **a** Listen to the questions and mark the main sentence stress.

1 Wie lange sitzen Sie schon hier?
2 Wie lange werden Sie noch hier sitzen?
3 Warum sitzen Sie hier?
4 Wie alt sind Sie?

b Listen again and repeat.

8 **a** Listen to the questions in 7a again. Mark the changed stress.
b Why are other words stressed?
c How do we express a change like this in English?

Sätze verbinden: *weil*

9 What is the answer to the *Warum* question? Complete.

Warum sitzen Sie hier? Weil ich ....

		1	2	
HS+NS		Ich	sitze	hier, **weil** ich Durst **habe**.
NS+HS	**Weil** ich Durst **habe**,		sitze	ich hier.

Use of *weil*
causal: sub-clauses with *weil* give a reason.
Question: Warum? Wieso?
In the spoken language the main clause is missed out in answers to questions with *Warum?* and *Wieso?*
Warum sitzen Sie hier? Weil ich Durst habe.

10 Match and make sentences with *weil.*

Er trinkt Bier, weil ...

1 Er trinkt Bier.
2 Er sitzt in der Kneipe.
3 Er trinkt nicht zu Hause.
4 Er war nie verheiratet.

a Er hat die Nase voll.
b Er hat seinen freien Tag.
c Er hat Durst.
d Das Bier schmeckt ihm nur in Gesellschaft.

11 a Answer the questions using *weil* clauses. Use the following expressions.

viel arbeiten müssen • noch etwas vorbereiten müssen • krank sein • fernsehen wollen

1 Warum fährt er zu seiner Mutter?
2 Warum hat er keine Zeit?
3 Warum geht er nicht aus?
4 Warum geht er nicht schlafen?

b Answer the questions.

1 Warum sind Sie manchmal schlecht gelaunt?
2 Warum gehen Sie (nicht) gern in die Kneipe?
3 Warum reisen Sie (nicht) gern?
4 Warum machen Sie (keinen) Sport?
5 Warum lernen Sie Deutsch?

12 Listen to a song. Note down the words that you hear often.
Where is the singer? Who is he talking to?

Der Mann am Klavier

Geben Sie dem Mann am Klavier
noch'n[1] Bier, noch'n Bier.
Sagen Sie ihm, 's wär[2] von mir,
's wär von mir, 's wär von mir.
Spielen soll er mir dafür,
mir dafür, mir dafür
das Lied von dem Mann am Klavier.
Dann kriegt er von mir dafür noch'n Bier.
Das Lied von dem Mann am Klavier,
dann kriegt er von mir dafür noch'n Bier.

Wenn Sie einmal tanzen gehen
und 'ne kesse Sohle drehen[3],
denken Sie erst nicht zum Schluss
an den braven Musikus.

Spielt er fast die ganze Nacht,
alles das, was Freude macht,
rufen Sie den Wirt heran
und bestellen dann:
Geben Sie dem Mann am Klavier
noch'n Bier, noch'n Bier.

Gießen Sie in das Klavier
noch'n Bier, noch'n Bier.
Sagen Sie ihm, 's wär von mir,
's wär von mir, dieses Bier.
Spielen soll es mir dafür,
mir dafür, mir dafür
das Lied von dem Mann am Klavier,
dann kriegt es von mir
dafür noch'n Bier.

Cornell-Trio 1954

[1] noch'n = noch ein
[2] 's wär = es wäre
[3] eine kesse Sohle drehen: shake a leg, trip the light fantastic

Aussprache: vokalisches *r*

13 a Listen and repeat.

am Klavier • von mir • noch ein Bier • Der Mann am Klavier – er kriegt von mir dafür noch ein Bier.

hören – er hört • buchstabieren – sie buchstabiert • fahren – du fährst • das Meer – die Meere • die Uhr – die Uhren • morgens – vormittags

b Where do you not hear an *r*? Put brackets round it.

hören – sie hö(r)t • das Jahr – die Jahre • Buchstabieren Sie bitte! – Buchstabier bitte! • die Uhrzeit • die Literatur • Das Bier schmeckt nur mir. • Ich höre mehr als andere.

r is spoken like a weak *a*:
- after a long vowel, when it belongs to the same syllable: hörst, Uhr, but: hö-ren, Uh-ren
- in prefixes: erklären, vergehen, vorbereiten …

Im Café

14 a You go into a café with two friends to have something to eat and drink. Note down in English what is said between you and the waiter/waitress.

b In a pub or restaurant you may hear and use the following sentences. Read the sentences and pick out those that match your notes from a.

Der Tisch dort ist noch frei. ● Die Rechnung bitte! ● Haben Sie reserviert? ● Kann ich bitte Pfeffer und Salz haben? Hier ist die Speisekarte. ● Dort hinten. ● Was macht das? ● Guten Appetit! ● Die Küche hat leider schon zu. ● Was willst du trinken/essen? ● Was wollen/möchten Sie trinken? ● 22 Euro 50. ● Was darf ich Ihnen bringen? ● Getrennt oder zusammen? ● Bringen Sie die Karte, bitte. ● Wie viele Personen? ● Ich möchte eine Tasse Kaffee. ● Ein Glas Apfelsaft, bitte. ● Ein kleines Mineralwasser. ● Wo ist bitte die Toilette? ● Bezahlen, bitte! ● Ein Omelett mit Schinken, bitte.

Die Zeit angeben: Präpositionen

seit, bis

Seit wann sind Sie hier? Wie lange sitzen Sie schon hier?	Seit fünf Minuten vor sechs.	**seit:** point of time in the past when something began
Wie lange sitzen Sie schon hier?	Seit einer Stunde.	**seit:** duration
Wie lange bleiben Sie noch hier? Bis wann bleiben Sie hier?	Bis Feierabend.	**bis:** up to a point in time

15 Which answers are possible for each of the questions? Match them.

1 b, ... 4 ....
2 .... 5 ....
3 ....

1 Wie lange sind Sie schon hier?
2 Seit wann sind Sie in München?
3 Wie lange bleiben Sie?
4 Bis wann bleiben Sie?
5 Wann haben Sie Zeit?

a Bis Weihnachten.
b Seit sechs Uhr.
c Bis acht Uhr.
d Zwischen fünf und sieben Uhr.
e Seit fünf Minuten.
f Zwei Monate.
g Seit dem 1. April.
h Zwei Jahre.
i Bis Montag.
j Seit zwei Monaten.

an, in, nach, von ... bis, zwischen, um, vor

Wann?

am	Montag Abend	**day, time of day**
am, vor dem, nach dem	9. März	
um, vor, nach	9 Uhr	**clock time**
von	7 Uhr **bis** 11 Uhr Montag **bis** Freitag	**duration**
zwischen	7 Uhr **und** 11 Uhr Montag **und** Freitag	**event within a period of time**
in	zwei Stunden einem Monat	**duration till the start of something**

16 Which time expressions fit which question? Please match.

1 .... 2 .... 3 .... 4 .... 5 .... 6 .... 7 ....

1 Wann beginnt die Woche?
2 Wie lange arbeiten Sie?
3 Wann spricht er mit dem Lehrer?
4 Wann kommt sie nach Hause?
5 Wann gehen Sie schlafen?
6 Wann kommt der Bus?
7 Wann beginnt der Unterricht?

a In einer Stunde.
b Um zehn Uhr.
c Nach der Arbeit.
d Von acht bis fünf Uhr.
e Am Montag.
f Vor dem Unterricht.
g Zwischen zehn und elf Uhr.

17 a Listen and answer the questions.

b Read the questions and check whether you answered correctly.

Wann müssen Sie an Wochentagen aufstehen?
Um wie viel Uhr gehen Sie zur Arbeit?
Von wann bis wann arbeiten Sie?
Wann machen Sie Mittagspause?
Bis wann schlafen Sie am Wochenende?
Um wie viel Uhr gehen Sie an Wochentagen schlafen?

c Listen to the questions again and repeat them.

18 Write a little story using the following items.

Frau Schulz ● 1975 ● Direktorin ● Büro ● Hotel ● Auto ● 8 Uhr ● Montag ●
Freitag ● 10 Minuten ● nach Hause ● Nachmittag ● Freundin ● Tennis

Herz verloren

Cultural information

The photographer and film-maker Bettina Flitner has one topic that she's particularly interested in: women and their relationships. She stopped them in the street and asked: "Haben Sie jemals Ihr Herz verloren? Und wenn ja: Welche Folgen hatte das?" (Have you ever lost your heart to someone? And if so: what were the consequences?) She asked a whole cross-section of women, in all walks of life: old women tending their memories, girls from the punk scene, foreigners from every country under the sun. The women told her about the love of their life, about pain, hope and depair, their wounds.

The role of women in the German-speaking countries differs little from that in other European societies. History has produced great female figures such as Empress Maria-Theresia von Habsburg (1717-1780), or the Polish-born Rosa Luxemburg (1870-1919) to name just two politicians. In general, however, women's role in public life remained very inconspicuous till well after the Second World War. In Switzerland, the very model of democracy, it was not till 1971 that men, who up till then had alone been eligible to vote, decided to grant women an active right to vote in federal elections. In some cantons this was not actually put into practice till 1990. Still, in 1999 a woman was elected President of the Federation.

A decisive change in the role of women began to make itself felt after 1968, when students in particular demanded a radical reform of society, and with it sexual equality, not only before the law but also in all spheres of social life. In companies, state organizations and parliaments, so-called Frauenbeauftragte (female representatives) were appointed. Quotas were fixed for the number of women to be represented in high-ranking positions and parliaments. And it worked sometimes. In practice, however, leading positions in business and the economy have remained in male hands.

Language

In the text there are several verbs with the prefix *ver-*: verlieren, verschenken. It is one of the strengths of the language that meanings can be defined more precisely through the use of prefixes and affixes. In this case, the prefix *ver-* means that something is no longer there.

Learning strategies

When you encounter new verbs, you should enter in your verb lists or on your index cards not only the different tenses, but also details of the objects and other special features, e.g.: gehören (D), geben (D, A), *sich* freuen (be pleased), *schief* gehen (go wrong). And of course an example sentence in each case: Das Haus gehört mir leider noch nicht. (Unfortunately the house doesn't belong to me yet.)

Haben Sie jemals Ihr Herz verloren?

1 Read the text without referring to a dictionary.

Haben Sie jemals Ihr Herz verloren?

Wenn ja, welche Folgen hatte das?

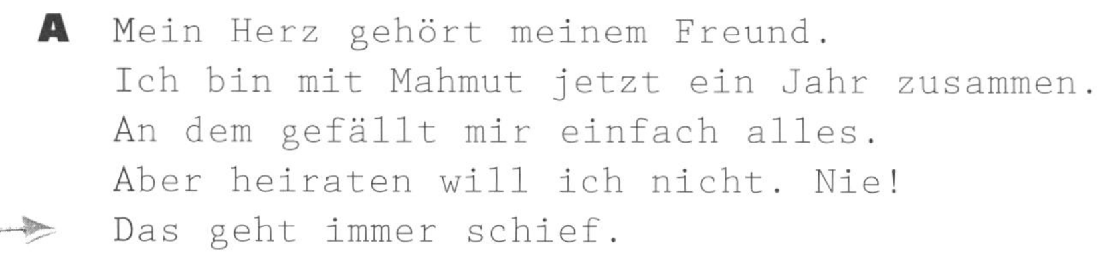

A Mein Herz gehört meinem Freund.
Ich bin mit Mahmut jetzt ein Jahr zusammen.
An dem gefällt mir einfach alles.
Aber heiraten will ich nicht. Nie!
Das geht immer schief.

B Sein Herz verschenken? Völliger Blödsinn!
Na ja, vielleicht einmal. In jungen Jahren,
da hatte ich so eine Affäre.
Die Frau sah ziemlich gut aus,
Liebe auf den ersten Blick, kurz und
stürmisch. Aber irgendwie war alles
wie ausgedacht.

C Ich hab mein Herz noch nie verloren.
Er hat mir in der Fleischerei immer mit
den schweren Kisten geholfen. Nach neun
Monaten war Mandy da. Erst hat er gesagt,
er freut sich drauf. Jetzt geht ihm das
Schreien auf die Nerven. Ich hatte mir
das alles anders vorgestellt!

D Ich würde mein Herz nie mehr verschenken,
ich würde es nur noch verborgen[1]!
Er ist weg, weil er noch ein Kind wollte,
eine eigene Familie. Ich hatte aber schon
eins und jeder hatte seinen Dickkopf.
Als er gegangen ist, hat mir das sehr wehgetan. Seither bin ich vorsichtig geworden.

Barbara Flitner

[1] verborgen: lend

2 Which of the four people once lost their heart to someone? Mark the relevant passage.

3 Answer the questions.

on A: What does she mean when she says "Mein Herz gehört meinem Freund"?
on B: What is meant by "Na ja, vielleicht einmal"?
on C: Who is Mandy?
on D: What does she mean when she says she would never give her heart away again?

4 Each text consists of two sections: 1 short answer to the question, 2 description of the situation and the experiences.

a Mark where each section begins.

b Try to express quite simply in one sentence what is said in the second part of each text.

5 Find verbs in the text in the infinitive, present, past and perfect. Make a table.

Infinitiv	Präsens	Präteritum	Perfekt
heiraten	gehört	hatte	habe verloren

6 Fill in the verbs *bekommen, fahren, gefallen, gehen, helfen, sagen, schreiben, verlieren, wehtun* in the perfect.

1 Er .... ihr einen langen Brief .... , aber noch keine Antwort ....

2 Ihr Freund .... ihr oft bei der Arbeit ....

3 Es war sehr schön in Osnabrück. Es .... ihnen dort sehr gut ....

4 Als das Kind da war, ... er zuerst .... , dass er sich freut.
Dann .... er .... Das .... mir sehr ....

5 Franziska .... immer wieder ihren Schlüssel ....

6 Herr und Frau Kunkel .... oft nach Griechenland ....

7 **a** Match appropriate answers to the questions.

1 ☐ 2 ☐ 3 ☐ 4 ☐ 5 ☐ 6 ☐ 7 ☐ 8 ☐ 9 ☐

1 Wie ist Ihr Name? Wie heißen Sie?
2 Woher kommen Sie?
3 Wie alt sind Sie?
4 Was machen Sie hier?
5 Was sind Sie von Beruf?
6 Sind Sie schon einmal verliebt gewesen?
7 Sind Sie verheiratet?
8 Möchten Sie heiraten?
9 Haben Sie Kinder?

a Aus ...
b Ich bin ... von Beruf. / Ich arbeite als ...
c Schon oft. / Noch nie.
d Nein. / Ich bin geschieden. / Seit fünf Jahren.
e Ja, einen Jungen und ein Mädchen. / (Leider) keine.
f Ich bin ... (Jahre alt).
g Ich denke, ja. / Ich glaube nicht. / Niemals.
h Mein Name ist ... / Ich heiße ...
i Ich studiere ...

b Select one of the people and ask them questions. Then answer the questions. Say the dialogue out loud with a partner.

c Write a biographical note about yourself for an information exchange on the internet. Start with: Mein Name ist ...

Verben mit Dativergänzung

Mein Herz gehört **meinem Freund**.
Er hat **mir** immer geholfen.

8 Fill in the dative object from the text..

			Dative object	
1	Mein Herz	gehört	..meinem Freund..........	
2	Alles	gefällt	....	an dem.
3	Er	hat	....	mit den schweren Kisten geholfen.
4	Das Schreien	geht	....	auf die Nerven.
5	Das	hat	....	sehr wehgetan.

Verbs with a dative object

antworten, auf die Nerven gehen, danken, gehen (Wie geht es dir?), gehören, gefallen, gratulieren, helfen, schmecken, wehtun

9 Complete the sentences.

1 Vater und Mutter gratulieren .... (ihre Tochter) zum Geburtstag.
2 Diese Musik geht ....(er) auf die Nerven.
3 Das Auto gehört .... (der Lehrer) und .... (seine Frau).
4 Wir haben ihm geschrieben, aber er hat .... (wir) nicht geantwortet.
5 Die Dias von Herrn Kunkel haben ....
(die Bekannten und Verwandten) sehr gefallen.
6 Ich danke .... (Sie) für die Einladung.
7 Hat es .... (sie) geschmeckt?

10 Fill in the endings and the personal pronouns in the right form.

1 Er hat d.ie..... Frau nicht gehört, deshalb hat er .ihr..... auch nicht geantwortet.
2 Der Film hat mein........... Freund nicht gefallen, er fand .... langweilig.
3 Sie haben ihr........... Chef zum Geburtstag gratuliert. Das hat .... sehr gefreut.
4 Er hat sein........... Schwester oft geholfen, aber sie hat .... nie gedankt.
5 Er fragt sein........... Kollegin immer, wie es .... geht. Das geht .... auf die Nerven.
6 Mein Herz gehört mein........... Freundin. An ihr gefällt .... alles.
7 Er hat sein........... Eltern nie verstanden. Das hat .... wehgetan.
8 Wir haben d........... Wein nicht getrunken, er hat .... nicht geschmeckt.

Das Verb: reflexive Verben (1)

Er hat gesagt, er **freut sich**.
Wir **verstehen uns** immer noch sehr gut.

Reflexivpronomen

11 a Underline the subject and the reflexive pronoun.

1 Ich muss mich beeilen.
2 Du willst dich mit deinen Freundinnen treffen.
3 Wir haben uns gut unterhalten.
4 Wo habt ihr euch kennen gelernt?
5 Verstehen Sie sich gut mit ihm?
6 Sie sehen sich jeden Tag.

b Fill in the missing reflexive pronouns.

Personalpronomen	Reflexivpronomen
ich	mich
du	....
Sie	....
er/sie/es/man	sich
wir	....
ihr	....
Sie	....
sie	....

Ich muss **mich** beeilen. Wir müssen **uns** beeilen.
The reflexive pronoun refers to the subject.

Karl und Maria **sehen sich** jeden Tag.
Karl sieht Maria. Maria sieht Karl.

With some verbs the reflexive pronouns in the plural (uns, euch, sich) express a reciprocal relationship and correspond to "each other"/ "one another" in English: sich sehen, sich unterhalten, sich mögen, sich lieben, sich verstehen, sich treffen, sich kennen lernen

12 a Complete the text with the following verbs.

sich treffen • sich kennen lernen • sich unterhalten • sich verstehen • sich sehen • sich rasieren • sich umziehen • sich freuen • sich beeilen

Harro ist verliebt

Wie spät ist es? Was? Viertel vor sieben? Um sieben .... ich .... (1) mit Claudia. Wir haben .... gestern in der Disko .... (2). Die ganze Zeit haben wir .... über Rockmusik .... (3). Wir haben .... sehr gut .... (4). Heute Abend .... wir .... (5) wieder. Ich muss schnell nach Hause, ... und .... (6). Ich .... (7) schon sehr auf sie. Oh Gott! Ich muss .... (8).

b Replace the parts underlined in the text with the following verbs.

sich treffen • sich unterhalten • sich mögen • sich fragen, ob • sich beeilen

Claudia schreibt in ihr Tagebuch

Heute Abend um sieben sehe ich Harro wieder …
Was machen wir wohl? Gehen wir wieder in die Disko? Sprechen wir wieder die ganze Zeit über Musik? Das war ein bisschen langweilig gestern. Ich mag ihn sehr, und er mag mich auch. Aber ich bin nicht sicher, dass er der Richtige ist. Na, jetzt denke ich nicht daran. Ich muss schnell machen. Es ist schon fast sieben Uhr.

Heute Abend um sieben treffen wir uns wieder …

Ich hab' mein Herz in Heidelberg verloren

13 What do you know about the German city of Heidelberg? Where is Heidelberg located?

14 a Listen to the chorus of the popular song "Ich hab' mein Herz in Heidelberg verloren".
b Read the text.

Ich hab' mein Herz in Heidelberg verloren
in einer lauen Sommernacht.
Ich war verliebt bis über beide Ohren
und wie ein Röslein hat ihr Mund gelacht!
Und als wir Abschied nahmen vor den Toren,
beim letzten Kuss, da hab' ich's klar erkannt,
dass ich mein Herz in Heidelberg verloren,
mein Herz, es schlägt am Neckarstrand!

Beda und Ernst Neubach

15 Fill in further expressions to do with the topic of *Liebe*.

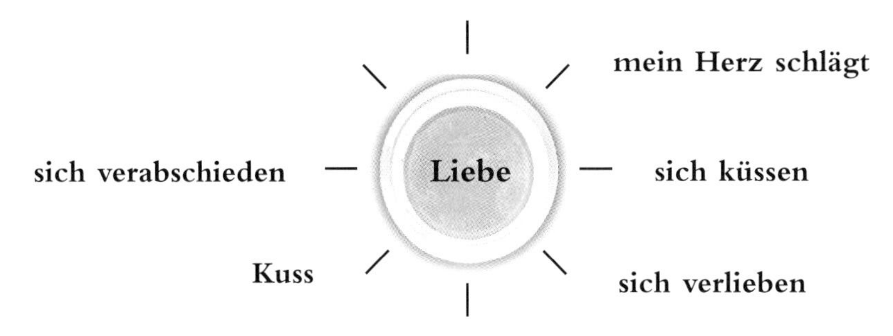

16 Listen to the song again and join in.

HALLO! HALLO!

Cultural information

The song "Hallo! Hallo!", in which a man is looking for a wife, is at first glance very simple and is one of those trivial texts to be found in many different countries. But when you find out that the song was composed in 1940 and broadcast by all German radio stations, the text suddenly has an explosive absurdity about it. Germany was at war. All young men over 18 were conscripted and sent off to fight. A large number of them died. Millions of women lost their husbands. Even in 1992 there were still 8.1 million women and only 4.3 men among the over 65s. So it wasn't women who were "in short supply", but men.

Language

In this unit you learn how to characterize and describe people. You will learn a number of adjectives (das Adjektiv), how to use them and what endings they have.

Adjectives are used to qualify or describe people and things:

a Deine Augen sind klar und dunkelblau.
(Your eyes are clear and dark blue.)
Adjective without endings

b Du hast klare und dunkelblaue Augen.
(You have clear, dark blue eyes.)
Adjective with endings

Adjective endings depend on the gender of the noun, the case and the determiners used with them. So it's not quite easy to learn them. On the other hand, comprehension is not dependent on the correctness of the adjectival endings. Statements will be understood anyway, especially when endings are slurred over, as is often the case in fast speech.

Learning strategies

First try and understand the essential elements of adjective declination. Always learn each new noun with its article. Note down on your vocabulary cards an appropriate adjective for each noun (e.g. ein jung**er** Mann, de**r** jung**e** Mann). Practise the endings by noting down examples and saying the words out loud.

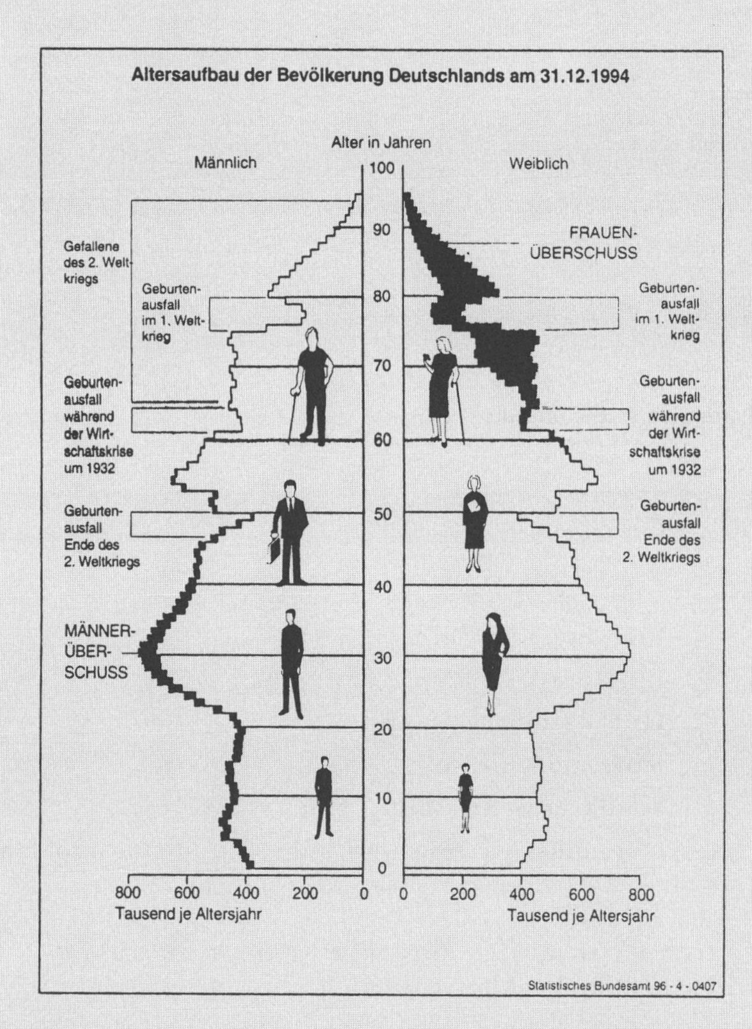

Hallo! Hallo!

1 Listen to the song and read it.

HALLO! HALLO! HALLO! HALLO!

Ich suche eine Frau,
eine süße, kleine und nette,
junge, liebe und hübsche Frau.
Ich wär so froh, ganz toll und froh,
das weiß ich ganz genau,
wenn ich sie bald hätte.
Mit Augen klar und rein und ganz dunkelblau.
Schön muss sie sein, aber auch klug,
lieb muss sie sein, das ist genug.

HALLO! HALLO! HALLO! HALLO!

Ich suche eine Frau,
eine süße, kleine, nette,
aber nicht so sehr kokette,
eine junge, liebe, hübsche, kleine Frau.

Joschi Neck

2 **a** What is the woman supposed to be like? Underline the adjectives.
b Match the adjectives.

Appearance ....

Age ....

Character ....

Intelligence ....

3 Copy down the words with an umlaut, *ä*, *ö*, *ü*. Make a list, and add to it words that you already know.

4 Listen to the song again. Pay special attention to the umlauts.

Aussprache: ö, ü

5 Listen and repeat.

lieb – jung – hübsch
lieb – klug – süß
klug – froh – schön

Lieb muss sie sein.
Jung muss sie sein.
Hübsch muss sie sein.
Klug muss sie sein.
Schön muss sie sein.
Nett muss sie sein und hübsch und süß und schön.

6 Listen and repeat.

pünktlich • natürlich • fünf • früh • Wir müssen zurück. • Kommst du früh? •
Sei doch pünktlich! • Pünktlich um fünf. • Aber natürlich müssen wir pünktlich sein.

7 a When do you hear a long ö as in *schön*? When do you hear a short ö as in *öffnen*?
Mark them with — or •.

Wir hören das Lied. Er hat drei Söhne und zwei Töchter. Um zwölf Uhr. So viele Wörter. Können Sie mich hören? Mögen Sie Frau Böhm? Ich komme aus Österreich.

b Listen and repeat.

Das Adjektiv: vor dem Nomen, beim Verb

8 Complete the sentences.

1 Sie muss ....klug.......... sein. (klug)

2 Ich suche ein...... .... Frau. (hübsch)

3 .... und .... muss sie sein. (schön, klug)

4 Ich wäre .... (froh)

5 Ich suche ein..... .... und .... Frau. (jung, lieb)

before a noun: adjective with ending	after a verb: adjective without ending
Er ist ein klug**er** Mann.	Ihre Augen sind klar.
Er sucht ein schön**es** Mädchen.	Ich bin froh.
Sie hat klar**e** Augen.	Das Kind ist intelligent.

Das Adjektiv: Nominativ, Akkusativ

9 Compare the adjective endings. Which are the same?

Das ist	ein	kluger Mann.	Ich suche	einen	klugen Mann.
	eine	kluge Frau.		eine	kluge Frau.
	ein	kluges Mädchen.		ein	kluges Mädchen.
Das sind		kluge Männer.	Ich suche		kluge Frauen.

10 Fill in the adjectives from section 9 and underline the endings.

	Singular			Plural
	maskulin	**neutral**	**feminin**	**m, n, f**
N	ein klug<u>er</u>........... Mann	ein .... Mädchen	eine .... Frau	.... Männer/Frauen
A	einen .... Mann	ein .... Mädchen	eine .... Frau	.... Männer/Frauen

Adjectives after *kein* and possessive articles (mein, dein/Ihr, sein, ihr, unser, euer/Ihr, ihr) follow the same pattern.

11 Rewrite the song.

Hallo! Hallo! Hallo! Hallo!

Ich suche einen Mann,

Ich wär so froh, ganz toll und froh,

das weiß ich ganz genau,

wenn ich ihn bald hätte.

Mit Augen

12 Make sentences.

Ich suche eine nette Frau.

- suchen
- besuchen
- denken an
- fotografieren
- fragen
- heiraten
- lieben
- treffen
- sehen

- ~~nett~~
- hübsch
- lieb
- jung
- klug
- blöd
- alt
- groß
- dick
- dumm
- neu
- krank
- reich
- hässlich
- ledig

- Freund
- Mädchen
- Gast
- Frau
- Freundin
- Chef
- Mann
- Lehrerin
- Kellner

13 Look at the photo. Describe the woman. Use suitable adjectives from the list in sections 12 and 17 (Phantombild). Select some adjectives from section 17 that you want to learn.

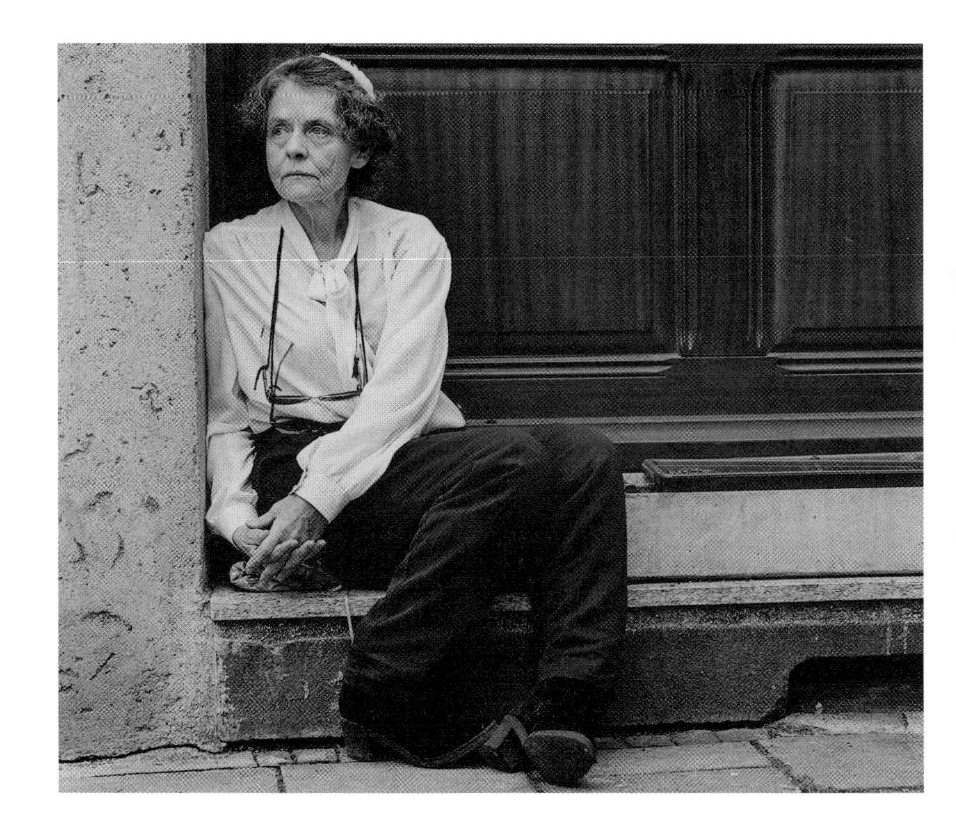

Das Verb: Konjunktiv II Gegenwart (1)

14 Complete from the text.

Ich suche eine Frau.

Ich .... so froh, wenn ich sie bald ....

Hätte and *wäre* are the forms of the subjunctive II present (Konjunktiv II Gegenwart) of the verbs *haben* and *sein*.
In these sentences they express an unreal condition:
Ich wäre froh, wenn ich sie bald hätte. (I would be glad if I had her soon.)
I haven't got her, so I'm not glad either.

15 Fill in the forms of the verb *haben*.

	sein	**haben**
ich	wär **e**	hätt **e**
du	wär (**e**) **st**	....
Sie	wär **en**	....
er/sie/es/man	wär **e**	....
wir	wär **en**	....
ihr	wär (**e**) **t**	....
Sie	wär **en**	....
sie	wär **en**	....

16 Complete the sentences with the following expressions. Use *hätte* and *wäre*.

dich alle gern haben • in der Kneipe sein • froh sein • jetzt wenig Zeit haben • jetzt in Italien sein • auch Geld haben

1 Wenn wir Urlaub ... hätten, wären wir jetzt in Italien. ....

2 Wenn du nett .... , ...

3 Wenn ich Feierabend .... , ...

4 Wenn ich Arbeit .... , ...

5 Wenn sie verheiratet .... und Kinder .... , ...

6 Wenn er jetzt hier .... , ... ich ....

Phantombild

17 With the aid of a questionnaire the police create an Identikit picture of a suspect.
A witness who saw the person marks the relevant characteristics.
Select a person that you know, or a photo.

a Mark appropriate words with a cross.

b Describe the person.

Der/Die Gesuchte
Alter
Größe
Geschlecht

Erscheinung
- ☐ gepflegt
- ☐ ungepflegt
- ☐ modisch
- ☐ seriös

Gestalt
- ☐ schlank
- ☐ muskulös
- ☐ dick
- ☐ sportlich

Gesicht
- ☐ oval
- ☐ länglich/schmal
- ☐ rund/voll
- ☐ breit
- ☐ eckig
- ☐ weich
- ☐ kindlich
- ☐ blass
- ☐ gerötet
- ☐ dunkel

Haare
- ☐ blond
- ☐ grau
- ☐ weiß
- ☐ braun
- ☐ dunkel
- ☐ schwarz
- ☐ glatt
- ☐ wellig
- ☐ kurz
- ☐ mittel
- ☐ dicht
- ☐ Glatze

Besonderheiten
- ☐ Zöpfe
- ☐ Pferdeschwanz
- ☐ Perücke

Augen
- ☐ groß
- ☐ klein
- ☐ dunkel
- ☐ hell

Ohren
- ☐ groß
- ☐ klein
- ☐ anliegend
- ☐ abstehend

Nase
- ☐ lang
- ☐ kurz
- ☐ breit
- ☐ schmal
- ☐ gerade
- ☐ schief

Mund
- ☐ klein
- ☐ mittel
- ☐ groß
- ☐ breit

Besonderheiten
- ☐ Sommersprossen
- ☐ Pickel
- ☐ Warzen
- ☐ Narben

Kinn
- ☐ kurz
- ☐ lang
- ☐ schmal
- ☐ breit
- ☐ spitz
- ☐ rund
- ☐ kantig
- ☐ Doppelkinn

Hals
- ☐ lang
- ☐ kurz
- ☐ dünn
- ☐ kräftig

Bart
- ☐ Vollbart
- ☐ Kinnbart
- ☐ Oberlippenbart
- ☐ hell
- ☐ dunkel
- ☐ dicht
- ☐ kurz
- ☐ lang
- ☐ spitz

18 a Ask a witness. Use the following expressions.

Wie alt ist …?
Hat deine/Ihre Person …?
Sieht er/sie … aus?
Trägt er/sie …?
Ist es ein Mann oder …?
Ist die Person / Heißt die Person …?
Hat er/sie … Gesicht?
Ist sein/ihr Gesicht …?

b Answer as a witness. Describe the suspect.

Der/Die Gesuchte ist etwa 35 Jahre alt und sieht gepflegt aus. …

Es war einmal ein Mann

Texts

The nursery rhyme "Es war einmal ein Mann" is an old favourite in all the German-speaking countries, and there are many different versions. In this unit we present two of them. The first was written down by someone as they remembered it being told to them in their childhood, the second is a redrafted version by the children's writer and artist Janosch.

Nursery rhymes are always rhythmic and melodic and help to practise language in an enjoyable, fun way. What we did as children with our mother tongue, we can do as adults too, with a foreign one.

Learning strategies

A lot of learners of a foreign language have the problem that they've mastered the vocabulary and grammar well enough, but can't in fact make themselves understood because their pronunciation is not right. It's usually less a question of inability than of not having the courage. Every language requires a different way of using your tongue, lips, teeth and gums, different rhythms and intonation patterns, and sometimes different tones. So you have to overcome your inhibitions and simply keep on practising till the articulation and intonation sound more or less authentic and, first and foremost, you are comprehsensible. By reciting unpretentious nursery rhymes with their rhythmic stress, you can get over any shyness about forming the correct articulation and intonation. It's more important at the beginning in fact to get the rhythm and intonation right than the articulation. So try to always practise the whole sentence first, and then pick out the individual sounds that are still a problem. It's probably best to learn the poem off by heart so that you can recite it any time you have a spare moment.

Language

In Unit 10 you learned the perfect as the first way of expressing past time. In this unit you meet the past, which is mainly used in written reports and narratives, while the perfect is more common in oral everyday speech. They both have the same status. When to use which is more a question of the situation and region. In oral colloquial speech most people, especially further south, prefer to use the perfect. The past, however, is predominant in written reports, and it is also to be heard as the narrative tense in lectures, oral narratives and public statements in front of an audience. Some verbs such as *haben* and *sein*, and modal verbs are mainly used in the past, also in speech. Take note of when which form is used in the texts that you come across.

Make sure that from now on you fill in the past forms in your verb list (→ S. 57). You can look them up in the Learner's Book.

Eier, Frau Meier ... Frau

in Köpfchen! Fall nur nicht

Es war einmal ein Mann

1 Look at the pictures. How does the story go. Note down the order.

2 Which people, objects and places play a role in the story? Note down the words.

3 The text begins *Es war einmal ...* (Once upon a time ...). What sort of texts in English have this sort of introduction? What sort of story are you expecting?

4 Listen to the text. Mark the words you hear in each verse.

Verse	1	2	3	4	5	6	7	8
Wald	☐	☐	☐	☐	☐	☐	☐	☐
Maus	☐	☐	☐	☐	☐	☐	☐	☐
Mann	☐	☐	☐	☐	☐	☐	☐	☐
Geschichte	☐	☐	☐	☐	☐	☐	☐	☐
Bett	☐	☐	☐	☐	☐	☐	☐	☐
Tirol	☐	☐	☐	☐	☐	☐	☐	☐
Schwamm	☐	☐	☐	☐	☐	☐	☐	☐
Berlin	☐	☐	☐	☐	☐	☐	☐	☐
Gass(e)	☐	☐	☐	☐	☐	☐	☐	☐
(da)heim	☐	☐	☐	☐	☐	☐	☐	☐

5 Listen to the text again. Note down which picture goes with verses 1, 2, 3 etc.

1 ☐ 2 ☐ 3 ☐ 4 ☐ 5 ☐ 6 ☐ 7 ☐ 8 ☐

6 Now read the poem.

Es war einmal ein Mann

Es war einmal ein Mann,
der hatte einen Schwamm.

Der Schwamm war ihm zu nass,
da ging er auf die Gass[1].

Die Gass' war ihm zu kalt,
da ging er in den Wald.

Der Wald war ihm zu grün,
da ging er nach Berlin.

Berlin war ihm zu voll,
da ging er nach Tirol.

Tirol war ihm zu klein,
da ging er wieder heim.

Daheim war's[2] ihm zu nett,
da legt'[3] er sich ins Bett.

Im Bett war eine Maus,
und die Geschicht'[4] ist aus.

Volksmund

[1] Gass = Gasse
[2] war's = war es
[3] legt' = legte
[4] Geschicht' = Geschichte

7 Why was the man never satisfied? Complete.

1 Der Schwamm ....
2 Die Gasse ....
3 Der Wald ....
4 Berlin ....
5 Tirol ....
6 Daheim ....

There are three degrees of intensity for characteristics:

normal	intense	too much / too little
nass	**sehr** nass	**zu** nass

8 Fill in *sehr* or *zu*.

1 Er ist .... jung, er kann das nicht verstehen.
2 Fast Food ist nicht .... gesund.
3 Diese Schokolade ist nicht .... süß.
4 Sie trinken .... viel Alkohol, das ist ungesund.
5 Deutschland ist heute .... groß, sagen viele Leute.
6 Sein Deutsch ist .... gut. Er spricht fast wie ein Deutscher.
7 Es ist hier .... dunkel, wir können nichts sehen.
8 Er ist .... nett, er hilft ihr oft.
9 In Kanada leben? – Nie, dort ist es mir .... kalt.

Ortsergänzung: Wohin? Woher?

9 Fill in prepositions and articles from the text.

Wohin? Der Mann ging ....nach.................. Berlin. .... Tirol.

.... Gass(e). .... Wald.

.... Bett.

Adverbials of place

Wohin?	nach	(only with place names and names of countries)	nach Berlin, nach Tirol, nach Amerika, nach Italien, nach Hause
	in +	accusative	ins Bett (in das = ins), in den Wald, in die Schweiz, in die Türkei
	auf +	accusative	auf die Gasse, auf die Straße
Woher?	aus +	dative	aus Amerika, aus der Schweiz, aus Berlin, aus dem Haus, aus dem Zimmer
	von +	dative	von dir, von einem Freund, von der Arbeit

10 Answer the questions.

Mallorca • Schule • Straße • Freund • Paris • Schwester • Schweiz • Kino • Türkei • Disko • Schweden • Hamburg • Park

1 Wohin fahren Sie im Urlaub?
2 Woher kommt seine Freundin?
3 Wohin fliegt ihr Freund?
4 Woher kennen sie sich?
5 Wohin laufen die Leute?
6 Woher hast du die Fotos?
7 Wohin geht ihr heute Abend?

Das Verb: Präteritum (2)

11 Fill in the missing verb forms.

	regelmäßige Verben		**unregelmäßige Verben**		
	legen	**warten**	**gehen**	**laufen**	**sprechen**
ich	leg **t e**	wart e **t e**	ging	lief	sprach
du	leg **t est**	wart e **t est**	ging **st**	lief **st**	....
Sie	....	....	....	....	....
er/sie/es/man	leg **t e**	wart e **t e**	ging	lief	....
wir	leg **t en**	wart e **t en**	ging **en**	lief **en**	....
ihr	leg **t et**	wart e **t et**	ging **t**	....	....
Sie	leg **t en**	wart e **t en**	ging **en**	....	....
sie	leg **t en**	wart e **t en**	ging **en**	....	....

regular verbs: Verb stem + past signal *t* + endings
irregular verbs: change of vowel (laufen – lief) or of vowel and consonant (gehen – ging) + endings
The *du*-form and *ihr*-form is rare in the past because the perfect is mostly used in speech.

12 Look up the past forms you don't know in a dictionary. Complete the table.

regelmäßige Verben			**unregelmäßige Verben**		
Infinitiv	**Präteritum**		**Infinitiv**	**Präteritum**	
	er/sie/es/man	sie (Pl.)		er/sie/es/man	sie (Pl.)
warten	....	....	lesen	....	....
sagen	sagte	sagten	schreiben	....	....
schmecken	....	....	rufen	....	....
legen	....	....	sitzen	....	....
machen	....	....	essen	....	....
arbeiten	....	....	trinken	....	....
besuchen	....	....	schlafen	....	....

13 Fill in the verbs in the past.

Mein Vater .... (1) als Kellner. Er .... (2) jeden Tag nach der Arbeit in seine Kneipe. Dort .... (3) er zwei bis drei Stunden, ... (4) drei Glas Bier und .... (5) Zeitung. Zu Hause .... (6) er nie. Dort .... (7) ihm das Bier nicht.

14 Fill in verbs in the past, prepositions and articles.

Wohin ist Ulla gegangen?

Es .... (sein) einmal eine schöne und kluge Frau, die .... (heißen) Ulla. Sie .... (wohnen) in einem großen Haus in Hamburg. Aber sie .... (haben) eine kleine Wohnung. Die .... (sein) ihr eines Tages viel zu klein und warm. Da .... (gehen) sie .... Straße und .... (laufen) .... Wald. Nach zehn Stunden .... (haben) sie die Nase voll und .... (gehen) wieder .... Hause. Aber da .... (haben) sie nichts zu essen, und sie .... (sein) allein.

Da .... (anrufen) sie im Reisebüro .... und .... (sagen): „Ich fliege .... Amerika. Schicken Sie mir ein Flugticket." Am nächsten Tag .... (fliegen) sie .... New York. New York aber .... (sein) ihr viel zu groß und zu laut. Auch .... (geben) es dort keinen Wald. Also .... (fliegen) sie wieder .... Hamburg und .... (gehen) sofort .... Bett. Und wenn sie noch nicht gestorben ist, liegt sie da heute noch.

15 **a** Read Janosch's version of the poem.
Look at the pictures and work out the meaning of the following words: Kahn, bauen, Floß, fallen, Dreck, Sau, Mauseloch.

b Write down the past forms and add the matching infinitive: war – sein.

baut = baute   kauft = kaufte

16 **a** Listen to Janosch's text.

b Read the text aloud.
Copy the rhythm.

17 Write a story about a man or a woman who is not content anywhere and goes from place to place as in section 14.
Begin like this:
Es war einmal ...

Simon Maier

Cultural information

An interview with the shepherd Simon Meyer gives us an insight into German agriculture, which has changed enormously over the last forty years. In 1950 one in three of the work-force was employed in agriculture, today it is just one in thirty. Nevertheless 83% of Germany's food requirement is produced at home. Only the larger farms have survived in farming villages, with efficient production methods using intensive farming and modern technology. Less fertile fields are left barren or are turned into golf courses.

All these unplanted fields and meadows provide excellent grazing for sheep. The result is that sheep farming is on its way back. In 1970 there were no more than 800,000 sheep in West Germany. In 1995 the figure was 1.7 million. Foreign immigrants from the Balkans and Turkey have played a role in this, as they want to eat fresh lamb at their festivals. The shepherd's romantic profession is in vogue again.

The text

The interview with a modern shepherd is a relatively long text with a lot of unknown words. But do your best to understand the text's most important statements. In our mother tongue too we keep coming across texts that we have to work our way into because we don't know the special terminology or because there's something else we don't understand.

Every text contains passages that are very important, and sections that add explanations, emphasis or atmosphere. To make it easier for you, we've highlighted the key information, and the tasks only relate to these sections. If you feel like it, there's nothing to stop you working on the whole text.

Learning strategies

Before you read a text it's a good idea to think about the topic and what details the text might contain information about. Our text is an interview, i.e. a text with a simple structure: it consists of questions and answers. If you understand the questions you already have an idea and can guess what the answers will be like. This unit therefore deals with the various ways of asking a question in German. When you ask a question in a foreign language, you should always think about what possible content the answers might have and what sort of language they might be couched in. If you only ask questions, the answers often mean nothing. And getting an answer is of course the actual aim of asking a question.

Simon Maier

1 **a** Look at the photo. What can you see?

b What do you learn about Simon Maier from the text and the photo?

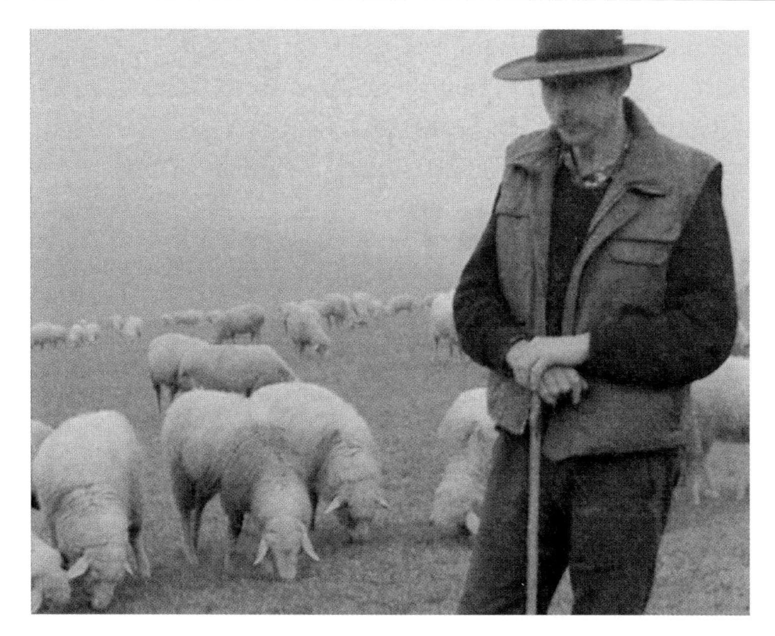

Simon Maier, 38, lebt seit 22 Jahren zusammen mit seinen Schafen unter freiem Himmel. Nicht nur steinerne Häuser sind ihm ein Gräuel[1]. Auch dass Schafe neuerdings Dolly heißen, macht ihm Angst.

[1]... sind ihm ein Gräuel: he loathes ...

2 Complete the word-spider on the topic of *Schafe*.

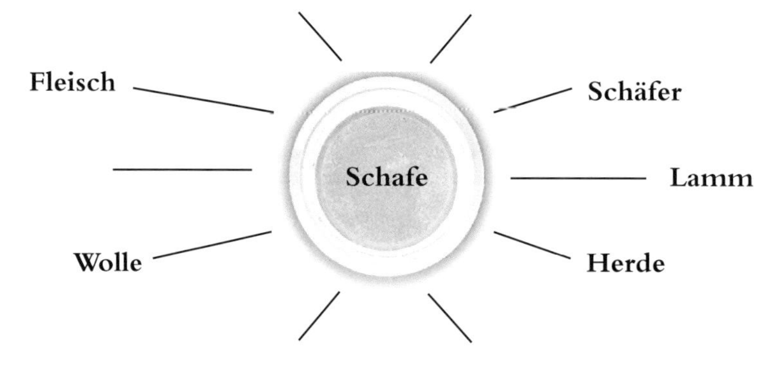

3 What questions would you ask the shepherd? Make a list in English.

4 **a** Here are some questions from the text. Which questions did you ask, which didn't you ask?

Stehen Sie den ganzen Tag?
Wie nennen Sie Ihre Schafe?
Wie wird man Schäfer?
Leben Sie vom Fleisch der Schafe oder von der Wolle?
Wo schlafen Sie?
Hören Sie Radio, lesen Sie Bücher?
Woran denken Sie den ganzen Tag?
Was geben Ihnen die Schafe?
Sie langweilen sich nie da draußen?
Haben Sie eine Freundin?

b Guess Simon Maier's answers to the questions.

c Read the highlighted sections of the text.

Simon Maier

Ein Schäfer darf auf der Wiese liegen, die Sonne scheint ihm auf den Bauch, er kaut an einem Grashalm, zwei Hunde halten die Herde zusammen – Sie haben eigentlich einen wunderbaren Beruf.

Na, ganz so romantisch ist es nicht. Ich habe schon zu tun. Ich muss die Klauen pflegen, und wenn eins humpelt, weil es in einen Stein reingetreten ist, muss ich den Stein entfernen.

Stehen Sie den ganzen Tag?

Ja, acht bis zehn Stunden. Ich habe immer die Schäferschippe dabei, da lehne ich mich drauf, wenn ich nicht wandere. Ich darf mich nicht hinlegen, sonst hören die Schafe auf zu fressen. Ein guter Schäfer muss die Schafe zum Fressen animieren. Wenn der Hirte sitzt und nicht aufpasst, dass die fressen, dann tun die Schafe auch nichts.

Kühe heißen meistens Rosie oder Marie. Wie nennen Sie Ihre Schafe?

Namen haben die keinen. Aber wenn man ständig beieinander ist, weiß man schon, wer da blökt. Jedes Schaf schaut anders aus, genau wie die Menschen auch. Das eine hat größere Augen, bei einem anderen sind die Lippen kleiner und der Kopf größer, das eine ist dick, das andere dünner.

Wie wird man denn Schäfer?

Mein Vater hat bereits Schafe gehabt und ich habe seine Herde übernommen. Irgendwer muss es ja machen, das Schafehüten ist mir angeboren. Da kann man sich nichts anderes mehr vorstellen.

Leben Sie vom Fleisch der Schafe oder von der Wolle?

Vom Fleisch der Lämmer, das Schaf muss ja die Lämmer bringen. Die Lämmer werden von einem Metzger in Rosenheim geschlachtet.

Fühlen Sie da nicht mit?

Wenn sie so klein sind, tut mir das schon sehr Leid.

Wo schlafen Sie, wenn Sie mit Ihren Schafen auf Wanderschaft sind?

Ich habe meistens einen Schäferkarren oder einen Wohnwagen dabei, aber oft fahre ich heim. Wenn es sein muss, schlafe ich auch draußen. Das ist schöner als jedes Bett.

Hören Sie inmitten Ihrer Herde Radio, lesen Sie Bücher?

Nein, höchstens mal eine Zeitung. Aber nie mitten unter den Schafen, man steht am Rand. Ich muss die Herde überblicken können.

Woran denken Sie, wenn Sie den ganzen Tag auf Schafe gucken?

Da komme ich oft auf dumme Gedanken. Wenn das Wetter schön ist, geht es ja, aber wenn es schlecht ist, denke ich: Warum machst du das? Andere Menschen in deinem Alter haben ein Dach über dem Kopf, du bist draußen. Da verzweifle ich manchmal. In solchen Momenten möchte ich am liebsten aufhören. Aber ich häng' halt so am Vieh, die sind wie Kinder für mich.

Was geben Ihnen die Schafe?

Ja mei[1], die Ruhe. Ich bin so froh, wenn ich nicht in die Stadt rein muss. Wenn mich die Schafe ärgern, dann weiß ich: Das sind Viecher, die können nichts dafür. Wenn aber der Mensch mich ärgert, macht er das absichtlich.

Sie langweilen sich nie da draußen?

Eigentlich nicht. Ich krieg' ja auch Besuch. Ich treffe so viele Kinder, die Schafe nur aus Büchern kennen. Die sind ganz aus dem Häuschen, wenn sie echte sehen.

Was ist Ihr Traum vom Leben?

Habe ich mich noch nie gefragt. Ich kann mir nichts Schöneres vorstellen als Schafehüten. Ich bin einfach froh, weg zu sein von der Straße.

Sie sind also kein geselliger Mensch?

Na ja, so gesellig bin ich nicht, nein. Ich bin jeden Tag bei den Schafen. Da kann ich nicht sagen, also heute habe ich keine Lust.

Haben Sie eine Freundin?

Nein. Frauen möchten heute frei sein und nicht mit einem Schäfer ziehen. So Frauen gibt es ganz selten. Vorerst sind mir die Schafe wichtiger.

aus: *Süddeutsche Zeitung, Magazin*

[1] Ja mei = Bavarian expression, used mostly to introduce a statement.

Frageformen

A	**Statement with question intonation**	
	Sie haben einen Namen?	Ja. / Nein.
	Sie haben keinen Namen?	Doch./Nein.
B	**Yes / no-question (Satzfrage)**	
	Haben Sie eine Freundin?	Ja. / Nein.
	Haben Sie keine Freundin?	Doch. / Nein.
C	**Alternative question**	
	Hat Simon Maier eine Freundin oder lebt er allein?	Er lebt allein.
D	**Wh-question (Wortfrage)**	
	Wo schlafen Sie?	Im Wohnwagen.
	Was geben Ihnen die Schafe?	Die Ruhe.
E	**Statement with question tag**	
	Sie sind Herr Maier. Nicht wahr?	Ja./Nein.

doch: positive answer / reaction to a negative question / statement.
- Ist Susanne **nicht** nett zu dir?
- **Doch.**
- Er kommt heute **nicht**.
- **Doch**, er kommt.

5 Find and note down one example of question forms A-D in the text.

A .... **B** ....

C .... **D** ....

6 **a** Note down all question words that you know for introducing a question.

Wer ? ....

b Form questions with the question words.

7 Prepare an interview with the woman in the photo on page 104.
Note down the questions you'd like to ask her. Use various question forms.

Intonation: Fragen

8 Listen and mark the intonation (↗ or ↘).

1 Sie langweilen sich nie? ___
2 Sie haben keine Freundin? ___
3 Sie lieben Ihren Beruf. ___ Nicht wahr? ___
4 Sie haben viel Zeit. ___ Oder nicht? ___
5 Sie haben einen schönen Beruf. ___ Hab ich Recht? ___
6 Langweilen Sie sich manchmal ↗ oder haben Sie immer viel zu tun? ↘
7 Stehen Sie den ganzen Tag ___ oder können sie sich auch hinlegen? ___
8 Leben Sie vom Fleisch der Schafe ___ oder von der Wolle? ___

Das Adjektiv: Vergleich (Grundform, Komparativ, Superlativ)

There are three ways of making a comparison:
- with the basic form: Der Beruf ist nicht **so romantisch, wie** viele glauben.
- with the comparative: Jedes Schaf schaut anders aus, das eine ist dick, das andere **dünner**.
- with the superlative: Dies ist **das kleinste** Schaf.

Grundform

9 What do the adjectives compare something with?

1 himmelblau blau wie der Himmel
2 grasgrün ....
3 schneeweiß ....
4 hundemüde müde wie ein Hund
5 haushoch ....
6 bildschön ....

Basic form
Dieses Schaf ist **schwarz wie** Kaffee.
Das eine Schaf ist (genau)**so groß wie** das andere.
Comparisons are formed with *wie*, *so* … *wie* or *genauso* … *wie*.

Komparativ

10 Find adjectives in the comparative form in the text, and note them down with their basic form.

kleiner - klein

Comparative = basic form + *er* (+ *als*)	klein**er**, schön**er**, hässlich**er**
with umlaut:	groß – gr**ö**ß**er**, alt – **ä**lt**er**, jung – j**ü**ng**er**
with ending before a noun:	Das eine Schaf hat **größere** Augen. Er hat einen **schöneren** Beruf **als** ich.
without ending after a verb:	Draußen schlafen ist **schöner als** jedes Bett.

Superlativ

11 a Read the poem and check the meaning of the unknown words.

Ferienerzählungen[1]

„Bin auf den höchsten Berg gestiegen."
„Bin im tiefsten Meer geschwommen."
„Bin durch die weiteste Ebene gefahren."

„Bin unterm Apfelbaum gelegen,
hab' meine Träume fliegen lassen:
Höher als die höchsten Berge,
tiefer als die tiefsten Meere,
weiter als die weitesten Ebenen."

Hans Manz

[1] Ferienerzählungen: holiday tales

b Underline the superlatives.

Superlative = article + basic form + *st* + ending or *am* + basic form + *sten*	
with ending before a noun:	Das ist **mein schönstes** Schaf. Er hat **den schönsten** Beruf.
after a verb:	Draußen schlafen ist **am schönsten**.

Unregelmäßige Formen

Some adjectives have irregular forms. Always learn the comparative and superlative forms with them.

1 The vowel has an umlaut:

a → ä	alt	ält**er**	der ält**este**	am ält**esten**
o → ö	groß	größ**er**	der größ**te**	am größ**ten**
u → ü	dumm	dümm**er**	der dümm**ste**	am dümm**sten**

2 Adjectives ending in *-t*, *-d*, *-s*, *-ß*, *-sch*, *-z* have *-est* in the superlative + ending or *-esten* (exception *groß*):

laut	laut**er**	der laut**este**	am laut**esten**
kurz	kürz**er**	der kürz**este**	am kürz**esten**
hübsch	hübsch**er**	der hübsch**este**	am hübsch**esten**
süß	süß**er**	der süß**este**	am süß**esten**

3 Adjectives ending in *-er*, *-el*:

dunkel	dunk**ler**	der dunkel**ste**	am dunkel**sten**
teuer	teu**rer**	der teuer**ste**	am teuer**sten**

4 Special forms:

hoch	**höher**	der **höchste**	am **höchsten**
nah	**näher**	der **nächste**	am **nächsten**
gut	**besser**	der **beste**	am **besten**
viel	**mehr**	die **meisten**	am **meisten**
gern	**lieber**	der **liebste**	am **liebsten**

12 Fill in the forms.

Grundform	Komparativ	Superlativ	Grundform	Komparativ	Superlativ
....	....	am ältesten	teuer	....	....
süß	....	....	....	....	am bittersten
....	dümmer	....	früh	....	....
....	....	am meisten	....	....	am nächsten
genau	....	....	hart	....	....
....	lieber	....	....	....	am klügsten
hoch	....	....	....	lauter	....
lang	....	....	groß	....	....

13 Complete the sentences with the adjectives given, in the basic form, comparative or superlative.

1 Ich hatte einen .... Freund. Einen .... findest du nicht. (gut)

2 Der Film Casablanca ist sehr .... Einen .... habe ich noch nie gesehen. (spannend)

3 Berlin ist die .... deutsche Stadt. Paris und London aber sind .... als Berlin. (groß)

4 In Frankfurt gibt es sehr .... Türken. Die .... Türken aber leben in Berlin. (viel)

5 S-Bahn und U-Bahn sind ziemlich .... bei meiner Wohnung.
Am .... aber ist die Bushaltestelle. (nah)

Ich & mein Bruder

Cultural information

Two texts about the family and society tell of conflicts between brothers and sisters and between a son and his parents. One text is a picture story, the other a song from the period of the so-called new German wave (Neue Deutsche Welle, NDW) at the beginning of the 1980s. Both are about a young man rebelling against his family and society in general telling him what to do. Both youths leave their family and the area where they grew up to make a new life for themselves. The song mentions the city of Osnabrück, which the young man leaves behind him. Osnabrück is a medium-sized city of 160,000 inhabitants in northwest Germany. Its most prominent characteristic is that, before the reunification of East and West Germany, it was statistically the average German city. Even the ratio of Protestants and Catholics corresponded to that of the whole of Germany. So if you know Osnabrück, you know just about everything there is to know about about German cities and German society. Osnabrück has a university, a civic theatre, a symphony orchestra, a conservatoire, 6 museums and galleries, 120 sports clubs, 9187 businesses, 4 hospitals and a zoo.

Language

In this unit you make the acquaintance of one of the peculiarities of German pronunciation, the glottal stop (der Knacklaut). It's not as bad as it sounds, because English has this feature too. A vowel at the beginning of a word or a syllable is preceded by a sound created right at the back of the throat, audible as a sort of light crack. Vowels are not linked to the sound that went before, but the voice starts afresh. The glottal stop (|) is an indication to the listener that a new word (Wie | alt | ist | er?) or syllable (Be | eil dich!) is beginning, which in many cases is important for comprehension.

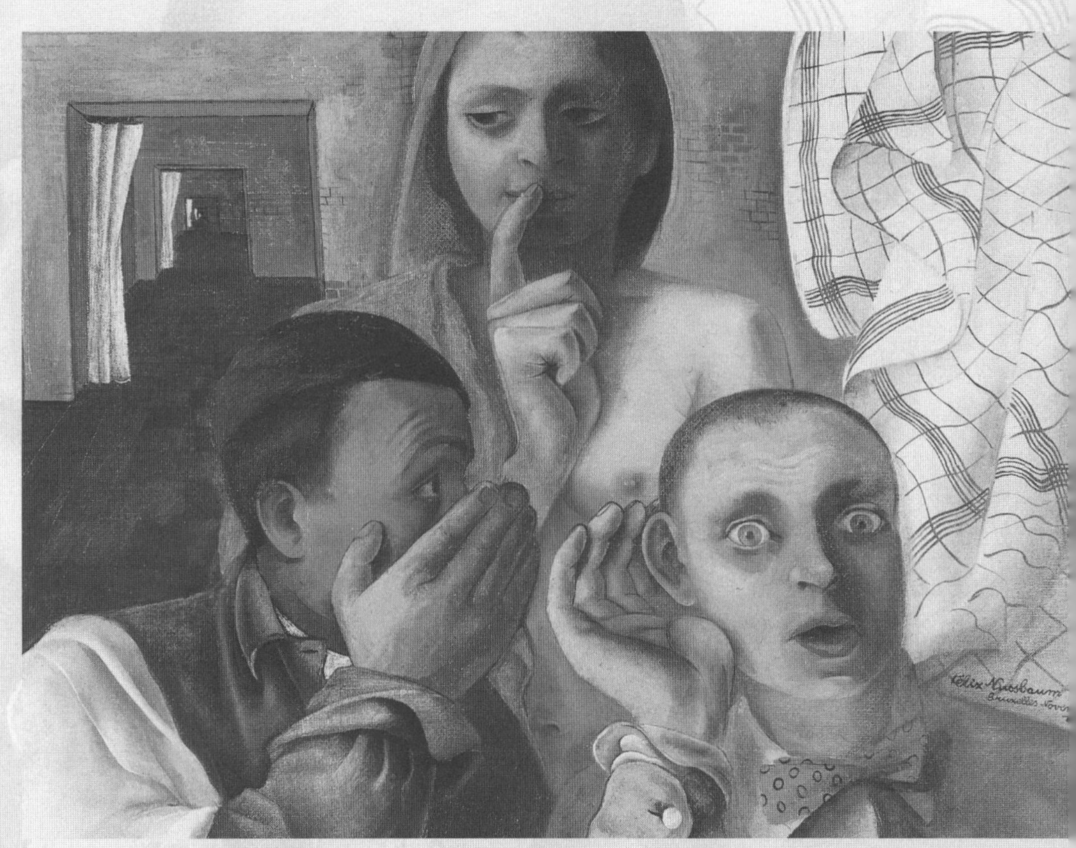

A gallery in Osnabrück is dedicated to the painter Felix Nussbaum, who was born here.

As a Jew he emigrated to Belgium as early as 1935, but was arrested there by the Gestapo in 1944 and murdered in Auschwitz together with his wife Felka Platek.

Ich & mein Bruder

1 Ich und mein Bruder: … Ich und meine Schwester: …
Continue this train of thought. Jot down some notes or a sentence or two.

2 Always look at the picture first, then read the text.

Als ich acht Jahre
alt war, kam
mein Bruder
zur Welt.

Als ich zehn war,
spielte ich mit ihm.

Als ich zwölf war,
erzählte ich ihm
Geschichten und las
ihm Bilderbücher vor.

Als ich vierzehn
war, wollte ich aus
ihm einen Muster-
knaben machen.

Als ich sechzehn
war, wollte ich, er
solle Klavier spielen
lernen.

Als ich achtzehn war, wollte ich,
er solle nicht mit fremden Kindern spielen
und nicht im Dialekt sprechen.

Als ich zwanzig war,
schenkte ich ihm eine
Krawatte.

Als ich vierundzwanzig war,
stritten wir,
weil er anderer Meinung war.

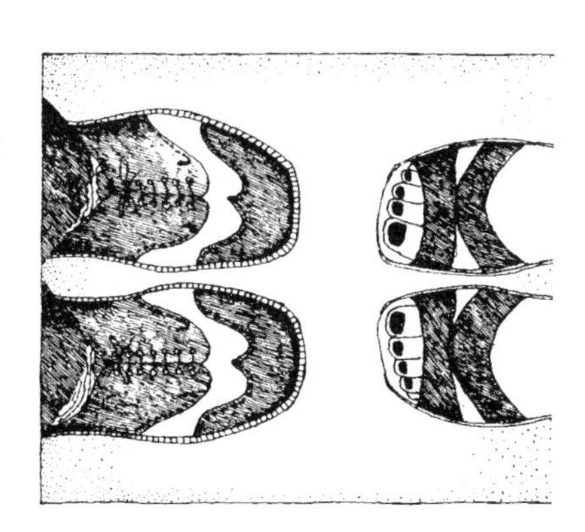

Als ich sechsundzwanzig
war, merkte ich nicht,
dass er erwachsen
geworden war.

Als ich achtundzwanzig war,
ging er irgendwohin,
um nicht wiederzukommen.

Angelika Kaufmann

3 Which terms are appropriate for the story? Mark them below and find others.

- ☐ Memory (Erinnerung)
- ☐ Tolerance (Toleranz)
- ☐ Ambition (Ehrgeiz)
- ☐ Egoism (Egoismus)
- ☐ Sense of responsibility (Verantwortungsbewusstsein)
- ☐ Bad conscience (schlechtes Gewissen)
- ☐ Superiority (Überlegenheit)
- ☐ Envy (Neid)
- ☐ Pride (Stolz)

4 Underline all the verbs in the text.

Das Verb: Präteritum (3)

5 Fill in the missing verb forms.

	regelmäßige Verben	unregelmäßige Verben			Modalverben	
	spielen	**gehen**	**kommen**	**denken**[1]	**können**[2]	**wollen**[3]
ich	spiel **t e**	ging –	kam –	dach **t e**	konn **t e**	woll **t e**
du	spiel t est	ging **st**	kam **st**	dach **t est**	konn **t est**	woll **t est**
Sie	....	....	....	dach **t en**	konn **t en**	woll **t en**
er/sie/es/man	....	....	....	dach **t e**	konn **t e**	woll **t e**
wir	....	....	....	dach **t en**	konn **t en**	woll **t en**
ihr	....	....	....	dach **t et**	konn **t et**	woll **t et**
Sie	....	....	....	dach **t en**	konn **t en**	woll **t en**
sie	....	....	....	dach **t en**	konn **t en**	woll **t en**

[1] similarly: *wissen, ich wusste; bringen, ich brachte*
[2] similarly: *dürfen, ich durfte; müssen, ich musste; mögen, ich mochte*
[3] similarly: *sollen, ich sollte*

Irregular verbs
Change of vowel (k**o**mmen → k**a**m) or change of vowel and consonant (g**eh**en → g**ing**).
Some verbs also have the past signal *t* and the ending of a regular verb (d**enk**en → d**achte**).

6 Sort the verbs from the text into the table. Write down the infinitive as well.

regelmäßige Verben	unregelmäßige Verben	Modalverben
ich spielte (spielen)	ich war (sein)	....
....	....	
....	....	
....	....	
	....	

7 What is the past of these verb forms? Look them up in a dictionary.

ich fahre ⁄⁄ wir essen ⁄⁄ er schreibt ⁄⁄ sie nimmt ⁄⁄ du gibst ⁄⁄ wir finden ⁄⁄
sie laufen ⁄⁄ ich werde ⁄⁄ er weiß ⁄⁄ ich bringe

8 With separable verbs you have to look for the basic verb in the dictionary. Underline the basic verb.

anfangen ⁄⁄ anrufen ⁄⁄ ausgehen ⁄⁄ fernsehen ⁄⁄ vorlesen ⁄⁄ wiederkommen

9 What's the infinitive of the verbs?

1 Wir s**a**ßen zu Hause und l**a**sen Bilderbücher. ....
2 Er spr**a**ch nur im Dialekt. ....
3 Er beg**a**nn erwachsen zu werden. ....
4 Wir str**i**tten oft. ....
5 Wir s**a**hen viele schöne Filme. ....
6 Er n**a**hm seinen Rucksack und f**u**hr weg. ....
7 Ich verl**o**r einen Freund. ....
8 Ich d**a**chte immer an meinen Bruder. ....
9 Ich schr**ie**b ihm lange Briefe. ....
10 Das gef**ie**l ihm vielleicht nicht. ....

Irregular verbs
The most important vowel changes in the past:
Infinitive → past

e → a	**ei → ie/i**	**a → ie**
ie → o	**i → a**	**a → u**

10 Fill in the past form of the verbs in brackets.

1 Mit zwei Jahren .... meine Schwester mit mir. Das .... schön. (spielen, sein)
2 Mit vier Jahren .... sie mir Geschichten. Das .... sie gut. (erzählen, können)
3 Aber mit sechs Jahren .... ich ein Musterknabe sein. (sollen)
4 Mit acht Jahren .... ich Klavier spielen lernen. Ich .... es nicht. (müssen, wollen)
5 Mit zehn Jahren .... ich nicht mit fremden Kindern spielen. Das .... ich nicht verstehen. (dürfen, können)
6 Mit zwölf Jahren .... ich eine Krawatte tragen. Ich .... sie nicht schön. (sollen, finden)
7 Mit sechzehn .... ich immer mit ihr. Sie .... mich nicht verstehen. (streiten, wollen)
8 Mit achtzehn .... ich erwachsen, aber sie .... es nicht. (sein, merken)
9 Mit zwanzig .... ich weg. Ich .... endlich frei sein. (gehen, müssen)

11 Form sentences as in the example.

1 meinen Rucksack packen – Tschüs sagen – weggehen
Ich packte meinen Rucksack, sagte tschüs und ging weg.

2 10 Minuten warten – aufstehen – fortgehen
Wir ....

3 aufstehen – keine Sonne sehen – wieder ins Bett gehen
Ich ....

4 sie sehen – zu ihr laufen – ihr alles erzählen
Er ....

5 die Zeitung nehmen – ein paar Seiten lesen – Angst bekommen
Ich ....

6 den Brief aufmachen – ihn lesen – lachen
Sie ....

7 mir die Hand geben – freundlich lächeln – kein Wort sagen
Er ....

Titel, Schlagzeilen, Überschriften

Am Tag, als ...

Als ich ein kleiner Junge war

Als die Bilder laufen lernten

Am Tag, als der Regen kam

Als ...

12 Make up similar titles (titles of books, films, songs), headlines or headings.

Aussprache: Knacklaut

13 a Listen and repeat.

um ein Uhr ● heute Abend ● geöffnet ● in Europa ●
bei ihm oder bei ihr ● meine Großeltern ● Ich habe gearbeitet.

> Vowels or diphthongs at the beginning of a word (**a**m **A**bend, **i**n **Eu**ropa) or the beginning of a syllable (Groß-**el**-tern) are spoken with a glottal stop, i.e. you start again, without linking up with the preceding sound.
> The glottal stop separates off syllables and words.

b Listen and mark the glottal stop as in the example: heute | Abend.

Als ich acht war. ● Er ist erwachsen. ● Ich schrieb ihm Briefe ● Wir sahen uns oft. ●
Wie alt sind Sie? ● Beeil dich! ● am Wochenende ● das eine, das andere

Sätze verbinden: *als*

	1	2	
HS+NS	Meine Schwester	war	acht Jahre alt, **als** ich zur Welt **kam.**
NS+HS	**Als** ich zur Welt **kam**,	war	meine Schwester acht Jahre alt.

> **Use of *als***
> **temporal:** *Als* indicates that individual events and actions were simultaneous in the past.
> **Question:** Wann?
> Wann gingst du weg? / Wann bist du weggegangen?
> – Als ich zwanzig war.

14 Answer the questions.

Wann war für Sie ein besonders schöner Moment?
Ein besonders schöner Moment war, als ...

Wann war für Sie ein besonders peinlicher (embarrassing) Moment?
Wann war für Sie ein besonders aufregender (exciting) Moment?
Wann war für Sie ein besonders gefährlicher (dangerous) Moment?
Wann waren Sie mal so richtig wütend (really angry)?

15 Read again the last sentence of the text on page 121. What became of the brother? What do you think?

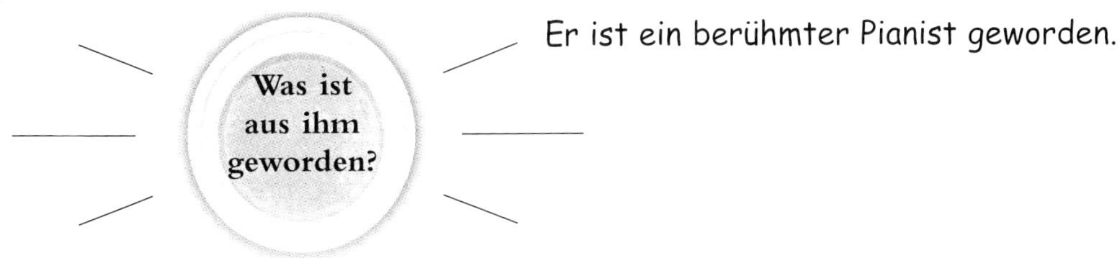

Hallo Vater!

16 Listen to the song. Who is talking to whom? Note down the answers.

.... ~~~ ....
~~~ ....
~~~ ....

17 Listen to the song again.

a Verse 1: Complete the sentences.

1 Aus ihm ist .... geworden, aber es geht ihm ....
2 Er .... jetzt in einer ....
3 Er ist .... Student, der pennt.

pennen (colloquial) = schlafen, nichts tun, faulenzen

b Verse 2: Complete the sentences.

1 Mutter und Sohn .... sich selten.
2 Wenn er .... ist, ... er ihr das rote Kleid.
3 Aber er ist leider .... so weit.

c Verse 3: What could *schwarz, rot* mean in these expressions?

Ich bin's, das schwarze Schaf,
das rote Luder.

das Luder = term of abuse for a person

18 Listen and read.

1 Hallo Vater! Ich bin's, dein Sohn.
Aus mir ist nichts geworden, mir geht's saugut[1]
denn ich singe jetzt in 'ner Band, bin kein Student, der pennt.

2 Hallo Mutter! Ich bin's, dein Sohn.
Danke schön, dass wir uns nur noch selten seh'n. Wenn ich reich bin, kauf' ich dir das rote Kleid, doch leider bin ich noch nicht so weit.

3 Hallo Schwestern! Ich bin's, euer Bruder,
das schwarze Schaf, das rote Luder.
Tut mir Leid, heut' hab' ich keine Zeit,
denn ich singe jetzt in 'ner Band, bin kein Student, der pennt.

4 Und komm' ich mal zurück nach Osnabrück, wenn dann mal irgendwann keiner mehr lacht, frage ich mich:
Hab' ich was falsch gemacht?

Gruppe „Clinch", Text: Wefel

[1] saugut (colloquial) = sehr gut

19 **a** What is his family's attitude to him?
Underline the sentences and words that tell you.

b What do his father, mother and sister really want from him?

20 How did you grow up? How was your relationship to your family / brothers and sisters, and how has it developed?

Und

Cultural information

Two women from different generations meet at a bus stop. One is young, the other old. The young one envies the old one, and the old one envies the young one.

The life of people in Central Europe has changed a great deal in the last 50 years. The old and the young rarely live together. In 1925 only 6.7% of old people lived alone, now it's 35.9%. So young mothers, who often go out to work, don't have a grandmother to take over the housework and look after the children. And the grandparents live on their own and don't have a task to satisfy them. On top of that, the average life expectancy is rising all the time. In the year 2000 it was 73 for men, and 80 for women. So there are a lot more old women, especially as there are many among them who lost their husbands in the war. Also people are healthier and nevertheless retire earlier. Things can get boring if you haven't got a goal. Some seniors (as they're called in Germany today) have got together and founded a party, the "Graue Panther" (the Grey Panthers). Many "young oldies" try to live together in shared accommodation and be of mutual assistance to each other; others volunteer to go to developing countries for a year or two to pass on their expertise and knowledge. Still others go back to school and study something they weren't able to when they were young. Courses of study are offered by universities and adult education centres, the latter offering a broad, varied educational programme for senior citizens, even in smaller towns.

Language

"Wenn ich doch so viel Zeit hätte" (If I only had that much time) one of the women in the text says, while the other laments "Wenn ich noch einmal so jung wäre" (If I were only young again). They speak of their wishes that cannot, however, be fulfilled and are therefore unreal. They do this by using the subjunctive II (Konjunktiv II) of the verb.

Other important uses of the Konjunktiv II are:
- unreal conditional sentences
  Wenn ich Zeit hätte, würde ich mitgehen.
  (If I had time, I would go along.)
- polite requests
  Ich hätte gern eine Tasse Kaffee.
  I would like a cup of coffee.

So it's a question of recognizing what function the Konjunktiv II fulfills. This can generally be deduced from the context.

Learning strategies

In this unit you'll also get used to the technique of only reading the first sentence in each paragraph of a longer text, making hypotheses about the rest of the content and then at the end comparing your assumptions with the whole text.

Und

1 Look at the photo? What do you see? What thoughts do you have?

2 a Read lines 1–5 of the text.

b "Dabei sehen sie sich an, einen Augenblick lang ... und ..." How might the sentence continue?

3 Read line 6 and line 19. Why do the women think like this? What do you think? Take notes.

4 Read the whole text. Take key notes.

Die junge Frau ist auf dem Weg zum Kindergarten. Sie zerrt ein kleines, widerspenstiges Mädchen neben sich her. Das stolpert und fällt hin, genau vor der alten Frau, die auf einer Bank an der Bushaltestelle sitzt. „Entschuldigung", murmelt die junge Frau. „Mir ist nichts geschehn. Hat das Kleine sich wehgetan?", sagt die alte Frau. Dabei sehen sie sich an, einen Augenblick lang ...

Die junge Frau denkt: Die hat's gut! Sitzt auf der Bank da, hat Zeit in Hülle und Fülle. Genau das, was mir fehlt. Hat auch keine widerspenstige Tochter in den Kindergarten zu zerren. Dabei hab ich's so eilig. Was ich heute noch alles machen muss! Wenn ich doch einmal so viel Zeit hätte wie die! Und heute Abend kommt Besuch, da muss ich etwas kochen: Hätte ich beinahe vergessen. Das wird dann sicher wieder spät. Dabei bin ich jetzt schon müde. Die alte Frau kann so früh schlafen gehen, wie sie will. Und ausschlafen kann sie auch. Ist ungerecht verteilt manchmal, wirklich.

und

Die alte Frau denkt: Die hat's gut! Hat wenigstens etwas zu tun den lieben langen Tag. Ich vertreibe mir ja bloß noch die Zeit. Wenn ich noch einmal so jung wäre ... Wie flink die laufen kann! Und das süße kleine Mädchen. Mit der jungen Frau würde ich gerne tauschen. Sie sicher nicht mit mir, kann ich verstehen. Ich hätte gern wieder einmal einen Tag vor mir, randvoll mit Sachen, die zu erledigen sind. Betrieb, Geschäftigkeit, Leben! Mittendrin möchte ich noch mal sein. Nicht so an den Rand geschoben, auf der Bank hier, immer bloß zusehn.

Susanne Kilian

5 Which expressions say roughly the same thing? Enter the appropriate letter.

1 ☐ 2 ☐ 3 ☐ 4 ☐ 5 ☐

1 Ich habe Zeit in Hülle und Fülle.
2 Mir fehlt Zeit.
3 Ich habe es eilig.
4 Ich hätte gern einen Tag, randvoll mit Sachen, die zu erledigen sind.
5 Ich möchte nicht an den Rand geschoben sein.

a Ich möchte mittendrin sein.
b Ich habe keine oder nur sehr wenig Zeit.
c Ich habe viel Zeit.
d Ich habe nicht genug Zeit.
e Ich möchte gern einmal viel zu tun haben.

6 Compare the two women. Fill in from the text.

Die junge Frau	**Die alte Frau**
hat keine Zeit.	hat ....
geht oft spät schlafen.	kann ....
muss früh aufstehen.	kann ....
hat's eilig.	vertreibt sich ....
möchte einmal Zeit haben und nichts tun.	möchte ....

7 Both women have wishes:

Wenn ich doch ... hätte/wäre!
Ich würde gern ... Ich hätte gern ...
Ich möchte ...

Underline the sentences with these forms in the text.

Das Verb: Konjunktiv II Gegenwart (2)

Mittendrin **möchte** ich noch mal sein.
- Was machen wir heute Abend? — **wish**
- Ich **möchte** (**gern**)/**würde gern** früh schlafen gehen.

Ich **möchte** eine Tasse Kaffee, bitte! — **request**
Ich **hätte gern** eine Tasse Kaffee.

8 Complete with a wish or a request.

Ich möchte ... Ich hätte gern ...

Wir möchten ... Ich würde gern ...

Möchtest du ...?

Wenn ich doch einmal so viel Zeit hätte wie die! — **unreal wish**
Wenn ich doch noch einmal so jung wäre!
(reality: Ich habe keine Zeit. Ich bin nicht mehr so jung.)

Also possible without *wenn*:
Hätte ich **doch** einmal so viel Zeit wie die!
Ich **hätte gern** einmal so viel Zeit wie die.
Wäre ich **doch** noch einmal so jung!
Ich **wäre gern** noch einmal so jung.

Ich **würde gern** mit der jungen Frau **tauschen**.
(reality: Wir können nicht tauschen.)

9 Form sentences.

Wenn ich doch ... hätte/wäre! Hätte/Wäre ich doch ...
Ich hätte/wäre gern ... Ich würde gern ...

Wenn ich noch einmal so jung **wäre**, — **unreal condition**
(dann) **würde** ich / **wäre** ich / **hätte** ich ... — **unreal consequence**

10 What might the old woman perhaps want to say? Complete this statement.

Wenn ich noch einmal so jung wäre, ...

Konjunktiv II Gegenwart: *sein, haben, werden,* Modalverben

11 a Fill in the missing verb forms.

b The Konjunktiv II forms are derived from the past forms. Compare the Konjunktiv II forms with the past forms and mark the differences.

				Modalverben		
	sein	**haben**	**werden**	**können**[1]	**wollen**[2]	**mögen**
ich	wär e	....	würd e	könnt e	wollt e	möcht e
du	wär (e) st	hätt est	würd est	könnt est	....	....
Sie	wär en	hätt en	würd en	....	....	....
er/sie/es/man	wär e	....	würd e	....	....	....
wir	wär en	....	würd en	....	....	....
ihr	wär (e) t	hätt et	würd et	könnt et	....	....
Sie	wär en	....	würd en	....	....	....
sie	wär en	....	würd en	....	....	....

[1] similarly: dürfen, müssen [2] similarly: sollen

würd- + Infinitiv

Die alte Frau	würde	gern mit der jungen Frau	tauschen.
Die junge Frau	würde	gern früh schlafen	gehen.
	würd-		**Infinitiv**

Satzklammer

Konjunktiv II: regular verbs	**Konjunktiv II: irregular verbs**
same as the past: ich machte, du machtest, ...	- Konjunktiv II signal ***e*** in the persons *ich, du, er/sie/es/man, ihr*
exception: brauchen (ich bräuchte, ...)	schreiben: ich schrieb**e**, du schrieb**e**st, er/sie/es/man schrieb**e**, ihr schrieb**e**t
	- often vowel change too *a → ä, o → ö, u → ü* fahren: ich f**ü**hr**e**, du f**ü**hr**e**st, Sie f**ü**hren, er/sie/es/man f**ü**hr**e**, ...

When is *würd-* + infinitive preferred, when the Konjunktiv II forms?

***würd-* + infinitive:**	**Konjunktiv II forms:**
with regular and	- with the verbs *sein, haben, werden* and with modal verbs
irregular verbs	- also common with the irregular verbs *kommen, lassen, gehen, geben, wissen* and *bleiben* kommen: ich k**ä**m**e**, du k**ä**m**est**, Sie k**ä**m**en**, er/sie/es/man k**ä**m**e**, wir k**ä**m**en**, ihr k**ä**m**et**, Sie k**ä**m**en**, sie k**ä**m**en** similarly: ich ließ**e**, ich ging**e**, ich g**ä**b**e**, ich w**ü**sst**e**, ich blieb**e**

12 Complete the sentences.

1 Es wäre gut, wenn ...
sie – bald – kommen — Es wäre gut, wenn sie bald kommen würden/kämen.

2 Ich würde mich freuen, wenn ...
du – mich – anrufen — Ich würde mich freuen, wenn du mich anrufen würdest.

3 Ich würde mich freuen, wenn ...
du – zu meinem Geburtstag – kommen

4 Was würdest du sagen, wenn ...
ich – dir – einen Elefanten – schenken

5 Es wäre schön, wenn ...
wir – jetzt Urlaub haben

6 Ich wäre froh, wenn ...
ich – nicht so viel – zu tun haben

7 Es wäre schön, wenn ...
er – jetzt – bei uns - sein

8 Würdest du ihnen helfen, wenn ...
sie – dich – fragen

13 Select some of the sentences and complete them.

Wenn ich mein Chef wäre, ...

Wenn ich heute noch arbeiten müsste, ...

Wenn ich 70 Jahre alt wäre, ...

Wenn er nicht immer so lange schlafen würde, ...

Wenn wir es nicht immer so eilig hätten, ...

Wenn ich schon perfekt Deutsch sprechen würde, ...

14 Write down what the people are thinking. Use the following expressions.

Wenn ich doch ... hätte/wäre! ● Hätte/Wäre ich doch ...! ●
Könnte/Dürfte ich doch ... ! ● Wenn ich doch nicht ... müsste! ●
Ich würde gern ... ● Wenn sie/er/... doch ... würde!

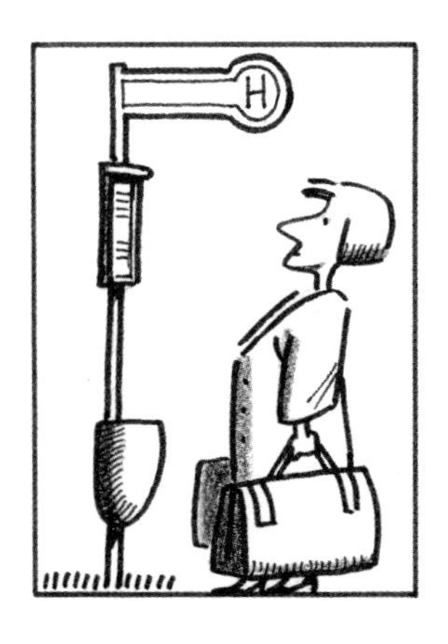

Höflichkeiten

15 **a** Listen and read.
b Mark the Konjunktiv II forms.

Verschiedene Höflichkeitsstufen

You would like somebody to give you the paper to read.

very polite:

Konjunktiv II (question form)	Würden Sie / Würdest du mir bitte die Zeitung geben? Könnten Sie / Könntest du mir bitte die Zeitung geben? Dürfte / Könnte ich bitte die Zeitung haben?

polite:

question form	Geben Sie / Gibst du mir bitte die Zeitung?
können, dürfen	Können Sie / Kannst du mir bitte die Zeitung geben? Darf ich bitte die Zeitung haben?
ich hätte gern	Ich hätte gern die Zeitung, bitte.

direct:

ich möchte	Ich möchte die Zeitung, bitte.
imperative + bitte (mal)	Geben Sie / Gib mir bitte (mal) die Zeitung!

impolite:

imperative	Geben Sie / Gib mir die Zeitung!
no verb	Die Zeitung (bitte)!

Note that the tone also indicates what is intended.

16 How could the requests in the picture story be expressed differently?

Würdest du mir mal einen Gefallen tun?
Würdest du bitte mal ein Stück zurückgehen?

17 Are these demands/requests: very polite (++), polite (+), direct (O), impolite (–)?

1 Könnten Sie / Würden Sie / Könntest du / Würdest du mir bitte einen Kaffee geben/bringen? ☐

2 Einen Kaffee! ☐

3 Ich hätte gern einen Kaffee, bitte. ☐

4 Können Sie / Kannst du mir einen Kaffee geben/bringen? ☐

5 Bringen Sie / Bring mir einen Kaffee! ☐

6 Ich würde gern einen Kaffee trinken. ☐

7 Wärst du so nett / freundlich und würdest mir bitte einen Kaffee geben / bringen? ☐
Wären Sie so nett / freundlich und würden mir bitte einen Kaffee geben / bringen?

8 Ich möchte einen Kaffee bitte. ☐

9 Kann ich bitte einen Kaffee haben? ☐

10 Einen Kaffee bitte! ☐

11 Bringen Sie / Bringst du mir einen Kaffee, bitte? ☐

18 What requests from section 17 are appropriate in these situations?

Höflichkeit im Alltag und im Unterricht

19 Imagine a situation in which you have to express requests and demands more politely and reformulate them.

Nach 20 Minuten

Even a very polite request is not always meant that way.

1 Sprechen Sie bitte etwas lauter.

2 Bring mir bitte die Zeitung!

3 Wiederhol / Wiederholen Sie das bitte.
Sag / Sagen Sie das bitte noch einmal.

4 Kann ich bitte deinen Schirm haben?

5 Sprich / Sprechen Sie bitte etwas langsamer.

6 Seid bitte leise!

7 Ich möchte Sie etwas fragen.

8 Buchstabieren Sie bitte das Wort.

9 Geben Sie mir bald Antwort.

10 Schreib / Schreiben Sie mir das bitte auf.

Der kleine Prinz

The text

The fairy tale "Der Kleine Prinz" by the French author Antoine de SAINT-EXUPÉRY appeared in 1943 and immediately after the war became a huge success in the German-speaking countries. Saint-Exupéry, who was a great aviator, gets to know the Little Prince after being forced to make an emergency landing in the middle of the desert. He has left his tiny planet because he got into "trouble" with the proud, vain rose and began to doubt her worth. On his travels to the other planets he meets people with all the weaknesses and vices typical of us human beings: the lonely tyrannical king, the vain man thirsting only for the admiration of others, the dulled alcoholic, the businessman, the lamp-lighter and the geographer. The latter advises him to travel to earth. There he first encounters the snake, who tells him about mankind's loneliness.

In the end the fox teaches him the secret of friendship and love. It consists of taking on responsibility for others: "You only know the things you tame," it says, i.e. that you develop a relationship to. Relating to other people, rediscovering love and friendship was a great need felt by the people in the period after the war. Death, loneliness and isolation were the experiences they had behind them. The fairy tale expressed their inner wish to retreat into the smallest cosmic units and to see and experience the world with their heart. "You can only see properly with your heart. The essential is hidden from our eyes," the fox teaches us.

Language

"Ich bin für dich nur ein Fuchs, der hunderttausend Füchsen gleicht." (For you I am only a fox, no different than a hundred thousand other foxes.) The subordinate clause explains who the fox is in greater detail. The subordinate clause is a relative clause (der Relativsatz). The relative clause begins here with the relative pronoun (das Relativpronomen) *der*, which is dependent on the word it refers to in the main clause, *ein Fuchs*, and on the verb in the relative clause, *gleichen* (Der Fuchs gleicht hunderttausend Füchsen). Relative clauses are ways of creating more precision; they describe the noun (person or thing) mentioned in the main clause. Through the relative clause the reader realizes what persons, things or abstract terms are meant.

The future tense (das Futur), which you also meet in this unit, is of little importance for expressing future events and actions. Usually German employs the present with a time adverbial. When the future tense is used for something future, it usually expresses a promise or a prophecy.

Der kleine Prinz

 **1** Listen and read.

In diesem Augenblick erschien der Fuchs.
„Guten Tag“, sagte der Fuchs.
„Guten Tag“, antwortete höflich der kleine Prinz, der sich umdrehte, aber nichts sah.
5 **„Ich bin da“,** sagte die Stimme, **„unter dem Apfelbaum ...“**
„Wer bist du?“ sagte der kleine Prinz. **„Du bist sehr hübsch ...“**
„Ich bin ein Fuchs“, sagte der Fuchs.
„Komm und spiel mit mir“, schlug ihm der kleine Prinz vor. **„Ich bin so traurig ...“**
„Ich kann nicht mit dir spielen“, sagte der Fuchs. **„Ich bin noch nicht gezähmt[1]!“**
10 **„Ah, Verzeihung!“** sagte der kleine Prinz.
Aber nach einiger Überlegung fügte er hinzu:
„Was bedeutet ‚zähmen‘?“
„Du bist nicht von hier“, sagte der Fuchs, **„was suchst du?“**
„Ich suche die Menschen“, sagte der kleine Prinz. **„Was bedeutet ‚zähmen‘?“**
15 **„Die Menschen“,** sagte der Fuchs, **„die haben Gewehre[2] und schießen. Das ist sehr lästig. Sie ziehen auch Hühner[3] auf. Das ist ihr einziges Interesse. Du suchst Hühner?“**
„Nein“, sagte der kleine Prinz, **„ich suche Freunde. Was heißt ‚zähmen‘?“**
„Zähmen, das ist eine in Vergessenheit geratene Sache”, sagte der Fuchs.
„Es bedeutet, sich ‚vertraut machen‘[4].“
20 **„Vertraut machen?“**
„Gewiss“, sagte der Fuchs. **„Noch bist du für mich nichts als[5] ein kleiner Junge, der hunderttausend kleinen Jungen völlig gleicht[6]. Ich brauche dich nicht und du brauchst mich ebensowenig. Ich bin für dich nur ein Fuchs, der hunderttausend Füchsen gleicht. Aber wenn du mich zähmst, werden wir einander brauchen. Du wirst für mich einzig sein**
25 **in der Welt.[7] Ich werde für dich einzig sein in der Welt ...“**
„Ich beginne zu verstehen“, sagte der kleine Prinz. **„Es gibt eine Blume ... ich glaube, sie hat mich gezähmt ...“**
„Das ist möglich“, sagte der Fuchs. **„Man trifft auf der Erde alle möglichen Dinge ...“**
„Oh, das ist nicht auf der Erde“, sagte der kleine Prinz.
30 Der Fuchs schien sehr aufgeregt:
„Auf einem anderen Planeten?“
„Ja.“
„Gibt es auch Jäger[8] auf diesem Planeten?“
„Nein.“
35 **„Das ist interessant! Und Hühner?“**
„Nein.“
„Nichts ist vollkommen[9]!“ seufzte der Fuchs.

Antoine de Saint-Exupéry

1 zähmen: tame
2 das Gewehr, -e: gun
3 das Huhn, Hühner: chicken
4 sich vertraut machen: get acquainted
5 nichts als = nur
6 gleichen: be like
7 Du wirst für mich einzig sein auf der Welt.: You will be unique in the world for me.
8 der Jäger, –: huntsman
9 vollkommen: perfect

2 Read the dialogue again (lines 1–17).

Was sucht der kleine Prinz auf der Erde?

Ich ....

Ich ....

Was sagt der Fuchs über die Menschen?

Sie haben ....

Sie ....

Das ist ihr ....

3 Now read the second part of the dialogue (line 18 to the end). What does *zähmen* mean for the fox? Mark the passage.

4 a Look for examples of different types of question in the text.

Wortfrage

....

....

....

Satzfrage

....

Aussagesatz mit Frageintonation

....

b Look for abbreviated questions in the text and complete them.

Intonation: Satzakzent

5 a Listen and mark the main sentence stress.

- Komm und spiel mit mir!
- Ich kann nicht mit dir spielen.

- Das ist möglich. Man trifft auf der Erde alle möglichen Dinge.
- Das ist nicht auf der Erde.
- Auf einem anderen Planeten?
  Gibt es auch Jäger auf diesem Planeten?

- Was bedeutet „zähmen"?
  Was heißt „zähmen"?

The main stress in a sentence is on the word that is most important in the utterance.

Komm und spiel mit mir! Ich kann nicht mit dir spielen.	Main sentence stress on the modal verb means: I want to, but it's not possible.
Ich kann nicht mit dir spielen.	In a neutral statement the modal verb doesn't have the main stress.
Das ist möglich. Man trifft auf der Erde alle möglichen Dinge. Das ist nicht auf der Erde. Auf einem anderen Planeten? Gibt es auch Jäger auf diesem Planeten?	The course of the conversation determines which word in the utterance carries the main stress.
Was bedeutet „zähmen"?	neutral question
Was heißt „zähmen"?	(impatient) repetition of the question

b Listen again and repeat.

Der Satz: Relativsatz (1)

Du bist für mich nichts als ein kleiner Junge, der hunderttausend kleinen Jungen gleicht.

6 What do *der, dem, die* refer to? Add arrows as in the example.

Ich bin für dich nur ein Fuchs, der hunderttausend Füchsen gleicht.
Auf dem Planeten, auf dem der kleine Prinz wohnt, gibt es keine Jäger, aber auch keine Hühner.
Aber es gibt eine Blume, die den kleinen Prinzen gezähmt hat.

Das Relativpronomen: *der, das, die*

	Singular			Plural
	maskulin	**neutral**	**feminin**	**m, n, f**
Nominativ	der	das	die	die
Akkusativ	den	das	die	die
Dativ	dem	dem	der	denen

A relative pronoun introduces a relative clause and refers to a noun (person or thing) in the main clause.

7 Compare the relative pronoun with the definite article (→ p. 36 and p. 77).
Where do you see a difference?

8 Underline the relative clauses in section 6 as in the example.
Du bist für mich nichts als ein kleiner Junge, der hunderttausend kleinen Jungen gleicht.

Der Relativsatz

Singular, maskulin

Das ist der kleine Prinz, der von einem Planeten zum anderen reist. (Der kleine Prinz reist ...)

Nominativ (Subjekt)

Singular, maskulin

Das ist der Fuchs, den der kleine Prinz auf der Erde trifft. (Der kleine Prinz trifft den Fuchs ...)

Akkusativergänzung

Plural

Der Fuchs kennt Menschen, die Gewehre haben und schießen. (Die Menschen haben Gewehre ...)

Nominativ (Subjekt)

Singular, maskulin

Das ist der Fuchs, mit dem der kleine Prinz spielen will. (Der kleine Prinz will mit dem Fuchs spielen.)

Ergänzung mit Präposition im Dativ

9 Complete the rule.

A relative clause is a subordinate clause which describes a person or thing.

A relative pronoun is placed .... of the relative clause.

The verb is placed ....

Number (singular, plural) and gender (m, f, n) of the person/thing to be described determine the number and gender of the relative pronoun: **der** Fuchs, **der ...** ; **die** Menschen, **die ...**

The verb in the relative clause determines the case (nominative, accusative, dative) of the relative pronoun. If the verb has a preposition, this is placed in front of the relative pronoun:
(spielen mit) Der Fuchs, **mit dem** der kleine Prinz **spielen** will.

10 Make two main clauses into a main clause + relative clause, as in the example.

1 Auf welcher Seite steht der Text? — Wir sollen ihn bis nächste Woche lesen.
Auf welcher Seite steht der Text, den wir bis nächste Woche lesen sollen?

2 Wie heißt das Buch? — Das Buch machte ihn weltberühmt.
Alle sprechen von dem Buch.
Sie hat das Buch für ihren Freund gekauft.

3 Wer ist die Frau? — Er ruft sie jeden Tag an.
Er schreibt ihr jede Woche einen langen Brief.
Er geht oft mit ihr aus.
Er macht alles für sie.

4 Wer sind die Leute? — Sie hat sie eingeladen.
Er fotografiert sie.
Er spricht mit ihnen.
Wir sollen ihnen gratulieren.

11 Select terms and define them using a relative clause.

Ein Optimist ist ein Mensch, der positiv denkt.

ein Pessimist ● ein Träumer ● ein Elefant ● eine Autorin ● ein Kellner ● ein Grüner ● ein Freund / eine Freundin ● ein Synästhetiker ● ein Musterknabe ● ein Schaf

Das Verb: Futur

12 a In his explanation, the fox uses the form *werd-* + infinitive. Underline these forms in the text on page 136, lines 24–25.

Wir	werden	einander	brauchen.
Du	wirst	für mich einzig	sein.
	werd-		**Infinitiv**

Satzklammer

The future doesn't just express an event in the future, but also a prophecy, a promise. If you only want to express the temporal aspect of the future, it is sufficient to use the present, generally in connection with time expressions, e.g.: bald, morgen, am Montag, nächste Woche, dann, ...
Nächste Woche fliege ich in die Karibik.

b Complete the rule.

Future: .... + ...

13 Express the future events using the present and a time adverbial.

1 Ich werde wiederkommen. — Ich komme in einer Stunde wieder. In einer Stunde komme ich wieder.
2 Sie wird Sie anrufen.
3 Ich werde dich besuchen.
4 Wir werden Urlaub machen.
5 Ich werde den Bericht schreiben.
6 Ich werde dir helfen, die Übung zu machen.
7 Er wird pünktlich da sein.

morgen früh ● in einer Stunde ● am Wochenende ● nächste Woche ● heute Abend ● morgen Nachmittag ● nächsten Monat ● um 5 Uhr

14 What do we promise so lightly? Express these promises using the future.

1 Ich vergesse dich nie.
2 Ich komme bald zurück.
3 Ich bin immer für dich da.
4 Ich schreibe dir viele Briefe.
5 Ich denke immer an dich.
6 Ich rufe dich jeden Tag an.

Nachdenken

„Weißt du, warum der Wind immer von da kommt? – Weil Adler nie rückwärts fliegen."

„Wie soll ich das verstehen?"

Nachdenken

1 What do you do in the morning when you wake up? Here are some of the possibilities in German. Check the meaning of unknown words and mark the statements that are true for you.

- ☐ Ich drehe mich noch einmal um und schlafe noch ein bisschen weiter.
- ☐ Ich gehe ins Bad unter die Dusche.
- ☐ Ich stehe sofort auf und mache Gymnastik.
- ☐ Ich frühstücke im Bett.
- ☐ Ich gehe in die Küche und mache mir einen starken Kaffee.
- ☐ Ich spreche ein Morgengebet.
- ☐ Ich wecke die anderen.
- ☐ Ich bleibe noch einige Minuten liegen und denke darüber nach, was ich heute machen muss.
- ☐ Ich ziehe mich an und hole frische Brötchen.

2 Read the text.

Nachdenken

Ich bleibe in der Früh immer gern
noch ein paar Minuten liegen.
Du nicht?
Dann denke ich ein bisschen nach.
5 Ich denke:
Ich bin ein Mensch
und bin im Bett,
und das Bett ist im Zimmer,
und das Zimmer ist im Haus,
10 und das Haus ist am Weg,
und der Weg ist in der Stadt,
und die Stadt ist im Land,
und das Land ist auf der Erde.
Und auf der Erde ist ein anderes Land,
15 und im anderen Land ist eine andere Stadt,
und in der Stadt ist ein anderer Weg,
und am Weg ist ein anderes Haus,
und im Haus ist ein anderes Zimmer,
und im Zimmer ist ein anderes Bett,
20 und im anderen Bett
ist auch ein Mensch.

Hans Manz

3 Explain briefly what the author Hans Manz has written a whole poem about. The questions will help you.

Was macht der Autor in der Früh?
An was oder an wen denkt er?
Wo ist diese Person?

4 Write out lines 10–13 of the text again, and use real names for *Weg, Stadt, Land.* Sometimes you'll have to change the prepositions: e. g. *am Weg* → *im Goetheweg.*

5 Write a few sentences about your morning habits. Say what you do in the morning when you wake up. The following words will help you.

Morgens stehe ich immer ... auf.

sich waschen • sich die Zähne putzen • sich ausziehen • aufstehen • ein Bad nehmen • sich anziehen • Kaffee machen / trinken • Radio hören

Aussprache: Vokal e

6 Listen and mark: e (long) or e (short).

Ich liege gern im Bett / Ich denke: Ich bin ein Mensch. /
auf der Erde, am Weg / Ich trinke Kaffee, manchmal Tee.

Short *e* is spoken like *ä*: der Mensch – die Männer.

7 Listen and repeat.

Den musst du kennen. / Hast du eine Idee? / Ruf doch den Kellner! /
Kannst du das lesen? / Wie die Zeit vergeht! / Hast du es vergessen? /
Ich möchte dich sehen. / Jetzt ist die Übung zu Ende.

Ortsergänzung: Wohin? Wo?

8 What do the verbs and the prepositions in section 1 and in the text "Nachdenken" express: Movement/Direction or state/position? Put them into a table and add A (accusative) or D (dative).

Movement/direction: Wohin?	State/position: Wo?
ins Bad gehen A	
ins = in das	im = in dem am = an dem

9 Complete the table in section 8 with the verbs and prepositions from the following text.

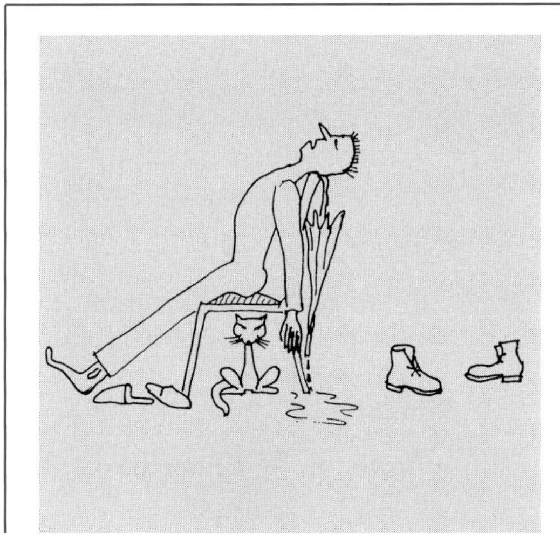

Draußen regnet es. Peter kommt müde nach Hause. Der Kater Wenzel springt unter den Stuhl. Peter hängt den nassen Schirm an den Stuhl. Der Schirm hängt jetzt am Stuhl. Die Schuhe zieht er aus und wirft sie hinter den Stuhl; jetzt stehen sie hinter dem Stuhl. Peters Mutter hat ihm die Pantoffeln vor den Stuhl gestellt. Sie stehen immer noch vor dem Stuhl. Peter ist zu müde, er kann sie nicht anziehen. Erschöpft setzt er sich auf den Stuhl. Nach wenigen Minuten ist er auf dem Stuhl eingeschlafen. Der Kater Wenzel sitzt immer noch unter dem Stuhl.

Ulrich Engel

10 Accusative or dative? Please complete.

The prepositions *an, auf, hinter, in, neben, über, unter, vor, zwischen*
take .... in answer to the question *Wo?*
and .... in answer to the question *Wohin?*

11 a What do the following verbs express: movement/direction (Wohin?) or state/position (Wo?)?

arbeiten ∅ gehen ∅ liegen ∅ sein ∅ fliegen ∅ laufen ∅ reisen ∅ fahren ∅ sitzen ∅ bleiben ∅ stehen ∅ kommen ∅ wohnen ∅ fallen ∅ legen ∅ schlafen ∅ stellen ∅ setzen

b Make questions with the verbs in a and answer them. Use the prepositions from section 10 and the following nouns.

Bett ∅ Büro ∅ Garten ∅ Haus ∅ Kino ∅ Slowakei ∅ (Schreib)tisch ∅ Schule ∅ Schweiz ∅ Schwimmbad ∅ Sessel ∅ Stadt ∅ Straße ∅ Stuhl ∅ Theater ∅ Türkei ∅ Wald ∅ Zimmer

Wo arbeiten Sie? — Ich arbeite im Büro.
Wohin soll ich die Bücher legen? — Lege sie auf den Schreibtisch.

12 a Which sentences answer the question *Wo?*, which the question *Wohin?* Sort them into the table.

1 Opa saß auf der Bank vor dem Haus.
2 Der Hund Fido lag gerne unter dem Bett.
3 Sein Bild hing immer über dem Klavier.
4 Die Jacke hängt am Stuhl.
5 Der Kellner hat das Bier auf den Tisch gestellt.
6 Sie setzte sich auf die Bank.
7 Wir haben lange in der Sonne gelegen.
8 Das Auto hat den ganzen Tag vor der Schule gestanden
9 Peter hängte den Schirm an den Stuhl.
10 Er legte das Buch auf den Tisch.

Wo?	**Wohin?**
Opa saß auf der Bank vor dem Haus.	Sie setzte sich auf die Bank.
....	....
....	....
....	....
....	
....	

b Complete the table with the forms from a.

Wo?			**Wohin?**		
Infinitiv	**Präteritum**	**Perfekt**	**Infinitiv**	**Präteritum**	**Perfekt**
sitzen	....	hat gesessen	(sich) setzen	....	hat (sich) gesetzt
liegen	....	hat gelegen	legen	....	hat gelegt
hängen	....	hat gehangen	hängen	....	hat gehängt
stehen	stand	....	stellen	stellte	....

Der Weitgereiste

What is the blue Flower?

Everywhere there are people with itchy feet who can't stick it out at home and just have to travel far away, to discover other people, other countries, landscapes and cultures. The poem "Der Weitgereiste" is contemporary and treats this topic in an ironical way. The song at the end is one of the countless German hiking songs. It treats the topic from the point of view of romanticism. Here the term blaue Blume appears and gives you an opportunity to think about why this course has this title.

Cultural information

The topic of this unit is the longing people have for foreign parts, the secrets of nature, for adventure far away. German writers have returned again and again to the figure of the runaway, those who opt out. People who wanted to give up the comforts of their native country, family, friends and possessions and who set off to seek the blaue Blume, the secret of happiness, in nature and places far away.

In times gone by, people who did so were usually on foot, following where adventure led them, but they also set forth to educate themselves, to add to their knowledge and learn manual craftsmen's skills. The custom has been preserved up till the present day whereby artisans spend their years of apprenticeship away in various places before they are allowed to establish themselves as a master craftsman. The Hamburg carpenters with their traditional costumes can still be seen on building sites all over Europe. For three years they are not allowed to set foot in Hamburg. Only after that may they be granted the master craftsman's diploma which allows them to open their own business and train apprentices.

Journeying on foot is an educational process, strengthens the feeling of solidarity, makes you feel close to nature, and sensitive to your body. These were the ideals of the Wandervogelbewegung (the German Wandervogel youth movement) in which hundreds of thousands of youths participated at the beginning of the 20th century.

Learning strategies

This is a reminder about the verb lists that you started in Unit 10. The main thing now is to add the past forms, and extend the list gradually as you proceed. Of course they exist in every grammar too. But if you do it yourself, you make the words easier to remember.

Language

In the poem there are sequences of words that don't quite follow the rules of German grammar. But in poetry everything is allowed, because of the rhyming. That's where the term poetic licence comes from.

Der Weitgereiste

1 Add to the word-spider on the topic of *Reisen*.

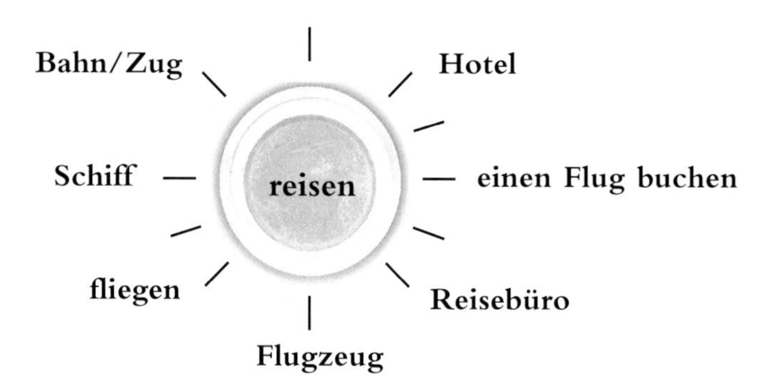

2 Listen to the poem with your book closed.
Where did the man travel to? What was the first, and what was the last stop? Take notes.

3 Read the poem and compare with your notes.

Der Weitgereiste

Es war vor Zeiten ein Mann,
der wohnte in Lausanne.
Und obwohl es ihm da nicht übel gefiel,
übersiedelte[1] er eines Tages nach Kiel.
5 Doch blieb er auch dort wohnen nicht
und zog, auf Neues stets erpicht,
nach Amsterdam, nach Rotterdam,
nach Osnabrück, nach Kehl, nach Hamm,
nach Basel, Iserlohn, Paris,
10 wo er sogar
ein ganzes Jahr
sich niederließ.
Das war ihm wider die Natur,
er fuhr per Schiff nach Singapur
15 und dort verlor sich seine Spur,
bis endlich man in Samarkand
den Weitgereisten wiederfand.
Er wohnte, jetzt an achtzig alt,
noch kurze Zeit in Mittenwald,
in Oberunterammergau 20
(wie lange, weiß man nicht genau),
und zog dann wieder nach Lausanne –

da starb der Mann.

Drauf sagten, die ihn dort begraben:
„Das konnte er bequemer haben." 25
Der Tote aber lächelte weise
und begab sich auf seine weiteste Reise.

Rudolf Otto Wiemer

[1] übersiedeln = umziehen: to move

4 Answer the questions.

1 Wie heißen die Länder, in denen die Städte liegen?
2 Welche Sprachen spricht man dort?
3 Wie heißen die Menschen, die dort leben?

Samarkand liegt in Usbekistan.
Man spricht dort Usbekisch.
Dort leben vor allem Usbeken.

5 Write down what it says in the text.

1 Es gefiel ihm da gut. ....
2 Er wollte alles Neue kennen lernen. Er war..........
3 Das gefiel ihm nicht. ....
4 Man fand ihn dort nicht mehr. ....

fahren – gehen

Wir **fahren** für zwei Wochen nach Amerika.
Er **ging** 1945 nach Amerika und blieb dort 10 Jahre.

fahren = reisen gehen = move, change place of residence and work

6 *Fahren* or *gehen*? Complete.

Mein Onkel Willibald ist ein sehr unruhiger Mann. Er kann in keiner Stadt für längere Zeit bleiben. Schon als Kind .... (1) er viel mit seinem Fahrrad. Er wollte immer weite Reisen machen und blieb aber immer nur einen Tag. Als er dann seine Schule beendete, ... (2) er nach Amerika, um dort zu studieren. Zuerst .... (3) er an das Oberlin College, dann an die Berkeley Universität. Eines Tages .... (4) er zu Besuch nach Hollywood. Dort gefiel es ihm so gut, dass er dorthin .... (5), um Schauspieler wie Jack Nicholson zu werden. Nun lebt er schon seit vielen Jahren in Hollywood und spielt mit großem Erfolg immer wieder die gleiche Rolle, die des Willy Wanderer. Das ist ein Mensch, der nie in einer Stadt bleiben kann und alle zwei Wochen in eine andere Stadt .... (6).

7 a Make questions in the past and the perfect. Give a short answer.

1 wohnen – der Weitgereiste – Wo?
Wo wohnte der Weitgereiste?
Wo hat der Weitgereiste gewohnt?
In Lausanne.

2 gefallen – es ihm dort – Wie?
3 umziehen – er – Wohin?
4 ziehen – er dann – Wohin?
5 bleiben – er ein ganzes Jahr – Wo?
6 fahren – er nach Singapur – Wie?
7 verlieren – sich seine Spur – Wo?
8 wieder finden – man ihn – Wo?
9 sterben – er – Wo?
10 lächeln – er – Warum?

b Add the verbs from a to your verb list and fill in the forms from section 10 on page 60, section 5 on page 97, section 12 on page 111 and section 6 on page 122.

Infinitiv	Präsens	Präteritum	Perfekt
fahren	fährt	fuhr	ist gefahren

8 Read and check the meaning of the words in the word-spider *Natur*. Add to it.

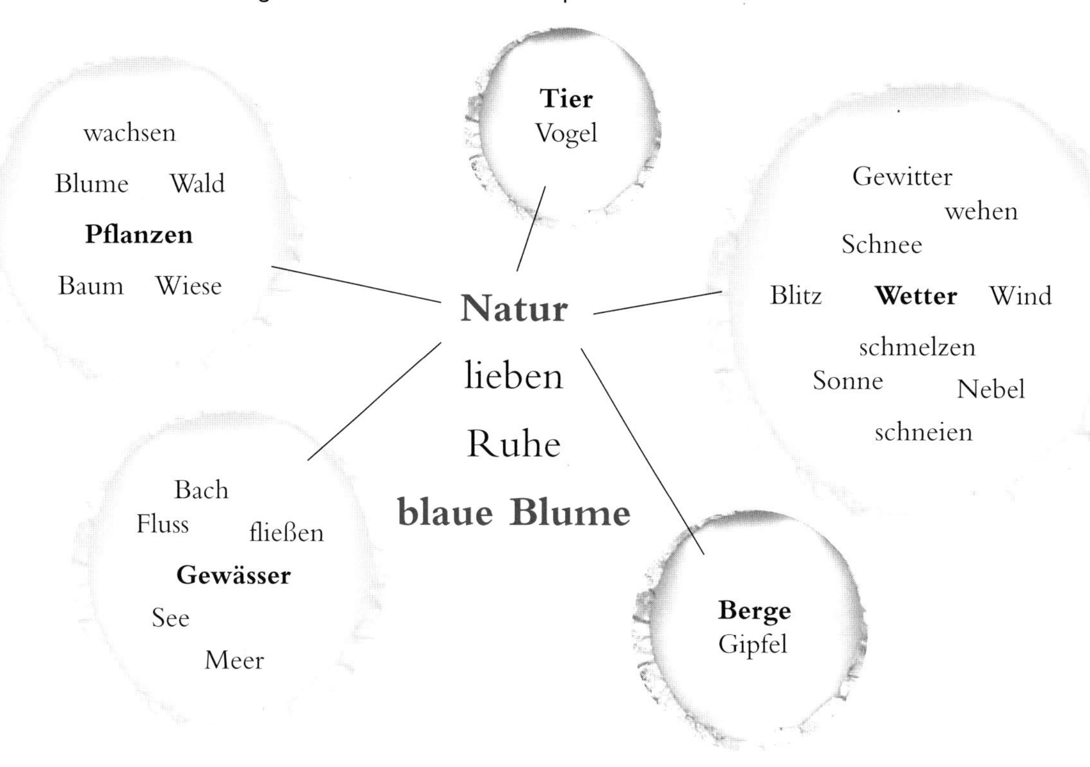

Wir wollen zu Land ausfahren

9 **a** Read the two verses of the song.

I.	IV.
Wir wollen zu Land ausfahren über die Berge weit, aufwärts zu den klaren Gipfeln der Einsamkeit. Horchen woher der Bergwind braust, sehen was in den Wäldern haust, und wie die Welt so weit, und wie die Welt so weit.	Es blühet im Walde tief drinnen die blaue Blume fein, die Blume zu gewinnen, ziehn wir in die Welt hinein. Es rauschen die Bäume, es murmelt der Bach, und wer die blaue Blume finden will, der muss ein Wandervogel sein, der muss ein Wandervogel sein. *Volkslied*

b What can the words *horchen, brausen, hausen* in verse 1 mean? Note them down in English.

c Give a brief answer to these questions about verse 1:

1. Wohin wollen diese Menschen reisen?
2. Was wollen sie hören?
3. Was wollen sie sehen?

d What can the words *gewinnen, ziehen, rauschen, murmeln, Wandervogel, blaue Blume* in verse 4 mean? Note the meanings down in English.

10 Listen to both verses of the song and sing along.

Der schöne 27. September

The texts

Life for most people is an on-going routine. Nature has predetermined this through the fact that the sun takes its leave every day at more or less the same time, as a reminder, as it were, that it's time to stop work and go to bed. So it's understandable that most people's day follows a steady pattern. A lot of things are the result of the rhythms of nature and life, but a lot of things can be classified as rituals. These are of especial interest because they are dependent on the culture of the individual country. In Germany it's still the case in many families that the soup is served on Sundays at midday sharp and grace is then said together. After the meal comes the family afternoon walk, and then coffee time with cake from the nearest confectioner's. A lot of young people no longer go along with these rituals, but it still requires a little courage to drop such social customs.

Both texts are about violation of such rituals. The author of the little poem thinks the 27th September is a wonderful day because he did something out of the ordinary. The little radio play excerpt at the end of the unit focusses on the ridiculousness of a fairly everyday scene the artist Sepp Buchegger has drawn two cartoons about. He lives and works in the provincial city of Tübingen in southwest Germany, famous mainly for its ancient university. Buchegger is a regular contributor to the "Schwäbische Tagblatt", Tübingen's regional daily paper. He is also known for the satirical cartoons he does for German television. Otherwise it's only big national dailies like the "Welt" or the "Frankfurter Allgemeine" that have their own artists doing political cartoons. It's a great exception that a small local paper should have its own cartoonist. But the Schwäbische Tagblatt has among its discriminating readership a large number of professors and students at the university, who expect a little more from their daily paper than just local news.

Learning strategies

This unit deals with various articles and determiners (Artikelwörter) such as *mein, kein* and the pronouns (Pronomen) derived from them, such as *meine, meiner, meins; keine, keiner, keins.*

He, das ist **mein** Ball!
Stimmt doch gar nicht, das ist **meiner**.

The example shows two different uses of *mein*: as a possessive adjective (mein Ball) and as a possessive pronoun (meiner). Take care with the different forms (mein – meiner) and the way they are used.

Der schöne 27. September

1 A nice day. What would that be for you? Write down some thoughts.

2 Read the text and mark all the nouns and verbs that you know. Then check the meaning of the words you don't know (→ p. 73, Learning strategies).

3 a Compare your notes from section 1 with the text. What differences are there?

b Who is meant by *keinem* in lines 4, 6 and 7? Add a noun.

c Why does the author only list what he didn't do, and why only these things? Try to find an explanation.

Der schöne 27. September

Ich habe keine Zeitung gelesen.
Ich habe keiner Frau nachgesehn.
Ich habe den Briefkasten nicht geöffnet.
Ich habe keinem einen Guten Tag gewünscht.
5 Ich habe nicht in den Spiegel gesehen.
Ich habe mit keinem über alte Zeiten gesprochen und mit keinem über neue Zeiten.
Ich habe nicht über mich nachgedacht.
Ich habe keine Zeile geschrieben.
10 Ich habe keinen Stein ins Rollen gebracht.

Thomas Brasch

Er ... jeden Tag ...   ... ist/sind für ihn wichtig.   Er ... oft/immer/meistens ...

Er muss jeden Tag sehr viele Zeitungen lesen. Das ist sein Job.

4 The last sentence is an idiom. What could it mean? Choose from these answers.

1 I didn't work. ☐ **2** I achieved nothing. ☐ **3** I didn't set anything in motion. ☐

Das Nomen: *n*-Deklination

In lines 4, 6 and 7 of the text *keinem* can be complemented, for example, by *Freund/Mensch/Kollege*.

5 Compare the nouns in the following sentences. Mark the change.

Kein Freund / Mensch / Kollege hat mit mir gesprochen.
Ich habe mit keinem Freund / Menschen / Kollegen gesprochen.

A few nouns belong to the *n*-declination.

Singular

Nominative: Wie ist Ihr Name?

Accusative: Ich habe Ihren Name**n** nicht verstanden.

Dative: Eine Person mit diesem Name**n** arbeitet nicht hier.

also: der Herr (den Her**rn**, dem Her**rn**)
der Mensch (den Mensch**en**, dem Mensch**en**)
masculine nouns with the ending *-e*: der Kollege, der Junge, der Grieche/Franzose ..., der Friede, der Gedanke **-n**

Words from Latin ending in: *-and*, *-ant*, *-ent*, *-ist*, *-oge*: der Student, der Präsident, der Pädagoge, ... -(**e**)**n**

one neuter noun in the dative: das Herz **-en**

6 Fill in the nouns.

1 Name Wie ist Ihr .... ? Sagen Sie mir bitte Ihren ....

2 Herr Kennen Sie den .... ? Ich habe gestern mit dem .... gesprochen.

3 Herz Ich wünsche dir von ganzem .... alles Gute.

Der Artikel: mit Nomen, als Pronomen

7 Fill in the missing endings.

		Singular			**Plural**
		maskulin	**neutral**	**feminin**	**m, n, f**
N	mit Nomen	der ein Brief kein	das ein Wort kein	die ein........ Zeitung kein......	die Briefe – Zeitungen kein...... Bücher
	als Pronomen	der, ein**er**, kein**er**	das, ein**s**, kein**s**	die, ein**e**, kein**e**	die, **welche**, kein**e**
A	mit Nomen	d.......... ein........ Brief kein......	das ein Buch kein	die ein........ Zeitung kein......	die – Briefe kein......
	als Pronomen	de**n**, ein**en**, kein**en**	das, ein**s**, kein**s**	die, ein**e**, kein**e**	die, **welche**, kein**e**
D	mit Nomen	d.......... ein**em** Freund kein.......	d.......... ein**em** Buch kein......	d.......... ein**er** Freundin kein......	d**en** – Freunden kein**en**
	als Pronomen	de**m**, ein**em**, kein**em**	de**m**, ein**em**, kein**em**	de**r**, ein**er**, kein**er**	de**nen**, **welchen**, kein**en**

also: jeder, jedes, jede; dieser, dieses, diese; mancher, manches, manche

8 There's a saying: *Einmal ist keinmal.* Fill in *kein* as a pronoun in the right form.

Einer ist .... Eins ist .... Eine ist ....

9 Fill in the article/determiner as a pronoun in the right form.

ein • kein • der • jeder • dieser • mancher • welche

1 ■ Wo ist ein Briefkasten? ▲ Ich habe .... gesehen.
Dort ist ....

2 ■ Ich suche ein Café. ▲ Dort ist ....

3 ■ Es gibt so viele verschiedene Zeitungen. ▲ Ich lese selten ....

4 ■ Nehmen wir ein Taxi? ▲ Ja, dort steht schon ....

5 ■ Brauchst du Briefmarken? ▲ Ja, hast du ....

6 ■ Wer hat einen Schirm? ▲ Tut mir Leid, ich habe ....

7 ■ Wer ist der Mann dort? ▲ .... kenne ich nicht.

8 ■ Kennst du denn jede Frau hier? ▲ Nicht ...., aber .... kenne ich, ich war mal mit ihr verheiratet.

9 ■ Gehen dir alle Kollegen auf die Nerven? ▲ Nicht alle, aber .... schon.

jemand – niemand; etwas – nichts

positiv		negativ	
jemand	(Nominativ)	niemand	(Nominativ)
jemand(en)[1]	(Akkusativ)	niemand(en)[1]	(Akkusativ)
jemand(em)[1]	(Dativ)	niemand(em)[1]	(Dativ)
etwas		nichts	

[1] usually without an ending, especially in speech

10 a How can *keinem* in the text on page 150, lines 4, 6, 7 be expressed in another way?

b Fill in *jemand, niemand, etwas, nichts.*

1 ■ Siehst du etwas? ▲ Nein, ...

2 ■ Hast du mit jemandem gesprochen? ▲ Nein, mit ....

3 ■ Warum weißt du das nicht? ▲ .... hat mir etwas gesagt.

4 ■ Komm mal her! ▲ Warum? Willst du mir .... sagen?

5 ■ So viele Leute! Kennst du .... hier? ▲ Nein, ...

Zahlen: Ordnungszahlen

11 a Which number do you hear? Mark the figures.

10. 1. 31. 7. 6. 2. 8. 23. 30. 3. 14. 17. 4. 15. 16. 18. 13. 11.

1. der **erste**
2. der zwei**te**
3. der **dritte**
4. der vier**te**
5. der fünf**te**
6. der sechs**te**
7. der sieb**te**
8. der ach**te**
9. der neun**te**
10. der zehn**te**

11. der elf**te**
12. der zwölf**te**
13. der dreizehn**te**

...

20. der zwanzig**ste**
22. der einundzwanzig**ste**

...

30. der dreißig**ste**
40. der vierzig**ste**

erst**ens**, zweit**ens**, dritt**ens**, viert**ens**, ...

b Listen to the numbers again and repeat.

Datum, Monate, Jahreszeiten

- Der wievielte ist heute?
- Der siebenundzwanzigste September.

12 a Listen and put the months in order from 1–12.

Juni ◯ März ◯ Januar ◯ Juli ◯ Oktober ◯ November ◯ Mai ◯ Dezember ◯ April ◯ September ◯ Februar ◯ August ◯

b Ask and note down the date.

- Wann haben Sie Geburtstag?
- Am dritten Februar.

13 Sort the months into the four seasons.

Meiner oder deiner?

14 Listen and read. Pay attention to the main sentence stress.

Possessivartikel als Pronomen

15 Fill in the missing endings.

	Singular			Plural
	maskulin	**neutral**	**feminin**	**m, n, f**
N	der Fuß	das Buch	die Zeitung	die Füße, Bücher, Zeitungen
Pronomen	**mein......**	**meins**	**mein......**	**mein......**
A	den Fuß	das Buch	die Zeitung	die Füße, Bücher, Zeitungen
Pronomen	**mein......**	**mein......**	**mein......**	**mein......**
D	dem Fuß	dem Buch	der Zeitung	den Füßen, Büchern, Zeitungen
Pronomen	**mein......**	**mein......**	**mein......**	**mein......**

also: dein/Ihr, sein, ihr, unser, euer (**eurer**, euer**s**, **eure**)/Ihr, ihr

16 Fill in the endings.

1 ■ Dort liegt eine Handtasche. ▲ Das ist mein....... .
2 ■ Ist das euer oder unser Schirm? ▲ Eur....................... . Wir haben keinen mitgenommen.
3 ■ Das ist mein Bier. Ihr....... steht dort, sehen Sie das nicht?
4 ■ Ist das ihr neuer Freund? ▲ Ihr.................... ? Das ist doch mein Freund!
5 ■ Fahren sie zu ihren oder seinen Eltern? ▲ Zu ihr................ , seine leben ja hier.
6 ■ Wem gehört das Geld hier? ▲ Das ist dein....... .

17 a Listen and mark the main sentence stress. Repeat.

■ Gibst du mir bitte meine Zéitung? ▲ Das ist méine Zeitung!
1 ■ Ist das dein neues Auto? ▲ Nein, das ist seins.
2 ■ Kennst du den Mann dort? ▲ Nein, den kenne ich nicht.
3 ■ Hast du ihr den Brief gegeben? ▲ Nein, ich hab ihn ihm gegeben.
4 ■ Wir wollten doch ins Kino gehen. ▲ Nein, du wolltest ins Kino, nicht ich.

b Make further mini-dialogues.

Articles/Determiners and pronouns are not accentuated in a neutral reporting utterance. But they can bear the main stress if a contrast is being expressed.

Feierabend

18 a Look at the pictures on page 149. What can you see in the top picture, what in the bottom one?
b What do you think happens between the two scenes?

19 a Listen to the conversation and pay special attention to the intonation and the emotional form of expression.
b Listen again and take notes in German or English.
Then say what the story is about.

Die roten Balkons

Cultural information

The song about the red balconies is a lament about one of the misguided developments of our time, satellite towns and suburbs. Just as everywhere else in the world, the old towns in Central Europe became too small, the more so as some of them were destroyed in the war. A lot of people were no longer able to find work in the country and had to move to the towns. At the same time, the demand for more accommodation grew as people became more and more prosperous. And so politicians in the 1970s thought it was a brilliant idea to create huge satellite towns from nothing, out in the green belt beyond the city limits.

They didn't realize till it was too late that housing developments like Mümmelsmannsberg in Hamburg were just dormitory suburbs that gave rise to many problems. The people who had been tossed together found it difficult to make contact. The planners had forgotten to provide for places where people could meet, such as pubs and cafés. The young people felt lost, the women isolated. Gradually a lot of families moved back into the towns or right out into the country. Those who couldn't afford to do so got left behind. The empty flats were often taken over by foreigners, refugee families and asylum seekers with lots of children. So such suburbs are now inhabited mainly by people whose lives are not the easiest. High unemployment often leads to youth drug addiction, crime, racism and right-wing extremism.

The second text is from the magazine BISS, a monthly publication produced by and for people in social need. In Munich, BISS is sold by the homeless; they can keep half of their takings, a step on the road to being able to find and afford their own four walls.

Language

One of the most interesting features of German is the way it is possible to link various words together, thus creating new terms and expressions. The word *Bilderbuch* consists of two nouns, and even to those who have never met the word before, it is clear that it signifies a book that contains pictures. The fact that it's just for children is something to be deduced from the context. *Krankenschwester, Krankenhaus, Krankenwagen, Krankengymnastik, Krankenkasse* are words formed from the adjective *krank* and a noun. Guess what meaning they have.

Learning strategies

On your vocabulary index cards always note down verbs with a fixed preposition such as *denken an, sich freuen über, träumen von* in a complete sentence so that you learn the right case:

Er denkt an den Vater.
(He's thinking about his father.)
Ich freue mich über das Geschenk.
(I'm pleased about/with the present.)
Sie träumt von einem schönen Mann.
(She dreams of a handsome man.)

Die roten Balkons

1 a What can you see in the photo? Jot down key words.
b Say what you think.

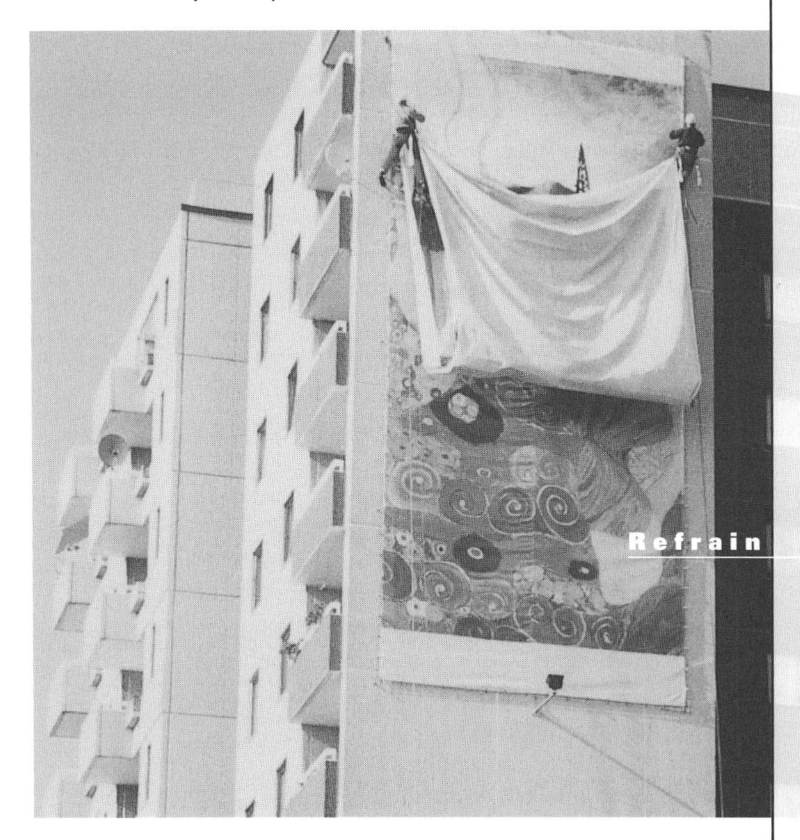

2 a First read the questions.

Wer spricht in dem Lied?
Von wem spricht er?
Was erzählt er?
Was geschieht am Ende?

b Listen to the song and answer the questions.

c Read the text of the song.

Sie wohnt auf dem Mond

(Die roten Balkons ...)

Der Abend war zu Ende.
Wir hielten unsre Hände.
Ich zahlte unsre Brause[1]
und bat sie: Sag nicht nein.
Ich bring dich noch nach Hause,
wo immer das mag sein.

Wir fuhren wie im Himmel.
Sie führte mich zum Mümmel-
mannsberg[2], dem Häusermeer
am Stadtrand. Und wir standen
vor den Betongiganten.
Da sagte sie zu mir:

Refrain

Erst kommen die roten Balkons.
Dann kommen die gelben Balkons.
Dann kommen die blauen Balkons.
Dann kommen die grünen Balkons.
Dann kommen die braunen Balkons.
Dann kommen die roten Balkons.
Dann kommen die gelben,
die blauen,
die grünen –
und dann die roten Balkons,
die sechste Reihe –
acht Reihn von unten
und von oben zweie:
da irgendwo wohn′ ich.

Verliebte träumen vom Mond.
Doch ich, ich wohn′ auf dem Mond.

Sie sprach beim Sternenscheine:
Den Rest geh ich alleine.
Als ich nach tausend Küssen
ihr noch zweitausend gab,
hab ich versprechen müssen:
Ich hol dich morgen ab.

Jedoch ich kleiner Dummer,
ich weiß nicht ihre Nummer
und wie sie hinten heißt.
Ich such seit sieben Stunden.
Ich habe sie nicht gefunden.
Ich glaub, mein Herz zerreißt.

Refrain **Erst kommen die roten Balkons . . .**

Hans Scheibner

[1] die Brause = die Limonade: lemonade
[2] Mümmelmannsberg = Trabantenstadt in Hamburg

3 The two people are in love. Mark the passages that make this clear.

4 What expression is there in the song for:

1 viele Häuser ....
2 große Häuser ....
3 nicht im Zentrum ....
4 ihren Familiennamen ....
5 sehr traurig ....

5 What does the woman mean when she says "Ich wohne auf dem Mond"?

6 What would you do in a situation like this? Jot down some ideas.

Das Adjektiv: Nominativ, Akkusativ, Dativ

Erst kommen die rot**en** Balkons. In den rot**en** Häusern wohnen viele jung**e** Menschen.
Ilona wohnt in einer klein**en** Wohnung in dem groß**en** Haus mit einem rot**en** Balkon.

7 Fill in the endings.

	Singular			**Plural**
	maskulin	**neutral**	**feminin**	**m, n, f**
N	der rot**e** Balkon	das rot**e** Haus	die klein**e** Frau	die klein........ Balkons
	ein rot........ Balkon	ein rot........ Haus	eine klein........ Frau	klein........ Balkons
A	den rot**en** Balkon	das rot**e** Haus	die klein**e** Frau	die klein**en** Balkons
	einen rot........ Balkon	ein rot........ Haus	eine klein........ Frau	klein........ Balkons
D	dem rot**en** Balkon	dem rot........ Haus	der klein**en** Frau	den klein........ Balkons
	einem rot........ Balkon	einem rot**en** Haus	einer klein........ Frau	klein**en** Balkons

8 Select the appropriate adjective and fill in the adjective and article endings.

bequem ✎ berühmt ✎ dumm ✎ fremd ✎ gefährlich ✎ gut ✎ lang ✎
langweilig ✎ neu ✎ peinlich ✎ spannend ✎ traurig

ein ...guter........ Gedanke, d........ .... Kuss, aus ei........ .... Stadt, d...... .... Politiker,
ei.... .... Unterricht, d........ .... Sessel, ei........ .... Geschichte, ei........ .... Augenblick,
für ein........ .... Freund, ei........ .... Beruf, ei........ .... Mensch, für d...... .... Chef

9 a This is how the story of the two young people might finish. Complete the sentences with suitable adjectives.

Der verliebte Mann sucht seit sieben Stunden. Er geht von den .... Balkons zu den .... Balkons. Er findet die .... Frau nicht. Er kommt wieder zu den Häusern mit den .... Balkons. Er fragt .... Leute nach ihr. Er geht zu der .... Bar, wo sie die .... Brause getrunken hatten. Dort kennt man die Frau nicht. Er hat eine .... Idee. Er gibt eine .... Anzeige in der Zeitung auf: „Ilona, schreibe mir. Ich finde dein Haus nicht." Ein Brief kommt. Sie schreibt: „Wo bist du denn, du Dummer? Erst kommen die .... Balkons, dann kommen die ...., die ...., die .... und dann die .... Balkons, die sechste Reihe: Da wohne ich."

b Now tell the story in the past.

Der verliebte Mann suchte seit sieben Stunden. ...

c Now make a real text out of it by adding linking words.

dann ● am nächsten Abend ● aber ● endlich ● erst ● danach ● zum Schluss

Am nächsten Abend suchte der verliebte Mann ...

10 Read the following text and make a list of the people. Note down in each case what expressions (including pronouns) are used to denote and describe the people.

Mutter, unsere Mutter, sie

Kleiner Wurm, was nun?

Geschichte eines unverhofften Wiedersehens

„Entschuldigung, kennst du mich?" Eine kleine, gut aussehende Frau mit roten Haaren fragt mich das. „Ich habe Sie noch nie gesehen", antworte ich. „Ich bin deine Schwester, die Rosi." Ich bin sprachlos – ich stehe in der Weinstraße, um BISS zu verkaufen und plötzlich steht meine Schwester vor mir. Ich glaubte immer, sie sei längst gestorben. „Ich habe dein Foto in der Zeitung gesehen", erzählt sie. „Es war ein Bericht über die Weihnachtsfeier in der Residenz. Dein Name stand da und dass du BISS[1]-Verkäufer bist. Seit drei Wochen laufe ich nun schon von einem zum anderen und suche dich." Ich muss mich erst an den Gedanken gewöhnen, dass die Frau vor mir meine Schwester ist. Das letzte Mal habe ich sie vor 43 Jahren gesehen.

Wir gehen zusammen Kaffee trinken und erzählen uns von früher und von zu Hause. Wir sind in Anklam in Vorpommern aufgewachsen. Es war Krieg und Vater, der Offizier war, lag verwundet im Lazarett. Ich war fünf Jahre alt und meine Schwester war noch ein ganz kleiner Wurm. Eines Tages ist unsere Mutter mit dem Fahrrad zum Einkaufen gefahren und ist nicht wieder zurückgekommen. Meine beiden Brüder und ich haben ihr Grab nie finden können. Wahrscheinlich ist sie bei einem Bombenangriff umgekommen. Unsere Großeltern haben uns dann zu sich genommen. (...)
Eines Tages stand Vater mit unserer neuen Mutter vor der Tür. Er hatte sie im Lazarett kennen gelernt, wo sie als Krankenschwester gearbeitet hatte. Sie haben uns drei Jungs mitgenommen nach Kulmbach in Oberfranken. (...)

In Kulmbach hatten wir Ziegen, Hasen und Tauben. Es gefiel mir dort. Einige Zeit nach dem Krieg kam Rosi, der kleine Zwerg, auch zu uns. Sie konnte sich aber nie so richtig an das neue Zuhause gewöhnen. Nach dem Tod unseres Vaters war die Stiefmutter nicht mehr dieselbe. Sie wollte nur mit Bonzen und Offizieren zu tun haben. Mit denen habe ich mich aber nicht so gut vertragen.

Weil es keine Arbeit gab, bin ich 1953 von Kulmbach weg, zuerst nach Nürnberg, dann nach München. Das war auch das letzte Mal, dass ich Rosi, die gerade elf Jahre alt war, gesehen habe. 1957 war ich noch einmal daheim und hatte gehört, dass sie weg sei und Krankenschwester lernte. Sie ist nie wieder nach Hause zurück. Wir Kinder sind ja alle in die Fremde. Rosi hat in München geheiratet und zwei Kinder bekommen. Ich lebe mit meinem Hund Bello in einem Wohnwagen in der Nähe von Ismaning.

aus: BISS

[1] BISS = Bürger in sozialen Schwierigkeiten: people in social need

11 The text contains a number of compound words. Make a list of these words and determine what the component parts are. Write down the English meaning next to them.

die Krankenschwester   krank + die Schwester   nurse

Wortbildung: Suffix *–los*

12 a Form adjectives with the suffix *-los*. Then look in a dictionary to find out what exact meaning they have. Write down the meaning in English.

die Sprache	sprachlos	speechless	das Herz	....	....
das Obdach	....	....	der Wert	....	....
der Atem	....	....	die Hilfe	....	....
der Grund	....	....	das Ende	....	....
das Wort	....	....	der Schmerz	....	....
der Schlaf	....	....			

b Complete with compound adjectives from a.

1 Grundlos .... ließ er seine Frau sitzen und ging nach Amerika.

2 Er rannte so schnell, dass er .... an der Bushaltestelle ankam.

3 Es war sehr .... von ihr, dass sie ihn nicht sehen wollte.

4 .... ging sie aus dem Zimmer.

5 Dieses Bild ist völlig ...., es ist nur eine schlechte Kopie.

6 Wir alle waren ...., als wir die weißen Berge voll Schnee sahen.

7 Ich hatte eine .... Nacht.

8 Das war eine .... Operation.

9 Er hat keine Wohnung. Er ist ....

10 Er wusste nicht, was er machen sollte. Er war .... wie ein Kind.

11 Sie haben .... über das Problem diskutiert.

13 Describe the encounter from the point of view of sister Rosi.

a First mark all the passages that express the sister's point of view or relate to her.

b Now write the letter in which Rosi tells a girlfriend about her unexpected encounter with her brother and remembers her childhood.

Ergänzung mit Präposition (1)

Der junge Mann träumte von dem Mädchen. — **Von wem** träumte er?

Verliebte träumen vom Mond. — **Wovon** träumen Verliebte?

Er denkt an den Vater. — **An** wen denkt er?

Sie dachte an den Urlaub. — **Woran** dachte sie?

Some verbs form a fixed collocation with a preposition:
bitten um, denken an, erzählen von, fragen nach, sich freuen auf, gehen um (es geht um …), sich gewöhnen an, sprechen über, sich unterhalten mit … über, träumen von, warten auf, …

14 People or things? Complete.

This is how you ask about prepositional objects:

preposition + ***wen/wem***
Mit wem? An wen? … with ....

wo(r) + **preposition**
Wovon? Woran? Worüber? … with ....

If the preposition begins with a vowel, an *r* is added:
wo + *r* + preposition.

15 Make questions about the words that are underlined.

1 Er denkt an morgen. Woran denkt er?
Er denkt nur an seine Freundin. An wen denkt er?

2 Ein Kunde hat nach dem Chef gefragt.
3 Ich muss noch auf meinen Freund warten.
4 Wir freuen uns schon sehr auf den Urlaub.
5 Ich habe mich gut mit deinem Bruder unterhalten.
6 In dem Lied geht es um zwei verliebte junge Leute.
7 Er hat von ihren Küssen geträumt.
8 Sie haben immer nur über ihre Arbeit gesprochen.
9 Sie hat gesagt, dass er sie um Geld gebeten hat.
10 Sie haben von ihren Verwandten erzählt.

16 Answer the questions.

1 ■ Mit wem hast du dich unterhalten? (Schwester, ihr Mann) ▲ Mit meiner Schwester und ihrem Mann.

2 Worüber habt ihr gesprochen? (mein Bekannter, seine Probleme)

3 Woran denkst du gerade? (die Geschichte von Rosi, ihr Wiedersehen mit dem Bruder)

4 Worauf freuen Sie sich? (das lange Wochenende, der Besuch von meinem Freund)

5 Auf wen wartet er denn? (seine Frau, ihre Eltern)

6 Woran denken Sie oft?

7 Wovon träumen Sie manchmal?

Blaulicht

Cultural information

It is something of a tradition in the German-speaking countries to take on some honorary duties and do some service to society without being paid. Hundreds of thousands of people are active in sports club and musical associations, help out in old people's home or when anniversaries are coming up for celebration or when someone has died and is to be buried, and take on the job of firefighting or building flood-prevention dykes as voluntary members of the local fire brigade that almost every village has. This voluntary work by the population for the community has a long tradition and was organized to complement and support the organs of state.

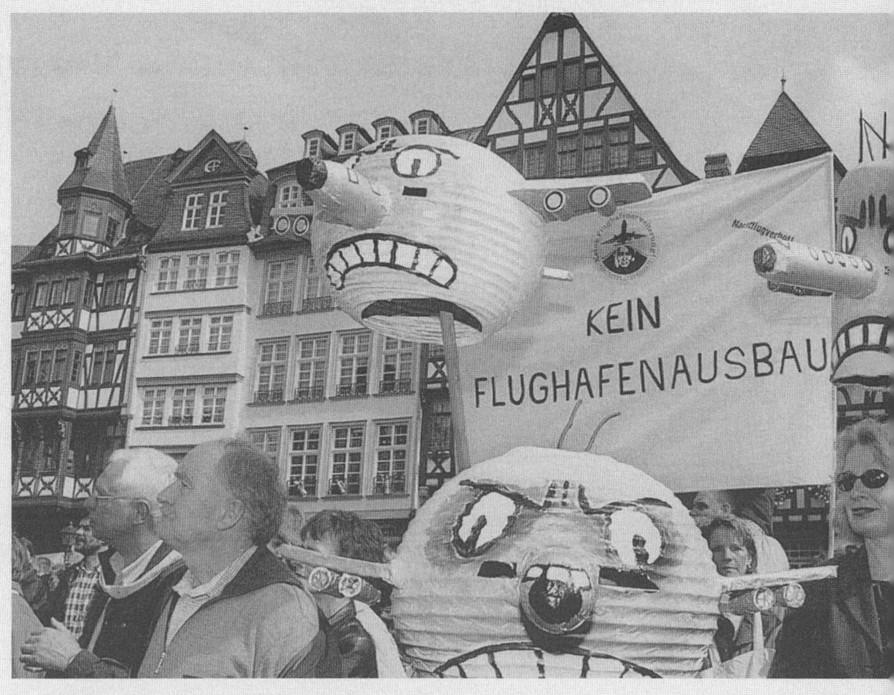

Pressure group protesting against the enlargement of Frankfurt Airport

Since the mid 1970s, however, people have also become more and more involved in pressure groups with the aim of influencing political decisions, fighting for reform or preventing or easing damage to the environment. It is from groups such as these (formed in support of foreigners, sufferers from AIDS, centres for women, or to fight against atomic power etc.) that the Green Party evolved.

In the past, most voluntary work was within the framework of a club or church organization. But things have changed. Voluntary work has become more and more separated from clubs and social institutions, and much more open. And another thing: in the past it was mainly people from the working population who were involved in this sort of voluntary work, nowadays, however, it is mainly done by older people. One in six of the retired population does some sort of voluntary work, compared with only one in ten of the working population. A country where social responsibility and initiative plays a greater role than almost anywhere else in the world is Switzerland. You'll find out more about it in Unit 40.

Language

Linguistic links between statements/sentences are an aid when producing text, but also when understanding texts. In this unit further sub-clauses are presented, especially relative clauses (der Relativsatz), as well as a summary of all conjunctions learned to date, with their function. It is always worthwhile analysing sentences with conjunctions, noting the position of the verb and possibly translating them into English so that you gradually get a clear idea of their precise meaning and they slowly become part of you ("in Fleisch und Blut übergehen", as this process is described in German).

Blaulicht

1 Look at the photo. Where are the men? At what time of day is the scene taking place? What do you think they are doing?

"Wenn wir einen Verletzten aus einem Wrack schneiden, und der kommt durch – dann war mein Leben nicht umsonst."

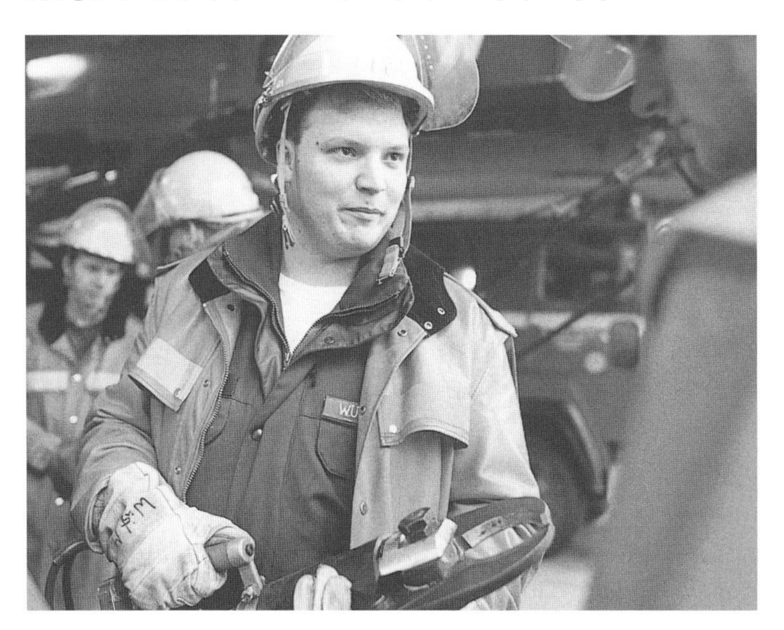

Michael Wüst, 24, Vertriebskaufmann, ehrenamtlicher Mitarbeiter beim Technischen Hilfswerk (THW), Freising

aus: *Brigitte*

2 Read the caption. What does it say about the man in the front. Fill in.

1 name	**4** function ....
2 age	**5** organization ....
3 profession	**6** location of the organization ....

3 a Read the heading above the photo.

b Read these explanations in German of the unknown words.

der Verletzte	Bei dem Autounfall gab es zwei Verletzte und einen Toten. Man hat die Verletzten ins nächste Krankenhaus gebracht.
das Wrack	Autowrack; Das Wrack der Titanic liegt 2000 m tief im Meer.
schneiden	Man kann Papier, Fleisch, Brot schneiden.
durchkommen	Er war schwer verletzt, aber er kam durch. Er lebt.

c What does *umsonst* mean here? Note down the meaning in English.

4 Read the whole text.

Ich hab' vor neun Jahren in der Jugendgruppe des THW angefangen, weil mich so ein Blaulicht gnadenlos fasziniert hat. Das tut's immer noch, aber inzwischen bedeutet mir das viel mehr. Ich habe hier gelernt, dass meine Grenzen viel weiter sind, als ich gedacht habe. Was ich allein nicht schaff', schaff' ich nämlich im Team. Mit Freunden zusammenzuarbeiten, auf die ich mich blind verlassen kann, das ist ein tolles Gefühl. Die Einsätze sind meistens echte Knochenarbeit, und obwohl wir für alle möglichen Katastrophen- und Hilfseinsätze gut ausgebildet sind, kommt die Angst, nicht schnell genug zu sein oder zu versagen, immer wieder, aber mir macht's auch heute noch total Spaß. Spaß gehört auch zum Lebenssinn, aber man muss sich doch auch darüber hinaus einen Sinn schaffen. Wenn wir jemandem geholfen haben, der sich selbst nicht helfen kann, dann macht das Sinn für mein Leben. Egal, ob das ein alter Mensch ist, der sich in seiner Wohnung eingeschlossen hat und befreit werden muss, ob es ein Hochwassereinsatz ist oder ob wir einen Lastwagenfahrer zwei Stunden lang aus seinem Wrack schneiden und der dann überlebt. Selbst wenn ich im Beruf und im Familienleben mal scheitere, habe ich doch was Sinnvolles getan. Dann war mein Leben nicht umsonst.

aus: *Brigitte*

5 How does Michael Wüst express his outlook and point of view? Complete.

1 Das Blaulicht hat ....

2 Mit Freunden zusammenzuarbeiten ist ....

3 Immer wieder kommt ....

4 Es macht mir auch heute noch ....

5 Jemandem zu helfen, der sich selbst nicht helfen kann, macht ....

6 The text contains a number of compound words. Underline them and note down their component parts. In the right-hand column write what you think the meaning in English is.

der Vertriebskaufmann	vertreiben / der Vertrieb, der Kaufmann	sales and marketing executive

Der Satz: Relativsatz (2)

Was ich allein nicht schaffe, (das) schaffe ich im Team.
Ich schaffe (das) im Team, **was** ich allein nicht schaffe.

Ich schaffe viel im Team, **was** ich allein nicht schaffe.
Ich schaffe alles im Team,
Ich schaffe etwas im Team,

Was introduces a relative clause and refers back to *viel, das, alles, etwas, nichts*. *Was* is not declined.

Wer im THW arbeitet, (der) gibt seinem Leben einen Sinn.
Wen wir aus dem Wrack schneiden, (den) kennen wir nicht.
Wem die Arbeit Spaß macht, (der) hat auch Erfolg.
(In Freising), **wo** Michael Wüst lebt, gibt es ein Technisches Hilfswerk.

Wer and *wo* also introduce relative clauses. *Wer* is declined (*wen, wem*). *Wo* is invariable and refers to a place.
Relative clauses with *was, wer* (*wen, wem*) and *wo* often precede the main clause. As they can be used to make generalizing statements, they are often found in proverbs.

7 Match the parts of the proverbs and sayings. Check the meaning of unknown words.

1	Was Hänschen nicht lernt,	**a**	fällt selbst hinein.
2	Was ich nicht weiß,	**b**	hat die Qual.
3	Wer A sagt,	**c**	ist des Talers nicht wert.
4	Wer andern eine Grube gräbt,	**d**	lacht am besten.
5	Wer den Pfennig nicht ehrt,	**e**	lernt Hans nimmermehr.
6	Wer die Wahl hat,	**f**	macht mich nicht heiß.
7	Wer nicht hören will,	**g**	muss auch B sagen.
8	Wer zuletzt lacht,	**h**	muss fühlen.

1 [e] 2 [ ] 3 [ ] 4 [ ] 5 [ ] 6 [ ] 7 [ ] 8 [ ]

Rüstige Alte

8 Describe the photo.

Was und wen sehen Sie?
Wer sind die Personen?
Was machen die Personen?
Worüber sprechen die Personen wohl?

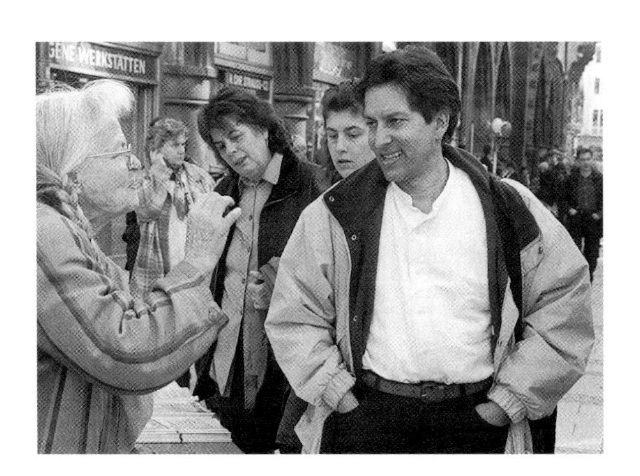

9 **a** Listen and read the beginning of a radio broadcast.
b What is the topic of the broadcast?

> Also bleiben Sie bei uns; denn am Ende dieser Notizbuchstunde werden Sie sich überlegen, welche unserer Geschichten könnte Ihre Geschichte werden. Ich blättere die Notizbuchseiten um. Mein Name ist Claudia Decker.
>
> Den Geschichten, die Sie jetzt hören, ist eines gemeinsam: Die Menschen erzählen von einer Arbeit, obwohl sie im Ruhestand leben. Und für die Arbeit bekommen sie kein oder kaum Geld. Anerkennung und Ehre bekommen sie. Deshalb heißt ihre Arbeit ehrenamtliches Engagement. So ein Engagement hat viele Facetten. Hier ist eine ...

10 The following text summarizes the most important statements of the interview. Check the meaning of the words underlined, using the context, your general knowledge and the regularities of word formation as clues.

Aktivistin — What internationalism is it from?
What does the ending *-in* tell you?
Who does it denote?
Which sections of the text explain the characterization *älteste Aktivistin*?

Ingrid Wagner ist mit 85 Jahren die älteste Aktivistin von Greenpeace in Deutschland. Greenpeace heißt auf Deutsch „grüner Friede“, das heißt Gewaltfreiheit. Sie gehört zum Team 50-Plus, das nur aus Senioren im Ruhestand besteht. Mit ihrem Engagement versuchen sie, die Umwelt zu schützen. Sie suchen nicht die „heile Welt“, aber sie wollen die Welt heilen helfen: Dort, wo die Umwelt krank ist, soll sie wieder gesund werden. Da Ingrid Wagner und ihre Freunde nicht mehr jung und sportlich sind, versuchen sie die Jungen bei ihren oft spannenden Unternehmungen zu unterstützen, aber sie beteiligen sich oft auch direkt an diesen Aktionen. Für ihre Arbeit bekommen sie kein Geld, aber Ehre und Anerkennung.

11 Listen to the second part of the broadcast. What do we find out about Ingrid Wagner and her family? What activities do Ingrid Wagner and her friends carry out?

12 Listen to Ingrid Wagner's statements again and fill in the gaps with the verbs. Check any unknown words.

aufgestellt ◆ aufgestellt ◆ beteiligen ◆ einsetzen ◆ klar zu machen ◆ können ◆ machen ◆ sagen ◆ sammeln ◆ schreiben ◆ schützen ◆ sind ◆ tun ◆ unterstützen ◆ versuchen ◆ versuchen ◆ versuchen ◆ verteilen

In dieser Gruppe .... (1) wir die Jungen zu .... (2) in ihren Unternehmungen. Und die .... (3) sehr viele waghalsige Dinge, wo sie teilweise sogar ihr Leben .... (4). Das .... (5) wir natürlich nicht mehr. Also wir .... (6) auf der Straße, wenn da ein Infostand .... (7), Informationsstand .... (8) wird. Dann .... (9) wir uns daran und .... (10) Zettel oder .... (11) Unterschriften. Und wir .... (12) viele Briefe an Politiker und Firmenchefs, Unternehmer und .... (13) ihnen ...., (14) dass es wichtig ist, die Umwelt zu .... (15). Und falls sie das gar nicht .... (16), ... (17) wir ihnen unsere Meinung darüber zu .... (18).

Sätze verbinden: *obwohl, falls, da*

1	2		
In der Radiosendung	erzählen	Menschen von ihrer Arbeit,	**obwohl** sie im Ruhestand **leben.**
Ingrid Wagner	spricht	mit den Politikern,	**falls** ihre Briefe nichts **nützen.**
Michael Wüst	hat	im THW angefangen,	**da** ihn das Blaulicht so fasziniert **hat.**

1	2	
Obwohl wir gut ausgebildet **sind,**	sind	die Einsätze viel Knochenarbeit.
Falls ich im Beruf **scheitere,**	habe	ich was Sinnvolles getan.
Da mich das Blaulicht fasziniert **hat,**	habe	ich beim THW angefangen.

Use of *obwohl*: A sub-clause with *obwohl* expresses a contradiction of what is said in the main clause.

Obwohl es nicht regnet, nehmen wir einen Schirm mit. (contrary to expectation)

(**Weil** es regnet, nehmen wir einen Schirm mit. = expectation)

Use of *falls*: The conjunction *falls* is used in place of *wenn*, if there is some doubt that the condition will be fulfilled.

Wir nehmen einen Schirm mit, **falls** es regnet. (It may be that it will rain.)

Use of *da*: The conjunction *da* is sometimes used instead of *weil*.

Da es regnet, nehmen wir einen Schirm mit.

13 Complete these sentences with your own ideas.

Da ich oft Besuch bekomme, fühle ich mich nicht allein.

Obwohl ich sehr müde war, ……………………

Obwohl ……………………, hat es uns Spaß gemacht.

Da ich es ihm versprochen habe, ……………………

Da ……………………, konnte ich ihn nicht besuchen.

Falls er noch einmal anruft, ……………………

Falls ……………………, holen wir Sie ab.

Sätze verbinden: Konjunktionen (Übersicht)

14 a Add example sentences to the table of conjunctions. Look for sentences in the texts or make up your own.

b Fill in the meaning of the individual conjunctions.

a	addition	**e**	contrary to expectation
b	alternative	**f**	contrast
c	condition	**g**	time
d	reason	**h**	no meaning

conjunction	example	meaning
1 aber		
2 da		
3 dass		
4 denn		
5 deshalb		
6 deswegen/daher		
7 falls		
8 obwohl		
9 oder		
10 sondern		
11 und		
12 weil		
13 wenn (temporal)		
14 wenn (konditional)	Wenn wir einen Verletzten aus dem Wrack schneiden, und er kommt durch, war mein Leben nicht umsonst.	c

Intonation: Satzmelodie in Satzverbindungen

15 a Listen and read. Pay attention to the intonation and the pauses.

Das ist Michael Wüst, → / der beim THW Freising arbeitet. ↘
Er hat dort vor neun Jahren angefangen, → / weil ihn so ein Blaulicht fasziniert hat. ↘
Wer beim THW arbeitet, → / gibt seinem Leben einen Sinn, → / sagt er. ↘
Er hat manchmal Angst, → / nicht schnell genug zu sein → / oder zu versagen. ↘

b Read the text aloud.

16 a Listen: from which sentence (a or b) can you expect the information on the right, which sentence is complete? Fill in the punctuation.

1 a Das ist Ingrid Wagner ☐
die älteste Aktivistin von Greenpeace in Deutschland.
b Das ist Ingrid Wagner ☐

2 a Greenpeace heißt auf Deutsch „grüner Friede" ☐
das heißt Gewaltfreiheit.
b Greenpeace heißt auf Deutsch „grüner Friede" ☐

3 a Für ihre Arbeit bekommt sie kein Geld ☐
aber Ehre und Anerkennung.
b Für ihre Arbeit bekommt sie kein Geld ☐

b Read the sentences out loud.

17 You want to appeal to people to form a section of Greenpeace (Team 50-Plus, Youth Group, or Neighbourhood Group). Draft a leaflet or flyer (for example, for the Internet) in German. The leaflet contains the following information: who are you? what do you want? what would you like to do? where should people write to?

Here is some material you can use.

aktiv werden bei Greenpeace – mitmachen
sich für die Umwelt interessieren – die Welt heilen helfen – sich einmischen
Protestschreiben an Politiker und Unternehmer – Unterschriften sammeln –
Zettel verteilen – Informationsstände aufstellen
im Team schaffen – mit Freunden zusammenarbeiten
tolles Gefühl – sich verlassen können auf – etwas Sinnvolles tun –
Spaß machen/haben – Sinn für das Leben machen
ehrenamtliches Engagement – kein Geld – Ehre und Anerkennung
schreiben – anrufen – faxen – eine E-Mail schreiben

Die Suche nach den **D**eu t**sch** en

Cultural information

Germans differ from all other nations in their strange sense of national identity. There are Germans who, when they're abroad, only go where other Germans are, but there are other Germans who avoid their compatriots wherever they can. The former want to have their German food and German popular music even when away from home, while the latter behave in such a way that you don't recognize them as German at all. The latter think they are better because they have a bad conscience and think they are model Germans. There are two sayings that take this divide to extremes. The first was created by the Nazis: "Am deutschen Wesen sollen sie genesen" (roughly: They – other nations – should regain their strength by modelling themselves on the German character, the spirit of German-ness). The other is by the poet Heinrich Heine (1797-1856): "Denk ich an Deutschland in der Nacht, dann bin ich um den Schlaf gebracht" (If I think of Germany in the night, I'm robbed of my sleep).

Ever since the 19th century Germany's history has been burdened by the fact that the development of healthy partrotism has been disturbed by a number of factors. Germany had always been a mosaic of politically, culturally, linguistically and religiously autonomous regions that had always had to gravitate towards various different centres of power. Thus there was a lack of orientation and identification. Then when nationalism swelled up, people vacillated between an inferiority complex and delusions of grandeur, one of the chief causes of the catastrophe of the Third Reich. Many Germans are still stricken and bewildered by what happened between 1933 and 1945, and feel shame. The text "Die Suche nach den Deutschen" (the search for the Germans) describes what this frame of mind led to. It's from the book "Ein Brasilianer in Berlin", in which the author Ribeiro tells of the surprises he experienced as a foreigner in the city, "surprises" which the Germans consider the most normal things in the world.

Language

We have usually acquired what we know from others, things we've read, things we've heard. In this unit you learn how to report what other people have said. This is most precisely done by quoting direct speech.

Maria sagt: „ Ich habe keine Zeit."

But you can't and don't always want to report something this way. So you use indirect speech (indirekte Rede). In indirect speech alongside the indicative (der Indikativ)

Maria sagt, sie **hat** keine Zeit.

we use the subjunctive (der Konjuktiv).

Maria sagt, sie **habe** keine Zeit.

Indirect speech allows us to distance ourselves from what we are reporting. Statements by politicians in particular are reported in newspapers in indirect speech in the subjunctive. Because it's difficult to overcome a feeling of mistrust.

George Grosz, Karikaturist: Weit von Berlin

Die Suche nach den Deutschen

1 **a** Read the text.
b Answer the questions.

What do you find out about Ribeiro's German friend? Where was he born? What does he look like? What's his mother tongue? Where does he live? What does he speak at home with his grandmother?

„Ich bin kein Deutscher."
„Wie bitte? Entweder bin ich verrückt oder du machst mich erst verrückt. Hast du nicht gerade gesagt, du seist in einer wirklich deutschen Gegend 5 geboren?"
„Ja, aber das will in diesem Fall nichts heißen. Die Gegend ist deutsch, aber ich fühle mich nicht als Deutscher. Ich finde, die Deutschen sind ein düsteres, unbeholfenes, verschlossenes Volk.
10 Nein, ich bin kein Deutscher, ich identifiziere mich viel mehr mit Völkern wie deinem, das sind fröhliche, entspannte, lachende Menschen, die offen sind ... Nein, ich bin kein Deutscher."
„Also, laß[1] mal gut sein, Dieter, natürlich bist du 15 Deutscher, bist in Deutschland geboren, siehst aus wie ein Deutscher, deine Muttersprache ist Deutsch ..."
„Meine Sprache ist nicht Deutsch. Ich spreche zwar deutsch, aber in Wahrheit ist meine Muttersprache 20 der Dialekt aus meiner Heimat, der ähnelt dem Deutschen, ist aber keins.
Obwohl ich jahrelang hier wohne, fühle ich mich wohler, wenn ich meinen Dialekt spreche, das ist viel unmittelbarer. Und wenn ich zu Hause nicht den 25 Dialekt unserer Heimat spreche, dann versteht meine Großmutter kein Wort."
„Halt mal, du bringst mich ja völlig durcheinander. Erst sagst du, deine Heimat sei wirklich deutsch, und jetzt sagst du, dort spricht man nicht die Sprache Deutschlands. Das verstehe ich nicht." 30
„Ganz einfach. Was du die Sprache Deutschlands nennst, ist Hochdeutsch, und das gibt es nicht, es ist eine Erfindung, etwas Abstraktes. Niemand spricht Hochdeutsch, nur im Fernsehen und in den Kursen vom Goethe-Institut, alles gelogen. Der wirkliche 35 Deutsche spricht zu Hause kein Hochdeutsch, die ganze Familie würde denken, er sei verrückt geworden. Nicht einmal die Regierenden sprechen Hochdeutsch, ganz im Gegenteil, du brauchst dir nur ein paar Reden anzuhören. Es wird immer deutlicher, 40 daß[2] du die Deutschen wirklich nicht kennst."
Nach dieser Entdeckung unternahmen wir verschiedene Versuche, einen Deutschen kennenzulernen, aber alle, auch wenn wir uns noch so anstrengten, schlugen unweigerlich fehl. 45
Unter unseren Freunden in Berlin gibt es nicht einen einzigen Deutschen. In Zahlen ausgedrückt ist das etwa so: 40% halten sich für Berliner und meinen, die Deutschen seien ein exotisches Volk, das weit weg wohnt; 30% fühlen sich durch die Frage beleidigt 50 und wollen wissen, ob wir auf irgend etwas anspielen, und rufen zu einer Versammlung gegen den Nationalismus auf; 15% sind Ex-Ossis[3], die sich nicht daran gewöhnen können, daß[3] sie keine Ossis mehr sein sollen; und die restlichen 15% fühlen sich 55 nicht als Deutsche, dieses düstere, unbeholfene, verschlossene Volk usw. usw.

João Ubaldo Ribeiro

[1] laß = lass [2] daß = dass [3] Ossi = Ostdeutscher: East German (citizen of the former GDR)

2 **a** What is characteristic of Germans in the opinion of the author's German friend? Jot down key phrases. (lines 1–13)
b What does he say about their language? (lines 14–41)
c What group of Berliners does the German friend belong to? (lines 42–57)

3 Check the meaning of the following verbs. Note down the meaning in English and copy out a sentence from the text or form a sentence of your own.

1 sich fühlen als (N)	to feel (like)	Ich fühle mich als Schweizer.
2 sich identifizieren mit (D)	....	....
3 aussehen wie (N)	....	....
4 sich halten für (A)	....	....
5 sich beleidigt fühlen durch (A)	....	....
6 anspielen auf (A)	....	....
7 aufrufen zu (D)	....	....
8 sich gewöhnen an (A)	....	....

Sätze / Satzteile verbinden:
wenn ... (dann), zwar ... aber, entweder ... oder, sowohl ... als auch

4 a Read the sentences.

Entweder bin ich verrückt **oder** du machst mich verrückt.
Jemand ist hier verrückt – **entweder** du **oder** ich.

Ich spreche **zwar** Deutsch, **aber** in Wahrheit ist meine Muttersprache ein Dialekt.
Er spricht **zwar** Deutsch, **aber** nicht sehr gut.

Wenn ich zu Hause nicht Dialekt spreche, (**dann**) versteht meine Großmutter kein Wort.

Dieter ist **sowohl** Deutscher **als auch** Berliner.
Die Deutschen sind **sowohl** düster **als auch** unbeholfen.

b Complete the rule.

The conjunction ....
links the main clause and the sub-clause,

The conjunctions ....
link main clauses or parts of clauses (e. g. pronouns, nouns, adjectives).

The conjunction ....
links parts of clauses.

5 Match.

1 ☐ 2 ☐ 3 ☐ 4 ☐ 5 ☐ 6 ☐

1	Er spricht sowohl Hochdeutsch als auch	**a**	sie macht mir Spaß.
2	Wenn er Dialekt spricht, dann	**b**	sie schreibt mir einen Brief.
3	Diese Arbeit ist zwar nicht einfach, aber	**c**	schafft sie es nicht.
4	Entweder ruft sie an oder	**d**	Dialekt.
5	Zwar fühlt er sich nicht als Deutscher, aber	**e**	versteht sie ihn nicht.
6	Wenn wir ihr nicht helfen, dann	**f**	er spricht nur Deutsch.

Redewiedergabe: direkte und indirekte Rede (1)

6 Fill in verb forms from the text.

line 1	„Ich .... kein Deutscher."
lines 3–5	Hast du nicht gerade gesagt, du .....seist................ in einer deutschen Gegend geboren?
line 28	Erst sagst du, deine Heimat .... wirklich deutsch, ...
lines 48/49	40% meinen, die Deutschen .... ein exotisches Volk, ...

Er sagte: „Ich **bin** kein Deutscher."	direct speech: indicative
Er sagte, er **ist** kein Deutscher. dass er kein Deutscher **ist**.	indirect speech: indicative
Er sagte, er **sei** kein Deutscher. dass er kein Deutscher **sei**.	indirect speech: subjunctive I

The reported words are generally introduced by verbs like *denken, finden, hören, lesen, meinen, sagen, schreiben*.

The direct speech is placed between inverted commas. Note the style of them: „..."
The introductory reporting verb is followed by a colon, not a comma.
The verb is in the indicative.

The indirect speech can be in the indicative or the subjunctive, with or without *dass*.

Konjunktiv I: *sein*

7 Fill in the verb forms.

sein

ich	sei	wir	sei **en**
du	....	ihr	sei **et**
Sie	sei **en**	Sie	sei **en**
er/sie/es/man	sei	sie	....

8 a Put the following sentences into direct speech. Note that you have to change the person and possessive adjectives. Pay attention to the punctuation.

Er sagte, das sei nicht seine Heimat.	Er sagte: „Das ist nicht meine Heimat."
Sie sagte, das sei nicht ihre Heimat.	Sie sagte: „Das ist nicht meine Heimat."
Er sagte, er sei kein Deutscher.	Er sagte: „Ich bin kein Deutscher."

Mein Freund sagte, seine Sprache sei kein Deutsch, sondern ein Dialekt.
Er meinte auch, die Deutschen seien ein verschlossenes Volk.

Michael Wüst sagte, es sei ein tolles Gefühl, mit Freunden zusammenzuarbeiten.
Die Einsätze seien jedoch schwere Arbeit. Er denkt dann immer, sein Leben sei nicht umsonst gewesen.

b Change the clauses into *dass* clauses.

Er sagte, er sei kein Deutscher. — Er sagte, dass er kein Deutscher sei.

Einwenden – Widersprechen

9 a Check the meaning of the proverbs and sayings.

Das will nichts heißen.
Das heißt gar nichts.

Lass mal gut sein.
Hör auf damit.

Das bringt mich (völlig) durcheinander.

Das ist alles gelogen.
Das stimmt doch nicht.
Das ist doch nicht wahr.

Das macht mich verrückt.
Du machst mich verrückt.
Mach mich nicht verrückt!

b Complete with sayings and proverbs from a.

1 ■ Die sieht mich mit ihren schwarzen Augen immer so intensiv an.
▲ Das will nichts heißen. Die sieht doch nicht gut.

2 ■ Er sagt, er kann sehr gut Deutsch.
▲ .... Er lernt Deutsch erst seit zwei Monaten.

3 ■ Ich höre auf zu studieren.
▲ .... Gestern hast du noch gesagt, dass es dir großen Spaß macht.

4 ■ Sie ist wahrscheinlich Berlinerin.
▲ .... Hast du nicht gesagt, sie kommt aus München?

5 ■ Seine Frage hat mich beleidigt.
▲ .... Er wollte nur wissen, wie du dich als Ex-Ossi fühlst.

Das Verb: Partizip I und Partizip II

	with ending	without ending
Partizip I	die **lachenden** Menschen = Menschen, die lachen Das war eine **beleidigende** Frage.	Sie kamen **lachend** aus dem Zimmer. Die Frage war **beleidigend**.
Partizip II	ein **beleidigter** Deutscher das **entspannte** Gespräch	Er fühlte sich **beleidigt**. Das Gespräch war sehr **entspannt**.

der **sprechende** Papagei = der Papagei, der spricht
die **gesprochene** Sprache = die Sprache, die gesprochen wird

The present participle (Partizip I) has an active meaning. It is formed from the infinitive of the verb + *d*. The past participle (Partizip II) usually has a passive meaning.
Present and past participle can be placed in front of a noun like an adjective, and then have adjectival endings. If they are after a verb, they have no ending.

10 Mark the endings of the participles in the table above.

11 Underline the participles in the following examples. What verbs are they derived from?

Wenn wir einen Verletzten aus dem Wrack schneiden, ...
Den Weitgereisten fand man in Samarkand wieder.
Wir bitten die Reisenden, ihre Koffer abzuholen.

Nouns are often derived from the forms of the present and past participle.
They are declined like adjectives: der Verletzt**e**, für den Verletzt**en**, ...

12 Form a present or past participle as in the example and translate it into English.

1 gut aussehen – ein Mann   ein gut aussehender Mann ....
2 sprechen – die Sprache   die ....
3 diskutieren – die Politiker   die ....
4 verletzen – ein Kind   ein ....
5 fehlen – das Geld   das ....
6 schreiben – die Sprache   die ....
7 warten – der Kunde   der ....
8 arbeiten – eine Mutter   eine ....

Deutschland ist ...

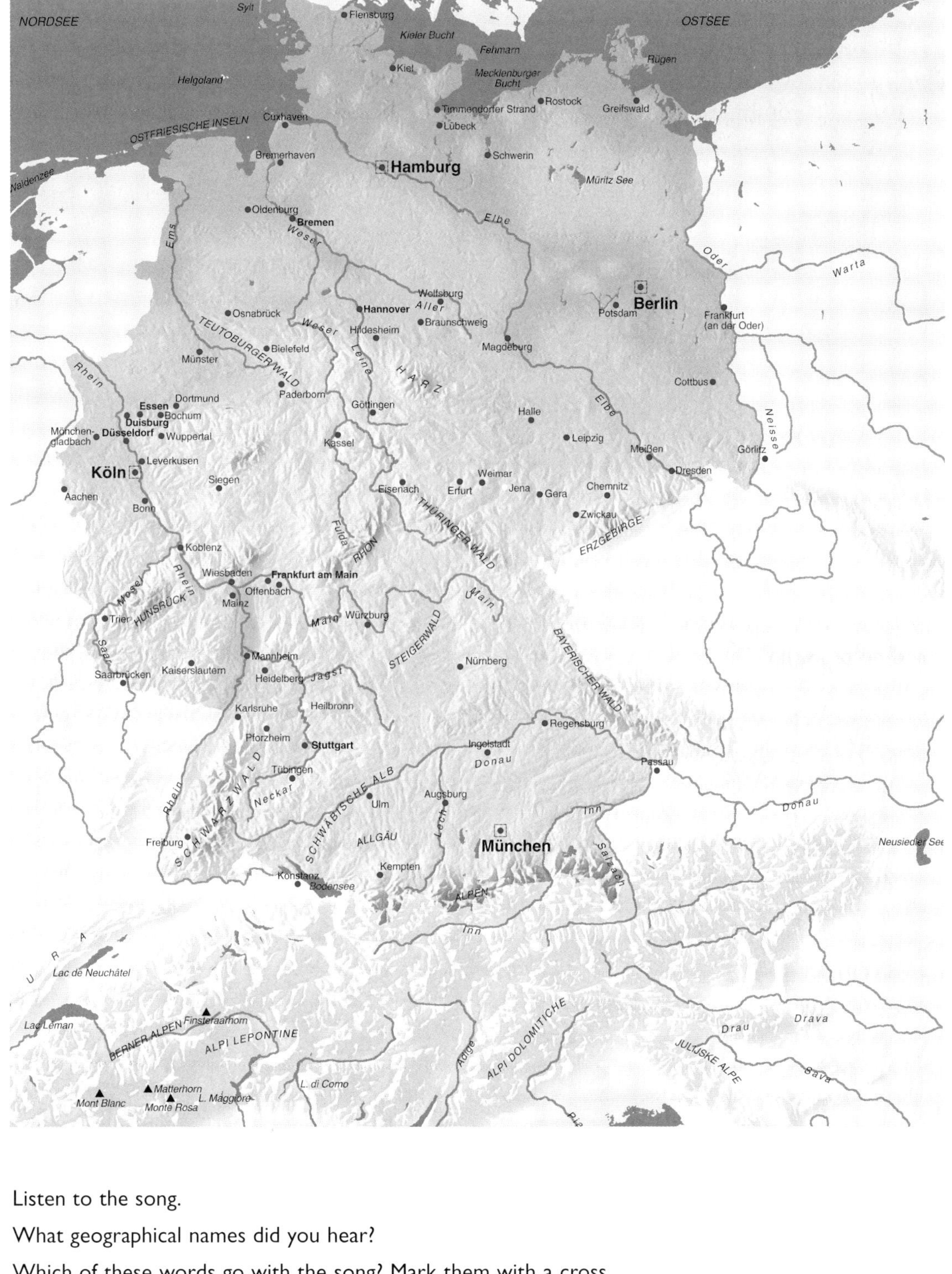

13 Listen to the song.

a What geographical names did you hear?

b Which of these words go with the song? Mark them with a cross.

Industrie ☐ Fußball ☐ Theater ☐ Religion ☐ Geografie ☐

Tiere ☐ Literatur ☐ Porzellan ☐ Politik ☐ Farben der Nationalfahne ☐

14 a Listen again and read.

1
Deutschland ist die Elbe bei Cuxhaven,
das grüne Gras im Allgäu,
der Timmendorfer Strand,
der rote Fels von Helgoland.

2
Deutschland ist Goethes Haus in Weimar,
das Porzellan aus Meißen,
und die Fische von Schwerin,
und der Ku'damm in Berlin.

3 Refrain
Schwarz wie die Kohlen im Revier,
Rot wie die Lippen der Mädchen hier,
Gold wie der Weizen und das Bier,
das sind die Farben, die Farben von dir.

4
Deutschland ist Bundesligaspiele
der HSV und Bayern,
Köln und Werder Bremen,
FKK und sich nicht schämen.

Gunter Gabriel

b Which words from 13b go with which verse?

1 ....
2 ....
3 ....
4 ....

15 a Read the information.

Allgäu: Landschaft östlich vom Bodensee, Allgäuer Alpen, Voralpenland, Seen, Wiesen, Landwirtschaft (Milch und Käse), Spielzeug aus Ravensburg

Ku(rfürsten)damm: großer Boulevard in Berlin, Geschäfte, Kinos, Theater, Café Kranzler

Ruhrgebiet (Revier): größtes Industriegebiet Europas, an den Flüssen (der) Rhein und (die) Ruhr, Kohlerevier, Schwerindustrie, Stahlwerke, Essen, Bochum, Dortmund, gutes Bier

Timmendorfer Strand: Badeort im Norden von Deutschland, Ostseeküste, zwischen Lübeck und Kiel, FKK = Freikörperkultur = Nacktbadestrand

Meißen: bei Dresden mit Villen und Porzellanmanufaktur, Weinberge, Land Sachsen

Helgoland: Insel, Nordsee, roter Fels, Zerstörung durch Bomben nach dem Zweiten Weltkrieg, Wiederaufbau, Ausflüge

Bundesliga: 1. Fußballliga seit 1966 in Westdeutschland, 18 Vereine, z.B. FC Bayern München, HSV, Werder Bremen, Borussia Dortmund

b Formulate texts as in the example.

Das Allgäu ist eine Landschaft. Es liegt östlich vom Bodensee. Dort gibt es viele Berge und grüne Wiesen. Das Allgäu ist bekannt für seine Milch, seine Kühe und seinen Käse.

Liebe und Tod

Cultural information

One way of finding out about a country and its culture is to visit its graveyards, old and new, because then you see how people deal with the phenomenon of death. The love of people for one another often only becomes visible when they have been separated by death.

Violent death in war is part of this. Before the Second World War every village had, alongside its graveyard, a war memorial at which wreaths were laid on particular days. After the Second World War most of these memorials were pulled down in Germany and Austria because they glorified nationalism and war. In Switzerland, however, which has not waged war against another country for 200 years, such memorials are still preserved. Most of the graves of soldiers killed in the Second World War are outside Germany and are tended by the War Graves Association. When a former soldier is buried today, salutes are still fired and a brass band plays the song "Ich hatt' einen Kameraden, einen besseren find'st du nicht". (I had a comrade, you won't find a better one.)

In the whole of the German-speaking area the dead are remembered on All Saints' Day (Allerheiligen), the first of November. On this day families pay a visit to the graveyard and place flowers and candles on the graves. People who live a long way away order a floral arrangement or wreath from a florist or nursery.

As old people usually no longer live with their children, they go into old people's homes and usually die in the anonymous atmosphere of a hospital, without any psychological support. That is grim for those who die, but also for young people, for whom death has become an unfamiliar, unknown phenomenon that they are never confronted with. This state of affairs has initiated a sort of counter-movement with the foundation of hospices for people approaching death. The dying are supported and not left alone with complicated medical machinery till they breathe their last.

Language

"Ich freue mich doch so darauf", says sister-in-law Hilde to Herr Kunkel when he invites her to his slide show. The little words, so called particles (Partikeln), such as *doch* in this sentence, play a special role in German. Most of them, such as *denn, doch, ja,* only make a minimal change to the basic meaning of the sentence. And sentences could remain without them. But they give a hint of the situation and the relationship between the people who are communicating with each other. They indicate the tone of the exchange. It is often these little words that show what the speaker really means. And there's something else about a lot of the words: depending on how they are used, they can fulfil different functions and meanings. This is why they are mainly used in the spoken language.

Liebe und Tod

1 What do you expect from a text entitled "Liebe und Tod"?

2 a Check the meaning of the unknown terms.

Angst ⊘ Trauer ⊘ traurig ⊘ Freude ⊘ Leben ⊘ lebendig ⊘ lieben ⊘ sterben ⊘ Grab ⊘ Kuss ⊘ fröhlich ⊘ kalt ⊘ gern haben ⊘ lieb haben ⊘ Mitleid haben ⊘ tot sein ⊘ warm

b Where do the words belong, to *Liebe* or to *Tod*? Sort them.

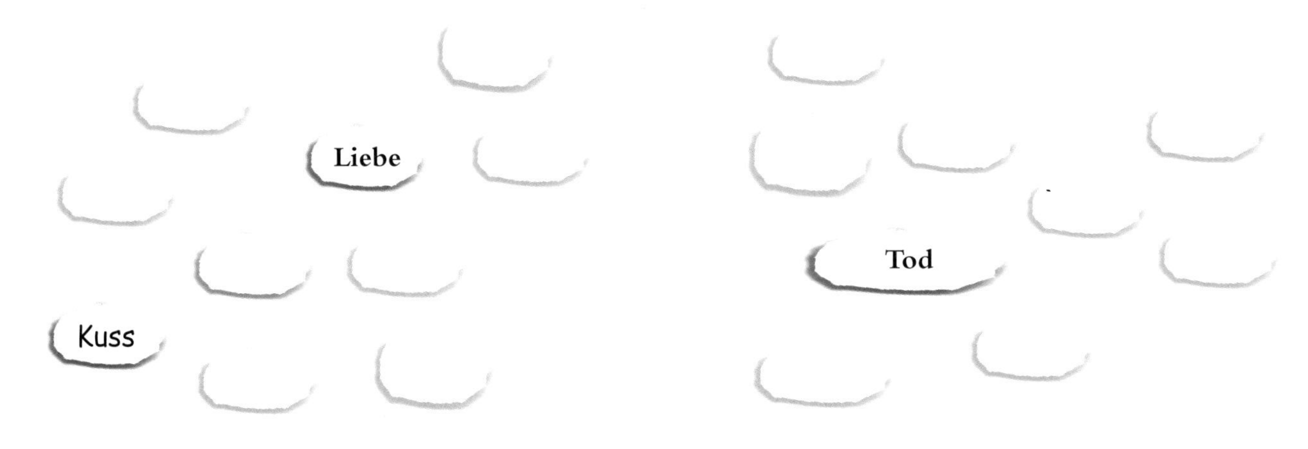

3 a Read the text.

b Who is talking to whom and what about?

Liebe und Tod

Den würd ich aber nicht mehr mit ins Bett nehmen. Der ist doch schon ganz kalt.
    Heut morgen war er ganz warm.
Das ist d e i n e Wärme, nicht seine.
    Na und?
5 Verstehst du denn nicht: Er ist tot.
    Eben. Deswegen nehme ich 'n ja mit ins Bett.
Aber das ist unhygienisch.
    Unwas?
Ungesund, schmutzig.
10 Wieso is' Liebhaben schmutzig?
Kein Wort von[1] gesagt.
    Du hast gesagt, der Goldhamster[2] is' schmutzig.
Der tote.
    Ja.
15 Na bitte.
    Und dass ich ihn lieb hab?
Du kannst ja immer lieb an ihn denken.

Warum?
Na, weil du ihn lieb gehabt hast.
20 Den lebendigen?
Genau.
Hab ich ja gar nicht.
Aber du hast es doch eben gesagt!
Ich hab gesagt, ich hab ihn lieb, weil er tot is'.
25 Du meinst, du hast Mitleid mit ihm.
Wieso denn? Jetzt isser[3] ja tot.
Na, aber dann nützt ihm doch jetzt auch dein Liebhaben nichts!
Nee.
Und warum hast du ihn dann trotzdem noch lieb?
30 Weil ich traurig bin.
Über seinen Tod.
Nee.
Aber worüber denn d a n n ?
Weil ich nich mehr nett zu ihm sein kann.
35 Mach ihm doch ein schönes Grab.
Findste[4] das nett?
Du kommst nicht drum rum[5]. Für was Gestorbenes muss man das tun.
Und was tu ich dafür, dass ich ihn lieb hab?
Dafür pflanzt du ihm Blumen drauf.
40 Und was hat er davon?
Vielleicht hast d u was davon.
Wie kann ich was von haben, wenn er nichts von hat?
Das kann man nicht vergleichen.
Eben.

Wolfdietrich Schnurre

1 von = davon
2 Goldhamster: hamster
3 isser = ist er
4 Findste = Findest du
5 um etw. nicht herumkommen: you can't avoid it

4 Underline all the words in the text where letters are missing. On the left write down how the words would be written in the standard language.

würde Den würd ich aber nicht mehr mit ins Bett nehmen.

Textzusammenhang verstehen

5 What do the following refer to: *deswegen* (line 6), (*da*)*von* (line 11), *dafür* (line 38 and 39), *d*(*a*)*rauf* (line 39), *davon* (line 40 and 41)? Draw arrows to make the reference clear.

Verstehst du denn nicht: Er ist tot.
Eben. Deswegen nehme ich ihn ja mit ins Bett.

Wieso ist Liebhaben schmutzig?
Kein Wort von gesagt.

Ergänzung mit Präposition (2)

■ Du hast gesagt, der Goldhamster ist schmutzig.
▲ Der tote.
■ Und dass ich ihn lieb hab?
▲ Du kannst ja immer lieb **an ihn** denken.

Preposition + personal pronoun
- instead of a noun denoting a living organism (people, animals).

■ Und was tu ich **dafür**, dass ich ihn lieb hab?
▲ **Dafür** pflanzt du ihm Blumen drauf.
■ Und was hat er **davon**?
▲ Vielleicht hast du was **davon**.

Die Blumen waren sehr schön. Sie freute sich **darüber**.

da(r) + **preposition**
- refers to a statement following (in a sub-clause).
- refers to a preceding statement.
- instead of nouns denoting things or abstract ideas

r is added to *da* before a vowel: da**r**auf, da**r**über, da**r**in.

6 Complete the sentences.

denken an • sich freuen auf • sich gewöhnen an • halten von • hören von • nachdenken über • sich verlassen auf • warten auf

1 Morgen muss ich noch zwei Briefe schreiben. ...Daran...... habe ich nicht mehr ...gedacht.......

2 ■ Wo ist Herr Haslinger? ▲ Er ist noch nicht hier. Ich .warte............... auch ..auf..ihn..................

3 ■ Er kommt immer zu spät. Das macht mich wütend.
▲ .... habe ich mich schon längst ....

4 Es scheint, dass der neue Kollege nett ist. Was .... du ....?

5 ■ Sie macht immer, was sie verspricht. ▲ Ja, ... kann man sich immer ....

6 ■ Am Wochenende soll schönes Wetter sein. ▲ Ja, ich .... mich auch schon sehr ...., dass ich wieder im Garten arbeiten kann.

7 ■ Sie wollen ihr neues Haus verkaufen. ▲ .... habe ich nichts ....

8 ■ Wird sie den neuen Job nehmen? ▲ Sie .... noch ....

Aussprache: Konsonanten

b, d, g – stimmlos oder stimmhaft

7 a Listen and read. Pay special attention to the consonants that are marked.

Ich ha**b** ihn lie**b** geha**b**t. • Mach ihm doch ein Gra**b**. • Er ist gestor**b**en. • Er stir**b**t. • Du hast gesa**g**t, das ist ungesun**d**, schmutzig. • Wieso ist Lie**b**ha**b**en schmutzig?

b Listen again and repeat.

8 a Listen and read. Where are *b, d, g* voiceless (*p, t, k*)? Mark with a cross.

1 Ich blei**b**e. ☐
2 Blei**b**st du noch? ☐
3 Blei**b** hier! ☐
4 sie**b**en ☐
5 sie**b**zehn ☐
6 Schrei**b**st du mir? ☐
7 A**b**er **b**itte **b**ald! ☐
8 der Freun**d** ☐
9 die Freun**d**e ☐
10 freun**d**lich ☐
11 Tut mir Lei**d**. ☐
12 lei**d**er ☐
13 Das war spannen**d**. ☐
14 Ein spannen**d**er Film. ☐
15 der Erfol**g** ☐
16 ver**g**leichen ☐
17 fol**g**endes Beispiel ☐
18 Ich gehe weit we**g**. ☐
19 Zei**g**en Sie es mir! ☐
20 Sa**g** doch etwas! ☐
21 Ich sa**g**e nichts dazu! ☐

At the end of a word or syllable (*ab • holen*) *b, d, g* are voiceless (cf. *s* voiced or voiceless, → p. 38).

b Listen and repeat.

Schreib doch mal!
Er kommt aus Berlin und sie aus Dresden.
Muss man sich das merken?
Glaubt sie, dass das möglich ist?
Sind Sie aus Dortmund?
Sag das noch einmal, bitte!
Frag doch!
Es geschah am Abend.
Tschüs, bis bald!
Mein Freund bringt mir Blumen.

9 a Listen and read. Pay attention to the consonants marked.

Hilfs**t** **d**u mir? • Gefäll**t** **d**ir die Musik? • Gehs**t** **d**u mi**t** **T**ina? •
Sie kommt au**s** **S**alzburg. • Der Zug fährt a**b** **P**otsdam. • Wir fliegen a**b** **B**erlin. •
Wa**s** **s**in**d** **d**enn das für Leute? • Was wills**t** **d**u denn heute Aben**d** **t**un?

When two consonants, e.g. *t+d, t+t, d+d, s+s, b+p, b+b, g+g* (*weggehen*), *m+m* (*am Montag*), *n+n* (*in Norddeutschland*) follow one after another, they are spoken as one sound.

b Listen and repeat the old saying.

Lernst du was, dann kannst du was. Kannst du was, dann wirst du was.
Wirst du was, dann bist du was. Bist du was, dann hast du was.

Die kleinen Wörter

10 Compare the following sentences with the text. Note down what is missing and mark the place √.

1 Der ist schon ganz kalt. ....

2 Verstehst du nicht? ....

3 Du kannst √ immer lieb an ihn denken. ....ja.........

4 Wieso? ....

5 Jetzt ist er tot. ....

6 Dann nützt ihm jetzt auch dein Liebhaben nichts. ....

7 Mach ihm ein schönes Grab. ....

Deswegen nehme ich ihn ja mit ins Bett. Wieso denn? Jetzt ist er ja tot.	**ja**	Both speakers know this.
Du kannst ja immer lieb an ihn denken.	**ja**	The speaker gives cautious advice and is looking for agreement.
Hab ich ja gar nicht.	**ja**	The speaker expresses a gentle contradiction.
Der ist doch schon ganz kalt. Da nützt ihm doch jetzt auch dein Liebhaben nichts.	**doch**	The speaker wants agreement, but with a certain degree of pressure or contradiction.
Aber du hast es doch eben gesagt.	**doch**	The speaker contradicts his/her conversation partner.
Mach ihm doch ein schönes Grab.	**doch**	reinforcement of a demand, request or advice
Verstehst du denn nicht? Wieso denn? Aber worüber denn dann?	**denn**	expression of impatience or interest

11 Complete the statements using *doch*.

gar nicht stimmen • immer zu spät kommen • nicht mehr modern sein • immer lügen • immer alles weitererzählen • gefährlich sein • sich nicht verlassen können • todlangweilig sein • es nicht wissen • ihr ein Buch schenken • heute Abend zu mir kommen • mal nachsehen

1 Das würde ich nicht sagen. Wieso? Das stimmt doch gar nicht.

2 Den würde ich nicht fragen. Wieso? Der …

3 Dem würde ich nicht glauben. Wieso? Der …

4 Ich weiß nicht, was ich ihr schenken soll. …

5 Das Kleid würde ich nicht anziehen. Wieso? Das …

6 Mit dem würde ich nicht zusammenarbeiten. Wieso? Auf den …

7 Ich verstehe das alles nicht. … Ich erkläre es dir dann.

8 Der würde ich es nicht erzählen. Wieso? Die …

9 Auf den würde ich nicht warten. Wieso? Der …

10 Mit dem würde ich mich nicht unterhalten. Wieso? Der …

11 Das würde ich nicht machen. Wieso? Das …

12 Da ist jemand vor der Tür. …, was er will.

Lebenszeit

12 **a** The sections of the text on page 184 are not in the right order. Read each section and give it a heading. The key words, i.e. the words that occur more often (people, animals, numbers) should guide you.

b How does the text really fit together? Note down the letters marking the individual sections in the right order.

☐ ☐ ☐ ☐ ☐

c Which words or sentences helped you find the right order? Mark them.

Lebenszeit

A Der Esel ging weg und der Hund erschien. „Wie lange willst du leben?", sprach Gott zu ihm, „dem Esel sind dreißig Jahre zu viel, du wirst aber damit zufrieden sein." „Herr", antwortete der Hund, „ist das dein Wille, denke daran, was ich laufen muss, das halten meine Füße so lange nicht aus; und habe ich erst die Stimme zum Bellen verloren und die Zähne zum Beißen, was bleibt mir übrig, als aus einer Ecke in die andere zu laufen und zu knurren?" Gott sah, dass er Recht hatte, und erließ ihm zwölf Jahre.

B Also lebte der Mensch siebzig Jahre. Die ersten dreißig sind seine menschlichen Jahre, die vergehen schnell, da ist er gesund und fröhlich. Darauf folgen die achtzehn Jahre des Esels, da wird ihm eine Last nach der andern aufgelegt: Er muss das Korn tragen, damit andere das Brot essen können, und er bekommt noch Schläge für seine Dienste. Dann kommen die zwölf Jahre des Hundes, da liegt er in den Ecken, knurrt und hat keine Zähne mehr zum Beißen. Und wenn auch diese Zeit vergangen ist, so kommen zum Schluss die zehn Jahre des Affen. Da ist der Mensch schwachköpfig und närrisch, treibt alberne Dinge und die Kinder lachen über ihn.

C Als Gott die Welt geschaffen hatte und allen Kreaturen ihre Lebenszeit bestimmen wollte, kam der Esel und fragte: „Herr, wie lange soll ich leben?" „Dreißig Jahre", antwortete Gott, „ist dir das recht?" „Ach Herr", antwortete der Esel, „das ist eine lange Zeit. Denke doch an mein mühseliges Leben: vom Morgen bis in die Nacht schwere Lasten tragen, Kornsäcke in die Mühle schleppen, damit andere das Brot essen, immer wieder Schläge kriegen! Erlass mir einen Teil der langen Zeit!" Da schenkte ihm Gott achtzehn Jahre.

D Endlich erschien der Mensch, war freudig, gesund und frisch und bat Gott ihm seine Zeit zu bestimmen. „Dreißig Jahre sollst du leben", sprach der Herr, „ist dir das genug?" „Welch eine kurze Zeit!", rief der Mensch. „Wenn ich mein Haus gebaut habe, wenn ich Bäume gepflanzt habe, die blühen und Früchte tragen, und ich mich meines Lebens freuen möchte, so soll ich sterben! O Herr, verlängere meine Zeit!" „Ich will dir auch noch die achtzehn Jahre des Esels schenken", sagte Gott. „Das ist nicht genug", antwortete der Mensch. „Du sollst auch die zwölf Jahre des Hundes haben." „Immer noch zu wenig." „Nun gut", sagte Gott, „ich will dir noch die zehn Jahre des Affen geben, aber mehr bekommst du nicht." Der Mensch ging weg, war aber nicht zufrieden.

E Darauf kam der Affe. „Du willst wohl gerne dreißig Jahre leben?", sprach der Herr zu ihm. „Du brauchst nicht zu arbeiten wie der Esel und der Hund und bist immer guter Dinge." „Ach Herr", antwortete er, „das sieht so aus, ist aber anders. Ich soll immer lustige Streiche machen, Gesichter schneiden, damit die Leute lachen, und wenn sie mir einen Apfel geben und ich beiße hinein, so ist er sauer. Dreißig Jahre halte ich das nicht aus." Gott schenkte ihm zehn Jahre.

nach: *Brüder Grimm*

 **13** Now listen to the whole text and read it.

Licht macht Laune

Cultural information

On 2nd February, the Catholic Church in southern Germany celebrates the feast of Candlemas, a festival that takes place exactly 40 days after Christmas (Weihnachten) and which similarly goes back to old Roman and Germanic festivals. These old festivals, like Easter, have to do with the changing seasons and the movement of the sun and the moon. While Christmas falls almost exactly on the winter solstice, Candlemas (Lichtmess) signals the first breath of spring. The days are getting longer, the sunlight is getting stronger. The farmers awake from their winter period of rest and begin preparing the cultivation of their fields. For centuries Candlemas was the day when farmers took on their helpers, farm labourers and maids. So this is also the festival of those employed in agriculture, and hundreds of years older than 1st May, Labour Day. This aspect has been forgotten.

The rituals of light, however, have been preserved as part of the yearly festivals: Easter candles, the tree with candles on it at Christmas. In the German-speaking regions, Christmas is the most important festival of the church year, preceded by the four weeks of Advent (Advent, stress on "-vent"). The advent wreath and advent calendar are part of it all. On each of the four Sundays before Christmas, a new candle is lit, and each day the children are allowed to open another window of their advent calendar. The way this tradition is still cultivated is the subject of a newspaper article from the Black Forest close to the Swiss and French borders.

Language

Der neue Kollege wurde nicht eingeladen.
(The new colleague was not invited.)
In this sentence the verb is in the passive (das Passiv). It could be in the active (das Aktiv), too. The fact that the passive is used shows us that the person who didn't invite the colleague is deliberately not being mentioned.
Alternative:
Man hat den neuen Kollegen nicht eingeladen.
Unlike in English, where the passive is more frequent, German normally uses an active form, and the passive is much less frequent. When it is used, this is mainly in the written language, in non-fiction texts, in instructions, regulations and rules. The passive is used when the person doing the action is obvious, or when, for whatever reason, the speaker doesn't want to or cannot mention them.

Advent wreath

Licht macht Laune

1 **a** Read lines 1–8. Underline key words: nouns (months, times of day), adjectives.
b Fill in the opposites from the text.

unglücklich ...heiter...... jeden Morgen ....

kürzer .... ein wenig früher ....

hell ....

2 Now read lines 9–20.
a What does *Licht* mean? Fill in the nouns.
b Then complete the matching idioms.

das Lebenslicht brennt ● jd. ist ein großes Licht ● das Licht der Welt erblicken ● das leuchtet mir ein ● Licht am Ende des Tunnels sehen

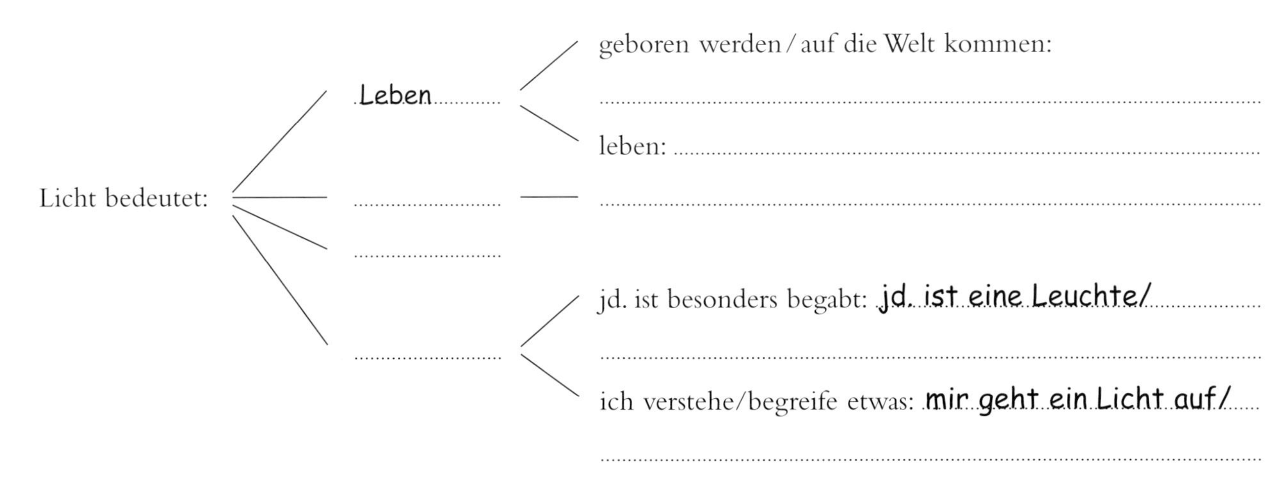

3 Read lines 21 to the end.
a What idioms are used to explain the following verbs?

jdn. täuschen: ...jdn.........., jdn..........

etw. aufklären: ...etw..........

b Translate the verbs into English.

Licht macht Laune

Jedes Jahr Ende Juni verkündete meine Oma unglücklich, dass die Tage jetzt wieder kürzer werden. Und pünktlich ein paar Tage vor Weihnachten erklärte sie heiter, von nun an würden sie wieder länger. Ich konnte das als Kind nie so recht verstehen, war es doch Mitte Juni immer nur hell und um Weihnachten fast immer dunkel. Natürlich hatte Oma
5 Recht. Vom 21. Dezember an wird es jeden Morgen ein wenig früher hell und jeden Abend ein bisschen später dunkel. Nur jetzt, Anfang Januar, merken wir alle noch nicht viel davon. Wenn ihr am Morgen aufsteht, dann ist für viele von euch noch finstere Nacht. Wie gut, dass es heutzutage auf Knopfdruck hell wird.

Habt ihr euch schon einmal überlegt, was das bedeutet? Licht? In unserer Sprache
10 steht das Wort für lauter Gutes. Wenn jemand geboren wird, erblickt er das „Licht der Welt", solange er lebt, brennt sein „Lebenslicht". Wenn jemand das „Licht am Ende des Tunnels" sieht, dann schöpft er neue Hoffnung. Der Spruch „Wenn du meinst, es geht nicht mehr, kommt irgendwo ein Lichtlein her", der drückt so ungefähr das Gleiche aus.

Licht bedeutet Leben, Hoffnung, Wärme – und Klugheit. Auch dafür gibt es viele Aus-
15 drücke in unserer Sprache. Sicher habt ihr schon einmal gehört (oder gesagt?), jemand sei unterbelichtet. Das ist ein reichlich unfreundlicher Ausdruck dafür, dass man ihn nicht für sonderlich intelligent hält. Auf der anderen Seite ist es ein Kompliment, wenn jemand als „Leuchte" oder als „großes Licht"[1] bezeichnet wird – der ist dann nämlich besonders begabt. Dazu gehört übrigens auch, dass einem etwas „einleuchtet" oder „ein Licht auf-
20 geht", wenn man etwas begreift. Alles klar?

Jetzt wird's ein bisschen schwieriger: Warum sagt man anstatt „täuschen" auch „hinters Licht führen"? Ursprünglich hieß das „jemanden ins Dunkle führen" – also dorthin, wo er nichts sieht und deshalb leicht zu täuschen ist. „Dunkelmänner" oder „dunkle Gestalten" machen das mit Vorliebe – „Lichtgestalten" dagegen tun natürlich nur Gutes. Wenn
25 etwas ans Licht gebracht wird, dann wird es aufgeklärt.

Bei Licht betrachtet[2] gibt es sicher noch viel mehr solche Ausdrücke in unserer Sprache und auch in anderen.

Sabine Ehrentreich

[1] The idioms *ein großes Licht sein, eine große Leuchte sein* are most usually in the negative today: *jd. ist keine große Leuchte / er ist nicht gerade eine Leuchte / er ist kein großes Licht.* The expression *jd. ist eine Leuchte* is often used ironically to denote someone too clever by half, who thinks he knows it all.

[2] bei Licht betrachtet: seen in the (cold) light of day / dawn

4 a Read these extracts from a dictionary. How are the idioms from the text labelled?
ugs. = umgangssprachlich: *colloquial* geh. = gehoben: *elevated* salopp: *casual, informal*

b What expressions with *Licht* exist in your language, or how are they expressed?

***das L. der Welt erblicken** (geh.; *geboren werden*); **ein bestimmtes L. auf jmdn. werfen** *(auf jmds. Ansehen bestimmte [negative] Auswirkungen haben);* **L. in etw. bringen** *(eine Angelegenheit aufklären);* **jmdn. hinters L. führen** *(jmdn. täuschen;* eigtl. = jmdn. nach der Seite führen, nach der hin der Lichtstrahl einer Lampe abgeschirmt ist); **jmdn., etw. ins rechte L. rücken/setzen/stellen** *(dafür sorgen, dass jmd., etw. vorteilhaft o. ä. erscheint);* **etw. in rosigem, im rosigsten L. sehen/darstellen** *(etw. sehr positiv beurteilen);*

***grünes L. geben** *(die Erlaubnis geben, etw. in Angriff zu nehmen;* nach dem grünen Licht von Verkehrsampeln o. Ä.);

un|ter|be|lich|ten ⟨sw. V.; hat⟩ (Fot.): *zu wenig belichten* (a): er unterbelichtet die Filme öfter; man muss vermeiden, die Filme unterzubelichten; Ü er ist [geistig] wohl etwas unterbelichtet (salopp; *geistig nicht auf der Höhe*)

***in einem guten, günstigen, schlechten o. ä. L. erscheinen/stehen** *(einen guten, günstigen, schlechten o. ä. Eindruck machen).* **2. a)** ⟨Pl. -er⟩ *Lampe, Lichtquelle:* ein spärliches, helles L.;

etw. ans L. bringen/ziehen/zerren/holen *(etw. [Verheimlichtes] an die Öffentlichkeit bringen);* **ans L. kommen** *([von etw. Verheimlichtem, Verborgenem] bekannt werden, offenbar werden);*

***kein/nicht gerade ein großes L. sein** (ugs.; ↑Kirchenlicht); **jmdm. geht ein L. auf** (ugs.; *jmd. versteht, durchschaut plötzlich etw.*); **sein L. leuchten lassen** *(sein Wissen, Können zeigen, zur Geltung bringen;*

‚Es geht ihm ein Licht auf'

Textzusammenhang verstehen

5 The words underlined refer to something already mentioned in the text or which will be referred to later. If you can't tell what the words refer to, ask the questions (see right-hand column).

Licht bedeutet Leben, Hoffnung, Wärme – und Klugheit. Auch dafür gibt es viele Ausdrücke in unserer Sprache. Sicher habt ihr schon einmal gehört, jemand sei unterbelichtet. Das ist ein unfreundlicher Ausdruck dafür, dass man ihn nicht für besonders intelligent hält. Auf der anderen Seite ist es ein Kompliment, wenn jemand als „Leuchte" oder als „großes Licht" bezeichnet wird – der ist dann nämlich besonders begabt. Dazu gehört übrigens auch, dass einem etwas „einleuchtet" , wenn man etwas begreift.

dafür: Wofür gibt es auch viele Ausdrücke?

das: Was ist ein unfreundlicher Ausdruck?

dafür: Wofür ist das ein unfreundlicher Ausdruck?

der: Wer ist dann besonders begabt?

dazu: Wozu gehört auch, dass einem etwas „einleuchtet"?

6 What do the underlined words refer to? Indicate the references as in section 5.

Lebenszeit

Der Esel kam zu Gott und fragte: „Herr, wie lange soll ich leben?" „Dreißig Jahre", antwortete Gott, „ist dir das recht?" „Ach Herr", antwortete der Esel, „das ist eine lange Zeit. Erlass mir einen Teil davon!" Da schenkte ihm Gott achtzehn Jahre.

Der Hund erschien. „Wie lange willst du leben?", sprach Gott zu ihm, „dem Esel sind dreißig Jahre zu viel, du aber wirst damit zufrieden sein." Darauf antwortete der Hund: „Herr, ist das dein Wille, denke daran, was ich laufen muss, das halten meine Füße so lange nicht aus."

Dem Menschen gab Gott siebzig Jahre. Die ersten dreißig sind seine menschlichen Jahre. Die vergehen schnell. Darauf folgen die achtzehn Jahre des Esels, das ist eine schwere Zeit. Dann kommen die zwölf Jahre des Hundes, ohne Zähne zum Beißen. Dazu kommen noch die zehn Jahre des Affen, in denen er närrisch ist und ausgelacht wird.

man

Wenn **man** etwas begreift, geht **einem** ein Licht auf.

Man denotes a person or group of people that the speaker doesn't want to or can't define.
Heutzutage kann **man** Licht machen, wann **man** will.
Man lernt viele Dinge. Viele interessieren **einen** aber gar nicht.
Die Grammatik kann **einem** ziemlich auf die Nerven gehen.

man	
Nom.	man
Akk.	einen
Dat.	einem

7 Fill in *man* in the correct form and translate the sentences into English (where you will need "you", "people" or the passive).

1 Kann .... sich auf ihn wirklich verlassen? Macht er auch, was er verspricht?
2 Diese Arbeit ist doch todlangweilig. Wie kann .... so etwas Spaß machen?
3 Jetzt sagst du wieder etwas anderes. Du kannst .... wirklich durcheinander bringen.
4 Wie soll .... das erklären? Das ist ziemlich kompliziert.
5 Sie ist nie pünktlich. Auf sie muss .... immer warten.
6 Ich glaube nie, was er sagt. Er kann .... so leicht täuschen.

Das Verb *werden*

8 When do the days get shorter, when do they get longer?

Ende Juni .... die Tage ....Vom 21. Dezember an .... sie wieder ....
Es .... jeden Morgen ein wenig .... und jeden Abend ein bisschen ....

Es ist dunkel.	Es wird hell(er).	Es ist hell.
Es ist Nacht.	Es wird Tag.	Es ist Tag.

werden + adjective (often in the comparative), *werden* + noun: describes a change.

9 a Describe the change.

1 Die Tage sind kurz. Die Tage .... Die Tage sind lang.
2 Es ist noch Nacht. Bald .... Dann ist es Tag.
3 Wir sind jung. Aber wir .... Irgendwann sind wir alt.
4 Das Kind ist klein. Schnell .... Bald ist es erwachsen.

b Describe other changes you can think of.

10 Fill in the verb forms.

	3. Person Singular (er/sie/es/man)		
Infinitiv	**Präsens**	**Präteritum**	**Perfekt**
werden	....	....	....

11 **a** Complete the sentences with the following expressions in the perfect.

wütend werden ⊘ verrückt werden ⊘ rot werden ⊘ alt werden ⊘ Geschichtslehrer werden ⊘ Bäcker werden ⊘ Vater werden

1 Dein Bruder studiert ja. Ich dachte, er ist Bäcker geworden.
2 Als er sagte, dass er mich liebt, ... ich ganz ...
3 Dein Mann hat immer sehr jung ausgesehen. In der letzten Zeit ... er jedoch ziemlich ...
4 Er fand Geschichte doch immer langweilig. Wieso ... er ...?
5 So ein Kleid kannst du doch nicht anziehen! ... du ...?
6 Warum ... du ...? Ich habe doch nur die Wahrheit gesagt.
7 Er wollte doch nie heiraten und jetzt ... er sogar ...!

b React to the statements in a.

- Dein Bruder studiert ja. Ich dachte, er ist Bäcker geworden.
- Er hat eine Zeit lang in einer Bäckerei gearbeitet, aber es hat ihm nicht gefallen. Jetzt möchte er Chemiker werden.

12 **a** Fill in *werden* in the past.

Tomi Ungerer war neun Jahre alt, als deutsche Truppen 1940 das Elsass besetzten. Deutsch .... die offizielle Sprache, aus den elsässischen Lehrern .... deutsche Lehrer, aus Jean-Thomas, von allen Tomi genannt, ... Hans, der in der Schule in Sütterlinschrift[1] schreiben musste.

[1] → S. 73

Tomi Ungerer, French artist, Cartoonist, * 1931

b What changes have there been in your life? Jot down some notes and talk about them.

Das Verb: Aktiv, Passiv (1)

13 Write down the forms *werden* + past participle from the text "Licht macht Laune".

Line 10: jemand ......wird....................

Line 18: jemand ....

Line 25: etwas .... ans Licht ...., es ....

Aktive: The agent (person, thing or event initiating the action) and the action are important.
Ein Journalist hat die Affäre aufgeklärt.
Sein Buch hat die Wahrheit ans Licht gebracht.

Passive: The focus in on the action. The agent (initiator of the action) is not of primary interest (is less important, known, or cannot or shouldn't be named).
Die Affäre wurde aufgeklärt. Die Wahrheit wurde ans Licht gebracht.

man is an alternative to the passive, especially in speech.
Dass wird mit zwei *s* geschrieben. → *Dass* schreibt man mit zwei *s*.

14 **a** Check the meaning of the following expressions to do with *Christmas*.
Glocken läuten ❀ Adventskalender ❀ Glühwein ❀ Heiligabend ❀ Weihnachten ❀ Weihnachtsgebäck ❀ Advent ❀ Kirche ❀ Christbaum ❀ schmücken

b Read the following newspaper article.

Dorf-Adventskalender in Gallenweiler

Jeden Abend um 18 Uhr wird ein neues Fenster geöffnet

ABEND FÜR ABEND wird in Gallenweiler ein Adventsfenster geöffnet, das von den Hausbewohnern weihnachtlich geschmückt wurde.

HEITERSHEIM-GALLENWEILER (mo). Einen Dorf-Adventskalender öffnen die Bürgerinnen und Bürger in dem kleinen Dorf Gallenweiler jedes Jahr im Dezember. Abend für Abend, Fenster für Fenster.
Nach einem genau festgelegten Plan schmücken 24 Familien aus dem Ort der Reihe nach ein Fenster ihres Hauses. Jeden Abend pünktlich um 18 Uhr wird ein anderes gezeigt und beleuchtet. Dazu läuten die Glocken der Kirche.
Zu dieser täglichen Adventsfreude treffen sich immer zahlreiche Kinder und Erwachsene vor dem Haus mit dem neuen Adventsfenster. Der Hausherr bietet den Besuchern Tee, Punsch oder Glühwein sowie Kuchen und Gebäck an. Man kommt ins Gespräch. Manchmal wird auch ein Gebet gesprochen oder ein Lied gesungen.
Wer einmal sein geschmücktes Fenster „geöffnet" hat, lässt es jeden Abend leuchten. Damit soll für alle Menschen im Dorf ein Zeichen des Lichts auf dem Weg zur Weihnacht gesetzt werden. Eine schöne Art, sich gemeinsam auf Heiligabend zu freuen.

Sabine Model

c Underline the passive forms in the text.

Passive = *werden* + past participle

Present:	Jeden Abend **wird** ein neues Fenster **beleuchtet**.
Past:	Jeden Abend **wurde** ein Fenster **geöffnet**.
Perfect:	Die Fenster **sind** jeden Abend um 18 Uhr **geöffnet worden**.
Infinitive:	Die Fenster müssen/mussten pünktlich um 18 Uhr **beleuchtet werden**.

15 Change the following text. What would you express in the passive?

Ein Lebenslauf

Ein Mensch erblickt das Licht der Welt – er wird geboren.

Er lernt gehen und sprechen – seine Eltern schicken ihn in die Schule.

Er lernt lesen und schreiben – seine Lehrer und Mitschüler bezeichnen ihn als „Leuchte" oder halten ihn für unterbelichtet.

Er täuscht oft andere Menschen – sie führen ihn aber auch oft genug hinters Licht.

Wenn er Glück hat, dann lieben ihn seine Mitmenschen.

So lebt er sein Leben und irgendwann begraben sie ihn.

Vielleicht vergessen sie ihn nicht. Oder haben sie ihn schon vergessen?

16 Read the sentences. How is *werden* used? Enter P (Passiv), F (Futur) or V (Veränderung: change) in the box.

1 Im Sommer wird es schon um 5 Uhr hell. ☐
2 ■ Was ist aus ihrer Diplomarbeit geworden? ☐
▲ Ich werde sie danach fragen, wenn ich sie sehe. ☐
3 Er wird für einen begabten Schauspieler gehalten. ☐
4 Wer wird es uns erklären, wenn wir etwas nicht verstehen? ☐
5 Um wie viel Uhr willst du abgeholt werden? ☐
6 Das Verstehen der Texte wird immer leichter. ☐
7 Das werde ich wohl nie begreifen. ☐
8 Das kann auch anders ausgedrückt werden. ☐

17 What have you always liked doing / What would you like to have done in your life, and what did others do to you? Jot down some ideas, then report.

Mit 13 habe ich am liebsten am Computer gesessen,	leider	wurde ich dreimal pro Woche in einen Sportclub geschickt.
Als Kind wollte ich immer schon Gitarre spielen,	aber	ich bin in die Klavierstunde geschickt worden. Mit 30 habe ich dann endlich Gitarrenunterricht genommen.
Ich wollte/wäre/hätte gern ...,	aber	ich wurde ... / ich bin ... worden.

Zoff oder *Zärtlichkeit*

Cultural information

German has a number of sayings and proverbs about morning.

Morgenstund hat Gold im Mund.
The early bird catches the worm.
(literally: The morning hour has gold in its mouth.)

Früher Vogel fängt den Wurm.
The early bird catches the worm.

schön wie der junge Morgen
as fair as a rose
(literally: as beautiful as the early morning)

Morgenluft wittern
see one's chance
(literally: scent, i.e. smell morning air)

These sayings and proverbs about morning all have a positive tone to them, there are no similar expressions about evening. Anyone who reads this might be forgiven for thinking that only if you do something in the morning are you on the right road and likely to be successful. But this fails to take into account the fact that a lot of people are not at all full of life in the morning, and that it's in fact better to just get out of their way, as the two texts in this unit describe. So you get the sneaking feeling that these sayings were made up to jolly people along and get them off to their day's work bright and early.

It's a fact that farmers, especially in the unfavourable growing conditions of the Alps, had to get up in the middle of the night in the summer to till their fields. Industrialization led to shift work, which was not just a chore, but also led to quite considerable health problems.
A lot of people don't really liven up till the sun goes down and are extremely creative all through the night. There is in fact a very close link between the Protestant work ethic and capitalist industrial society, as the famous German sociologist Max Weber demonstrated at the beginning of the 20th century. At about the same time, Dr. Wilhelm Fliess recognized in his patients' medical history that they followed certain constant rhythms. From these biological rhythms active in a person's bodily functions, intellect and spiritual realm, he developed the theory of biorhythms. They can be used to deduce when a person is in a good or poor state of health. Now in fact a lot of doctors look at a person's biorhythms before fixing the date for an operation, and trainers fix the training sessions of their athletes to coincide with their biorhythm. A lot of companies have recognized the importance of this phenomenon and have introduced flexitime.

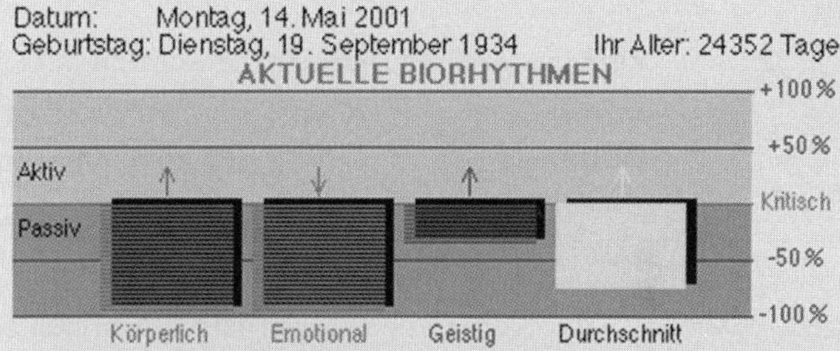

Gestern war ich schlecht gelaunt, und alles ging daneben.
Heute bin ich ganz erstaunt, wie schön ist es zu leben.

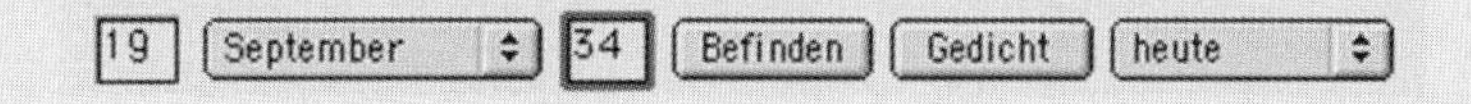

Learning strategies

If you want to find out more about biorhythms, try visiting the website depicted above (www.biochart.com). There you can get your personal rhythm for the day and a poem to go with it. Another way of improving your German day by day.

Zoff am Morgen

1 a Read the words and sort them into two groups.

sprechen

schweigen = nicht sprechen

plappern, *ugs.* = viel und schnell reden, nichts Wichtiges sagen

der Zoff, *ugs.* = der Streit
mit jdm. Zoff haben/bekommen;
es gibt Zoff

der Krach, *ugs.* = der Streit
mit jdm. Krach haben/anfangen/bekommen
Es gibt Krach.

sich unterhalten

der Streit

streiten

reden = sprechen
Sie redet/spricht kein Wort mit mir.
Er redet nur von Autos.

to speak	to quarrel
...	...

b Translate the following verbs and verbal expressions into English.

schlafen ....
müde sein ....
aufwachen/erwachen ....
wach sein ....
munter sein ....
ausgeschlafen sein ....

2 Read the texts and underline the words from section 1.

Zoff am Morgen

„Morgens um sieben bin ich putzmunter, ausgeschlafen und würde mich liebend gern unterhalten."

Ernsthafte Krisen entstehen im Bett – wenn ein fröhlicher Mensch die Augen aufmacht und losplappert. Vergebens versucht der Morgenmuffel[1], die Decke über den Kopf zu ziehen und konsequent zu schweigen. Doch die Morgenblüte[2] an seiner Seite redet unbeeindruckt weiter: Über die Party am Vorabend oder was man wohl der Schwiegermutter zum Geburtstag schenken könnte.

Der Krach am Morgen ist perfekt – allerdings in leisen Tönen. Denn der Morgenmuffel ist zum Lautwerden viel zu müde.

Die Zeit der süßen Rache kommt für ihn am Abend: Er ist wach, der Partner müde. Und der Morgenmuffel fragt sich, wo die allgemeine Entrüstung über den Abendmuffel bleibt.

Elna Utermöhle

Nächtliches Tagebuch

„Er beschloss, sein Leben zu ändern, die Morgenstunden auszunutzen. Er stand um sechs Uhr auf, duschte, rasierte sich, zog sich an, genoss das Frühstück, rauchte ein paar Zigaretten, setzte sich an den Arbeitstisch und erwachte am Mittag."

Ennio Flaiano

[1] Morgenmuffel = someone who is ill-tempered in the morning and doesn't say much
-muffel = someone who doesn't like (doing) something (Krawattenmuffel, Tanzmuffel, Modemuffel, Sportmuffel, ...)

[2] Morgenblüte = the opposite of Morgenmuffel

3 *Die Morgenblüte* and *der Morgenmuffel*: What are they like? What do they do?

Morgenblüte	Morgenmuffel
ist morgens um sieben putzmunter	zieht die Decke über den Kopf

4 What passages in the texts do these statements go with?

A „Wer morgens früher aufsteht, hat auch nicht mehr vom Tag."
B „Wer morgens länger schläft, hält abends länger aus."

5 Standard language – colloquial? Make a list and sort the words into it.

Streit – Krach – Zoff • Maloche – harte Arbeit • dumm – blöd • durchkommen – überleben • sehen/schauen – gucken • pauken – lernen • kriegen – bekommen • beginnen – loslegen • Klar! – Natürlich!/Sicher!

standard	colloquial
	Zoff

Infinitiv mit *zu*

Vergebens **versucht** der Morgenmuffel, die Decke über den Kopf **zu ziehen**.

6 Underline the sentences in the text that have a verb in the infinitive with *zu*.

> **Infinitive with *zu* after verbs**
> z. B.: anfangen/beginnen, aufhören, beschließen, bitten, sich freuen, sich schämen, vergessen, versuchen, versprechen, sich etw. wünschen
> Ich habe vergessen(,) dich an**zu**rufen.
> In separable verbs *zu* is placed between the prefix and the infinitive.
> The comma at the beginning of the infinitive clause is optional.

7 a Complete the sentences with the items given.

1 Ich bitte dich(,) ...
(erzählen – ihm – nichts)

2 Sie freut sich(,) ...
(treffen – ihre alten Freunde – wieder)

3 Er hat vergessen(,) ...
(vorbereiten – den Unterricht)

4 Ich höre sofort auf(,) ...
(denken – an den Infinitiv)

b Complete with your own ideas.

Ich habe beschlossen(,) ... Ich versuche immer(,) ... Ich vergesse oft(,) ...

> **Infinitive with *zu* after adjectives with *sein/finden***
> z. B.: Es ist / Ich finde es schön/gut/wichtig/interessant, ...
> Es ist schön, dich **zu** treffen. Ich finde es wichtig, viele Sprachen **zu** verstehen.
> If the main clause contains *es*, the comma is compulsory.

8 Complete the sentences.

Es ist langweilig, ... Ich finde es gefährlich, ... Ich finde es schwer, ...

Infinitive with *zu* after nouns and verb

e. g.: Zeit haben/finden; Angst haben; es macht mir/dir/... Freude;
es hat keinen/wenig Sinn; es macht (mir/dir/...) Spaß; es ist ein tolles Gefühl

Es macht ihm Freude, mich immer **zu** korrigieren.
Ich habe jetzt keine Zeit(,) auf deine vielen Fragen **zu** antworten.

9 Complete the sentences.

Heute habe ich Zeit(,) ... Es macht (mir) Spaß, ... Du hast keinen Grund(,) ...

Infinitiv mit *zu* statt Nebensatz mit *dass*

Es ist schön / Ich finde es schön, **dass ich dich treffe**.
Es ist schön / Ich finde es schön, **dich zu treffen**.

An infinitive clause with *zu* is often used instead of a sub-clause with *dass*, when the subject in the main clause and sub-clause are identical.

Ich habe beschlossen(,) in Zukunft früher aufzustehen.
(**Ich** habe beschlossen, dass **ich** in Zukunft früher aufstehe.)

but: **Ich** habe beschlossen, dass **wir** in Zukunft morgens gemeinsam schweigen.

10 In which of the sentences can the *dass*-clause be replaced with an infinitive clause with *zu*?

1 Ich freue mich, dass wir in zwei Wochen in Urlaub fahren.
2 Er genießt es, dass er ein paar Tage allein ist.
3 Ich bin es gewohnt, dass ich so früh aufstehen muss.
4 Ich habe dir doch versprochen, dass wir dich vom Hotel abholen.

Infinitiv ohne zu

Die Morgenblüte **möchte sich** liebend gerne schon um sieben Uhr **unterhalten**.

Infinitive without *zu*

- **after modal verbs**
  Der Morgenmuffel kann um sieben Uhr morgens noch nicht reden.
- **after the verbs *hören*, *sehen*, *bleiben*, *gehen*, *fahren*, *kommen*, *lassen*, *helfen***
  Kommst du mit uns einen Kaffee trinken?

11 Complete the sentences with the items given.

arbeiten – sehr gut – am Abend ● besuchen – mich – am Wochenende ●
liegen – den ganzen Tag – im Bett ● einkaufen – ein paar Dinge – für mich

1 Der Morgenmuffel kann ...
2 Gehst du bitte ...
3 Ich bleibe heute ...
4 Meine Freundin kommt ...

Versuche mit Liebe

12 Read the text and look for the German equivalents of the following words/expressions.

feelings	....	enjoy sth.	....
caresses	....	sth. annoys me	....
dissembling	....	sth. is unbearable	....
think oneself lucky	....	bear sth.	....

Ich will es nicht anders und schätze mich glücklich, allein zu wohnen, meines Erachtens[1] der einzig mögliche Zustand[2] für Männer, ich genieße es, allein zu erwachen, kein Wort sprechen zu müssen. Wo ist die Frau, die das begreift? Schon die Frage, wie ich geschlafen habe, verdrießt mich, weil ich in Gedanken schon weiter bin, gewohnt voraus zu denken, nicht rückwärts zu denken, sondern zu planen. Zärtlichkeiten am Abend, ja, aber Zärtlichkeiten am Morgen sind mir unerträglich und mehr als drei oder vier Tage zusammen mit einer Frau war für mich, offen gestanden, stets der Anfang der Heuchelei, Gefühle am Morgen, das erträgt kein Mann. Dann lieber Geschirr waschen!

Max Frisch

[1] meines Erachtens: in my opinion

[2] der Zustand, Zustände: state

13 Note down.

Was gefällt ihm?	**Was gefällt ihm nicht?**

14 Write about yourself on the topic of "Am Morgen" or "Am Abend"

a First note down time expressions from the text, and add others you know.

... / morgens ... / abends vor dem Frühstück ...

b Select some of the following beginnings of sentences and complete them, also with time expressions from a.

Ich schätze mich glücklich(,) ... Ich genieße es, ... Ich bin (es) gewohnt, ... Ich ertrage kein(e) ... / Ich ertrage es nicht, wenn ... Es ärgert mich, wenn ... Es ist für mich unerträglich, ...

Ich bin es gewohnt, morgens im Bett eine Tasse Kaffee zu trinken.
Vor dem Frühstück ertrage ich es nicht, wenn ...

c Now write a short, continuous text with the sentences from b.

Indirekte Frage

	Direct question	**Indirect question**
Wh-question	**Wo bleibt** die allgemeine Entrüstung über den Abendmuffel?	Der Morgenmuffel fragt sich, **wo** die allgemeine Entrüstung über den Abendmuffel **bleibt**.
yes/no-question	**Hast** du gut **geschlafen**?	Ich möchte morgens nicht gefragt werden, **ob** ich gut **geschlafen habe**.

An indirect question is possible after verbs or verbal expressions like: (sich) fragen, sagen, erzählen, wissen, verstehen, sehen, hören, es ist nicht klar, es ist nicht sicher.

15 Form indirect questions from the direct ones.

1 Warum haben viele Menschen morgens gute Laune? Ein Morgenmuffel versteht nicht, ...
2 Soll ich aufstehen oder liegen bleiben? Er fragt sich, ...
3 Soll ich mein Leben ändern? Ich weiß nicht, ...
4 Was hast du gesagt? Ich habe nicht gehört, ...
5 Wen soll ich einladen? Kannst du mir sagen, ...
6 Ist das ein *n* oder ein *m*? Ich kann nicht sehen, ...

Fragewörter (Übersicht)

■ Guck mal, ein Morgenmuffel!
▲ Welchen von den beiden meinst du?
■ Na den, der so schlecht gelaunt aussieht. Was für ein Typ bist du eigentlich?

16 Sort the question words into the table.

Was? ⊘ Wer? ⊘ Wann? ⊘ Wie lange? ⊘ Wem? ⊘ Wen? ⊘ Wohin? ⊘ Wo? ⊘ Welches? – Welche? ⊘ Welchem? – Welchem? – Welcher? ⊘ Welchen? – Welches? – Welche? ⊘ Wie? ⊘ Woher? ⊘ Warum? ⊘ Worüber? – Womit? – Wovon? ⊘ Wie viel/viele?

Person	Sache	Was für ein ...? Welch- ...? Person oder Sache			
.... (Nom)	.... (Nom/Akk)	**m**	**n**	**f**	
.... (Akk)	wo(r) + Präp.	Was für ein ...? *	Was für ein ...? *	Was für eine ...? *	(Nom)
.... (Dat)	....	Welcher ...? **	....	....	
Wessen ...?	....	Was für einen ...?	Was für ein ...?	Was für eine ...?	(Akk)
(Gen)	....	....	....	....	
		Was für einem ...?	Was für einem ...?	Was für einer ...?	(Dat)
		....	....	....	

* Plural Nom., Akk., Dat.: Was für ...?
without a noun: Was für einer? Was für eins? Was für eine?; Plural: Was für welche?

** Plural Nom., Akk.: Welche ...?; Dat.: Welchen ...?; without a noun: the same forms

Zeit	Grund	Zweck	Art/Weise	Quantität	Ort (Position, Richtung)
....	....	Wozu?	....	....	....
....		Wofür?			....
					....

17 Listen and ask.

a Sometimes you don't understand everything and have to ask and check.
■ Christian und ich haben gestern noch lange über den Film diskutiert. ▲ Worüber habt ihr diskutiert?

b Sometimes you have to ask because you want to know the exact details.
■ Ich brauche unbedingt 10.000 Euro. ▲ Wozu brauchst du denn so viel Geld?

18 a What questions annoy you?
Die Frage, ..., ärgert mich.

b What questions wouldn't you answer?
Auf die Frage, ..., würde ich nicht antworten.

Former German Finance Minister at Carnival

Cultural information

The Germans have the reputation of having little or no sense of humour. It's true in fact that German theatre literature includes few comedies, and that in business and employment a sense of humour is considered relatively unimportant; work, after all, is something deadly serious, not to be laughed about, like religion. And statistics suggest humour is having a harder and harder time of it: according to the 5.12.1997 edition of the Süddeutsche Zeitung, people in 1956 laughed an average of 16 minutes a day, but now it's only 8 minutes.

Foreign business people have a good opinion of their German partners, but it's often not much fun negotiating with them because everything that is not relevant to the conversation is excluded. That includes certain rituals of conversation that Germans just don't participate in. Often they just get straight down to business and go straight to the point, giving their trading partners, the people they're talking to, quite a shock. But things are changing. In seminars German business people now learn that a light word or humorous remark can ease negotiations forward in the global market, where everyone has to adapt to survive and where humour is a matter of course.

But if you look elsewhere in other spheres of life, there's humour to be found in all the German-speaking countries. People laugh a lot more than is generally believed, and not only where laughter is spurred on by alcohol.

Strangely enough, humour has a different style in the three German-speaking countries. German wit often takes the form of satire and also earthy jokes, Austrian humour often has a touch of the macabre, while the Swiss favour self-irony.

In all three countries there is political cabaret (das Kabarett), not as elsewhere in colourful revue style, but mostly produced in small theatres where satirical scenes from society and politics are put on stage with lots of pep. Once a year the "Orden wider den tierischen Ernst" (award against dead seriousness) is awarded, usually to a politician. And in fact there are quite a number of politicians who are snappy and good at making witty remarks. At the end of the 1990s Regine Hildebrandt's sense of humour made her one of the most popular politicians in Germany, despite the fact that her political status in comparison to others was relatively low.

Manager sollen wieder das Lachen lernen

1 **a** Analyse the title. What could the text be about? Take notes in English.
b Read lines 1–4. Who should do more for his soul?

2 Check the meaning of these words about the state of the soul.

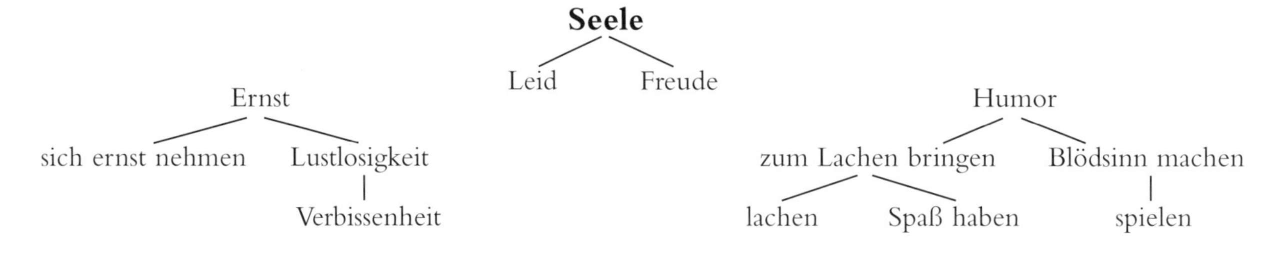

3 Read the text and underline the terms in section 2.

Manager sollen wieder das Lachen lernen

Wer den ganzen Tag im Büro sitzt, sollte nicht nur etwas für seinen Körper tun, sondern auch etwas für die Seele. Firmenberater C.W. Metcalf aus Fort Collins (US-Bundesstaat Colorado) veranstaltet „Humaerobics"-Seminare: Er zeigt Managern, wie sie ihren Humor trainieren.

Der Komiker Karl Valentin

Humor hilft im Kampf gegen Verbissenheit und Lustlosigkeit. Wer viel lacht, sei motiviert und kreativ, so Metcalf. „Uns wird eingeredet, Lachen, Spaß und Spielen seien unerwachsen, unintelligent und unprofessionell", sagt der ehemalige Lehrer und Schauspieler. Nichts sei weiter von der Wahrheit entfernt. Viel habe er von krebskranken Kindern gelernt, die trotz ihres Leids Blödsinn machen. Ein Mädchen klebte sich, bevor sie zur Operation gerollt wurde, einen Zettel auf den Bauch: „Lieber Doktor, wenn Sie meinen Tumor rausnehmen, entfernen Sie mir auch den Leberfleck im Gesicht – ich will Schauspielerin werden!"

Ein tibetanischer Mönch habe ihm einmal eine Übung erklärt, so Metcalf, mit der man lernen könne, sich selbst nicht ernst zu nehmen und die Absurdität des Lebens zu akzeptieren: Man stelle sich nackt vor einen Spiegel, breitbeinig, Hände in den Hüften, und lache über sich.

Andere Übungen:

- Lassen Sie mal einen Freudenschrei heraus.
- Machen Sie Fotos von sich und Kollegen beim Grimassenschneiden[1] und hängen Sie diese auf.
- Machen Sie alberne Geräusche.
- Erstellen Sie eine Liste von komischen Erinnerungen, die Sie zum Lachen bringen.

aus: *Die Welt*

[1] das Grimassenschneiden: pulling faces

4 What does C.W. Metcalf think managers should do? What tips does he give them? Note down your answers.

5 Which of the four definitions fit the concept of humour that the author of the text means?

Hu•mor

[hu'mo:ɐ] *der*, -s; nur Sg;

1 *die Fähigkeit, unangenehme Dinge heiter und gelassen zu ertragen*: jemand hat viel, wenig, keinen Humor; etwas mit Humor ertragen/nehmen. Auch in den schwierigsten Situationen behält er seinen Humor.

2 *die Fähigkeit, selbst Witze zu machen u. zu lachen, wenn andere Witze über einen machen*: (keinen) Sinn für Humor haben

3 *die gute Laune*: Der ewige Regen kann einem wirklich den Humor/ die Laune verderben!

4 *die Fähigkeit haben, kurze, sehr passende (oft ironische od. sarkastische) Bemerkungen zu machen*: einen trockenen Humor haben

1–3 **hu•mor•los** *Adj*; **Hu•mor•lo•sig•keit** *die*; **hu•mor•voll** *Adj*.

6 Which definitions go with which statements?

1 Michaela hat immer gute Laune und versteht auch Spaß.
2 Jürgen ist ein sehr lustiger Mensch. Er lacht viel.
3 Großmutter kann über sich selbst lachen. Sie erträgt auch schwierige Dinge mit Humor.
4 Dieser Politiker ist sehr witzig und humorvoll.
5 Sei doch nicht so ernst, nimm's mit Humor.

Redewiedergabe: indirekte Rede (2)

7 Fill in verb forms from the text.

1 Humor .... im Kampf gegen Verbissenheit und Lustlosigkeit. Wer viel lacht, ... motiviert und kreativ, so Metcalf.

2 Uns wird eingeredet, Lachen, Spaß und Spielen .... unerwachsen.

3 Der ehemalige Lehrer sagt, nichts .... weiter von der Wahrheit entfernt.

4 Viel .... er von krebskranken Kindern gelernt, die trotz ihres Leids Blödsinn machen.

5 Ein tibetanischer Mönch .... ihm einmal eine Übung erklärt, so Metcalf, mit der man lernen ...., sich selbst nicht ernst zu nehmen.

Indirect speech is mainly in the 3rd person singular and plural of the indicative and subjunctive.

Indirekte Rede: Konjunktiv I, Konjunktiv II

Gegenwart

Er sagte, man **habe** Angst zu lachen.
die meisten Menschen **hätten** zu wenig Humor.
man **lache** zu wenig.
die Menschen **würden** zu wenig **lachen**.

If the subjunctive I is identical with the indicative, subjunctive II is used in indirect speech. In speech *würd-* + infinitive is mainly used, except with *haben, sein* and modal verbs.

Singular		**Plural**		
er/sie/es/man	sei	sie	seien	
	habe		~~haben~~	hätten
	werde		~~werden~~	würden
	könne		~~können~~	könnten
	lache		~~lachen~~	lachten, würden lachen
	fahre		~~fahren~~	führen, würden fahren

Vergangenheit

8 Change the sentences into direct speech.

Metcalf sagt, er **habe** viel von krebskranken Kindern **gelernt**.

Die Freunde sagten, er **sei** unerwachsen und unprofessionell **gewesen**.

Er sagte, sie **hätten** trotz ihres Leids dabei viel **gelacht**.

Sie sagten, sie **seien** damals sehr kreativ und motiviert **gewesen**.

In indirect speech, the past is formed with *habe/sei* + past participle for the singular, and *hätten/seien* + past participle for the plural.

Intonation: Pausen

9 Listen and read. Mark the pauses /.

1 Metcalf sagt, ein tibetanischer Mönch habe ihm einmal eine Übung erklärt.
2 Metcalf, sagt ein tibetanischer Mönch, habe ihm einmal eine Übung erklärt.

Who explained the exercise in the first sentence, and who in the second?

10 a Listen and put in commas where the speaker makes a pause.

1 **a** Marion sagte Melanie kommt nicht mit. **b** Marion sagte Melanie kommt nicht mit.
2 **a** Warum schreibst du nicht mal Michael? **b** Warum schreibst du nicht mal Michael?
3 **a** Gehst du mit Hanna? **b** Gehst du mit Hanna?

4 Vor der Tür stand Otto auf dem Kopf einen schwarzen Hut in der Hand eine rote Rose im Mund eine Zigarette hinter dem Ohr ...

b Put the commas in sentence 4 in another place.

c Read the sentences in a out loud.

11 **a** Listen and read. Mark the pauses / .

Heute, meine Damen und Herren, lernen wir das Leben und die Arbeit von ihrer lustigen Seite zu nehmen. Was können wir alles tun?

Stellen Sie sich vor einen Spiegel, breitbeinig, Hände in den Hüften, und lachen Sie über sich. Lassen Sie auch ab und zu mal einen Freudenschrei heraus oder machen Sie alberne Geräusche. Machen Sie Fotos von sich und Kollegen beim Grimassenschneiden und hängen Sie diese auf. Erstellen Sie eine Liste von komischen Erinnerungen, die Sie zum Lachen bringen.

Wenn Sie nur zweimal die Woche solche Übungen machen, wird sich das Leben bald von seiner guten Seite zeigen.

b Listen again and mark the main stresses.
c Take ten minutes and learn the text by heart.
d Speak the text without looking in your book.

12 You are preparing a seminar for colleagues, sales personnel, teachers, ... What should the participants do? Formulate some sentences and speak them out loud, as in a lecture.

Redewiedergabe: Redeeinleitung

Er sagt: „Man lacht heute zu wenig."	**Er sagt**, man lacht/lache heute zu wenig. **Er sagt**, dass man heute zu wenig lacht/lache.
„Man lacht heute zu wenig", **sagt er**.	Man lacht/lache heute zu wenig, **meint er**.
„Man lacht", **so Metcalf**, „heute zu wenig."	Früher, **meinte er**, hat/habe man viel mehr gelacht.

The reporting verb can be before, after or in the middle of the reported speech. In direct speech the statement is placed between inverted commas („...").

13 Change the following text into direct speech. Remember that you also have to change personal and possessive pronouns.

„Ich bin unschuldig. Ich habe ..."

Karl Wildinger erklärte, er sei unschuldig. Er habe die Uhr nicht gestohlen. Vom Richter gefragt, wie sie denn in seine Tasche gekommen sei, meinte er, jemand habe sie ihm wohl in die Tasche getan, als er durch das Kaufhaus gegangen sei. Er sei kein Uhrendieb. Der Richter wisse doch, dass er bereits eine Uhr besitze und keine zweite brauche. Was er dann in dem Kaufhaus gemacht habe, fragte der Richter, wo er doch kein Geld in der Tasche gehabt habe und ein Einkauf unmöglich gewesen sei. Das, sagte Karl Wildinger, habe ihm wohl ein anderer gestohlen. So einen Unsinn habe er schon lange nicht mehr gehört, meinte der Richter.

Sätze/Satzteile verbinden: *nicht nur ... sondern auch*

Wer den ganzen Tag im Büro sitzt, sollte **nicht nur** etwas für seinen Körper tun, **sondern auch** etwas für die Seele.

14 Form sentences with *nicht nur ... sondern auch.*

1 Karl Scholl – ein sehr guter Schauspieler – ein guter Mensch
Karl Scholl ist nicht nur ein sehr guter Schauspieler, sondern auch ein guter Mensch.

2 Marina – viel lachen – andere zum Lachen bringen
3 Metcalf – Firmen beraten – Seminare veranstalten
4 Helmut – intelligent – gut aussehend
5 Der Taxifahrer – arbeitet von Montag bis Freitag – am Wochenende
6 das Hotel – schmutzig – teuer

Sätze/Satzteile verbinden: *sondern, aber*

C.W. Metcalf ist kein Kabarettist, **sondern** Firmenberater.

Lachen und Spaß bei der Arbeit sind nicht unprofessionell, **sondern** machen kreativ.

Die Arbeit ist nicht schwer, **aber** gefährlich.

Die Arbeit ist nicht schwer, **sondern** leicht.

Sondern tends to introduce a contrast to a preceding statement, *aber* an alternative or an addition.
Sondern is only used after a negative statement.

15 Link the sentences with *aber* or *sondern.*

Man soll das Leben nicht so ernst nehmen, sondern auch mal verrückte Sachen machen.

1 Man soll das Leben nicht so ernst nehmen, ... einen Dialekt, der dem Deutschen nur ähnelt.
2 Er lacht oft über andere, ... er hat nicht nach ihrer Adresse gefragt.
3 Er sagt, er spricht nicht Deutsch, ... sie gibt seinem Leben einen Sinn.
4 Die Arbeit beim THW ist schwer, ... er hat es nicht gern, wenn Witze über ihn gemacht werden.
5 Die Senioren sitzen nicht passiv zu Hause, ... auch mal verrückte Sachen machen.
6 Er wollte sie am nächsten Tag abholen, ... sie unterstützen Greenpeace in seinen Aktionen.

16 Look at the cartoon and read the texts that go with each picture.
What sort of person is it about? Try and characterize him.

Nein,

KAMAGURKA

Lachen

17 What do these expressions to do with laughter and laughing mean?
Which expressions go with 1–5? Match them and translate the expressions into English.

Das ist ja lächerlich! ☐

Da gibt's nichts zu lachen. ☐

Wer zuletzt lacht, lacht am besten. ☐

Dass ich nicht lache! ☐

Lachen ist die beste Medizin. ☐

1 Lachen ist gesund.
2 Das ist eine sehr ernste Sache.
3 Das ist unmöglich. / Das glaube ich nicht.
4 Man soll sich nie zu früh freuen.
5 Das ist unsinnig. / Das kann man nicht ernst nehmen.

18 Complete the sentences with expressions from section 16.

1 Er hat gesagt, er kommt heute pünktlich um acht Uhr.

....

Er kommt doch immer zu spät.

2 Gut, ich habe das Spiel verloren. Aber beim nächsten Mal verlierst du.

....

3 Obwohl es so schwer krank ist, lacht dieses Kind den ganzen Tag.

....

4 Was? Sie meinen, ich hätte eine Uhr gestohlen? ....

.... Ich habe doch eine.

5 Das Leben ist kein Witz.

....

Samstag nacht in Deutschland

Cultural information

The first 30 years after the Second World War were characterized by an almost unbelievable continuity and stability in West German society. The average citizen just wanted to forget or make forgotten what happened before and during the war. The media also played their part in creating this "intact world" from which the recent past was excluded. Both public broadcasting channels made a point of focussing predominantly on harmless entertainment. For decades they kept to the pattern they had established. Neither the content nor the people changed. In many families the unchanging structure of the programming gave rise to matching rituals. So, for example, water consumption was regularly at its peak every Saturday about 10 pm, because this was the time when the first part of the evening's entertainment finished with the drawing of the lottery numbers and people used the break to go to the bathroom or the toilet. The article from the popular illustrated weekly "Stern" presents an average West German family in the 1970s that followed these customs like millions of other Germans. The critical text illustrates the typical German characteristics linked to this kind of life, such as diligence, tidiness, cleanliness and punctuality.

Language

German follows certain rules that make it possible to form long, complex sentences such as are to be found in many German texts.

1st rule:
The verb is always second in a main clause.
Ihr Mann wartet vor dem Büro.

2nd rule:
The information that has the focus and which is new is at the end.
Ihr Mann wartet vor dem Büro. (Wo?)
Vor dem Büro wartet ihr Mann. (Wer?)

So changes in the sequencing of clauses and clause elements have different effects. Dividing the sentence up into three areas sheds some light on the different word order possibilities: initial position (das Vorfeld), central part (das Mittelfeld) end-position (das Nachfeld).

Position 1	Satzklammer			
Jeden Morgen	ging	sie schnell an mir	vorbei,	ohne zu grüßen.
Vorfeld	**Mittelfeld**			**Nachfeld**

Initial position is the beginning of the sentence, the verb with its ending is in position 2 and opens the central part. With compound verb forms (e.g. perfect, modal verb + infinitive, separable verbs) the second part of the verb closes the central part (verbal bracket).
In this unit you'll have a chance to familiarize yourself a bit with the initial position, and find out what sentence elements can be placed there and with what effect. The central part is the topic of Unit 40, the end-position is dealt with in Unit 43.

Samstagnacht in Deutschland

1 a Describe the cartoon.

Welche Gegenstände gibt es in dem Bild?
Wie viele Personen sehen wir?
Was erfahren wir über die Personen, die wir nicht sehen?
Warum sind sie nicht da?

b Find a title for the cartoon.

Zeichnung: Ernst Hürlimann

2 Read the text on page 209. What section does each of the following statements belong to?

1. Für die meisten Leute beginnt der normale Arbeitstag um sechs Uhr morgens. ☐
2. Das Haus steht in einem Vorort von München. ☐
3. Wenn die Familie fernsieht, hat jede Person ihren Platz. ☐
4. In dem Haus wohnen Menschen jeden Alters. ☐
5. Herr Hellwig sieht sich jeden Samstag mit einem Freund Fußballspiele im Fernsehen an. ☐

3 Make a list of all compounds in the text. What word classes are the component parts?
Note down the meaning in English.

Verb + Nomen	Nomen + Nomen	Adjektiv + Nomen	Englisch
Gehminuten			minutes on foot
	Samstagabend		Saturday evening

4 What is the difference between the Hellwig family's flat and the one in the cartoon, how is the situation different? Note down the differences and talk about them.

Samstagnacht in Deutschland

A Das Haus: Es steht achtzehn S-Bahn- und einige Gehminuten vom Münchener Zentrum entfernt im Vorort Unterhaching, ist neun Jahre alt und sechs Stockwerke hoch. Die 52 modernen Wohnungen mit ein bis vier Zimmern kosten monatlich zwischen 330 und 900 Mark[1] Miete, Heizungskosten inbegriffen. Den betonierten Parkplatz über der Tiefgarage dürfen die Kinder der Anwohner zum Rad- und Rollschuhfahren benutzen, bis die von der Arbeit kommenden Väter ihre Autos darauf parken.

B Die Mieter: Die älteste Hausbewohnerin ist 90 Jahre, die jüngste 17 Monate alt. Die meisten Familien haben ein mittleres Einkommen (um 2500 Mark netto) und mittleres Alter, ein bis zwei Kinder sind die Norm. Einige halten sich einen Kanarienvogel, manche eine Katze. Im Lift grüßt man sich, zwischen einigen Mietern bestehen freundschaftliche Kontakte. Welche von den jüngeren Paaren verheiratet sind, fragt man nicht. Garantie für einen guten Namen sind eine immer saubere Wohnung und genügend Vorhänge vor den Fenstern.

C Der Samstagabend: Wie überall ist er auch in Unterhaching bestimmt vom Ablauf der Arbeitswoche, die für die meisten hier um sechs Uhr früh beginnt. „Den Samstag", so sagen die meisten,„lassen wir faul zu Ende gehen." In der Regel verbringt die Familie den Abend vor dem Fernsehapparat, der gegenüber der Couchgarnitur steht.

[1] entspricht 160 bzw. 450 Euro

D Klaus Hellwig, 37, und seine Frau Manuela, 32, wohnen mit ihren Söhnen Harald und Martin seit neun Jahren hier. Ein Umzug innerhalb des Hauses von einer Drei- in eine Vierzimmerwohnung im letzten Sommer hat am Ritual ihres Samstagabends nichts verändert, machte aber eine neue Sitzordnung nötig. Bei Hellwigs wie auch bei den anderen Familien im Haus hat jeder seinen Stammplatz. Der Vater hat den Sessel mit direktem Blick zum Fernseher. Die Mutter sitzt auf der Couch, weil sie dann besser einschlafen kann, und die Kinder verteilen sich auf die übrigen Sitzmöglichkeiten oder liegen auf dem Boden. Ist der Vater außer Haus, nimmt die Mutter seinen Platz ein und die Kinder den ihren. Ist auch die Mutter außer Haus, bestimmt das Alter die hierarchische Sitzordnung der Kinder.

E Klaus Hellwig, der eine Firma für Altbausanierung betreibt, beginnt seinen Samstagabend um 18 Uhr. Da trifft er sich mit seinem Freund und Nachbarn Paul Wittwer mal im eigenen, mal in dessen Wohnzimmer zum gemeinsamen Anschauen der Sportschau. Bei Bier aus Gläsern, die mit „Paul" und „Klaus" beschriftet sind, schreien die beiden um die Wette, wenn ein Tor fällt. Zum anschließenden Hellwigschen Farb-TV-Samstag gehören außerdem die Aufschnittplatte, eine Literflasche nicht zu sauren Weins, Knabbernüsse. Der Vater sitzt im Morgenmantel da und die Kinder dürfen bis zu den Lottozahlen aufbleiben. Die Pause zwischen den Lottozahlen und dem Spätkrimi nutzt Manuela Hellwig für die Vorbereitungen auf die Nacht: zum Abschminken, Zähneputzen, Bettfertigmachen.

nach: *Stern*

Sätze/Satzteile verbinden: *Wenn*-Satz ohne *wenn*

Ist der Vater außer Haus, nimmt die Mutter seinen Platz ein.
oder

Wenn der Vater außer Haus ist, nimmt die Mutter seinen Platz ein.
Die Mutter nimmt seinen Platz ein, **wenn der Vater außer Haus ist**.

Sub-clauses with *wenn* can appear without *wenn* and are then placed before the main clause. A sentence like this starts with the verb, followed by the clause subject.

5 Transform into sentences without *wenn*.

1 Die beiden schreien um die Wette, wenn ein Tor fällt.
Fällt ein Tor, schreien die beiden um die Wette.
2 Die Miete ist höher, wenn die Heizungskosten inbegriffen sind.
3 Die Kinder können auf dem Parkplatz spielen, wenn die Väter in der Arbeit sind.
4 Wenn die Mutter auf der Couch sitzt, kann sie besser einschlafen.
5 Die Kinder dürfen den Parkplatz nicht mehr benutzen, wenn ein Auto darauf parken will.

Nomengruppen

Nomengruppe als Subjekt

Die		**Wohnungen**		kosten monatlich ...
Die	**52**	**Wohnungen**		kosten monatlich ...
Die	**52 modernen**	**Wohnungen**	**mit ein bis vier Zimmern**	kosten monatlich ...
Die	**52 modernen**	**Wohnungen,**	**die ein bis vier Zimmer haben,**	kosten monatlich ...
Article	Attribute	Noun	Attribute	Verb

left of the noun: modernen (adjective as attribute), 52 (number as attribute)
right of the noun: mit ein bis vier Zimmern (preposition + noun as attribute)
die ein bis vier Zimmer haben (relative clause as attribute)

Nomengruppe als Ergänzung

Die Kinder	benutzen	**den**	**betonierten**	**Parkplatz**	**über der Tiefgarage ...**
	Verb	Article	Attribute	Noun	Attribute

The subject or object often have an attribute (Attribut) as well as a noun. They are placed to the left and/or right of the noun and describe it more closely. The whole is called a *Nomengruppe* (noun group, i.e. phrase). The noun (with its article) is the head of the noun phrase.

6 Underline the nouns in the noun phrases (their head).

1 ... den betonierten Parkplatz über der Tiefgarage ...
2 ... die von der Arbeit kommenden Väter ...
3 Garantie für einen guten Namen ...
4 ... eine immer saubere Wohnung und Vorhänge vor den Fenstern.
5 ... vor dem Fernsehapparat, der gegenüber der Couchgarnitur steht.
6 ... den Sessel mit direktem Blick zum Fernseher ...

7 Make a table and enter the noun phrases from section 6. Decide what the attributes to the left and right of the head consist of (adjective, present and past participle used as an adjective, preposition + noun).

attribute left of the noun	head (noun as subject or object)	attribute right of the noun
den betonierten (past. part.)	Parkplatz	über der Tiefgarage (prep. + noun)
die von der Arbeit kommenden (pres. part.)	Väter	

8 Form noun phrases.

1 Kunkel (weit gereist - mit seinen Bekannten und Verwandten)

der weit gereiste Kunkel
der weit gereiste Kunkel mit seinen Bekannten und Verwandten

2 die Balkons (viel – bunt – an den Häusern)
3 der Brief (schön – lang – von dir)
4 das Buch (sehr interessant – über Griechenland)
5 die Frau (allein lebend – aus unserem Haus)
6 der Herr Hellwig (auf dem Stuhl – eingeschlafen)
7 der Vorort (10 Gehminuten entfernt – vom Zentrum)

9 a Underline the noun phrases in section E of the text.
b Write down whether they are Subjekte (S) or Ergänzungen (E).

Architektur von Sätzen: Vorfeld

10 a Note down in which sentences in the following table the subject is not in position 1.
b What is in initial position (position 1) in each case? Subject, accusative object, time phrase, sub-clause, a comparison? Note it down in the fourth column.

	Vorfeld 1	Verb 2		Was steht im Vorfeld?
1	Die 52 modernen Wohnungen mit ein bis vier Zimmern	kosten	monatlich zwischen 330 und 900 Mark Miete.	subject
2	Die älteste Hausbewohnerin	ist	90 Jahre alt.	....
3	Welche von den jüngeren Paaren verheiratet sind,	fragt	man nicht.	....
4	Den betonierten Parkplatz über der Tiefgarage	dürfen	die Kinder zum Radfahren benutzen.	....
5	Klaus Hellwig, der eine Firma für Altbausanierung betreibt,	beginnt	seinen Samstagabend um 18 Uhr.	....
6	Da	trifft	er sich mit seinem Freund und Nachbarn Paul Wittwer.	....
7	Wie überall	ist	der Samstagabend auch in Unterhaching bestimmt vom Ablauf der Arbeitswoche.	comparison

The following can be placed in initial position: the subject, an object (e.g. accusative object, place adverbial), an expression of time, a subordinate clause or a comparison.
This is done to achieve:

- more variation: if the subject is always in position 1, the text gets monotonous.
- emphasis of sentence elements, e.g. Im Lift grüßt man sich.
- link to the preceding sentence, e.g. ... beginnt seinen Samstagabend um 18 Uhr. Da trifft er sich mit ...
- avoidance of too many objects after the verb, e.g. Die Pause nutzt M. Hellwig für die Vorbereitungen.

11 a Read the following text and check the meaning of the words.

in Rente gehen • Künstlerin • Fest • U-Bahn • Erdgeschoss • Treppe • Treppenhaus

b Divide the sentence up into its individual elements.

Die Wohnung des früh in Rente gegangenen Herrn Eichelstiel / liegt / fast im Zentrum von München, / in der Parkstraße 29.

c In this text, the subject is in initial position in all the sentences. Take some of the sentences and put another element in position 1.

Herr Eichelstiel muss von dort nur wenige ... Von dort muss Herr Eichelstiel nur wenige ...

Die Wohnung des früh in Rente gegangenen Herrn Eichelstiel liegt fast im Zentrum von München, in der Parkstraße 29. Herr Eichelstiel muss von dort nur wenige Minuten zur U-Bahn und zu den Bussen 62 und 66 und zum Oktoberfest gehen. Er geht meist nur im September auf das Oktoberfest, um ein oder zwei Glas Bier zu trinken. Das Haus in der Parkstraße 29 hat 6 renovierte Wohnungen mit zwei bis vier Zimmern. Frau Doris Kunz, eine allein stehende Künstlerin, wohnt im Erdgeschoss, der Rentner Eichelstiel im ersten Stock und die 1914 im Haus Parkstraße 29 geborene Frau Leimsieder im dritten Stock. Niemand weiß, wer die anderen Mieter sind. Man hört sie nur, wenn sie am Morgen die Treppe herunterkommen. Der Rentner Ludwig Eichelstiel fragt sie, wenn er sie im Treppenhaus trifft, wie es ihnen geht. Er bekommt darauf immer die gleiche Antwort: „Danke, gut." Aber Herr Eichelstiel weiß nicht, wer diese Mieter sind.

12 Write an e-mail to a German friend saying how you usually spend your Saturday evening.

zu Hause bleiben • vor dem Fernseher/Computer sitzen • Briefmarken sortieren • Zeitung/Bücher lesen • Briefe schreiben • ein Bad nehmen • sich mit ... unterhalten • kochen • faulenzen • telefonieren • Musik hören/machen • ausgehen • Freunde treffen • ins Kino/Theater/Konzert/in die Diskothek/in eine Bar gehen • spazieren gehen • einen Stadtbummel machen • schwimmen gehen • Billard spielen • tanzen gehen • ...

Here are the beginning and the end of the e-mail.

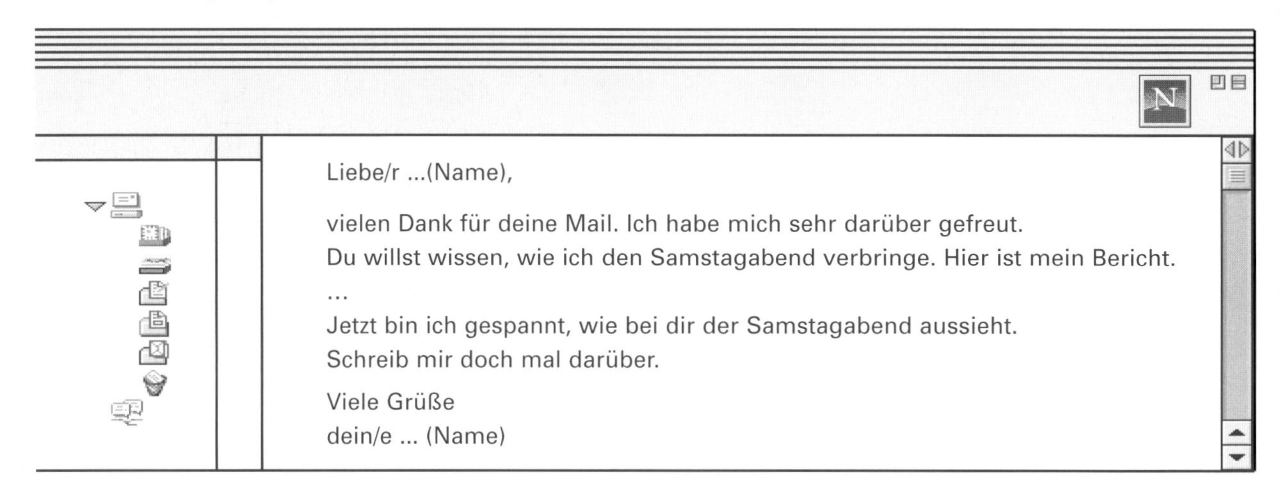

Liebe/r ...(Name),

vielen Dank für deine Mail. Ich habe mich sehr darüber gefreut.
Du willst wissen, wie ich den Samstagabend verbringe. Hier ist mein Bericht.
...
Jetzt bin ich gespannt, wie bei dir der Samstagabend aussieht.
Schreib mir doch mal darüber.

Viele Grüße
dein/e ... (Name)

Was macht die **Liebe** ?

Text

The interview with Irmgard and Herbert, an elderly couple, has two aspects to it: the fact that they got to know each other at the end of the Second World War, and the fact that their marriage has lasted a long time; the couple speak about their conflicts and their love.

The beginning of the story reminds us of the war and what it meant for many Germans and Austrians. The Russian winter forced Hitler's army into retreat, as it had done with Napoleon's. Appeals were made to the population to support the starving, freezing soldiers on the eastern front (Ostfront) with so-called *Liebesgabepakete* (loving gift parcels) and the winter relief organization. In vain. The retreat (der Rückzug) with many casualties was unavoidable. The war instigated by Hitler and his cohorts was lost.

Worldwide 60 million people lost their lives in the war, 20 million lost their homes and were made refugees. What the Germans had done to other nations, they now had to suffer in part themselves. The following figures are provided by *WASt* in Berlin (Wehrmachtsauskunftsstelle für Kriegerverluste und Kriegsgefangene – Wehrmacht information office for war losses and prisoners of war) for Germany and Austria, which had united with Germany in the war: 3,100,000 soldiers and 3,075,000 civilians lost their lives. 1,200,000 were registered as missing. These figures include the 300,000 Germans who were victims of racial, political and religious persecution and killed by the Nazis. Most of the German population of areas that are now Russian, Polish and Czech were forced to leave, so that many soldiers returning from the war found that they had lost both their possessions and their families. The search organizations of the Red Cross had more than enough to do for 30 years after the end of the war.

The old Germany was broken up. East Prussia and Silesia were ceded to the Soviet Union and Poland. Austria again became an independent republic. The rest of Germany was divided into two separate states opposing each other as enemies during the forty years of the Cold War.

Language

The text "Was macht die Liebe?" is an interview in which the interviewer just asks brief questions and the two interviewees answer in conversation. The conversation contains many deictic reference forms which help to avoid repetition, keep the text together and make the links clear. You have already learned various ways of making references in earlier units (→ p. 24, p. 45, p. 179, p. 188). In this unit there is an overview of the most frequent forms for doing this.

Was macht die Liebe?

1 What can you see on the poster of 1936? Who is the poster aimed at?
Check the meaning of the words *Strickopfer* and *Winterhilfswerk*. What is the goal of this poster?

2 First just read the questions put by the interviewer from the magazine "Brigitte". What does she want to know? What do you think the answers will be?

3 a The following interview consists of several topic blocks. Find where the blocks begin.
b Find headings for the individual topic blocks.

A Herbert und Irmgard lernen sich kennen. / Begegnung

Herbert (76) und Irmgard (74) sind seit 47Jahren verheiratet. Doch erst seit acht Jahren können sie über ihre Gefühle reden.

Brigitte: Wie haben Sie sich kennen gelernt?

Herbert: Ich war Soldat an der Ostfront. Kurz vor Weihnachten 1944 bekamen wir Liebesgabenpakete aus der Heimat. In meinem war ein Paar handgestrickter Socken, mit denen ich auch gleich den Rückzug antreten musste. 20 Stunden marschieren. Irgendwas tat mir am linken Fuß furchtbar weh.
Als wir dann mal rasteten, zog ich Stiefel und Socken aus. In dem Socken war ein kleines Kärtchen. Lieber unbekannter Soldat, stand drauf, vielleicht meldest du dich mal bei der Strickerin. Name und Adresse.

Irmgard: Im Februar 1945 standest du dann an unserer Gartentür in Backnang[1].

Herbert: Ja. Weil es die einzige Adresse war, die ich bei der Entlassung aus der Kriegsgefangenschaft angeben konnte. Ich war aus Königsberg[2] und hatte keine Ahnung, was aus meiner Familie geworden war. 1949 haben wir geheiratet.

Brigitte: Die große Liebe?

Irmgard: Für mich schon.

Herbert: Für mich auch.

Irmgard: So was hast du mir aber nie gesagt.

Herbert: Wir Ostpreußen sind schweigsam.

Irmgard: Darunter habe ich oft gelitten. Als ich mal in einer ernsten Krise steckte, haben wir kein Wort darüber geredet.

Herbert: Aber inzwischen haben wir uns doch ausgesprochen.

Irmgard: Ja. 30 Jahre danach. Über Gefühle können wir erst seit acht Jahren reden, seit meiner Krebsoperation. Ich bedaure, dass wir uns damit so lange Zeit gelassen haben.

Brigitte: Was war das für eine Krise?

Irmgard: Ich hatte einen anderen Mann kennen gelernt. Einen Kollegen von Herbert, Lehrer am selben Gymnasium, in der damaligen Situation mein Traummann. Einen, bei dem es eben diese Schranke der Zurückhaltung nicht gab. Er hat mir etwas vermittelt, das ich bis dahin nicht kannte: Nähe und Wärme. Wir konnten bei einem Glas Wein sitzen und bis nach Mitternacht diskutieren. Außerdem sah er schick

aus, sehr gut angezogen, immer. Da ist mir aufgestoßen, dass du damals zu Hause immer im Trainingsanzug rumgelaufen bist.

Herbert: Aber ich war Sportlehrer ...

Irmgard: Schon. Aber es hat mich genervt. Eigentlich wollte ich in dieser Zeit nichts wie weg. Ein neues Leben anfangen. Aber da waren die Kinder, unsere zwei Söhne. Und dich mochte ich ja auch. Ich wusste, dass du viel empfindsamer warst, als du zeigtest. Irgendwie habe ich es nicht über mich gebracht, dir wehzutun.

Brigitte: Also hat Ihr Mann gar nichts gewusst von dieser Beziehung?
Irmgard: So glaubte ich. Als dieser Mann sich nach zwei Jahren in eine andere Stadt versetzen ließ, dachte ich, wenigstens hat Herbert nichts gemerkt.
Herbert: Natürlich habe ich es gemerkt, so was kann doch nicht verborgen bleiben. Du warst sehr verändert auf einmal. Und nicht alle deine Ausreden waren hieb- und stichfest. Einmal bin ich sogar zu dem Hotel gefahren, in dem du mit ihm eine Nacht verbracht hast. Angeblich warst du bei deiner Schwester, aber dafür hast du dich zu hübsch gemacht. Das fiel sogar mir auf.
Brigitte: Und Sie sind nicht in dieses Hotel hineingegangen?
Herbert: Aus einem ganz einfachen Grund nicht. Ich dachte, dann muss ich sagen, er oder ich. Und ich hatte Angst, du entscheidest dich für ihn.
Irmgard: Dass du es die ganze Zeit gewusst und mit dir rumgetragen hast – als du mir das sagtest, war ich vollkommen fertig. Was hab' ich dir angetan! Und wie hast du das bloß ausgehalten?
Brigitte: Viel später konnten Sie aber darüber sprechen. Warum?
Herbert: Vor acht Jahren hatte meine Frau eine sehr schwere Operation. Nierenkrebs. Ich saß tagelang an ihrem Bett. Sie erholte sich nur langsam, musste bestrahlt werden. Alles, unser ganzes Leben, war auf einmal anders. Ich konnte mir nicht vorstellen, kann es immer noch nicht, dass ich sie verliere. Bei diesem Gedanken stehe ich vor einer Wand.
Irmgard: Ja, und da haben wir zum ersten Mal – na, wie sagt man – unser Herz aufgemacht. Und da ist ganz viel zum Vorschein gekommen. Manches hat wehgetan, zum Beispiel über diese Geschichte zu reden. Aber vieles war auch einfach wunderbar. Weil wir gemerkt haben, wie sehr wir uns lieben. Nicht wahr?
Herbert: Sehr wahr.
Irmgard: Es klingt blöd, ich weiß. Aber irgendwie bin ich meiner Krankheit heute fast dankbar. So vieles hat sich durch sie verändert – auch positiv. Auf der anderen Seite ist immer die Angst da vor dem Tod, dem Ende. Dagegen kann man nichts machen.
Herbert: Wir versuchen, unsere Zeit besser zu nutzen. In unserem Alter verreist man nicht mehr so gern. Wir hören viel Musik, wir reden. Ich glaube, wir haben uns noch nie so gut verstanden. Nur in einer Hinsicht vernachlässigst du mich.
Irmgard: Wie bitte?
Herbert: Du hast mir nie wieder Socken gestrickt.
Irmgard: Ich wüsste überhaupt nicht mehr, wie das geht.

aus: *Brigitte*

[1] Small town in Baden-Württemberg
[2] German city in former East Prussia, since 1945 Kaliningrad (Russia)

4 Now read the text carefully.

Line 1–32	Underline all numbers and the words they refer to. Work out the meaning of the sentences.
Line 33–51	What words are significant for this section?
Line 52–79	What characteristics did the other man have? What characteristics did Herbert have in contrast? Take notes.
Line 80–111	How did Herbert notice his wife's affair with the other man? Note down all the verbs that express supposition and knowing!
Line 112–156	What period is decribed in this section? What events were significant for this period?

Textzusammenhang verstehen (Übersicht)

5 Lines 36–53: Determine what the words *so was*, *darunter*, *darüber*, *danach*, *damit* refer to. Draw arrows.

Wir Ostpreußen sind schweigsam. Darunter habe ich oft gelitten.

6 Deictic items (reference words) always refer to a word or sentence which gives them a meaning. Write down in the third column of the table what the underlined words refer to in the text.

Personal pronoun	sie, er, mit ihm …	1 einen anderen Mann Er hat mir etwas vermittelt, ... (lines 58-59)
Relative pronoun	der, die, mit dem, was, wo …	2 ... ... , mit denen ich den Rückzug antreten musste (lines 11-12)
Articles and determiners	dieser, der, mit diesen, mein, in meinem ...	3 ... ... , wie das geht. (line 156) 4 ... In meinem war ein Paar ... (lines 9-10)
Paraphrase	Da kam ein Auto. Der Wagen, dieser Wagen ...	5 ... Einen Kollegen von Herbert, ... (lines 53-54)
Certain adjectives	damalig, folgend	6 ... in der damaligen Situation (lines 55-56)
Other	hier, dort, dafür, dagegen, darüber, deshalb, darum, so etwas, so jemand ...	7 ... So was hast du mir aber nie gesagt. (lines 36-37) 8 ... Dagegen kann man nichts machen. (lines 142-143)

Die Zeit angeben: Hinweise zur Zeit

Herbert und Irmgard sind **seit 47 Jahren** verheiratet.
Doch **erst seit acht Jahren** können sie über ihre Gefühle reden.

In statements, time references are placed in the initial position or in the middle of the sentence.
Time references tell us about:

- a point in time — Wann? — jetzt, in diesem Moment, als ich mal ... steckte
- duration — Wie lange? — tagelang, seit 47 Jahren
- frequency — Wie oft? — nie wieder, immer wieder

Time references can consist of one word (heute, jetzt),
two words (erst jetzt, bis dahin, noch nicht, nicht mehr, nie wieder)
or a sub-clause (Als du es mir sagtest, ...).

7 a Underline the time references in the sentences.
b How are they expressed in English? Note down the answers.

Herbert und Irmgard sind seit 47 Jahren verheiratet.	....
In meinem war ein Paar handgestrickter Socken, mit denen ich auch gleich den Rückzug antreten musste.	....
Als wir dann mal rasteten, zog ich Stiefel und Socken aus.	....
1949 haben wir geheiratet.	....
Aber inzwischen haben wir uns doch ausgesprochen.	....
Er hat mir etwas vermittelt, was ich bis dahin nicht kannte.	....
Da ist mir aufgestoßen, dass du damals zu Hause immer im Trainingsanzug rumgelaufen bist.	....
Eigentlich wollte ich in dieser Zeit nichts wie weg.	....
Viel später konnten Sie darüber sprechen.	....
Ich konnte mir nicht vorstellen, kann es immer noch nicht, dass ich sie verliere.	....
Ich glaube, wir haben uns noch nie so gut verstanden.	....
Du hast mir nie wieder Socken gestrickt.	....

Time references can also be combined, for example as follows:

erst viel noch immer	später	schon	seit 1995 früher immer	immer	schon noch wieder erst, wenn ...
nie	wieder mehr	noch	einmal nie immer	viel noch	früher/später

8 Complete the sentences with the following expressions.

noch nie ● schon immer ● noch einmal ● erst jetzt ● nie wieder ● viel später

Katharina Wolfsleben schreibt an ihre Freundin Bettina: Liebe Bettina, Karl ist seit zwei Monaten weg. Ich wusste .... (1), dass Karl gerne allein sein will. Aber er ist .... (2) mehr als drei Tage weggeblieben. .... (3) ist mir klar geworden, dass er .... (4) kommen wird. Erst .... (5) bekam ich einen Brief aus Argentinien, in dem er mir schrieb: „Ich wollte allein sein. Deshalb bin ich nach Argentinien gegangen. Ich weiß nicht, ob wir uns .... (6) sehen werden.“ Du kannst dir denken, wie mir das wehgetan hat.

9 Think up an answer to the question "Liebst du mich?".

Gefühle ausdrücken

10 a Underline the expressions that can be used to express positive feelings.

Es tut mir gut, wenn … ◆ Es tut weh, wenn … ◆
Ich bin sehr froh, dass … ◆ Ich bin glücklich/unglücklich über … ◆ Es nervt mich, wenn … ◆
Ich bedaure, dass … ◆ Ich freue mich, dass ... ◆ Ich bin traurig über … ◆ Ich werde wütend, wenn … ◆
Ich habe Angst vor … ◆ Es macht mich fertig, wenn … ◆ Ich fühle mich beleidigt, wenn … ◆
Ich habe ein schlechtes Gewissen, wenn …

b Select some of the questions and answer them using expressions from a.

Was tut Ihnen gut? Was beleidigt Sie? Wann haben Sie ein schlechtes Gewissen?
Was macht Sie wütend? Wovor haben Sie Angst? Was bedauern Sie? Worüber sind Sie froh?
Was nervt Sie?

Mozart war ein armer Schlucker

The text about the composer Mozart and his poverty is from the book mentioned in Unit 6, "Lexikon der populären Irrtümer".

Cultural information

Wolfgang Amadeus Mozart was one of the greatest musicians of all time, but for all his success he was one of life's victims, thwarted by its practicalities. He lived for only 35 years, from 1756 to 1791. All his biographers have wondered how he managed to create thousands of compositions in this short time. As the infant prodigy his father had made him, he wrote a minuet for piano at the age of six and travelled all over Europe with his father and his sister, giving concerts to huge acclaim. Yet, despite his successes as a child, he didn't manage to find a permanent post with one of the music-loving rulers. And so he left his home town of Salzburg for Vienna where he lived as a freelance composer.

The tradition has been preserved to the present-day that the state and all large cities have their own theatre and their own orchestra. There are 121 concert halls and 141 professional symphony orchestras. The members of these ensembles have the status of life-long civil servants. A flautist appointed to the Munich or Berlin Philharmonic is free of any money worries for the rest of his or her life. However, exceptional talent, diligence and hard work is required from anyone hoping to apply to an orchestra like these. They are such an attractive proposition that they count among their number many outstanding musicians from countries like the USA, Japan and Russia.

Mozart's last opera, "Die Zauberflöte", opened in a local theatre in Vienna on 30th September 1791. The conservative Viennese were not particularly enthralled by the critical tone and the humanitarian ideals expressed in it. The facts that the opera contained Freemasonry images and the texts were sung in German was another cause of annoyance; public opinion was that the German language was unsuitable for operatic singing.

Reading skills

An indication of the content of a text is given by the headings and the beginning of the paragraphs. It's sometimes enough to read and understand just the first sentence of a section. It usually sets out the question that will dominate the section. As the answer to the question is often given in the last sentence of a section, it's worth working out the meaning of this too. Only then should you have a closer look at the filling in between.

1 a Check the meaning of these terms from the topic area *Geld*, and write the meaning in English underneath.
b Fill in the missing verbs next to the nouns marked with an asterisk (*).

Geld

- die Einnahmen* ... einnehmen ... / ... earnings ... earn ...
- die Einkünfte / das Einkommen ...
- die Ausgaben* ... / ... ...
- der Lohn ... / das Gehalt ...
- verdienen ...
- die Kosten* ... / ... ...
- der Verlust* ... verlieren ... / ... ...
- die Rechnung* ... / ... ...
- bezahlen ...
- das Erbe* ... / ... ...

Mozart war ein armer Schlucker

2 Read only the first sentence of each of the three paragraphs and then complete the following statements.

1 Mozart war .... armer Schlucker. **2** Mozart verdiente ....

3 Er verdiente zwar ...., aber ....

Mozart war alles andere als ein armer Schlucker[1]. Er gilt zwar vielen als klassisches Beispiel, wie große Künstler von den Herrschenden ausgebeutet, schlecht bezahlt und schließlich fallen gelassen werden, aber diese Legende hält den Tatsachen nicht stand.

Nach heutigen Maßstäben war Mozart ganz im Gegenteil ein Großverdiener. Er berechnete für eine Klavierstunde zwei Gulden Honorar (zum Vergleich: Mozarts Magd bekam 12 Gulden für das ganze Jahr); für einen öffentlichen Auftritt als Pianist bekam er nach eigenen Angaben „wenigstens 1000 Gulden", was bei durchschnittlich 6 Auftritten pro Jahr zusammen mit seinen anderen Einkünften ein Jahreseinkommen von rund 10 000 Gulden ergab, nach heutiger Kaufkraft etwa 130 000 Euro.

Dass er dennoch oft in Geldverlegenheiten steckte[2] und Bettelbriefe schreiben musste, lag einfach daran, dass er zwar viel einnahm, aber noch mehr ausgab, von seiner Frau Constanze bestens unterstützt. Die Mozarts hielten sich in guten Zeiten ein Dienstmädchen, eine Köchin und einen eigenen Friseur, und wenn Mozart bei seinem Tod so hohe Schulden hatte, dass seine Frau das Erbe ausschlug und ihren Mann in einem Armengrab bestatten ließ, so war das nicht die Schuld des Kaisers oder anderer böswilliger Notabeln[3], es war vor allem eine Folge seiner eigenen häuslichen Misswirtschaft, gepaart mit einer Leidenschaft für Kartenspiel und Billard, wo er vermutlich (denn er war ein schlechter Billardspieler) mehr Geld verlor, als er durch seine Musik verdienen konnte.

aus: *Lexikon der populären Irrtümer*

[1] ein armer Schlucker: a poor devil
[2] in Geldverlegenheiten stecken: be in financial difficulties
[3] die Notabeln: Notables

3 Now read the whole text. Which words from section 1 occur in the text? Underline them.

4 What did Mozart get money for, what did he spend it on? Make a list.

Einnahmen	Ausgaben

als

5 How do you express the underlined parts in English? Write the answer down next to the sentences.

1 Schon als Kind gab Mozart Konzerte und galt als sehr begabt. ....as a child..........

2 Als 11-Jähriger komponierte er seine erste Oper. ....

3 Mozart war alles andere als ein armer Schlucker, aber seine Ausgaben waren größer als seine Einnahmen.

....

4 Er verlor mehr Geld (beim Kartenspiel und Billard), als er (durch seine Musik) verdienen konnte.

....

5 Als Mozart starb, hatte er hohe Schulden. ....

6 Mozart arbeitete an einem Requiem, als er 1791 starb. ....

Use of *als*

1 *Als* introduces a sub-clause and indicates that single (i.e. not repeated, habitual) events or actions occurred simultaneously in the past.
Als Mozart geboren wurde, war Goethe sieben Jahre alt.

2 *Als* introduces a comparison.
Mozart fand berühmte Billardspieler **interessanter als** berühmte Musiker.
Er hatte **mehr** Geld, **als** man lange Zeit geglaubt hat.

3 *Als* explains a person or thing: before a noun or adjective, sometimes also in connection with verbs like *gelten als, bezeichnen als*.
A noun does not have an indefinite article after *als*.
Mozart bekam für einen Auftritt **als Pianist** 1000 Gulden Honorar.

6 How is *als* used in the sentences in section 5? Enter the numbers of the explanations.

7 Make a table.
a Sort the terms from the word-spider in section 1 into the fields "private life" and "work".
b Collect terms for the field "bank".

Privat	Arbeit	Bank
bezahlen		

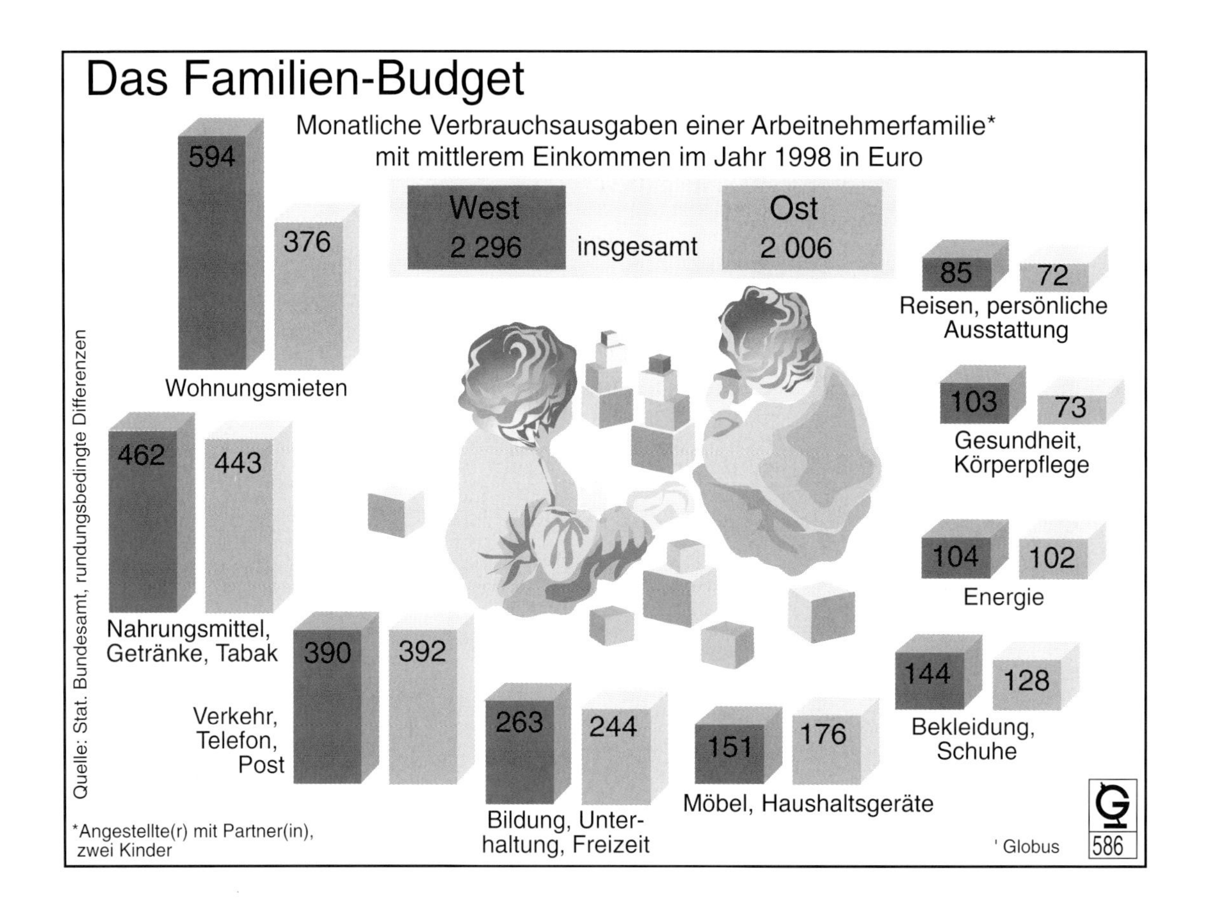

8 a What do West German / East German families spend most money on, what least? Sort the following items into the lists.

Nahrungsmittel, Getränke, Tabak ● Miete ● Bildung, Unterhaltung, Freizeit ● Gesundheit, Körperpflege ● Bekleidung, Schuhe ● Verkehr, Telefon, Post

westdeutsche Familien	**ostdeutsche Familien**
1	1 ....
2	2 ....
3	3 ....
4	4 ....
5	5 ....
6	6 ....

b Describe the two lists with the following expressions.

Auf Platz eins bei ... stehen die Ausgaben für ... ● Auf dem letzten Platz stehen bei ... die Ausgaben für ... ● Am meisten Geld geben die ... für ... aus. ● Die ... geben mehr Geld für ... aus als für ... ● Am wenigsten geben die ... für ... aus. ● Die ... geben mehr/weniger Geld für ... aus.

c What do you spend most/least on? Make a list and give a report.

Das Verb *lassen*

9 a Read the sentences.

1 1791 starb Mozart und seine Frau **ließ** ihn in einem Armengrab **bestatten**. ☐
2 Ich **habe** mir alle Klavierkonzerte von Mozart **schenken lassen**. ☐
3 ■ Warum **lässt** du mich nicht ins Konzert **gehen**? ☐
▲ Ich **lasse** dich doch, aber ich möchte auch mitgehen. ☐
4 Er war da, aber ich **habe** ihn nicht ins Haus **gelassen**. ☐
5 ■ Ich mag den Kaffee nicht.
▲ Dann **lass** ihn doch **stehen**. ☐
6 Wo ist mein Geldbeutel? **Habe** ich ihn im Restaurant **gelassen**? ☐
7 ■ Er geht und du **lässt** ihm deinen Computer? Das verstehe ich nicht. ☐
▲ Er **hat** mir seinen Fernseher **gelassen**. ☐
8 Das kannst du nicht machen. Bitte **lass** das! ☐

b Fill in the verb forms.

Infinitiv	3. Person Singular (er/sie/es/man)		
	Präsens	**Präteritum**	**Perfekt**
lassen	....	....	.... /hat ... lassen*

* with a second verb (hat stehen lassen)

Meaning of *lassen*
1 Have something done by another person: Ich lasse mir die Grammatik erklären.
2 allow something: Lass mich den Brief lesen.
not allow something: Er hat uns nicht sprechen lassen.
3 Somebody should stop doing something: Lass das Singen! (= Hör auf zu singen!)
4 leave something: Den Schirm lasse ich zu Hause; es wird schon nicht regnen.
5 forget something: Ich muss zurück, ich habe meinen Mantel hängen lassen.
6 let someone keep something: Ich lasse dir das Buch bis nächste Woche.

10 a What does *lassen* mean in the sentences in section 9 a? Write down the numbers from the explanations.
b Translate the sentences into English.

fixed expressions with *lassen*
jdn. sitzen lassen, jdn. stehen lassen,
jdn. fallen lassen, jdn. links liegen lassen
■ Peter spricht nicht mehr mit mir.
▲ Dann lass ihn doch einfach links liegen.

11 Make little dialogues with the different meanings of *lassen*.

■ Du hast einen Fleck auf deinem Rock.
▲ So ein Pech, jetzt muss ich ihn schon wieder reinigen lassen.

Das Nomen, das Adjektiv: Genitiv

Singular				**Plural**
m	**m** (Nomen der n-Deklination)	**n**	**f**	**m, n, f**
die Biographie de**s**/eine**s** berühmt**en** Künstler**s**/Mann**es**	das Bild de**s**/eine**s** klein**en** Junge**n***	die Folge de**s**/eine**s** schlecht**en** Billardspiel**s**	die Folge **der**/ein**er** groß**en** Spielleidenschaft	das Lexikon **der** populär**en** Irrtümer

also: dieser; jeder; kein; mein, dein, ...

* with: der Friede, der Gedanke, der Glaube, der Name: **-ns**; das Herz: **-ens** (→ S. 150)

Namen haben im Genitiv *s*: Mozart**s** Frau Constanze – die Entdeckung Amerika**s**

12 Mark the articles/determiners and nouns in the genitive, and the noun the genitive refers to.

1 Wenn Mozart kein Geld hatte, so war das nicht die Schuld des Kaisers, sondern die Folge seiner Misswirtschaft und seiner Leidenschaft für Kartenspiel und Billard.
2 Man soll sich selbst nicht ernst nehmen, man soll die Absurdität des Lebens akzeptieren.
3 Zu Hause spreche ich den Dialekt unserer Heimat.

13 Link the nouns and adjectives as in the example.

1 das Bild – berühmt – eine Frau   das Bild einer berühmten Frau

2 die Fahrerin – rot – das Auto
3 der Erfolg – neu – seine Firma
4 das Gehalt – jünger – ein Lehrer
5 die Folge – schwer – ihre Krankheit
6 die Höhe – monatlich – die Ausgaben
7 der Lohn – deutsch – ein Bäcker

Das Verb: Passiv (2)

Häufig wurden große Künstler von den Herrschenden ausgebeutet und schlecht bezahlt.
Mozart wurde durch seine Spielleidenschaft ruiniert.

The agent (person, thing or event initiating the action) can be mentioned in a passive sentence if it is of interest or important for understanding what's going on.
von + dative: mostly with people
durch + accusative: mostly with things and events

14 Mark the passive form and the agent.

1 Lange Zeit wurde Mozart von den Biographen als armer Schlucker beschrieben.
2 Viele Legenden werden durch das Buch „Lexikon der populären Irrtümer" aufgeklärt.

15 Who do you think did what? Make several speculations about each headline and write the headlines as full sentences.

Mehrere Babys nach der Geburt vertauscht

Hund aus fünf Meter hohem Baum gerettet

Bundespräsident nicht zum Jubiläum eingeladen

Zeit* ohne *Zeit

Cultural information

During the course of the last hundred years, the amount of free time a person has at his or her disposal has increased enormously, and this trend is set to continue. And yet the question of time has become a problem for a lot of people, as they register the fact that they have too little of it; busy managers are among them needless to say, but also retired people hastening from one commitment and one entertainment to the next. Unlike money, the amount of time available per day cannot be increased, the only thing you can do is make better use of it. This is the reason why philosophers of all periods have been drawn to the topic. For some years now it has also become fashionable to talk and write about it in non-philosophical circles. Working time, free time, time in relation to space. Albert Einstein, born in 1879 in the southern German city of Ulm, took this latter topic as the starting point of his theory of relativity. Einstein put an end to the false belief that the world can be comprehended in terms of only three dimensions. His discovery cost him his reputation in the eyes of his fellow-scientists for years. Thus he traipsed from the patent office in the Swiss capital, Berne, to the Technical University in Zurich, thence to the German-speaking university in Prague, then back to Zurich, before landing finally in Berlin in 1913. Soon afterwards, however, his fame began to spread, he became known internationally and in 1922 was awarded the Nobel prize for physics at the age of only 43. When the National Socialists came to power in Germany in 1933, he stayed in the USA where he was on a lecture tour. He died there in Princeton in 1955. Einstein had another passion: music. Whenever he could, he would play the violin. Is it a coincidence that music, of all the arts, is so dependent on the divisions of time we experience, the bars, beats and rhythms that carry the melody on through time?

Learning strategies

Language too contains musical elements, dependent as it is on stresses and melodic movement. Anyone who learns a language only as a logical structure, devoid of any musical element, will have a hard time of it and will find it almost impossible to match the rhythm of a partner in conversation and thus communicate effectively in the foreign language. The linguistic genius Heinrich Schliemann learned the twenty languages he mastered by learning texts by heart and reciting them aloud till he had the right feel for their sound and rhythm. Only then did he commit the individual elements to memory. Try following his example!

Zeit ohne Zeit

1 Skim through lines 1–7 of the text and complete these sentences.

Der zivilisierte Mensch hat .... Statt Zeit hat er ....

Er hat sie .... Aber der zivilisierte Mensch hat kein .... mehr.

2 a Read the explanations of the words.

die Weste, -n: waistcoat
der Mantel, Mäntel: coat
der Rock, obsolete for die Jacke/das Jackett: jacket

b Read lines 1–7 again, closely this time, and work out the meaning of the follwoing words from the context.

das Merkmal • trägt • aufknöpfen • außerdem • ohne

Reminder
When working out the meaning of unknown words from the context, it's useful to ask yourself the following questions:

- What word class is it?
- What other word is it linked with?
- What is the logical connection between the word and the rest of the sentence, the preceding or following one, or the topic of the text?

Check the word in the wordlist in the Handbuch or in a dictionary only right at the end.

3 Read the definition of *Urmensch* and write a definition for *Uhrmensch* (word made up by the author).

Urmensch, der; -en: eine frühere Form des Menschen, aus der sich die Menschheit entwickelt hat

Uhrmensch, der; -en: ....

....

4 Read from line 8 to the end. What statement of the author's do you disagree with?

Zeit ohne Zeit

Das Merkmal des zivilisierten Menschen: Er hat keine Zeit. Stattdessen hat er eine Uhr. Nicht nur eine. Er lebt zwischen den Uhren, mit den Uhren, gegen die Uhren. Er trägt sie nicht mehr in der Weste, braucht nicht Rock noch Mantel aufzuknöpfen. Er hat sie an der Hand, in der Hand. Außerdem auf dem Schreibtisch, auf der
5 Straße, im Auto, auf dem Nachttisch, überall. Nur nicht im Kopf.
Ohne Uhr wüssten wir nicht, ob wir Hunger haben, ob wir müde sind. Das Zeitgefühl ist uns abhanden gekommen[1].
Der Urmensch hatte Zeit, aber er wusste nichts davon.
Wir Uhrmenschen wissen darum[2] und haben die Uhren erfunden[3], die unsere Zeit
10 in Scheiben schneiden[4], ein Scheibchen hierfür, ein Scheibchen dafür, recht viele und recht dünne, wie man es bei Hartwurst[5] macht, wenn sie lange reichen soll. Die dünnen Blättchen schmecken nicht, in Wurst muss man hineinbeißen[6] können. Mit der Zeit ist es ebenso[7].

Heinrich Spoerl

1 abhanden gekommen = haben wir verloren
2 wir wissen darum = wir kennen das Problem
3 erfinden: invent
4 in Scheiben schneiden: cut in slices
5 die Hartwurst: hard sausage
6 hineinbeißen: bite into
7 ebenso: the same

Das Verb *brauchen*

- Der zivilisierte Mensch **braucht** eine Uhr, denn er hat sein Zeitgefühl verloren.
- Ich **habe** noch nie eine Uhr **gebraucht**, ich weiß immer, wann Feierabend ist.
- Ja, wenn du gehst, dann ist es genau vier Uhr. Da **brauche** ich **nicht** auf die Uhr **zu sehen**.
- Du **brauchst nur** ein gutes Zeitgefühl **zu haben**.

nicht brauchen + zu + infinitive (needn't) = nicht müssen
nur brauchen + zu + infinitive (only need to) = nur müssen

5 Replace *nicht/nur müssen* with *nicht/nur brauchen*.

1 Sie müssen nur anrufen, dann komme ich sofort.
Sie brauchen nur anzurufen, dann komme ich sofort.
2 Du musst mir nur die Adresse geben, ich finde das schon.
3 Das musst du mir nicht sagen, das weiß ich selber.
4 Sie müssen sich nicht jetzt entscheiden, nächste Woche reicht es auch noch.
5 Er muss sich die Regel nur genau anschauen, dann wird er sie gleich verstehen.
6 Du musst mir den Weg nicht lange erklären, ich war schon einmal da.
7 Sie müssen mich morgen nicht abholen, ich muss noch etwas erledigen.

Kleidung – tragen, anhaben, aufhaben

tragen/anhaben: Bluse, Hemd, Ring, ... tragen/aufhaben: Hut, Mütze, ...

6 Fill in the missing words.

die Strümpfe

der Anzug

das Hemd

die Jeans

der Pullover

....

....

die Bluse

....

....

das Kostüm

....

....

das T-Shirt

die Jacke

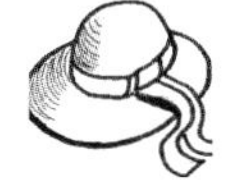
der Hut

der Ring

die Halskette

der Schal

das Halstuch

die Turnschuhe

die Mütze

....

....

....

....

7 Make suggestions as to how the people could dress. Describe the pieces of clothing too, using the following adjectives.

Texte erschließen: Lesetexte

8 **a** Select one text (A, B or C) from pages 229–230 and work on it.
Remember the various strategies.

Reading for gist

- take note of the type of text (newspaper article, poem, advert, ...)
- pay attention to the graphics and design of the text (photos, diagrams, ...)
- make deductions about the content from the heading: ask questions about the text (who? what? how? ...)
- work out the way the text is constructed (divide it into sections)
- skim through the whole text first and
  - check whether it contains internationalisms
  - note whether anything is emphasised in the text (special script, inverted commas, ...)
  - pick out key words, numbers, names, geographical terms
- once the text is divided into sections, read the first and possibly the last sentence in each section

Reading for detail

- take notes on everything you already understand
- work out the meaning of unknown words
  - from the context
  - by splitting compounds up into their component parts
  - through your knowledge of word formation
- split long sentences up (after the punctuation marks for example)
- note the meaning of conjunctions
- recognize the internal links: reference words and what they refer to

b Afterwards note down which techniques you used.

A

a Summarize the content of the text in a few sentences.
Who is talking to whom?
What about?
What is the outcome?

b Listen to the text.

Ganz einfach

Ein Mann fährt zu einem Blitzbesuch
zu seinem Vater auf das Dorf.
Der Vater füttert gerade die Katzen.
Der Mann sagt: „Tag! Ich bleib nicht lang,
hab eigentlich gar keine Zeit.
Ich weiß nicht mehr, wo mir der Kopf steht!
Ich hetz mich ab und schaffe nichts.
Ich bin nur noch ein Nervenwrack.
Woher nimmst du nur deine Ruhe?“
Der Alte kratzt sein linkes Ohr
und sagt: „Mein Lieber, hör gut hin,
ich mach es so, es ist ganz einfach:
Wenn ich schlafe, schlafe ich.
Wenn ich aufsteh, steh ich auf.
Wenn ich gehe, gehe ich.
Wenn ich esse, ess ich.
Wenn ich schaffe, schaffe ich.
Wenn ich plane, plane ich.
Wenn ich spreche, spreche ich.
Wenn ich höre, hör ich.“
Der Mann fragt: „Was soll dieser Quatsch?
Das alles mache ich doch auch
und trotzdem find ich keine Ruhe.“
Der Alte kratzt sein linkes Ohr
und sagt: „Mein Lieber, hör gut hin,
du machst es alles etwas anders:
Wenn du schläfst, stehst du schon auf.
Wenn du aufstehst, gehst du schon.
Wenn du gehst, dann isst du schon.
Wenn du isst, dann schaffst du.
Wenn du schaffst, dann planst du schon.
Wenn du planst, dann sprichst du schon.
Wenn du sprichst, dann hörst du schon.
Wenn du hörst, dann schläfst du.
Wenn ich schlafe, schlafe ich.
Wenn ich aufsteh, steh ich auf.
Wenn ich gehe, gehe ich.
Wenn ich esse, ess ich.
Wenn ich schaffe, schaffe ich.
Wenn ich plane, plane ich.
Wenn ich spreche, spreche ich.
Wenn ich höre, hör ich.“

Gerhard Schöne

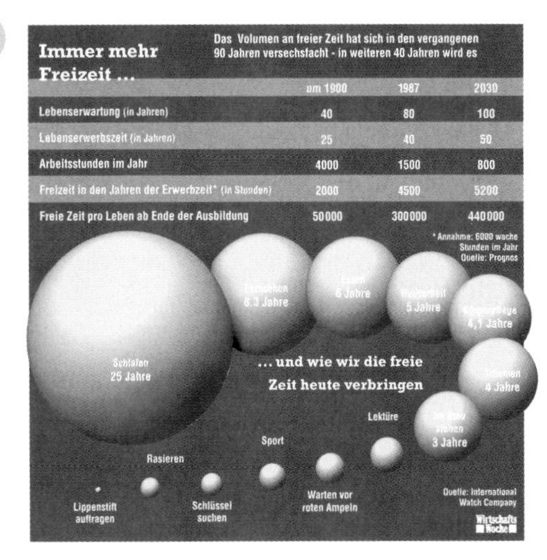

Immer mehr Freizeit ...

Das Volumen an freier Zeit hat sich in den vergangenen 90 Jahren versechsfacht - in weiteren 40 Jahren wird es

	um 1900	1987	2030
Lebenserwartung (in Jahren)	40	80	100
Lebenserwerbszeit (in Jahren)	25	40	50
Arbeitsstunden im Jahr	4000	1500	800
Freizeit in den Jahren der Erwerbzeit* (in Stunden)	2000	4500	5200
Freie Zeit pro Leben ab Ende der Ausbildung	50000	300000	440000

* Annahme: 6000 wache Stunden im Jahr
Quelle: Prognos

a Fill in information from the diagram/illustration.

Um 1900 lebten die Menschen durchschnittlich .... Jahre, ... Jahre und 2030 wird die Lebenserwartung auf .... steigen. Ab Ende der Ausbildung hatten die Menschen um 1900 .... Stunden Freizeit bis zum Ende ihres Lebens, ... Stunden und .... werden sie .... haben. Die Grafik zeigt auch, wie ...

b Select some activities that interest you and give a report.

25 Jahre verbringen die Menschen mit Schlafen, ...

Umgang mit der Zeit

Was Karlheinz Geißler seinen Kunden rät.

Langsamer ist oft besser

Geschwindigkeit ist als ökonomische Produktivkraft weitgehend ausgereizt. Dagegen ist das Langsame noch eine unentdeckte produktive Kraft. Haben Sie sich schon einmal überlegt, wie Sie die Vorzüge dieser Energie in Ihrem Unternehmen entwickeln können?

Warten lohnt sich

Warten ist weit mehr als nur Handlungsverzicht und oft produktiver als purer Aktivismus. Um etwa den richtigen Zeitpunkt für die Markteinführung von Produkten zu finden, muss man warten können.

Pausen sind kreativ

Machen Sie öfter eine kreative Pause. Nur so können Sie beurteilen, was gelungen ist und was nicht. Pausieren Sie auch beim Übergang von einer Arbeit zur nächsten und nehmen Sie sich Zeit, sich vom Alten zu verabschieden. Nur so kann das Neue richtig beginnen.

Verlieren Sie Anfang und Ende nicht aus den Augen

Projekte werden häufig aufgestockt, umdefiniert und erweitert. Am Ende weiß keiner mehr, wann sie begonnen wurden und wann sie eigentlich zu Ende gehen sollen. Wer aber Anfang und Schluss nicht mehr überblickt, der verliert auch den Mittelpunkt aus den Augen. Mit deutlich fixierten Anfängen orientieren und motivieren Sie Ihr Team; und mit klar markierten Abschlüssen machen Sie Erfolgseinschätzungen erst möglich.

Im Rhythmus arbeitet sich's besser

Im Arbeitsrhythmus – etwa dem Rhythmus von Arbeitszeit und Pause oder der Beschleunigung und Verlangsamung – drückt sich eine Arbeitskultur aus. Der heute herrschende Flexibilisierungsdruck macht die orientierende Kraft von Rhythmen notwendig. Nur wer einen klaren Rhythmus hat, kann problemlos flexibilisieren.

Zeitmanagement kostet Geld

Wie viel Zeit verbringen Sie eigentlich mit der Organisation Ihrer Zeit? Zeitmanagement verschlingt paradoxerweise Zeit. Je weniger Sie über Zeit nachdenken, desto mehr Zeit haben Sie.

aus: *Wirtschaftswoche*

a Explain the headings and pieces of advice in your own words.

b What do you think of the advice? Select those items that seem sensible for you in your own life.

Freiheit, die ich meine

As a result of the Second World War the smaller, eastern part of Germany became part of the sphere of influence of the Soviet Union, and the larger western part came under the influence of the other victorious powers, the USA, France and Great Britain. The result was that the so-called Iron Curtain hung right across Germany. Berlin was granted special status.

1949

The Basic Law of the **Bundesrepublik Deutschland** (BRD) was passed. In the preamble it states that the population of the three western occupation zones also acted for those Germans who were not permitted to be involved. The whole of the German people is called upon "to complete the unity and freedom of Germany in free self-determination".

The constitution of the **Deutsche Demokratische Republik** (DDR) was confirmed: "Germany is an indivisible democratic republic constructed from the German states ... There is only one German nationality."

1955

The Federal Government stresses that the Federal Republic alone has the right to represent Germany and threatens to break off diplomatic relations with states that recognize the GDR.

The period of occupation ended for the Federal Republic.

1961 Erection of the Berlin Wall

1968 The GDR gives itself a new constitution. "The German Democratic Republic is a socialist state of German nationhood."

1970

"The concept of the nation forms the link that binds divided Germany together. Nation means more than just a common language and culture, more than a state and social order. The nation has its foundations in the on-going sense of belonging together among the people. Nobody can deny that there is and there will be in this sense a German nation."

Willy Brandt, Chancellor of the FRG

"Today the socialist German Democratic Republic and the monopolistic capitalist Federal Republic exist as two separate independent states. Their citizens live and work under conditions completely opposed to one another. ... In reality, the two sovereign states, GDR and FRG, cannot be united, because social orders contrary to one another cannot be united."

Willi Stoph, Prime Minister of the GDR

The treaty covering the basis of the relationship **1972** between the Federal Republic of Germany and the German Democratic Republic was signed. In it both German states affirm the inviolability of the border between them and the fact that neither has the right to act in the other's name in its internal or external affairs.

November 1989 Fall of the Wall

October 1990 Reunification

Abreiß-Kalender, ein deutsch-deutsches Tagebuch

1 **a** Read the explanations of the words.

Maler, Malerin: painter
einen Antrag stellen: make an application (for permission)
einen Antrag ablehnen: refuse an application
die Haft, die Einzelhaft: custody, solitary confinement
die Haftanstalt/das Gefängnis: prison
die Stasi (der Staatssicherheitsdienst): stasi
die Republikflucht: illegal emigration

b Skim through the text.

1985
ENDE JUNI
Brigitte, eine Freundin, ist verhaftet worden. Auf dem Flugplatz Berlin-Schönefeld, als sie nach Bulgarien fliegen wollte. Es heißt, sie habe die DDR illegal verlassen wollen. Richtung Südfrankreich.
5 Ja, den Traum hatte sie. Schließlich ist sie Malerin. Sie wollte nach Südfrankreich, um dort zu malen – die warmen Farben, das warme Gelb zogen sie an. Immer wieder stellte sie von ihrem Mecklenburger Dorf aus Anträge.
Die wurden immer wieder abgelehnt.
MITTE OKTOBER
10 Ständig muss ich an Brigitte denken; sie sitzt nun schon seit dreieinhalb Monaten in Einzelhaft. In Neustrelitz, bei der Stasi. Darf keine Post empfangen, keinen Besuch.
1986
JANUAR
Muss an Brigitte denken. Sie sitzt nun seit fünf Monaten in Einzelhaft. Weil sie nach Südfrankreich
15 wollte.
ENDE FEBRUAR
Brigitte ist verurteilt und nach Hoheneck transportiert worden. Zwei Jahre und zwei Monate für Republikflucht, dazu sechs Monate für Verschiebung von Kulturgut: Sie hatte vor Fluchtantritt ihre Bilder von Freunden mit in den Westen nehmen lassen.
20 ENDE JUNI
Wir machen uns große Sorgen um unsere Freundin Brigitte. Die Staatsorgane wollen sie offenbar fertig machen. In der Haftanstalt Hoheneck liegt sie in einer Zelle mit neun weiteren Frauen. Sie ist die einzige „Politische", sechs der Frauen aus ihrer Zelle haben Kindesmord begangen. Es ist ein Trakt für Lebenslängliche, in dem sie untergebracht ist.
25 MITTE AUGUST
Zu Hause angekommen, finden wir eine Postkarte im Briefkasten.
Sie ist aus Paris. Und sie ist von Brigitte.
Wir fallen uns in die Arme, als wären wir selbst entlassen worden.
1987
30 14. Januar
Brigitte hat sich nun nicht nach Südfrankreich abgesetzt, sondern sich in einem ärmlichen Dorf in Süditalien niedergelassen. Hat noch immer schwer mit ihrer Haftpsychose zu kämpfen.

Freya Klier

2 **a** Underline the following words in the text and work out their meaning from the context or their component parts. Note down what they might mean in English.

1 line 4: verlassen **2** line 6: zogen sie an **3** line 3: verhaftet **4** line 17: verurteilt
5 line 22: fertig machen **6** line 24: Lebenslängliche **7** line 28: entlassen **8** line 32: Haftpsychose

b What other words and linguistic elements helped you understand the text?
What role did the place adverbials play in helping you understand?

c Read the text again closely and check your translations of the words in a.

3 Complete the sentences with words from the text.

Brigitte wohnte in .... Von Beruf ist sie ....

Sie hatte den Traum ....

Ende Juni 1985 wurde sie ...., Februar 1986 wurde sie zu

zwei Jahren und acht Monaten Haft ....

Im August wurde sie .... Seither lebt sie in ....

....

4 When do you think the texts were written, in the fifties, sixties, seventies, ...? Read the time line on page 231 again.

O aus
einem fremden land, sieh
die marken ... Wie
heißt das land?
– – –
Deutschland, tochter

Rainer Kunze

Auch heute wachsen
Kinder auf in den
beiden deutschen
Staaten. Fragen wir
uns denn ernst genug:
Wie sollen die,
wenn sie groß sind,
miteinander reden?
Mit welchen Wörtern,
in was für Sätzen
und in welchem Ton?

Christa Wolf

5 **a** Describe the photo and then read the text.

Freiheit, die ich meine

1990 standen plötzlich sechzehn Millionen Menschen, sobald sie nur einen Schritt vor die eigene Haustür taten, auf fremdem Terrain; nachdem die erste Euphorie verflogen war, spürten sie einen scharfen Wind, der ihnen ins Gesicht blies. Der Boden schwankte unter ihren Füßen, und dass jeder seines Glückes Schmied sei, war keine Floskel mehr, sondern oft unbarmherzige Realität, mit der viele nicht zurechtkamen. Sie hatten es nicht gelernt, weil sie es früher nicht lernen mussten.

Regine Hildebrandt

b What do the images in the text mean? Express them in your own words.

ein scharfer Wind blies ihnen ins Gesicht ⊘ der Boden schwankte unter ihren Füßen ⊘ jeder ist seines Glückes Schmied

6 Which of the following terms go with the picture, which with the text?

Freude ⊘ harte Realität ⊘ Optimismus ⊘ Enttäuschung ⊘ Unsicherheit ⊘ Hoffnung ⊘ Eigenverantwortung ⊘ Verlust von Illusionen

Vergangenheit – Gegenwart – Zukunft

7 Fill in the tenses and complete the explanations in the summary.

Vergangenheit

..........: .... or .... + ...	Brigitte **hat** sich nicht nach Südfrankreich **abgesetzt**. Brigitte **ist** nach Italien **gegangen**.
....	Brigitte **wollte** die DDR verlassen. 1990 **standen** plötzlich sechzehn Millionen Menschen, sobald sie nur einen Schritt vor die eigene Haustür **taten**, auf fremdem Terrain.
Past perfect: .... past of .... or .... + past participle. Describes what was already the past in the past.	Nachdem die erste Euphorie **verflogen war**, spürten sie einen scharfen Wind. Sie **hatten** es nicht **gelernt**, weil sie es früher nicht lernen mussten.

Gegenwart

....	
a now	a Die Bundesländer der ehemaligen DDR **nennt** man die „neuen Bundesländer".
b Something began in the past and still continues.	b Brigitte **lebt** seit 1987 in einem Dorf in Süditalien.

Zukunft

.... + time expression	Ich **komme nächste Woche zurück**.
..........: .... + ...	Ich **werde** dir jeden Tag **schreiben**.

Temporale Konjunktionen (Übersicht)

Gleichzeitigkeit

als: single action / event in the past	**Als** ich zwanzig war, war alles anders.
wenn: present, future	**Wenn** ich arbeite, bleibt er bei den Kindern. **Wenn** du ankommst, werde ich am Bahnhof sein.
(immer) wenn: repeated action / event in the past	**(Immer) wenn** sie anrief, unterhielten wir uns stundenlang.
während	**Während** du weg bist, kann ich ja endlich die Einladungen schreiben. **Während** das Radio läuft, kann ich nicht arbeiten.
solange	Wir können nichts tun, **solange** es keinen Beweis gibt. **Solange** das Radio läuft, kann ich nicht arbeiten.

zeitliche Abfolge

bevor	Kannst du mir helfen, **bevor** du gehst?
nachdem	**Nachdem** wir endlich alles erledigt hatten, gingen wir nach Hause.
als	**Als** der Besuch endlich gegangen war, gingen wir gleich schlafen. = Nachdem der Besuch ...
sobald	**Sobald** sie da ist, fahren wir los. **Sobald** ich die Schulden bezahlt habe, kann ich auch mal an Urlaub denken.

Anfang, Ende

seit(dem)	**Seit(dem)** ich es weiß, bin ich sehr vorsichtig.
bis	Er wohnte bei seiner Mutter, **bis** er endlich heiratete.

8 *Als* or *wenn*? Complete.

.... (1) Brigitte noch in ihrem Mecklenburger Dorf lebte, hatte sie einen Traum. Sie wollte nach Südfrankreich. .... (2) sie malte, dachte Brigitte an dieses Land, an seine warmen Farben. Aber .... (3) sie Reiseanträge stellte, wurden sie immer abgelehnt. .... (4) sie sich entschied nach Bulgarien zu fliegen, hat man sie auf dem Flugplatz verhaftet. Sie verbrachte mehr als ein Jahr im Gefängnis. .... (5) wir ihre Postkarte aus Paris im Briefkasten fanden, freuten wir uns sehr.

9 Complete the sentences paying attention to the content and context.

a Add sub-clauses using the conjunctions *als, wenn, während, bis.*

…, sind sie viel ausgegangen.
…, haben sie immer ihre Verwandten eingeladen.
…, hat er Ausflüge mit den Kindern gemacht.
Mit dem Kauf eines Hauses haben sie gewartet, …

b Add main clauses.

Nachdem er sie verlassen hatte, ...
Seitdem sie geschieden sind, ...
Solange sie genug Geld verdiente, ...
Bevor er auf ihren Brief geantwortet hat, ...
Sobald sie Zeit hat, ...

10 Change the sentences as in the example.

Nach dem Einkaufen gingen wir gemütlich einen Kaffee trinken.

Nachdem wir eingekauft hatten, gingen wir gemütlich einen Kaffee trinken.

Präposition	**Konjunktion**
vor (D)	bevor
nach (D)	nachdem
während (G/D)	während
seit (D)	seit(dem)
bis (zu) (D)	bis

1 Seit ihrem Urlaub reden sie nur wenig miteinander.
2 Während des Flugs über den Atlantik konnten wir Grönland sehen.
3 Vor dem Unterricht sollte ich noch einmal den Text lesen.
4 Mach schnell, es sind nur noch fünf Minuten bis zur Sportschau!
5 Erst nach einigen Jahren konnte ich über den Streit lachen.

Jahrgang 49 – aufgewachsen in zwei deutschen Staaten

Zwei Frauen, beide geboren am Tag der Gründung ihres Staates, geben in einem Interview Antwort auf verschiedene Fragen.

11 a First read the information about the people, then the questions.

Monika Röhm lebt in Köln. Über den Sport traf sie auf Menschen aus der DDR (DDR-Fechtmannschaft) – sie bekam aber keinen persönlichen Kontakt zu ihnen.

Petra Wecker stammt aus Dresden. Sie selbst hatte gar keinen Kontakt mit der Bundesrepublik, nur über ihren Mann, der 1982 dienstlich in die Bundesrepublik geschickt wurde.

1 Wann haben Sie erfahren, dass Ihr Geburtstag ein historisch bedeutsamer Tag ist?
2 Gibt es besondere Prägungen, die Sie aus ihrer Kindheit behalten haben?
3 Wann haben Sie zum ersten Mal von der Existenz eines anderen deutschen Staates gehört?
4 Hatten Sie irgendwelche Vorstellungen von den Menschen, die da drüben in der DDR lebten? Was für eine Vorstellung hatten Sie von den Menschen im Westen?
5 Mit welchen Gefühlen haben Sie den Fall der Mauer wahrgenommen?
6 Sind Sie nach der Vereinigung oft in den Westen gereist?

b Listen to the interview and take notes on the answers that interest you.

c Compare your notes.

Hand

Body language

"Der Körper sagt immer die Wahrheit" was the title of an article in the Süddeutsche Zeitung focussing on the problems a lot of managers have with body language. They don't know that their body posture, gestures and involuntary movements often make what they say appear false and untrue. While speaking or listening, everybody transmits a constant stream of messages with their body which often contradict what is being said. It would be difficult to control all this, because often it's not just the body, but also the legs, head, eyes and hands that are involved in communication. Scientific studies have shown that the impressions left by people meeting are determined much less by the choice of words (8%) than by the stress (23%) and body posture (69%). Certain elements of body language can be learned with a lot of practice, but bodily behaviour only appears genuine if it is really meant, says Horst Rückle in his book "Körpersprache für Manager". The best that can be achieved is to make the perception of the body language of others the subject of seminars and training programmes.

Language

It is above all our hands that betray us, as language itself knows. It's not for nothing that there are countless idioms and sayings, not just in German, to do with hands.

Eine Hand wäscht die andere.
You scratch my back, I'll scratch yours.

Das hat einfach Hand und Fuß, was er macht.
What he says makes sense.

Herr Müller ist meine rechte Hand.
Herr Müller is my right-hand man.

Er hat die Information aus erster Hand.
He has the information first-hand.

Es liegt (klar) auf der Hand, dass das nicht geht.
It's obvious (as plain as can be) that that's not possible.

Sie hat einen guten Techniker an der Hand.
She's got a good technician on hand.

Im Handumdrehen war das Auto repariert.
The car was repaired in no time at all.

Mein Vater hat das in die Hand genommen. Jetzt klappt es auch.
My father has taken charge of it. Now it's working out.

Dieser junge Mann hat einfach zwei linke Hände. Nichts gelingt ihm.
This young man is all thumbs. He can't do anything right.

Sie hatten nichts mehr. Sie lebten von der Hand in den Mund.
They had nothing left. They were living from hand to mouth.

Der Politiker musste sich die Hände schmutzig machen.
The politician had to get his hands dirty.

Die Mitglieder des Teams arbeiten Hand in Hand.
The members of the team work hand in hand.

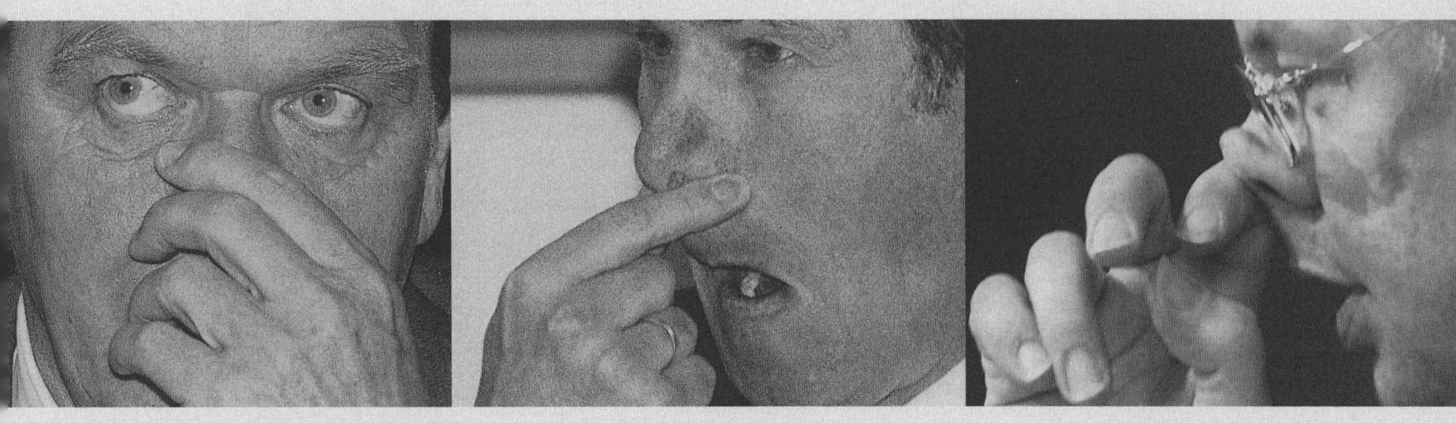

Drei prominente deutsche Politiker fassen sich an die Nase.

Fritz sagt

1 Read the picture story.

2 Add these expressions to the illustration.

das Auge, -n ● das Ohr, -en ●
der Mund ● der Kopf ● die Nase ●
der Hals ● das Gesicht

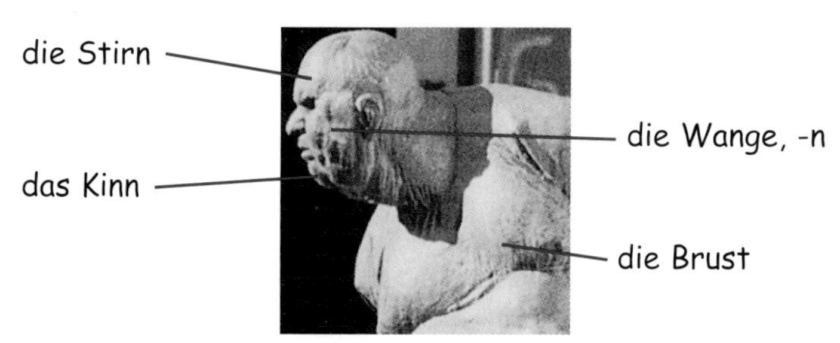

3 Write a sentence in the first and last speech bubble of the story.

4 Add these terms to the illustration.

der Körper ● der Arm, -e ●
der Finger, - ● der Bauch ●
das Bein, -e ● die Hand, Hände ●
der Fuß, Füße

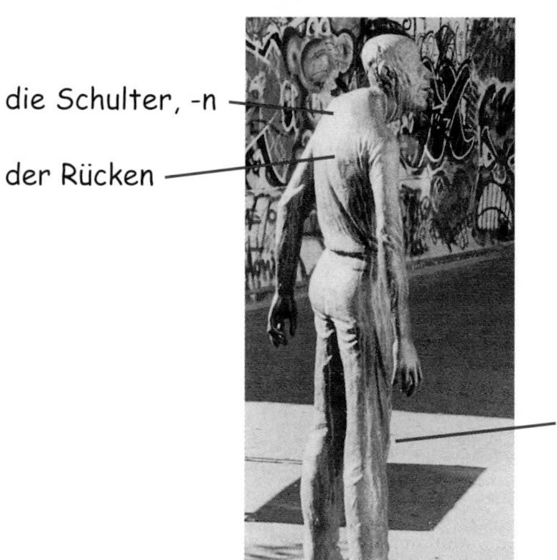

5 a Talk about the photo.

Who are the people?
What does their posture express?
What brought them together?
What are they talking about?
How are they talking to each other?

b Write a dialogue that might be going on between the two people.

6 What can people, legs, eyes, hands be like?
Sort the adjectives into the word-spiders and add additional ones of your own.

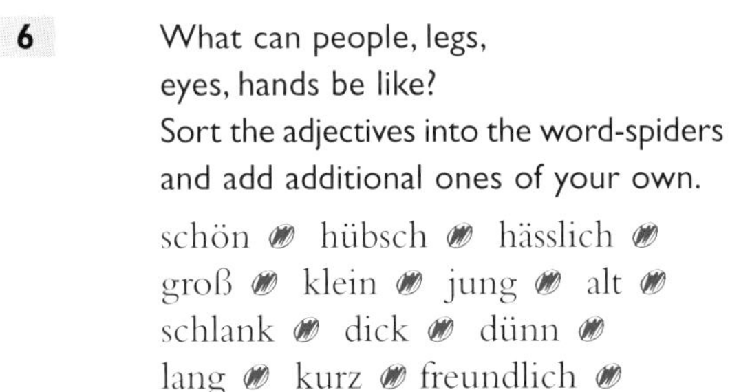

schön • hübsch • hässlich • groß • klein • jung • alt • schlank • dick • dünn • lang • kurz • freundlich • hell • dunkel • schwarz • rot • blau • grau • braun • grün • kalt • sympathisch • unsympathisch • schmal • breit • wütend • lustig • fröhlich • blond • traurig • ängstlich • schmutzig • gepflegt • sportlich • neidisch

Die Welt begreifen – eine kleine Kulturgeschichte der Hand

7 What do you like to touch, what don't you like touching? Why?

Ich fasse gerne/nicht gerne … an.
… fasse ich gerne/überhaupt nicht gerne an.

Wolle

Kuchenteig

Gras

Hundefell

Samt

Laub

Putzlumpen

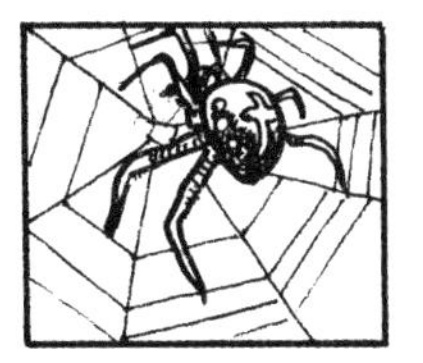
Spinnen, Spinnennetz oder …

8 What do you like doing with your hands? Why?

Katze streicheln

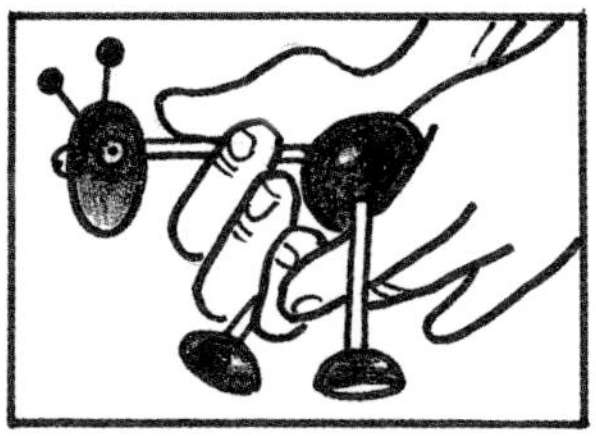

basteln

häkeln

spülen

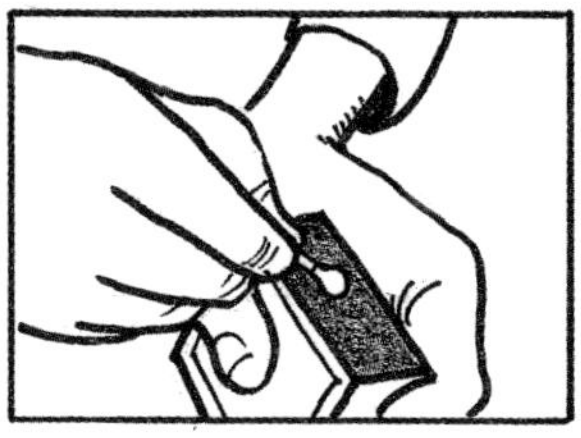

Streichholz anzünden

oder ...

9 In what situations when people are speaking do they use their hands as well?

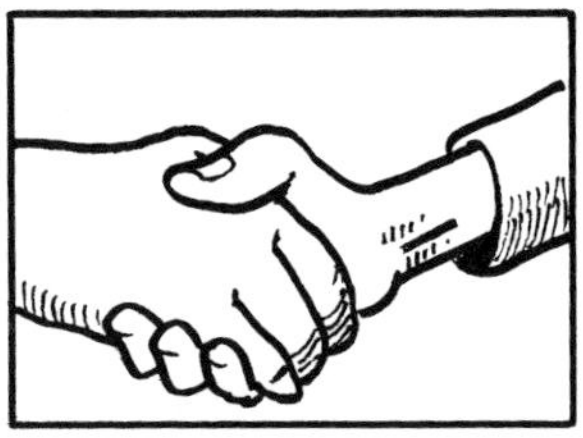

beim Begrüßen: Hände schütteln

vor Gericht: schwören; einen Schwur leisten

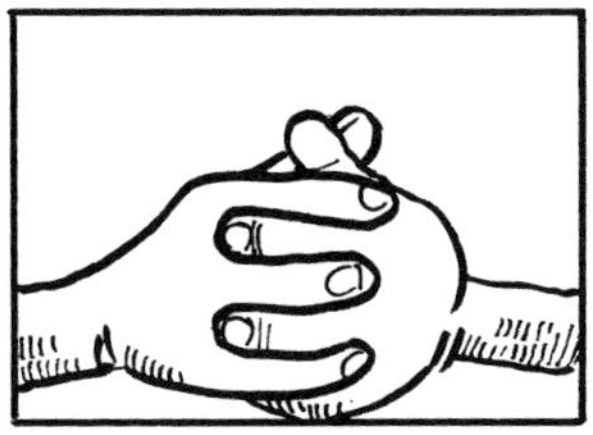

beim Gebet: die Hände falten

oder ...

10 Listen and take notes.

Was fassen die Personen gerne an?	Was fassen die Personen nicht gerne an?	Was machen die Personen gerne mit den Händen?
....	....	....
....	....	....
....	....	....

11 **a** First read the sentences that convey the main points from the text on page 241.

1 Der Autor ist der Meinung, dass die Hände uns sehr viel über eine Person sagen können.
2 Nach seiner Meinung ist es nicht wichtig, wie die Hände aussehen (gepflegt oder schmutzig), sondern wie sie etwas tun. Denn das kann eine Person nicht kontrollieren.
3 Er betrachtet bei Menschen immer nur die Hände, und zwar in allen Situationen.
4 Wenn er ihre Hände studiert hat, weiß er, wer sie sind und wie sie sind.

b Read the text. What passages do the sentences in a go with? Mark the passages and write down the line numbers.

1 line .... 2 line .... 3 line .... 4 line ....

Ein Dichter sieht Hände

Ich schwöre[1] auf die Hände der Menschen. Die Hände vermögen[2] zwar einen falschen Schwur zu leisten, sie können streicheln und wehtun, aber den Charakter ihres Trägers verraten sie dennoch. Die Hand mag[3] vom Alltagsschmutz beeinflusst werden, sie kann ungepflegt sein oder sie kann durch ausgezeichnete Maniküre zu
5 täuschen versuchen. Doch das sind Dinge, auf die ein Anfänger hereinfallen mag[3]. Die Hand verrät dich und verrät mich, weil sie im Augenblick der Beschäftigung unwillkürlich ist. Man achte doch einmal darauf, wie verschieden die Hände sich benehmen, wenn sie ein Streichholz anzünden oder wenn sie Geld zählen oder wenn sie sich zum Gebet falten. Wenn ich Menschen studiere, studiere ich ihre Hände, weil
10 wir die Seele im wahrsten Sinne des Wortes in den Händen tragen. Die Hand im Ganzen muss betrachtet werden: die Hand in der Ruhe, die Hand bei der Arbeit, die Hand beim Vergnügen. Stundenlang kann ich in einem Tanzcafé sitzen, möglichst nah an der Tanzfläche, mit nichts anderem beschäftigt, als die Hände der Tanzenden zu betrachten. Nachher vermag[2] ich nicht zu sagen, welche Kleidung die Damen tru-
15 gen, aber ich habe sie dennoch kennen gelernt.

Wolfram von Hanstein

1 auf etwas schwören = hier: etwas für sehr wichtig halten
2 vermag/vermögen = kann/können
3 mag/mögen = hier: kann/können

c What do the following verbs and adjective mean: *verraten* (line 3), *hereinfallen auf* (line 5), *achten auf* (line 7), *sich benehmen* (line 8), *beschäftigt sein mit* (*sich beschäftigen mit*) (line 13) und das Adjektiv *unwillkürlich* (line 7)? Work out the meaning from the context first, then check your translation in the wordlist in the handbook or a dictionary.

d Listen to the text.

Ich küsse Ihre Hand, Madame

12 Listen to the song and summarize its content.

Hauptsätze verbinden (Übersicht)

13 Underline the subject in each of the second main clauses.

Die Hand kann ungepflegt sein **oder** sie kann durch ausgezeichnete Maniküre zu täuschen versuchen.
Ich sitze oft stundenlang in einem Tanzcafé, **denn** ich betrachte gerne die Hände der Tanzenden.
Ich kann nicht sagen, welche Kleidung die Damen trugen, **aber** ich habe sie dennoch kennen gelernt.
Ich bin ja so galant, Madame, **doch** das hat seinen Grund,
Ihr Herz ist leider nicht mehr frei, **trotzdem** liebe ich Sie seit vielen Wochen.
Wir müssen jetzt gehen, **sonst** wird es zu spät.
Ich betrachte gern die Hände der Tanzenden, **deshalb/deswegen** sitze ich oft stundenlang in einem Tanzcafé.
Hände können streicheln, **außerdem** können sie wehtun.

14 What sentence model do the conjunctions in section 13 belong to? Enter the conjunctions here.

Hauptsatz				Hauptsatz		
Vorfeld	Verb	…	**Konjunktion** und, sondern, ...oder...........	Vorfeld	Verb	…

Hauptsatz			Hauptsatz		
Vorfeld	Verb	…	Vorfeld **Konjunktion** außerdem...........	Verb	…

Trotzdem, sonst, deshalb/ deswegen, außerdem können auch mitten im Satz stehen.
Wir müssen jetzt gehen, es wird **sonst** zu spät.

15 Change the position of *trotzdem, deswegen/deshalb, außerdem* in the sentences in section 13.

16 Write a story to go with the song on page 241: who are the people and what are they like? Where did they meet? What is the man dreaming about? How does the woman react? How does the story end?

Proceed as follows:

- Collect vocabulary (nouns, verbs, adjectives, connectors) on the individual points
- Formulate sentences (main clauses)
- Arrange the sentences in a sequence so that the structure is clear
- Link the sentences with conjunctions (→ table above and p. 167)
  Add reference words (→ p. 216)
- Give the story an appropriate title.

Die Hand in der Sprache

17 You might find the following text on the cover of a thriller.

a Read the text and underline all the words that contain *Hand*.

b Write down these words next to their translations.

c Fill in the missing translations.

Der Roman handelt von der Entführung[1] der Frau des Politikers K. Sonderbarerweise verlangen die Entführer kein Geld von K., sondern ein Handbuch zu einem ganz speziellen Computerprogramm, das K. in seinem Besitz hat. Von diesem Buch gibt es zwar nur wenige Exemplare, aber dass es so wertvoll sein soll? K. akzeptiert den Handel, aber noch bevor er den Entführern das Buch aushändigen kann, wird es ihm gestohlen. K. verhandelt mit den Entführern und bekommt einen Aufschub von 48 Stunden. Er muss schnell handeln, denn es handelt sich um das Leben seiner Frau. Die Zeit läuft …

handeln von.........:	be about
die Handlung:	....
............:	handbook
etw. handhaben:	deal with something
............:	deal
handeln mit etw.:	....
............:	hand sth. over to s.o.
............:	negotiate with s.o.
die Verhandlung:	....
............:	act
............:	concern

[1] die Entführung: kidnapping

draußen
Was passiert

Cultural information

In two texts we meet people who are ill, have to go to hospital and thus come into contact with the German health system. The average life expectancy of people in Central Europe has now climbed to 74 for a man and 81 for a woman. At the end of the 18th century the figure was between 35 and 40 years. The reason is a better way of life, but above all an improvement in medical care. In the past many people died at a young age, while today there are the appropriate medicines and cures for most illnesses. Medicine has not just gained in general esteem and importance, but has also become an important economic factor.

Not surprisingly, great attention is paid to the health services in the media. All the TV stations broadcast a steady stream of so-called doctors' series, which are far more popular than any thriller. The most popular of all was the series "Schwarzwaldklinik" which served up touching little stories of handsome doctors and good people. The two texts in this unit, however, show that illness, for all the progress that has been made and despite a well-functioning health service, can mean a lot of human hardship and misery.

Language

Maria Schmidt, Autorin,
32 Jahre, aus Bochum
So, 20 Uhr, Literaturhaus,
Platz reservieren!

If you go and study at a foreign university or have dealings with foreign business partners, you may well have to take a lot of notes in the foreign language. It's a good idea to learn techniques that help you take the right notes from what you hear and read, and construct texts from the notes once they're taken. Obviously you can't just leave things out at will. Usually it's the subjects or objects that are noted down, with or without attributes. It may also be necessary to note down a verb or the most important part of a verb phrase. You can usually miss out items that help to make the message into a text, such as conjunctions, adverbs and pronouns. As the most important information is usually at the end of a sentence, you should pay special attention to the end when you jot down your notes.

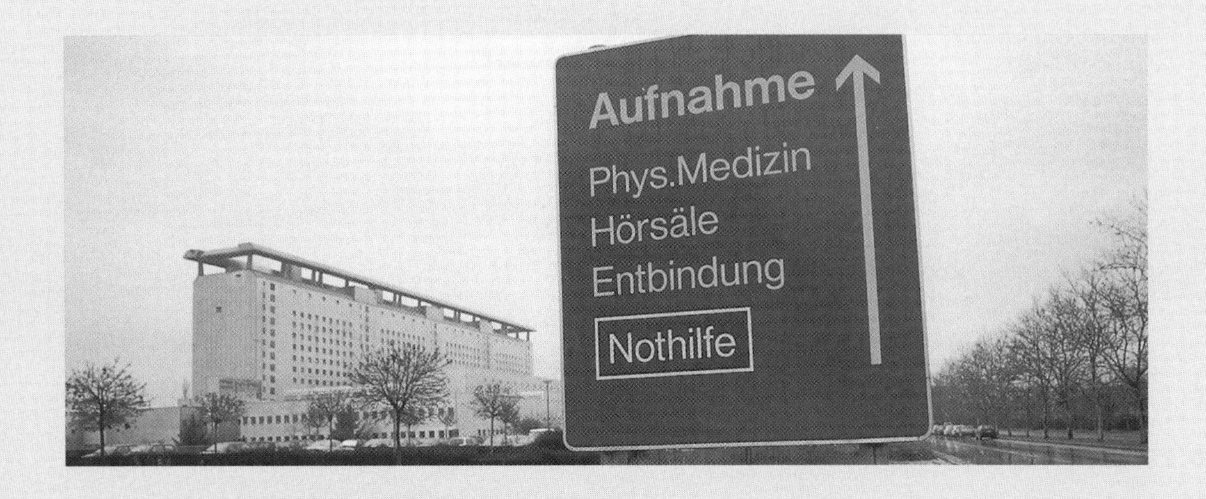

Was draußen passiert

1 Describe the picture.

2 Check the meaning of the words. Complete the word-spider.

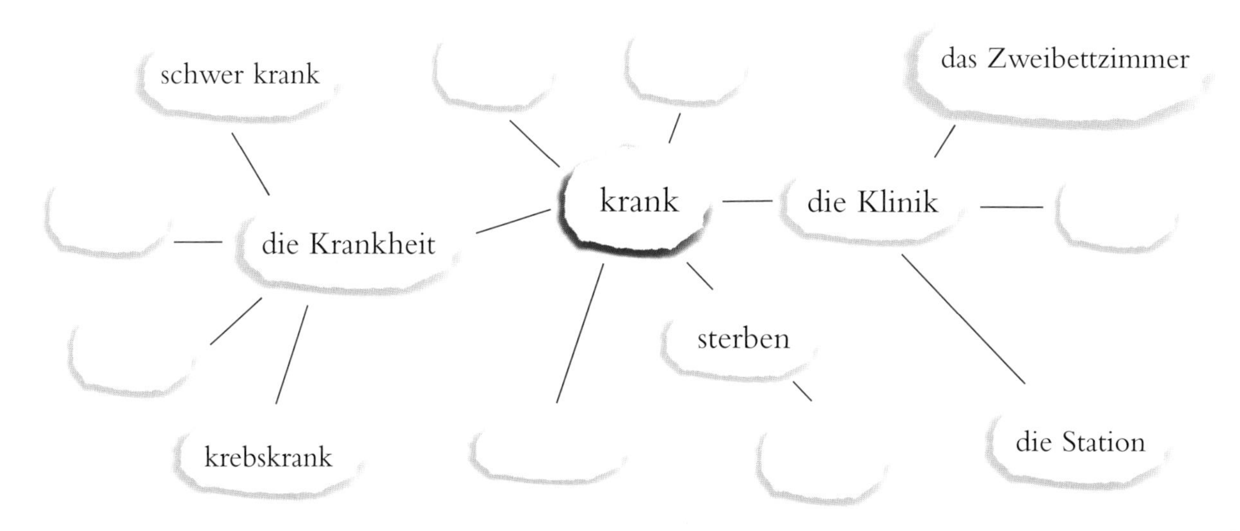

3 a Read the text and mark the noun (or a compound with it) that occurs most frequently.

b What does the man at the door want?

Was draußen passiert

Beste Geschichte meines Lebens. Anderthalb Maschinenseiten vielleicht. Autor vergessen; in der Zeitung gelesen.
Zwei Schwerkranke im selben Zimmer. Einer an der Tür liegend, einer am Fenster. Nur der am Fenster kann hinaussehen. Der andere keinen größeren Wunsch, als das Fensterbett zu erhalten. Der am Fenster leidet darunter.
Um den andern zu entschädigen, erzählt er ihm täglich stundenlang, was draußen zu sehen ist, was draußen passiert.
Eines Nachts bekommt er einen Erstickungsanfall[1].
Der an der Tür könnte die Schwester rufen. Unterlässt es; denkt an das Bett. Am Morgen ist der andere tot; erstickt.
Sein Fensterbett wird geräumt; der bisher an der Tür lag, erhält es. Sein Wunsch ist in Erfüllung gegangen. Gierig, erwartungsvoll wendet er das Gesicht zum Fenster.
Nichts; nur eine Mauer.

Wolfdietrich Schnurre

[1] Erstickungsanfall: choking fit

4 **a** Mark which sentences have the subject or verb missing.
b Determine in what part of the text there are the most complete sentences.
c Form complete sentences from the first four abbreviated ones.
d What sort of text is it? When do people write texts like this? Where do you find them?

5 What does *hinaussehen* mean? Deduce the meaning from its components and the context.

Verkürzte Sätze

Shortened sentences are used

- to describe events and circumstances very briefly when the rest of the sentence is clear anyway.

  Er wendet das Gesicht zum Fenster. **Nichts; nur eine Mauer.**

  Zwei Schwerkranke im selben Zimmer. Einer an der Tür liegend, einer am Fenster.

- to avoid repetitions, especially in speech.

  Warum? – Weil du ihn lieb gehabt hast. – **Den lebendigen?** – Genau. – **Hab ich ja gar nicht.**

- to make notes from a text (lecture, talk, conversation) or as a preparation for writing a text.

  Beste Geschichte meines Lebens. Anderthalb Maschinenseiten vielleicht. Autor vergessen.

6 Preparations for a party: Luise and Rudolf want to have a big party three weeks on Saturday to celebrate Rudolf's 30th birthday. They talk about all the things that have to be done.

a Read the following sentences and check the meaning of the unknown words.

Als Erstes müssen wir eine Liste mit allen Leuten erstellen, die wir einladen wollen. Dann fragen wir deine Schwester Ingrid, ob sie mir bei den Vorbereitungen helfen kann. Dann überlegen wir uns, was wir zum Essen anbieten, was wir selber kochen und was wir einkaufen. Vielleicht kann man den einen oder anderen fragen, ob er etwas mitbringen kann, Salate, Nachspeisen. Georg muss die Getränke besorgen und Eberhard Kassetten und CDs mitbringen, damit man auch tanzen kann. Die Personen, die ich einladen will, muss ich spätestens am Wochenbeginn anrufen, ob sie auch können und wollen. Die Telefonnummer von Ina und Jörg muss mir Franz besorgen, die sind nämlich umgezogen.

b Shorten the sentences and make them into notes.

1 Liste der Gäste
2 Ingrid fragen - Vorbereitung
3 ...

Domian – Eins Live

Im Westdeutschen Rundfunk Köln (WDR) gibt es jede Nacht von 1:00 bis 2:00 Uhr eine Sendung mit dem Titel „Domian". Die wird von vielen Tausenden von Menschen entweder im Radio (Eins Live) gehört oder im Fernsehen angesehen. Jürgen Domian, der Moderator dieser Sendung, lässt sich von seinen Hörern Geschichten erzählen. Meistens berichten sie über ihre Probleme. Einmal hat Hubert, ein 35 Jahre alter Mann, bei Domian angerufen. Er war leukämiekrank im Endstadium und hatte nur noch wenige Wochen zu leben. Hubert war sehr einsam. Er hatte weder Freunde noch Familie und er suchte Menschen, mit denen er reden konnte.
Einige Wochen später erreichte Jürgen Domian folgender Brief.

Hallo, Jürgen!

Ich schreibe dir noch einige Zeilen aus dem Uni-Klinikum, in dem ich nun doch liegen muss. Es ging nicht mehr zu Hause. Ich bin auf einer Station, die man in der Patientensprache die „Totenkopfstation" nennt. Es ist nicht gerade gemütlich hier, an einem Ort, wo nur Sterbende liegen.

Ich war überwältigt von der Briefflut, die mich von euch erreicht hat. Ich wusste gar nicht, wo ich anfangen sollte zu antworten. Und ich hatte ein paar sehr schöne Gespräche. Zur Zeit bin ich nur noch wenige Stunden am Tag wach. Und diese Zeit nutze ich, um die Natur zu bestaunen, denn die „Totenkopfstation" liegt im dritten Untergeschoss. Es ist schön, ein grünes Blatt in den Händen zu halten. Wie schön wäre es, richtig zu leben. Leben um zu leben. Grüße alle Hörer von mir und das Team von „Eins Live". Und ganz besonders grüße ich dich, lieber Jürgen.

Entschuldige meine schlechte Schrift, aber in der rechten Hand liegt eine Kanüle.
Und nun, lieber Jürgen, noch ein kleines Gedicht zum Abschied.

Ich wünsche dir nicht alle möglichen Gaben.
Ich wünsche dir, was die meisten nicht haben,
Ich wünsche dir Zeit,
dich zu freuen und zu lachen.
Und wenn du sie nutzt, kannst du etwas draus machen.
Ich hoffe, ich habe es bald geschafft.

Viele Grüße von der Factory of Death.

Bye Hubert

Du kannst diesen Brief auch gerne im Radio oder TV vorlesen - als Dank für alle Hörer.

7 **a** Take notes on the most important information about the programme and Hubert's letter.

Sendung: WDR Köln, „Domian", 1:00 bis 2:00 Uhr, ...
Huberts Brief: Uniklinik, Totenkopfstation, leukämiekrank, ...

b Give an oral report about Domian's programme and Hubert's letter, using your notes.

Zeit haben

8 Bavarian Radio's daily programme "Das Notizbuch" dealt with the topic "Zeit haben" on 14.12.1998. What do you think was said? Note down a few sentences or keywords.

9 **a** Read the introduction to the programme and check the meaning of unknown words.
b What effect do the pills have?

In der berühmten Geschichte „Der kleine Prinz" von Saint-Exupéry begegnet der kleine Prinz dem Händler, der höchst wirksame durststillende Pillen verkauft. Wer jede Woche eine Pille schluckt, spürt überhaupt keinen Durst mehr. Auf die Frage des kleinen Prinzen, wozu das nützlich sei, antwortet der Händler, dass damit 53 Minuten Zeitersparnis erzielt werden können und dass man mit dieser eingesparten Zeit frei sei, das zu tun, was man will. Wenn ich 53 Minuten übrig hätte, antwortete darauf der kleine Prinz, würde ich ganz gemächlich zu einem Brunnen laufen.

10 **a** Now listen to the whole text.
b Listen to the text again and note down key words and phrases.
c Use your notes to write a short summary of the text that will be used to describe the programme in a radio and TV magazine.

Zweck und Ziel: *damit, um ... zu* + Infinitiv

11 Compare the sentences.

Der Händler verkauft die Pille, **damit** die Leute keinen Durst mehr haben.
Man nimmt die Pille einmal pro Woche, **um** Zeit ein**zu**sparen.
Er erzählt, was draußen passiert, **um** den anderen **zu** entschädigen.
Diese Zeit nutze ich, **um** die Natur **zu** bestaunen.
Wie schön wäre es zu leben, **um zu** leben.
Der Esel muss das Korn tragen, **damit** andere das Brot essen können.
Der Affe soll immer lustige Streiche machen, **damit** die Leute lachen.

12 The same or different? Complete.

Purpose is expressed with *damit* or *um ... zu* + infinitive.
The conjunction *um ... zu* + infinitive can only be used when the subjects of both sentences are .... If the subjects are .... , the conjunction *damit* is used.

13 Finish the sentences using the following expressions.

sich informieren ◆ informiert sein ◆ sich erholen ◆ besser einschlafen ◆ Spaß haben ◆ nicht denken müssen ◆ Probleme vergessen ◆ sich nicht langweilen ◆ nicht immer zu Hause sitzen ◆ sich über die neuesten Filme/Theaterstücke unterhalten können ◆ nicht allein sein

1 Ich höre Radio, um ... Ich höre Radio, um mich zu informieren.
2 Ich sehe fern, um ...
3 Ich sehe mir die Sendung ... an, um ...
4 Ich lese Zeitung/Bücher, um ...
5 Ich gehe ins Kino / ins Theater / ins Konzert / in die Disko / in die Kneipe, um ...

14 *Um ... zu* + infinitive or *damit*? Link the sentences.

1 Domian lässt sich in seiner Sendung Geschichten erzählen. Viele Hörer können so von den Problemen anderer hören.

Domian lässt sich in seiner Sendung Geschichten erzählen, damit viele Hörer von den Problemen anderer hören können.

2 Hubert schrieb einen Brief an Domian. Er wollte ihm danken.
Hubert schrieb einen Brief an Domian, um ihm zu danken.

3 Wolfram von Hanstein beobachtet die Hände von Menschen. So lernt er sie kennen.
4 Brigitte stellte mehrere Ausreiseanträge. Sie wollte nach Südfrankreich reisen und dort malen.
5 Mozart berechnete für seine öffentlichen Auftritte als Pianist hohe Honorare. Er und seine Frau konnten viel Geld ausgeben.
6 Der Firmenberater Metcalf veranstaltet Seminare. Die Manager sollen ihren Humor trainieren.
7 Wir sollten mehr lachen und spielen. So werden wir motivierter und kreativer.
8 Morgenmuffel stehen spät auf. So sind sie abends wach und aktiv.

Möglichkeit ausdrücken

Was draußen zu sehen ist.	*sein* + *zu* + Infinitiv
Was man draußen sehen kann. / Was man da sehen könnte.	*können* + Infinitiv
Es kann/könnte sein, dass ich nicht mehr lebe, wenn	*es kann/könnte sein, dass ...*
Es ist (un)möglich, dass wir Zeit zum Diskutieren finden.	*Es ist (un)möglich, dass ...*
Wir haben möglicherweise keine Zeit.	*möglicherweise*

Awkward passive constructions can be avoided by using *sein* + *zu* + infinitive *Was draußen zu sehen ist* instead of *Was draußen gesehen werden kann.*

15 Write down all the things that are possible.

1 sehen – im deutschen Fernsehen – interessante Sendungen

Im deutschen Fernsehen kann man viele interessante Sendungen sehen.
Im deutschen Fernsehen sind viele interessante Sendungen zu sehen.

2 finden – das Fernsehprogramm – die Zeitschrift „Die Fernsehwoche“
3 sehen – „Domian“ – um 1 Uhr nachts
4 hören/sehen – Domians Sendung – sowohl im Fernsehen als auch im Radio
5 empfangen – viele ausländische Programme – über Satellit oder Internet

Des Schweizers Schweiz

Cultural information

What does the average European know about Switzerland? That they make good cheese, good chocolate and good clocks there, that the banks are so discreet that rich people and dictators can tuck away their money without fear, and that the Swiss mountains and lakes are a wonderful place to spend a holiday. In addition, Switzerland is considered one of the most boring countries in Europe, the Swiss conservative and clever business people. But if you go into things a bit more, you discover some very surprising facts about Switzerland. It is the only country with a direct democracy, every street, every law has to be passed by the whole population. The government therefore has more of an administrative role, and the State President is appointed on just a yearly basis. That's why nobody knows him or her. Switzerland is not a member of the European Union, not in NATO, not in the UN, and that in the middle of Europe! But Geneva is the seat of countless international organizations. The country has not been involved in any war for 200 years, and yet is heavily armed. Every man between the ages of 20 and 50 is liable to military service and is called up for exercises on a regular basis. This is the reason every adult Swiss man has his uniform and arms at home in his cupboard. The whole country is criss-crossed by an elaborate system of bunkers. It is said Hitler didn't attack Switzerland because he was afraid he wouldn't be able to capture it.

Language

Apart from its fixed position in a main clause, the verb has another peculiarity: it determines which items definitely have to be part of the sentence for it to be grammatically complete. Thus most verbs require, in addition to the subject, a compulsory object (accusative or dative object, prepositional object or locational object). Optional complementing elements are adverbials of time, of reason, of manner or place. A sentence does not need them to be grammatically complete.

The central part of the sentence

	Satzklammer			
Jeden Morgen	ging	**sie schnell an mir**	vorbei,	ohne zu grüßen.
Vorfeld		**Mittelfeld**		Nachfeld

The central part (Mittelfeld) contains the sentence's real message and thus often has several obligatory and/or optional complementing elements. Their position is determined by certain basic rules. What is known, has already been mentioned, is placed at the beginning of the central section, the new information goes at the end. The optional items are generally in the middle of the central section.

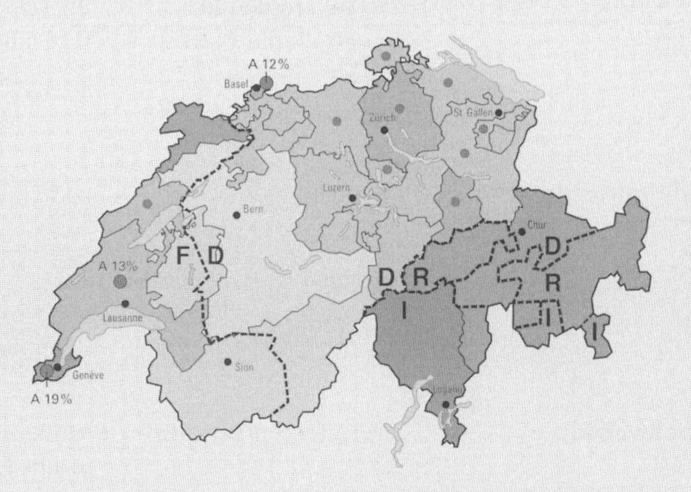

Schweizer Varianten

Velo = Fahrrad

Pult = Schreibtisch

absitzen = sich hinsetzen

Billett = Fahrkarte/Eintrittskarte

Morgenessen = Frühstück

zügeln = umziehen

Taxcard = Telefonkarte

Fürsprech = Rechtsanwalt

Des Schweizers Schweiz

1 **a** What does home (country) mean to you? Jot down in note form or whole sentences what the concept makes you think of.
b Rank your associations in order of importance.

2 **a** Read the sentences in the left-hand column. These sentences give you an idea of the content of the text on page 251.
b Check the meaning of the words/expressions on the right, read the relevant passage in the text and write down the English translation.

Ich lebe in diesem Land.
(line 1–7)

sich etw. einbilden
to imagine s.th. ....

das Gehaben (das Verhalten)
....

erkennen (eine Person an ihrer Stimme ~; etwas an der Farbe ~)
....

der/die Schüchterne
....

der/die Weltgewandte
....

unterscheiden (von/zwischen)
....

Ich fühle mich hier zu Hause.
(lines 8–10)

schwer fallen (Es fällt mir schwer.)
....

das Heimweh
....

Die Schweiz ist mir bekannt.
(lines 11–13)

etw. ist jdm. bekannt (etw. kennen)
....

angenehm
....

das Bekannte
....

etw./jdn. durchschauen
....

Ich fühle mich hier sicher.
(lines 14–16)

einordnen (z. B. eine Person als konservativ ~; etw. als gut oder schlecht ~)
....

die Regel (Norm)
....

das Außerordentliche (anders als die Norm)
....

überraschen (Das überrascht mich.)
....

die Heimat
....

... ich leide unter dem Föhn.
(lines 18–21)

der Nebel
....

leiden unter
....

das schlechte Gewissen
....

besteigen (z. B. einen Berg)
....

etw. sein lassen = etw. nicht tun
....

Ich bin Schweizer.
(lines 22–24)

ärgern (etw. ärgert jdn.)
....

Mühe machen (etw. macht jdm. Mühe)
....

beschäftigen (etw. beschäftigt jdn.)
....

Des Schweizers Schweiz

Ich lebe in diesem Land.
Es läßt sich in diesem Land leben.
Ich bin hier geboren. Ich bin hier aufgewachsen. Ich verstehe die Sprache dieser Gegend.
Ich weiß, was ein Männerchor ist, was eine Dorfmusik ist, ein Familienabend einer Partei.
5 Ich bilde mir ein, hier leidenschaftliche Briefmarkensammler auf der Straße an ihrem Gehaben erkennen zu können. Nur hier kann ich mit Sicherheit Schüchterne von Weltgewandten unterscheiden.
Ich fühle mich hier zu Hause. Auch mir fällt es schwer, mir vorzustellen, daß sich jemand so zu Hause fühlen kann wie ein Schweizer in der Schweiz.
10 Ich leide unter Heimweh; aber es ist bestimmt nur Heimweh nach dem Bekannten.
Die Schweiz ist mir bekannt. Das macht sie mir angenehm. Hier kenne ich die Organisation. Hier kann ich etwas durchschauen. Ich weiß, wie viel die Dinge hier ungefähr kosten, und ich brauche das Geld, mit dem ich bezahle, nicht umzurechnen.
Ich fühle mich hier sicher, weil ich einordnen kann, was hier geschieht. Hier kann ich unter-
15 scheiden zwischen der Regel und dem Außerordentlichen. Vielleicht bedeutet das Heimat.
Daß ich sie liebe, überrascht mich nicht.
...
Wir haben in dieser Gegend viel Nebel und ich leide unter dem Föhn. Der Jura und die Alpen machen mir vor allem ein schlechtes Gewissen, weil ich immer das Gefühl habe, ich müßte
20 sie besteigen und es doch immer wieder sein lasse. Ich habe mit nichts so viel Ärger wie mit der Schweiz und mit Schweizern.
Was mich freut und was mich ärgert, was mir Mühe und was mir Spaß macht, was mich beschäftigt, hat fast ausschließlich mit der Schweiz und mit den Schweizern zu tun. Das meine ich, wenn ich sage: „Ich bin Schweizer."

Peter Bichsel

3 Read the text again, this time closely.

a Find out the meaning of the compounds in the first section (lines 1–7) by breaking them down into their components.

ein Männer/chor, ein Welt/gewandter ...

Define them.

Männerchor: ein Chor, in dem nur Männer singen

b Divide the longer sentences into their elements (→ p. 77).

	Auch mir fällt es schwer,			
Was?		mir vorzustellen,		
Was?			dass sich jemand so zu Hause fühlen kann,	
Wie?				wie ein Schweizer in der Schweiz.

4 a Compare what it says about *Heimat* in the text with your notes from section 1. Add words and ideas from the text.

b Summarize in one or two sentences what the author understands by *Heimat*.

5 a How can you recognize *leidenschaftliche Briefmarkensammler, Schüchterne, Weltgewandte?*

b What type of people do you recognize straightaway and how?

6 What is the rule for you, what the exception? What rules should a foreigner who comes to your country know?

Obligatorische und fakultative Ergänzungen

Most verbs need an object as well as a subject to make a complete sentence: **compulsory complementation**.

Er schläft. Die Sonne scheint. Die Blumen blühen.	subject + verb
Sie wohnt in Bern.	subject + verb + place adverbial
Die Alpen machen mir ein schlechtes Gewissen.	subject + verb + dative object + accusative object
Verliebte träumen vom Mond.	subject + verb + preposition and prep. object

7 What are the compulsory complementing elements and the matching questions in the following sentences?

Akkusativergänzung ● Dativergänzung ● Ergänzung mit Präposition ● Ortsergänzung ● Nominativergänzung

Wo? ● Wem? ● Wohin? ● Woran? ● Was?

1. Peter Bichsel ist ein ziemlich bekannter Autor. Nominativergänzung – Was?
2. Er schrieb den Text „Des Schweizers Schweiz" 1967. ....
3. Die Schweiz ist ihm bekannt. ....
4. Er lebt in diesem Land. ....
5. Auch viele Ausländer leben dort ....

   und viele fahren in die Schweiz, um Urlaub zu machen. ....
6. Er schrieb auch: Kein Schweizer denkt an Demokratie, wenn er an die Schweiz denkt, er denkt nur an Prosperität. ....

There are complementing elements that are not necessary for the sentence to be grammatically complete. They provide references about time, reason, manner, place: **optional complementing elements.**

Die alte Dame sitzt **auf einer Parkbank.**	compulsory element
Sie hat viel Geld **auf einer Schweizer Bank.**	optional element (place reference)

8 Complete the list.

Hinweise zur Zeit: Wann? Wie lange? Seit wann? Bis wann?

1987 – vor einigen Wochen – morgen – seit drei Jahren – von acht bis zehn Uhr – immer im August – ...

Hinweise zum Grund: Warum?

aus diesem Grund – aus Angst – aus Liebe – wegen seiner Krankheit – ...

Hinweise zur Art und Weise: Wie?

langsam – herzlich – mit deiner Hilfe – auf dem kürzesten Weg – mit großer Freude – mit dem Zug – ohne Probleme – ...

Hinweise zum Ort: Wo? Wohin? Woher?

in Genf – aus Berlin – hier – dort – dorthin – in die Alpen – nach Italien – ...

9 a Cross out the optional complementing elements in the following sentences.

Peter Bichsel schreibt:

Ich bilde mir ein, hier leidenschaftliche Briefmarkensammler auf der Straße an ihrem Gehaben erkennen zu können.

Nur hier kann ich mit Sicherheit Schüchterne von Weltgewandten unterscheiden.

Wir haben viel Nebel in dieser Gegend.

Ich gestatte mir an einem Föhntag das Alpenpanorama zu ignorieren.

Schweizer tragen im Ausland ihr Geld in Beuteln unter dem Hemd oder eingenäht in der Unterwäsche.

b What do the optional elements give information about: time, manner, place?

Architektur von Sätzen: Mittelfeld

Vorfeld	Verb			**Mittelfeld**		Verb
		Subjekt	**obligatorische Ergänzungen**	**fakultative Ergänzungen**	**obligatorische Ergänzungen**	
			Nominativ Akkusativ (Bekanntes) Dativ		Nominativ Akkusativ/Dativ (neue Information) Erg. mit Präp. Ortsergänzung	
Der Autor	ist				Schweizer.	
Er	kann			in der Schweiz	alle Situationen	einordnen.
Dort	kennt	er	alles	seit vielen Jahren.		
Er	kann		Menschen	auf der Straße	an ihrem Gehaben	erkennen.
Die Alpen	machen		dem Autor	immer wieder	ein schlechtes Gewissen.	
Außerdem	leidet	er		oft	unter dem Föhn.	
Trotzdem	lebt	er		gern	in der Schweiz.	

There is a basic rule governing the order of optional complementing elements:
time – reason – manner – place.
If there are several optional elements, one of them is usually in initial position in the sentence.
Wegen des schönen Wetters gingen viele Touristen **gestern Abend im Park** spazieren.

10 Read the texts and add the time, place and manner adverbials.

Nach Informationen von „World Development Indicators 1998“ ist die Schweiz das reichste Land der Welt. Der durchschnittliche Bruttolohn lag bei monatlich 5 000 Franken. Die Schweizer arbeiten 40,5 Stunden pro Woche, 4,7 Stunden mehr als ihre Nachbarn. Sie liegen klar an der Spitze.	im Jahr 1996 in Deutschland in Europa

Wilhelm Tell – ein Mythos? Oder schoss er wirklich seinem Sohn den Apfel vom Kopf? Man ist sich nicht sicher. Aber Schillers Drama und Rossinis Oper machten ihn bekannt.	schon seit dem 18. Jahrhundert in der ganzen Welt

Esprit, Poesie, Zelebration: die Basler Fasnacht. Die „drei schönsten Tage“ beginnen mit dem „Morgestraich“ der Trommler und Pikkolospieler.	am Montag nach Aschermittwoch – um vier Uhr früh

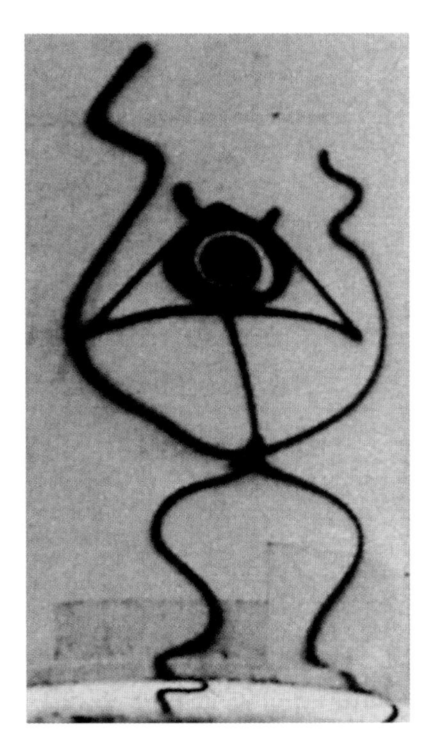

Für Harald Naegeli ist Zürich „ein geputztes Weltdorf, wo zahlreiche Saubermänner und -weiber mit ewigem Reinemachen beschäftigt sind“. Der poetische Anarchist sprayte seine Figuren auf Beton und ärgerte Polizei und Bürger.	zwei Jahre lang (1977–1979) – nachts – unbeobachtet
Dann flüchtete er nach Deutschland, wo die Heidelberger Stadtreinigung bedauerte, dass sie ein Werk von ihm entfernt hat. Er wurde zu neun Monaten Gefängnis verurteilt.	„irrtümlich“ in der Schweiz

Wie meinen Sie das?

11 Das meine ich, wenn ich sage: „Ich bin Schweizer."

a Read the sentences aloud paying attention to the stress (´) and intonation (↗ or ↘).
b Match the explanations to the sentences.

1 Wie meinen Sie das? / Was meinen Sie damit? ↘
2 Was meinen Sie (dazu)? ↗
3 Ich meine Sie/dich! ↘
4 Was meinen Sie? ↗
5 Haben Sie mich gemeint? ↗

a Man hat etwas nicht gut gehört/verstanden.
b Man spricht mit einer Person, aber die reagiert nicht.
c Man fragt eine bestimmte Person um ihre Meinung.
d Man weiß nicht, mit wem eine Person spricht.
e Man bittet um eine Erklärung.

Aussprache: *ch, ig, chs*

12 a Listen and read.
Ich lebe in der Schweiz. **Ich** bin hier aufgewa**chs**en.
Ich fühle mi**ch** hier si**ch**er. **Ich** verstehe die Spra**ch**e.
Nur hier kann **ich** mit Si**ch**erheit Schü**ch**terne erkennen.
Das alles ist wi**chtig** und beschäfti**gt** mi**ch**.

b Listen and read, repeat.
ich – auch schlecht – acht sprechen – gesprochen das Gespräch – die Sprache
Meinst du nicht? Ist das richtig? Ist das leicht?
Noch eine Woche. Das habe ich nicht gedacht. Du hast es nicht gesucht.

c Listen and read, repeat.
glücklich – ruhig glückliche Leute – ruhige Gegend
täglich – fleißig tägliches, fleißiges Training

d Note down other words in which *ig* is pronounced like *ch*.

e Listen and read, repeat.
sechs die sechste Reihe wachsen Ich bin hier aufgewachsen.
Sie ist schon erwachsen. Am nächsten Tag Höchstens zwanzig Euro

Jetzt reden wir – Mitbestimmung, Volksabstimmung

„Alle Staatsgewalt geht vom Volk aus", so steht es im Grundgesetz der Bundesrepublik Deutschland, aber nur alle vier Jahre bei den Wahlen. Ganz anders bei den Nachbarn in der Schweiz. Dort ist das Mitbestimmen bei staatlichen (eidgenössischen), kantonalen und die Gemeinde betreffenden Entscheidungen längst eine Selbstverständlichkeit.

13 Listen to the excerpts from an interview with representatives from Switzerland and Germany.
The Germans want to have more say. What reasons are given?
What form does participation take in Switzerland? Note down key words and phrases.

Die Schweiz – in Stichworten

14 Read the texts and match the headings.

Die Schweiz – ein Reiseland ● Ein Land, aber mehrere Kulturen ● So sagt man in der Schweiz ● Die Schweiz in Zahlen ● Kein Nationalbewusstsein?

1 ....

Die Schweiz ist ein Bundesstaat mit 26 souveränen Kantonen. Die Bundeshauptstadt ist Bern. Auf 41 285 km² leben 7 081 Millionen Einwohner (1996). 60% der Landesfläche entfallen auf die Alpen. Als letztes europäisches Land führte die Schweiz 1971 das Frauenwahlrecht auf Bundesebene ein – in den Kantonen wurde es erst 1990 überall realisiert. Die Währung ist der Schweizer Franken (CHF), er gilt seit langem als härteste Währung der Welt.
Im Jahr 1992 lehnten die Schweizer in einer Volksabstimmung den Beitritt zum Europäischen Wirtschaftsraum ab.

aus: *Munzinger Archiv*

2 ....

Die Schweizer differenzieren sich ethnisch und sprachlich in Angehörige der deutschen, französischen, italienischen und rätoromanischen Sprach- und Kulturgemeinschaft und bilden eine über Jahrhunderte gewachsene vielfältige Nation. Amtssprachen sind Deutsch, Französisch und Italienisch. Neben diesen drei Sprachen ist seit 1938 Rätoromanisch als vierte Landessprache anerkannt.

aus: *Munzinger Archiv*

3 ....

„Hier wurde bereits in der Mitte des 19. Jahrhunderts der moderne Tourismus erfunden. Nicht etwa von reiselustigen Eidgenossen[1], sondern von jenen allgegenwärtigen Engländern, die halsbrecherische Bergtouren unternahmen und Sonnenuntergänge bewunderten. Aber die Schweiz war schon lange vorher ein Reiseziel par exellence und sie ist es heute mehr denn je."

Paul L. Walser

[1] Eidgenossen = inhabitants of Switzerland

Fr. R. de Chateaubriand berichtete dagegen 1832: „Ich atme nicht besser, mein Blut läuft nicht schneller, mein Kopf ist nicht weniger schwer im Alpenhimmel als in Paris."

4 ....

Stellt man in der Schweiz die Routinefrage: „Wie geht's?", dann kann man immer wieder die Routineantwort hören: „Man kann nicht klagen." Man sagt nicht: „Es geht gut", sondern eben: „Man kann nicht klagen." Der ursprüngliche Zustand scheint das Klagen zu sein, und wenn es einem „besser" oder „gut" geht, nähert man sich jener Verfassung, die sich am ehesten als ein „Nicht-Klagen" umschreiben lässt.

Hugo Loetscher

5 ....

„Dieses Land ist human, weil es mir kein bestimmtes Maß an Patriotismus abverlangt. Hat nicht die Schweiz als vielleicht einziges Land der Welt ihre Nationalhymne so verloren, wie jemand seine Brille verlegt? Die jetzige Melodie ist ausdrücklich als Provisorium deklariert, singen kann sie keiner."

Markus Kutter

Nicht

Cultural information

In 1940, when the Italian dictator Mussolini issued an ultimatum to Greece with the aim of occupying northern Greece with Italian troops, he received a telegram from his Greek counterpart with just one word: no. Hitler took this "no" as his cue to occupy the small country with German troops, in what was the last of a series of blitzkrieg attacks and ultimately the beginning of the end of this dreadful war. Since then, one of Greece's two national holidays is dedicated to this "no". Something like that would be unthinkable in Germany. In German culture and society, negation has been regarded as an expression of evil for centuries. Even liberal Goethe felt this way, when he put the following words into Mephisto's mouth in his *Faust*.

Mephisto: Ich bin der Geist,
der stets verneint!
Und das mit Recht; denn alles,
was entsteht,
ist wert, dass es zu Grunde geht.
Drum besser wär's, dass nichts
entstünde,
so ist denn alles, was ihr Sünde,
Zerstörung, kurz das Böse nennt,
mein eigentliches Element.

Johann Wolfgang von Goethe, Faust

Mephisto: I am the spirit
that ever negates!
And rightly so; for all that
comes into being
deserves ruin and decay.
Thus it would be better
if nothing came into being,
and all that you call sin,
destruction, in short evil
is my true element.

As a German it is possible to identify with the doubter, megalomaniac Faust, but not with his seducer Mephisto. Thus Germans have become a nation of yes-men. If they are given a goal to work towards, they set out to achieve it, in a disciplined and imaginative way, but saying "no" and asserting themselves in their dissent is not one of their strengths. Maybe that's the reason they've never managed a real revolution.
On the other hand, the philosophers Friedrich Hegel, Karl Marx and Friedrich Nietzsche have grappled with negation and granted it an important function in dialectics.
As intellectuals often express the result of their deliberations in negative terms, they don't have such a high standing as in other cultures. This is the reason why it was easy for the National Socialists to drive practically the whole of the intelligentsia out of the country within the space of just a few years.

Text

The text in this unit is an essay about German grammar. You may well find certain passages difficult to understand fully because they contain technical terms and abstract concepts. The only thing that's important is what you learn from it about negation in German. The text deals with the question of where the little word "nicht" can be placed in a sentence. That depends above all on what is being negated – the whole sentence, part of a sentence or just a word.

1 a Skim through the text. What function do the sentences in inverted commas have?

NICHT

Es gibt in ausländischen Universitätsbibliotheken ganze Bände über das Wörtchen „nicht". Verfasst von Sprachwissenschaftlern verschiedener Fachgebiete, die sich alle zum Ziel gesetzt haben[1], diesem „Geist, der stets verneint" auf die Schliche zu kommen[2].

5 Allen voran zerbrechen sich die Syntaktiker den Kopf über die Standortstrategie[3] des verneinenden Adverbs. Sie möchten wissen – und dieses Wissen dann didaktisch, also lehrend, vermitteln –, warum „nicht" ständig seinen Platz wechselt und welche Auswirkungen diese außergewöhnliche Mobilität auf den Sinn des ganzen Satzes hat.

Da gibt es zunächst den grundlegenden Unterschied zwischen der globalen Ver-
10 neinung und der, welche sich auf nur ein Element des Satzes bezieht:

„Deutsch wird in der ganzen Schweiz nicht gesprochen." (nirgendwo)
„Deutsch wird nicht in der ganzen Schweiz gesprochen." (nicht überall)
„Nicht Deutsch wird in der ganzen Schweiz gesprochen." (sondern?)

Bei globaler Verneinung, heißt es weiter, steht „nicht" nach Objekten (Ergänzungen)
15 ohne Präposition, doch vor Objekten (Ergänzungen) mit Präposition:

„Er hat seinen Wagen nicht abgeschlossen."
„Er ist nicht mit dem Wagen gekommen."
„Er hat seinen Wagen nicht in die Garage gefahren."

Alles klar? Übung:

20 „Er hat (nicht) die Wahrheit (nicht) gesagt."
„Er wird sich doch (nicht) das Leben (nicht) nehmen!"
„Er hat (noch nie) Schach (noch nie) gespielt."

Lösung: In allen drei Fällen ist die zweite Verneinung falsch.

Obwohl es keine Präposition gibt. Denn „die Wahrheit sagen", „sich das Leben nehmen",
25 „Schach (Klavier, Fußball ...) spielen" sind so genannte feste Verbindungen.
Das heißt, dass das Objekt sich wie eine trennbare Verbpartikel verhält:

„Er sieht jeden Abend fern."
„Er hat heute nicht ferngesehen."
„Er sagt immer die Wahrheit."
30 „Er hat diesmal nicht die Wahrheit gesagt."

Beobachten wir nun folgende Sätze:

A: „Ich habe diesen Menschen noch nie gesehen."
B: „Ich habe noch nie einen Marsmenschen gesehen."

Hier geht es um die Anordnung von Bekanntem (Bezugteil) und Unbekanntem
35 (Informationsteil) im deutschen Satz. „Diesen Menschen" (A) habe ich zwar noch nie gesehen, es war aber schon von ihm die Rede[4], demnach ist er – laut Grundgesetz des deutschen Satzes – keine neue Information und wird also so früh wie möglich abgefertigt. Neu und wichtig ist die Verneinung des Verbs „gesehen". Anders beim Marsmenschen (B): Er ist die Antwort auf die Frage, was ich denn noch nie gesehen hätte
40 – also kommt er, der Marsmensch, so weit nach hinten wie möglich.

Dies zu den Standortbestimmungen der Verneinung.

Waltraud Legros

[1] sich etw. zum Ziel setzen: set oneself the goal of doing sth.
[2] jdm. auf die Schliche kommen: find s.o. out
[3] die Standortstrategie: positioning strategy
[4] es ist/war die Rede von: there is / has been mention of

b Find two sentences that state the topic of the text.

2 Read lines 1–8 and work out the meaning of new words:

- from the context
  e.g. Bände: Es gibt in ausländischen Universitätsbibliotheken ganze Bände über das Wörtchen „nicht".
- nouns from other nouns or the verb, verbs through the noun
  e.g. wechseln: Was für ein Verb passt zu *Platz* in diesem Kontext?
- by breaking the word down into its components, e.g.: Sprach/wissen/schaft, Ver/nein/ung

3 Read lines 9–13. In which example is the whole sentence negated (global negation), in which one just one element of the sentence?

4 What is negated here – the whole sentence or just one element? Mark the sentences where only one element is negated with a cross.

1 Sie brauchen nicht alle Wörter zu verstehen. ☐
2 Manchmal verstehen Sie mehrere Sätze nicht, aber Sie verstehen trotzdem den Text. ☐
3 Diese Musik gefällt nicht allen. ☐
4 Er will dich nicht sehen. ☐
5 Er wollte nicht dich sehen, sondern mich. ☐
6 Nicht er hat den Brief geschrieben, sondern sie. ☐

5 a Listen to the statements and mark the main sentence stress.
b Which statements can you follow up with a question asking for an explanation? Note down a or b and write down the relevant question.

Sondern was? ✱ Sondern zu wem? ✱ Sondern wann? ✱ Sondern welchen?

1 a Wir fahren heute noch nicht. ....b........ ....
b Wir fahren noch nicht heute.

2 a Sie hat nicht deine Adresse vergessen. ....
b Sie hat deine Adresse nicht vergessen.

3 a Ich habe diesen Text nicht gelesen. ....
b Ich habe nicht diesen Text gelesen.

4 a Ich habe das nicht zu dir gesagt. ....
b Ich habe das nicht zu dir gesagt.

6 *Vor* or *nach*? Read lines 14–30 and complete the rule.

> When the whole sentence is negated, *nicht* (*nie, niemals, noch nicht* ...) is placed .... the prepositional object, ... an object without a preposition.

7 Negate these sentences with *nicht, noch nicht.*

1 Er hat die Kinokarten gekauft.
2 Sie ist schon nach Hause gegangen.
3 Sie war mit ihnen in der Kneipe.
4 Du kannst dir viel Zeit lassen.
5 Es hat ihm sicher Leid getan.
6 Wir haben den Text begriffen.
7 Ich habe den Text schon ganz gelesen.
8 Hast du die Erklärung verstanden?

8 Read from line 31 to the end. Which sentence (A, B) matches the following questions better as an answer.

1 Gibt es etwas, was du noch nie gesehen hast? ☐ 2 Kennst du diesen Herrn dort? ☐

Möglichkeiten „Nein" zu sagen

Negation can be expressed with:
- words: *kein, nichts, niemand, ...*
- the suffixes *-frei, -los, -arm*: koffeinfrei, arbeitslos
- the prefix *un-*: unglücklich

9 a Opposites: What do the following words go with?

jemand, alle ● überall ● immer, oft ● etwas, alles ● ein ● mit ● viel ● auch ● und

kein	....	ohne	....	niemand	....
nichts	....	außer	...auch...	nie/niemals	....
wenig	....	weder ... noch	...und...	nirgends/nirgendwo	....

b Form negative and affirmative sentences as in the example.

Ich habe Zeit, außer am Mittwoch. Ich habe Zeit, auch am Mittwoch.
Sie hat weder ein Auto noch ein Fahrrad. Sie hat ein Auto und ein Fahrrad.

10 Collect examples of negation with the prefix *un-*.

11 a Form adjectives with the suffixes *-frei, -los, -arm* and translate them into English.

-los	-frei	-arm
Geist, Partei, Mühe, Rat, Witz, Humor, Gewalt, Charakter, Gefühl, Wort, Ziel, Grund, Sinn, Ende	Krise(n), Vogel, Verkehr(s), Alkohol	Gefühl(s), Wald, Kontakt

b Connect the adjectives from a to the following nouns.

Arbeit ● Revolution ● Spaziergang ● Beziehung ● Streit ● Mensch ● Bier ● Straße ● Gegend ● Politiker

geistlose, mühelose Arbeit, ...

Negation can be more precise:

reinforcement:	**gar/überhaupt** nicht	Ich habe das alles gar/überhaupt nicht verstanden.
comparison:	**auch** nicht	Wir auch nicht.
temporal:	**noch** nicht	Es ist schon der Erste und mein Gehalt ist noch nicht gekommen.
	nicht **mehr**	Ich warte schon drei Wochen und ich glaube, die Anwort kommt nicht mehr.

similarly with *kein, nichts, nie, niemand*

12 a Explain the meaning of the following sentences.

1 Er kommt heute auch nicht.
2 Er kommt heute überhaupt nicht.
3 Er kommt heute noch nicht.
4 Er kommt heute nicht mehr.

1 Er ist gestern nicht gekommen und er kommt heute nicht.

b Form negative sentences and then make them more precise.

Ich habe keine Lust zu arbeiten. Ich habe keine Lust mehr!!!

Den farbigen Firmen gehört die Welt

Cultural information

The further north you go, the more colourful the houses get. Whilst Egyptian villages with their habitations moulded from the mud of the Nile hardly stand out from their surroundings, and on the Aegean islands an almost monotonous white predominates, in North Germany there are many brightly coloured buildings. The weather conditions obviously play a part in this. In areas where blue sky is seldom to be seen and the sun doesn't provide for bright light so much, people feel forced to do something to create a patch of colour. The fact that light and colour play a great role in people's moods is well-known. But it's a relatively new idea to make use of this insight to influence productivity and creativity in the world of work. The text in this unit tells us about the Swiss Erich Chiavi who has made a highly successful career out of advising people in industry to surround themselves with lots of colour.

A particularly telling example that supports the theory that bright colours are linked to economic success is the Swiss clock and watch industry. It once led the world with its chronometers. But when quarz clocks and watches were invented, Swiss clockmakers with their expensive, handmade products were plunged into crisis. Until the businessman Hayek came up with the idea of producing cheap clocks and watches too, and giving them a colourful, unconventional design. He called this product Swatch, and since its invention in 1983 it has been a roaring success all round the worl. The Hayek company is now the largest watchmaker in the world and has sold more than 250 million watches since its foundation. The company began a cooperation with Daimler-Chrysler and developed a colourful little car on the same principle, the Smart. Both the watches and the cars are relatively cheap and colourful.

And it's no coincidence that all this has happened between Zurich and Stuttgart, probably the most creative industrial region in modern Europe. The region not only produces the largest numbers of patent registrations. With 23% of the workforce employed in high-tech industries, the Stuttgart region leads the whole of Europe.

And the Swiss industrial region centred on Basle, just two hours from Stuttgart by train, is the centre of the European chemical industry.

Language

More than other languages, German has the possibility of creating new words with the use of prefixes. Statistically the prefix *ver-* is the most common, e.g. *verstehen*. It can be linked to 130 verbs. The verb with the most prefixes (126) is *kommen*, e.g. *ankommen*. 11,356 new verbs are formed in German using prefixes.

Den farbigen Firmen gehört die Welt

1 The following names occur in the text: Schweiz, Zürich, Davos, Basel, Sindelfingen (Stuttgart), Bern.

a Find the places or regions on a map.

b Ask and answer.

Wo liegt Basel? - An der deutsch-schweizerischen Grenze.

2 Read the whole text and mark all the internationalisms.

„Crosstalk" stellt Ihnen den Schweizer Raum- und Farbpsychologen Erich Chiavi vor.

Wer sich mit Erich Chiavi an der Züricher Bahnhofstraße verabredet hat, muss keine Angst haben, er könnte den Bündner[1] übersehen. Inmitten der grau oder dunkel gekleideten Banker und 5 anderen Business-Leute fällt Chiavi auf. Er trägt ein dunkelblaues Hemd zu einer knallgelben Hose.

Erich Chiavi ist Farbpsychologe. Er berät Firmen bei der farblichen Gestaltung der Arbeitsräume, 10 er entwirft bunte Möbel, Teppiche, Bodenplatten. Und der Davoser findet Gehör. Neben Aufträgen für die Basler Chemie arbeitet er im Moment zum Beispiel mit Mercedes zusammen. Bekannt sind auch seine Auftritte an den 15 Davoser Management-Symposien. Seine Vorträge und Seminare haben ihm schon viele Türen geöffnet. „Farbigen Firmen gehört die Welt", sagt Erich Chiavi. „Wer nur linear denkt, ist nicht kreativ, nicht dynamisch, nicht tolerant." 20 Dass er, der bunte Vogel unter den grauen Mäusen, Respekt und Anerkennung findet, überrascht ihn nicht: „Die meisten Manager beneiden mich, ja sie bezeichnen ihre Kleidung selber als langweilig." Aber ihnen fehle der Mut, sich so 25 anzuziehen. „Dabei waren Farben immer schon Auslöser für die Kreativität. Buntes hat doch viel mehr Dynamik als graue Töne oder anthrazitfarbene", sagt Chiavi. „Schwarz und Grau bedeuten Rückzug, sich abschließen. Wer nur in 30 Schwarz-Weiß denkt, hat keine Ideen mehr." Die Kommunikation, das weiß Erich Chiavi aus eigener Erfahrung, funktioniere zudem viel besser, wenn man einander farbig begegne. Wenn Erich Chiavi in Fahrt gerät, zu erzählen beginnt, dann entstehen ganze Gedankengebäude. Von 35 riesigen runden Arbeitstischen erzählt er, die er für das Forschungsgebäude von Mercedes in Sindelfingen entwickelt habe. Anstatt hierarchisch geordnet an langen, eckigen Tischen, gruppiert er Führungsstäbe und Angestellte an seinen bun- 40 ten, runden Stehtischen. „Die Besprechungen werden so effizienter und sind belebter", sagt Chiavi. „Wer farbig denkt, ist nicht mehr Neinsager, sondern offen und bereit, auch das Ungewöhnliche zu wagen. Nur wer derart positiv 45 denkt, kann auch neue Produkte entwickeln." Aus seiner Tasche holt er Fotos hervor. Die europäische Vertriebszentrale einer weltweit tätigen Firma zeigt er. In den Räumen müsste man nach Grau und Schwarz suchen. Bunte Teppiche, bun- 50 te Stellwände, fast keine rechten Winkel. Chiavi zeigt Bilder eines Werks der Ciba Speciality Chemicals in Grenzach, ganz in der Nähe von Basel. Die Gebäude sind außen wie innen farbig. 55 „Man stelle sich vor, die Natur wäre nur grau und anthrazit ...", sagt er. „Die Natur ist doch überschwenglich, lebt die Farben aus."

Viel Spaß machen dem Bündner jeweils die Seminare mit Managern. Er lässt führende Geschäftsleute farbige Collagen basteln. 60 „Da erkennt man dann die Flachdenker, die Chaoten oder die Dreidimensionalen. Und man sieht ihnen die Freude am spielerischen Umgang mit den Farben an." Er habe, so Chiavi, diese Collagen nach dem Schluss der Seminare fein säuberlich in Schachteln verpacken und den Urhebern in alle Welt nachschicken müssen. „Nachher erhalte ich oft Anrufe und Aufträge, diesen Leuten auch für ihre eigenen Büros und Häuser Tipps zu geben." Nach einem Wunsch befragt, den er sich trotz seiner mittlerweile sehr guten internationalen Kontakte noch nicht hat erfüllen können, überlegt der Davoser kurz: „Ich würde gern einmal mit Parlamentariern und Bundesräten[2] in Bern ein Farbseminar machen. Da müssten sie sich exponieren."

aus: *Crosstalk*

[1] Bündner = inhabitant of the Swiss Canton of Graubünden
[2] der Bundesrat, die Bundesräte: Member of the Executive Federal Council

3 Note down all the expressions that have something to do with colour.

inmitten der grau oder dunkel gekleideten Banker, ein dunkelblaues Hemd zu einer knallgelben Hose, ...

4 Sort the expressions into the table.

ist langweilig • kann neue Produkte entwickeln • ist auf dem Rückzug • ist offen • denkt linear • kann besser kommunizieren • wagt das Ungewöhnliche • ist nicht tolerant • besitzt mehr Kreativität • ist nicht kreativ • ist ein Neinsager • hat keine Ideen • denkt positiv • dem fehlt Mut

Wer farbig oder bunt denkt,	Wer in Schwarz-Weiß (Grau, Anthrazit) denkt,
...	ist auf dem Rückzug, ...
...	...
...	...
...	...
...	...
...	...

5 Explain these images. Translate them into English.

Er findet Gehör. • Ihm haben sich viele Türen geöffnet. • Er ist ein bunter Vogel. • Er ist eine graue Maus. • Er kommt in Fahrt. • Er findet Respekt/Anerkennung. • Wer nur in Schwarz-Weiß denkt, ... • Er ist kein Neinsager. • Farbigen Firmen gehört die Welt. • Er erkennt die Flachdenker und die Dreidimensionalen.

Wortbildung: Präfixe

6 The text contains a lot of verbs with prefixes: *ab, an, auf, aus, be, ent, er, ge, hervor, nach, ver, vor, über, zusammen.*

a Find these verbs in the text and make a table.

Prefix	Verb	Example
vor	vorstellen	Crosstalk stellt Ihnen den Schweizer ... Erich Chiavi vor.
ver + ab	sich verabreden	Wer sich mit Erich Chiavi ... verabredet hat, ...

b Make sentences of your own with the verbs from the table.

7 Find prefixes for the verbs *kommen* and *sehen*.

a Complete the word-spiders.

b Make sentences.

Den Herrn Chiavi können Sie nicht übersehen.
Er ist gerade angekommen.

Sätze/Satzteile verbinden: *je ... desto/umso*

Je farbiger ein Mensch denkt, **desto/umso** kreativer ist er.

Je ... desto/umso link a subordinate clause to a main clause.
After *je ... desto/umso* the adjective is always in the comparative form..

Je später der Abend, desto/umso schöner die Gäste.
If the verbs are the same and have no special meaning, they can be omitted.

8 Complete the sentences.

tolerant sein ● dynamisch sein ● effizienter und belebter diskutieren ● die Kommunikation funktioniert gut ● die Mitarbeiter denken kreativ

1. Je bunter ein Raum ist, desto ....
2. Je farbiger man einander begegnet, umso ....
3. Je bunter sich jemand kleidet, ...
4. Je weniger hierarchisch die Angestellten gruppiert sind, ...
5. Je weniger einer linear denkt, ...

Das Verb: reflexive Verben (2)

9 Mark the reflexive verbs in the text (→ p. 99).

10 a Compare the sentences.

Mir fehlt der Mut, **mich** bunt anzuziehen.	Ich ziehe **mir** eine schwarze Jacke an.
Wasch **dich**.	Wasch **dir** deine Hände.

b Accusative or dative? Please complete.

The reflexive pronoun *sich* is in the ...., if the verb has an accusative object as well.

Die Menschen begegnen **sich** farbig. Die Menschen begegnen **einander** farbig.

Verbs expressing a reciprocal relationship such as *sich begegnen / grüßen / hassen / lieben / kennen lernen / küssen / treffen / sich etw. schenken* can be used with the pronoun *einander* instead of a reflexive pronoun.

11 **a** First check the meaning of these verbs.

sich anstrengen ◆ sich beschäftigen mit ◆ sich … erfüllen ◆ sich freuen über ◆ sich fühlen ◆ sich … kaufen ◆ sich kennen lernen ◆ sich kümmern um ◆ sich langweilen ◆ sich … nehmen ◆ sich … schneiden lassen ◆ sich schreiben ◆ sich sehen ◆ sich treffen mit ◆ sich … überlegen

b Complete the letter.

Liebe Anita,

vielen Dank für deinen lieben Brief, über den ich .... sehr .... (1) habe.
Es scheint mir, du .... (2) wohl in Baden-Baden.
Ich hoffe sehr, dass du .... viel Zeit .... (3) für die Therapie.

Es macht nichts, wenn du .... manchmal etwas .... (4).
Du hast .... in den letzten Monaten zu sehr .... (5) und
.... nur noch mit deinem Job .... (6). Jetzt ist es Zeit,
dass du .... deine Zukunft .... (7) und ....
auch mal wieder um dich selbst .... (8).

Gestern habe ich .... mit Gerlinde .... (9). Es geht ihr sehr sehr gut.
Sie hat einen neuen Freund. Sie haben .... in einem Café ....
.... (10). Jetzt .... sie .... (11) jede Woche
einmal und jeden Tag .... sie .... (12) mehrere E-Mails.
Sie ist glücklich wie noch nie.

Ich selber habe .... auch einen Wunsch .... (13) .
Ich habe .... ein wunderschönes Kleid .... (14). Heute Nachmittag
gehe ich zum Friseur und .... die Haare .... (15)
und abends geht es in die Oper „Ritter Blaubart" .

Ganz liebe Grüße
von deiner Annedört

c Where could *sich* be replaced with *einander*? Note down the verbs.

Wie wohnen Sie denn?

12

Answer the question where and how you live. You can give the information orally, or write to a pen-friend.

Wohnort	Wohnungstyp	Räume	Einrichtung/Möbel
Kleinstadt	Villa	Wohnzimmer	Sitzgruppe
Dorf	Einfamilienhaus	Schlafzimmer	Couchgarnitur
Zentrum	1-5-Zimmerwohnung	Kinderzimmer	Sofa
Innenstadt	Apartment	Arbeitszimmer	Sessel
Vorort	Reihenhaus	Küche	Esstisch
Siedlung	Mietshaus	Bad	Stühle
	Untermiete	Toilette/WC	Bett
	Eigentumswohnung	Keller	Schrank
	Altbauwohnung	Garage	Teppich
	Neubauwohnung	Garten	Vorhänge
	Studentenheim	Terrasse	Schreibtisch
	Wohngemeinschaft	Balkon	Bücherregal
			Stehlampe

www.ikarus.de

Wo wohnen Sie denn? Haben Sie eine Wohnung oder ein Haus?
Wohnen Sie auch in einem Mietshaus? Wie groß ist die Wohnung?
Hat sie Balkon, Garten, Terrasse? In welchem Stock/Stockwerk wohnen Sie?

Wir wohnen im Zentrum von ... in einer schönen Altbauwohnung.
Sie hat ein großes Wohnzimmer mit Balkon zur Straße und zwei kleinere Räume.
Dazu gibt es eine große Küche und ein Bad. Das Wohnzimmer besteht aus alten Möbeln von meiner Großmutter. Das sieht sehr gemütlich aus. Die Couch ist natürlich modern. Vielleicht ziehen wir einmal aufs Land, wenn wir Kinder haben.
Aber jetzt sind wir noch sehr zufrieden.

Ein Weg zurück

Cultural information

In wealthy Europe 14.3% of all households live under the poverty line. In Germany there are 1.3 million people with no permanent home, and 360,000 people live in the streets, under bridges, in gateways or parks. The reasons for homelessness are many. Unemployment, debt and alcohol are usually involved. Although there are lots of initiatives and charitable organizations doing their best to help, you get the impression that people living this way are populating our inner cities more and more, living of what ordinary society leaves them. In the listening text "Ein Weg zurück" a woman talks about how she ended up on the very edges of society. You will hear excerpts from a long interview, and all the ups and downs of the life she has led.

Learning strategies

The unit has two aims:

- understanding and working out the meaning of a longish listening text
- structuring an extensive piece of written text.

In order that both goals can be achieved, parts of the interview are printed word for word, other parts are summarised in note form.

Language

The end position in the sentence

	Satzklammer			
Jeden Morgen	ging	sie schnell an mir	vorbei,	**ohne zu grüßen.**
Vorfeld		Mittelfeld		**Nachfeld**

In contrast to the initial position and the central part of the sentence, the end-position (das Nachfeld) doesn't necessarily have to be filled. Its main purpose is to provide an opportunity to emphasise something. It also enables you to move an element of the sentence out, if the verbal bracket is too extended.

The sentence above might also be formulated like this:
Jeden Morgen ging sie *ohne zu grüßen* schnell an mir vorbei.
Then there would be seven words between the separable prefix *vorbei* and the conjugated verb *ging*. If *ohne zu grüßen* is in end-position, this statement has much greater weight.

Tramp under the Wittelsbach Bridge in Munich

Ein Weg zurück

 **1** **a** Listen to the conversation and read it at the same time.

■	Ich bin heute bei Doris, in ihrer Wohnung am Stadtrand von München. Die Wohnung ist nicht groß, vielleicht 30 Quadratmeter, aber hell und freundlich, ganz wohnlich eingerichtet, mit viel Holz, ein großes Holzregal mit Büchern, viele Pflanzen, an der Wand ein Poster, ein Bild von Buddha – sind Sie Buddhistin, Doris?	Wie lebt Doris jetzt?
Doris	Nee, eigentlich nich. Aber ich hab das Bild von der Sibylle, meiner Schwester, und der gefällt mir, der sitzt da so ruhig und ... ja, irgendwie zufrieden.	
■	Doris, vor ein paar Jahren war Ihr Leben ja noch völlig anders. Wo hätte ich Sie denn da gefunden?	
Doris	Ja, so vor drei Jahren war ich noch im Wohnheim für Obdachlose und vorher ... auch noch manchmal auf der Straße.	Was war vorher?
■	Sie haben damals ja auch über längere Zeit regelmäßig getrunken. Wie hoch war denn da Ihr Alkoholkonsum?	
Doris	Hm, na ja, so eine Flasche Wein oder 6, 7 Halbe, ja ... und Schnaps, Schnaps eigentlich immer ... ich weiß nich mehr so genau ...	
■	Woher hatten Sie den Alkohol? Hatten Sie denn Geld?	
Doris	Ich hab doch immer wieder mal irgendwelche Jobs gehabt: Putzen ... oder im Kaufhaus oder so ... das hast du natürlich kaum bezahlt gekriegt, aber was zu trinken und Zigaretten, das war kein Problem, das hatt ich eigentlich immer. Und wenn ich keinen Job hatte, hab ich halt Leute gefragt, ob sie mir was geben können.	
■	Möchten Sie vielleicht mal erzählen, wie es dazu kam? Sie sind ja von der Herkunft ... ja, man könnte sagen, eine höhere Tochter, oder?	
Doris	Na ja, wie man´s nimmt.	

b Jot down some notes in answer to the questions by the side of the text.

2 **a** Read the continuation of the conversation in note form.

Kindheit in einem Vorort von München ◆ Vater erfolgreicher Architekt, Mutter Hausfrau, von außen gesehen stimmt alles, Ehe ist aber kaputt ◆ Mutter fühlt sich allein, ist frustriert und nervös, schlägt Doris, wird wieder schwanger und möchte sich am liebsten umbringen ◆ immer Streit zwischen Mutter und Vater ◆ Vater lernt eine andere Frau kennen ◆ Mutter reicht die Scheidung ein ◆ Doris und ihre Schwester bleiben bei der Mutter, Bruder beim Vater ◆ Doris haut einmal von zu Hause ab ◆ Mutter fühlt sich mit Doris überfordert ◆ mit 13 ist Doris dann in einer Clique, raucht Joints, beginnt zu trinken ◆ Verhältnis zwischen Doris und ihrer Mutter ist manchmal schlimm ◆ kommt in ein Heim ◆ macht dort Realschulabschluss und kehrt zur Mutter zurück ◆ fängt Ausbildung im Büro an ◆ nimmt mit 18 ein eigenes Zimmer ◆ sieht keinen Sinn in der Arbeit ◆ fühlt sich leer ◆ versteckt sich in ihrem Zimmer

b Now listen to the conversation and note down further details.

Sprechen: berichten – erzählen

3 a Read the continuation of the conversation in note form.

Doris bekommt Schwierigkeiten in der Arbeit, beendet Ausbildung nicht ⊘ wird zeitweise von Mutter und Geschwistern finanziert, weil sie nicht auf eigenen Beinen stehen kann ⊘ trinkt regelmäßig Alkohol ⊘ lernt ihren Freund kennen, Helmut, einen Musiker ⊘ Helmut hat keine Wohnung, lebt zeitweise in London, „um Musik zu machen", und bei ihr in München.Ist auch Alkoholiker ⊘ sie leben von einem Tag auf den anderen, glauben, frei zu sein, lieben die Spontaneität ⊘ massives Trinken ⊘ Doris schafft Alltag nicht mehr, kann Wohnung nicht sauber halten, verliert Wohnung ⊘ wohnt zuerst bei Freunden, schläft dann manchmal draußen im Freien oder in Unterkunft für Obdachlose ⊘ ist nun sozial völlig abgestiegen ⊘ kein Kontakt zum Vater, telefonisch zur Mutter, bekommt immer die gleichen Vorwürfe ⊘ denkt, die Geschwister möchten nichts mehr mit ihr zu tun haben ⊘ Schwester geht glücklicherweise zu den Anonymen Alkoholikern – lässt sich beraten, wie sie sich verhalten soll

b Turn the notes into a complete text.

As the presenter of the programme, give a summary of this section of the conversation ...

Doris bekam Schwierigkeiten in der Arbeit und beendete ihre Ausbildung nicht.

- Note the tense: past
- Report in a neutral, detached way.
- Use words that make the time sequencing clear, such as zuerst, am Anfang, später, dann ...
- Join the sentences with conjunctions (→ p. 167, 235, 241, 242).
- Report what Doris says as indirect speech (→ p. 202).

or take over Doris' role.

Ich hab Schwierigkeiten mit der Arbeit bekommen und hab dann meine Ausbildung nicht beendet.

- You can switch between the present, perfect and past tense.
- Comment on what you are narrating with expressions that show your feelings and mood:
  Ich fand das sehr schön/traurig/...
  Ist das nicht schön/schlimm/...?
  Das hat mir sehr wehgetan/gut getan.
  Das war (sehr) (un)angenehm/schlimm/...
  ... glücklicherweise ... /... leider ...
- You can use main clauses; use words that show the time sequencing.
- Address your listeners sometimes:
  Können Sie sich vorstellen ...
  Wissen Sie ...
  Sehen Sie mal, ...
  ..., ja?/..., nicht wahr?

 **4 a** Listen to the conversation and read it at the same time.

■	Doris, was haben Sie überhaupt damals empfunden? Wie fühlt man sich in so einer Lage?
Doris	Ich weiß nich ... ich glaub, ich wollt mich spüren ... ich wollt endlich überhaupt irgendwas spüren ...
■	Sie waren aber auch mal trocken in diesem Zeitraum, oder?
Doris	Ja, und da hatt ich auch n Job und ... ja, und dann kam Silvester, und da hat jemand Champagner mit heimgebracht, dummerweise, ... jedenfalls ... das war´s dann. Schönes neues Jahr, nicht wahr?
■	Und was ist dann geschehen? Wie haben Sie es dann doch geschafft, nicht mehr zu trinken?
Doris	Ja, das war ... da hab ich n paar Wochen nur durchgesoffen. Irgendwann waren wir dann mal unter ner Brücke und ham da geschlafen und irgendwann, morgens, wollt ich mich hinsetzen und merk auf einmal, es geht nich ... und bin dann liegen geblieben und hab eigentlich immer nur gedacht: Das Leben is aus. Dann sterb ich eben. Es is o.k. Das Leben is o.k. und der Tod is o.k. Und das war überhaupt nich schlimm, das war unheimlich angenehm. Und dann hör ich nur noch, wie der Helmut sagt: He, was ist denn los mit dir? Ja ... und dann war ich weg.
■	Sie sind dann ins Krankenhaus gekommen ...
Doris	Ja, jemand hat den Notarzt gerufen ...
■	Die Ärzte konnten Ihren Körper retten. Und Ihre Psyche?
Doris	Ja, das war ganz eigenartig ... Ich war da schon fieberfrei, aber ich war auch total fertig und ... und ich hab aus dem Fenster geschaut, da war so ne schöne Aussicht, ein total schöner Baum vor dem Fenster ... und auf einmal war da was in mir, so ganz tief drin, so was wie ... ja ... ich will ja leben und ... vielleicht kann ich mich ja doch n bisschen lieb haben ... Und ... ich hab schon gewusst, ich schaff das alles nich allein, und hab mir, ja, so gewünscht, dass die Sibylle kommt, und das war noch am selben Tag, ich hatte sie nich so schnell erwartet, da hat's auf einmal geklopft und da stand sie doch tatsächlich da und hat mich erst nur angeguckt. und dann sagt die doch zu mir, meine liebe, große Schwester, sagt: "Du blöde Kuh!" Und irgendwie, da hab ich gedacht, ich kann's vielleicht schaffen.
■	Und Ihre Mutter?
Doris	Ja, die kam dann am nächsten Tag und ... ja, ich glaub, sie hat sich echt vorgenommen, ich sag jetzt nichts, ich bin einfach da und ...
■	Hat sie denn auch ... Schuldgefühle gegenüber Ihnen ... ja, den Kindern?
Doris	Ja, sicher. Sie hat schon eingesehen, dass ... ja, dass sie auch was falsch gemacht hat und ... Sie will jetzt alles wieder gutmachen und kommt manchmal da gar nich mehr weg davon ... na ja ... ich will eigentlich nur noch, dass es ihr gut geht ...

b Read the text again and note down key words.

5 a Read these notes about Doris' return from homelessness.

Doris ist entschlossen, ein neues Leben zu beginnen ⊘ macht Entziehungskur ⊘ findet danach mit Sibylles Hilfe Platz in Wohnheim ⊘ zieht nach einem Jahr dort aus und nimmt sich eigene kleine Wohnung ⊘ arbeitet wieder im Büro, möchte eine Umschulung machen ⊘ geht regelmäßig zu Treffen der Anonymen Alkoholiker ⊘ mit den Freunden von einst möchte sie nichts mehr zu tun haben ⊘ hat auch keinen Kontakt mehr zu Helmut, „in ihre Wohnung kommt er nicht rein" ⊘ wünscht sich Partnerschaft, aber noch nicht jetzt ⊘ materiell geht es ihr ganz gut, leistet sich auch mal was, manchmal Essengehen, Urlaub – möchte Skifahren lernen, zeichnet gern. ⊘ eigentlich geht es ihr auch seelisch ganz gut ⊘ ein Knacks ist da, man kann das nicht alles einfach wegradieren ⊘ hat eine richtige Odyssee hinter sich ⊘ hat manchmal Angst, dass sie es nicht schafft ⊘ Gespräche bei den Anonymen Alkoholikern haben ihr viel geholfen ⊘ ist körperlich ziemlich kaputt ⊘ lebt halt jetzt ⊘ findet, das ist schon viel

b Listen to Doris narrating the last section.

Architektur von Sätzen: Nachfeld

Vorfeld	Verb	Mittelfeld	Verb	**Nachfeld**
Doris	hat	sich richtig	versteckt	in ihrem Zimmer. (1)
Ihr Bruder	ist	ein Jahr jünger		als Doris. (2)
Sie	hat	irgendwelche Jobs	gemacht:	Putzen ... oder im Kaufhaus. (3)
Was	ist	denn	los	mit dir? (4)
Die Ehe ihrer Eltern	war	(eigentlich von Anfang an)	kaputt,	eigentlich von Anfang an. (4)
Doris	hat	die Chance (ihr Leben zu ändern)	genutzt	ihr Leben zu ändern. (5)
Doris	lernt	ihren Freund (, der auch Alkoholiker ist,)	kennen,	der auch Alkoholiker ist. (5)

The end-position in the sentence can be occupied by the following items:

- an adverbial of place (time/manner/reason) (1)
- a comparison (2)
- a list (3)
- a postscript (4)
- an infinitive clause/a sub-clause (5)

These items are placed in end-position if the speaker wants to emphasise them, or if the two parts of the verb would be too far apart – especially in speech.

6 In the following sentences put one of the items in the end-position.

1 Doris hat sehr früh – so mit 13 – angefangen zu trinken.
2 Doris ist in kurzer Zeit durch das massive Trinken sozial abgestiegen.
3 Doris' Mutter fühlte sich mit den drei Kindern überfordert.
4 Doris hat das Buddha-Poster von Sibylle, ihrer Schwester, bekommen.
5 Ihre Mutter fing immer von ihrer Angst zu reden an.
6 Dann hat Doris eine Ausbildung im Büro angefangen.
7 Im Krankenhaus hat Doris ihre Schwester, die sie lange Zeit nicht gesehen hatte, wieder getroffen.
8 Die Wohnung ist schön mit Holzregalen, Büchern, einem Buddha-Poster eingerichtet.
9 Doris hat in dieser Zeit gar nicht viel empfunden.
10 An Silvester hat jemand dummerweise Champagner mit heimgebracht.

Einen Text schreiben

7 Write a text about Doris' life. Select one of the two suggestions.

- Doris' story in a book entitled "Außergewöhnliche Lebensläufe".
- article about Doris in the magazine "Alcoholics Anonymous", a magazine for people with alcohol problems.

Proceed as follows:

collect

Read the conversations again and the summaries in note form. Write down what topics are dealt with (in such a way that you can add key words to them later on).

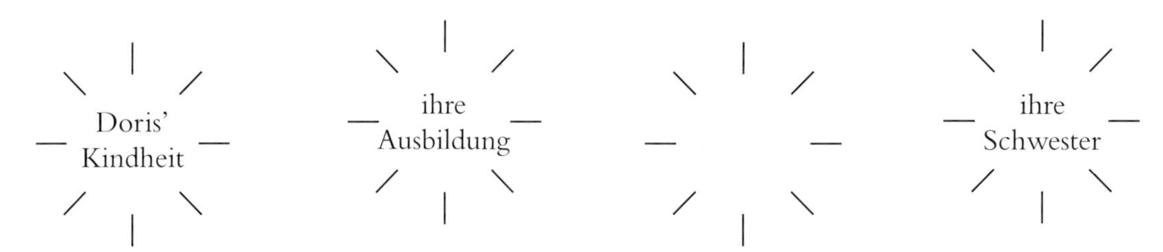

plan

Then think about

- why you are writing and for whom: what topics and key words are important for the text? Select the topics and note down the key words around them.
- how the text should be structured: chronologically or from the present perspective? Put the topics in the appropriate order.

formulate

It's best if first of all you just form main clauses covering your notes and then add suitable conjunctions afterwards (→ p. 167, 235, 241, 242).

correct

Finally check your text taking account of the notes on

- sentence structure (initial position → p. 211, central position → p. 253 and end-position → p. 271)
- the various deictic words for making references (→ p. 216).

Das wunderbare Volk

Cultural information

Romanies and Sinti are referred to as gypsies nearly all over the world. Although this term covers all the tribes and has been handed down to us through history, it is no longer in common usage or correct to refer to Romanies and Sinti in this way. Members of this race are to be found all over Europe, but also in Asia and in the USA. Although many of them are now sedentary, the concept of *fahrendes Volk* (travellers) is still very much alive. And there are plenty of people who follow the pattern and are constantly on the road in their caravan or mobile home, because they find more companionship and a busier social life on campsites, the modern gyspies' camps, than in a permanent home.

The "Gaje", the non-gypsies, know next to nothing about the the Romanies or Sinti living in Europe:

- Since 1979 gypsies have been recognized by the UN as an independent ethnic group.
- They rarely own land.
- They are members of many different religions, but nevertheless stick together on account of their common language and shared customs.
- They are the only people on the earth never to have waged war.

Maybe this is the reason they have always been the victim of discrimination and persecution, an ostracized minority that refused to live and think like the rest. In the Third Reich they were branded as racially inferior and deported to concentration camps and murdered. 500,000 lost their lives. And in many countries even today they are not only despised, but also subject to constant harassment by the population and the authorities.

It is not easy to gain access to the secretive world of this people. From 1934 to 1944 a young Belgian managed to join up with a Romany family. The son of an artist who was himself enthusiastic about the Romanies' way of life, Jan Yoors simply left home and went and lived with gypsies. Fortunately his parents never took it amiss. And so he was able to write a book about what he saw and experienced in those ten years.

Learning strategies

Whether we learn anything is always a question, too, of how curious we are. It's the same with a foreign langauge. Only learners who are curious about those who speak the language will be successful at learning it. Being tolerant of their way of life and thinking is part of it too. Learning a foreign language means also learning what tolerance is and how to practise it.

Das wunderbare Volk

1 Read a section from the introduction to the book "Das wunderbare Volk".

a Work out the meaning of the sentence in lines 3–5. Proceed as follows:
Einblick ... bekommen → in die Sitten und Bräuche dieses Volkes → er hatte Gelegenheit

b Clarify the meaning of the term *Unterwegssein* (line 6) from the context and the word formation.

c What could *liefern* (line 10) mean? And then *aufräumen mit* (line 9)?

d Who is the main character? Underline how he is referred to in various parts of the text.
Who was he involved with? Where did the story take place? When did it take place?

Der Belgier Jan Yoors wurde als Zwölfjähriger von einer angesehenen Familie der Lowara, eines der vier Hauptstämme der Rom[1], adoptiert und zog von da an zehn Jahre lang, von 1934 bis 1944, mit ihnen durch Europa. Als „Gajo", Nichtzigeuner, hatte er die seltene Gelegenheit, Einblick in die Sitten und Bräuche die-
5 ses Volkes zu bekommen. Er lernte ihre Sprache und schließlich auch ihre Philosophie des Unterwegsseins, die bedeutet, in der ewigen Gegenwart zu leben, auf die alle Erinnerungen, Träume und Wünsche bezogen sind.
Yoors will mit diesem Buch, geschrieben aus der seltenen Sicht des Insiders, die Distanz zu dem uns oft so fremden Volk verringern. Er räumt mit Vorurteilen auf
10 und liefert uns mit einem detaillierten und lebendigen Bericht eine ethnologische Fundgrube und faszinierende Lektüre.

[1] Rom = Roma

2 a Skim through the following text. Underline the parts that you can understand easily.

b What is the most important information in the text? Note it down.

„Eine Zeit lang fuhren wir gemächlich umher, ohne etwas von anderen Familien zu sehen. Für mich waren diese Tage in ihrem gelösten Frieden und ihrer ganzen Stimmung die schönsten Sommerferien, die ich je erlebt hatte. Die anfängliche Aufregung über mein seltsames Abenteuer schwand. Langsam wurde ich mit
5 den Tönen, Farben und Gerüchen um mich her vertraut. Und ich verlor allen Sinn für Zeit. Die Tage begannen mit dem Frühstück, für das es keine bestimmte Zeit gab, und endeten nach dem späten Abendbrot, dessen Zeitpunkt ebenfalls nicht festgelegt war. Eine andere Tageseinteilung gab es nicht. Es war immer vor und nach dem Frühstück und vor oder nach dem Abendessen. Da es auch keine
10 Sonntage oder andere Ruhetage gab, flossen die Tage und Wochen ohne Einschnitt ineinander. Keins der Kinder unterschied zwischen den aufeinander folgenden Monaten des Jahres oder kümmerte sich darum, was für ein Monat gerade war. Für sie war entweder Sommer oder Winter. Der Sommer war offensichtlich viel länger als der Winter. Und diese Unterscheidung hatte auch nur insoweit
15 Bedeutung, als die Roma während des Sommers weit umherfuhren, während sie im Winter infolge der ungünstigen Witterung weniger beweglich waren. Sie kannten die historische Zeitrechnung von Christi Geburt an nicht, sondern bezeichneten die ablaufende Zeit nur durch Ereignisse wie „in dem Sommer, als Pipish starb", „in dem Winter, als wir beinahe verhungert und erfroren wären
20 und von den Wölfen überfallen wurden" oder „in dem Jahr, als Zurka geboren wurde und wir drei Hengste verkauften".

Jan Yoors

3 Mark all the terms that have something to do with time.

Eine Zeit lang fuhren wir gemächlich umher ...

4 What is different about the way gypsies feel about time? Write down a few sentences.

5 Describe to a foreigner what people do in your country. Use the following expressions.

Die meisten Leute ... ✎ Einige ... ✎ In meiner Familie ... ✎ Ich persönlich ... ✎ aufstehen ✎ frühstücken ✎ schlafen ✎ Arbeitsbeginn ✎ Mittagspause und Mittagessen ✎ Nachmittag ✎ Feierabend ✎ Abendessen/Abendbrot ✎ Wochenende ✎ Feiertag

Sätze verbinden: *ohne ... zu, ohne dass, statt ... zu, (an)statt dass, während*

Sie fuhren umher, **ohne** etwas von den anderen Familien **zu sehen**.
Jan Yoors ging zu den Zigeunern, **ohne** seinen Eltern etwas davon **zu sagen**.
Jan Yoors ging zu den Zigeunern, **ohne dass** er seinen Eltern etwas **sagte**.
Jan blieb die ganzen Sommerferien bei den Zigeunern, **ohne dass** seine Eltern etwas davon **wussten**.

> *Ohne ... zu* + infinitive and *ohne dass* are used when what was expected (event, behaviour) did not in fact happen.
> If the subject in the main and subordinate clause is the same, you can use either *ohne ... zu* or *ohne dass*. If the subjects are different, only *ohne dass*. (→ p. 196)

Statt mit seinen Eltern vorher **zu sprechen**, ist Jan einfach mit den Zigeunern abgereist.
Statt dass er mit seinen Eltern **gesprochen hat**, ist Jan einfach mit den Zigeunern gegangen.
Statt dass der Vater mit dem Jungen **gesprochen hat**, hat die Mutter ihm seine Sachen gepackt.

> *Statt ... zu* + infinitive and *statt (anstatt) dass* are used to describe something that happened instead of something else.

Statt (sich) mit seinen Schulkameraden (zu treffen,) **traf** er sich mit den Kindern der Roma.

> Sentence elements that are identical (*sich treffen* occurs twice) can be omitted.

Während wir umherfuhren, sahen wir wenig von anderen Familien.
Die Roma fuhren im Sommer weit herum, **während** sie im Winter weniger beweglich waren.

> The conjunction *während* can have a temporal meaning (1st example) or express a contrast 2nd example).

Während sie umherfuhren, sahen sie die anderen Familien nicht.
Während der Fahrt sahen sie die anderen Familien nicht.

Conjunction	**Preposition**
während: temporal or adversative	*während* (G/D): temporal
ohne zu + infinitive / *ohne dass*	*ohne* (A)
statt zu + infinitive / *(an)statt dass*	*(an)statt* (G)

6 Join the sentences using *ohne ... zu / ohne dass, statt ... zu / statt dass* and the prepositions *ohne* and *statt.*

1 Er sagte nichts. Er verließ das Zimmer.

Er verließ das Zimmer, ohne etwas zu sagen.
Er verließ das Zimmer, ohne dass er etwas sagte.
Er verließ das Zimmer ohne Worte.

2 Sie hatte keine Freude daran. Sie lernte jeden Tag Vokabeln.
3 Wir haben ihr zum Geburtstag nichts geschenkt. Wir haben sie ins Restaurant eingeladen.
4 Er hatte nicht viel Interesse daran. Er hat über das Thema geschrieben.
5 Sie mussten ihm nicht helfen. Er hat es geschafft.

7 Form sentences with *während* as a conjunction.

a temporal

Während des Besuchs bei ihren Verwandten haben sie viel von ihrer Kindheit gesprochen.
Während sie ihre Verwandten besuchten, haben sie viel von ihrer Kindheit gesprochen.

1 Während seines Studiums an der Universität hat er viel mit seinen Freunden unternommen.
2 Er hat viel fotografiert während seiner Italienreise.
3 Während der Arbeit hat er nie geraucht.
4 Während der Diskussion hat er kein Wort gesagt.

b adversative (= expressing a contrast)

Sie isst viel Gemüse und Obst, während er lieber Fleisch isst.

1 Sie reist sehr gern, während er ...
2 Sie spricht Deutsch, Englisch und Spanisch, während er ...
3 Er lädt gern Freunde ein, während sie ...
4 Ihr Hobby ist Lesen, während er ...

–einander

8 Complete from the text.

Die Tage und Wochen flossen ohne Einschnitt ....

Die Kinder unterschieden nicht zwischen den .... folgenden Monaten.

Einander always indicates that several items, people or objects are involved. According to the situation it can be linked with various prepositions: übereinander, aufeinander, miteinander, zueinander, ...

Die Koffer lagen **übereinander**.
Bruder und Schwester kamen immer wieder **zueinander**.
Die Minister standen nicht **nebeneinander,** sondern **voreinander** bzw. **hintereinander**.
Untereinander haben die Roma keine Probleme.
Die beiden Politiker kämpften **gegeneinander**.
Miteinander leben!

9 Fill in suitable words from section 8.

„Wie sind Sie denn .... (1) gekommen?", fragte die Frau Allesweiß meine Frau und mich. „Ach", sagte ich, „das war ganz einfach. Wir saßen in der Schule jahrelang .... (2). Eines Tages sagte ich zu Eva: ‚Weißt du was, wollen wir nicht heiraten?' ‚Wenn du meinst!', war die Antwort von Eva. Da gingen wir gleich .... (3) in die Kirche. Seitdem sind wir ein Ehepaar." „Und das ist immer gut gegangen?" „Ach, wissen Sie", war meine Antwort, „man gewöhnt sich an alles. Leider ist es auch ein ständiger Kampf .... (4)."

10 **a** Listen to the song with your books shut.
b Read the text and underline the key words.
c Read the text and check the meaning of the unknown words.

Schwarzer Zigeuner

Du schwarzer Zigeuner, komm spiel mir was vor.
Denn ich will vergessen heut', was ich verlor.
Du schwarzer Zigeuner, du kennst meinen Schmerz,
Und wenn deine Geige weint, weint auch mein Herz.

Spiel mir das süße Lied aus gold'ner Zeit.
Spiel mir das alte Lied von Lieb' und Leid.
Du schwarzer Zigeuner, komm, spiel mir ins Ohr.
Denn ich will vergessen ganz, was ich verlor.

Heut' kann ich nicht schlafen geh'n, heut' find ich keine Ruh'.
Ich will Tanz und Lichterglanz und Musik dazu.
Grad weil ich so traurig bin, drum bleib ich nicht allein.
Will mein Herz betören bei Musik und Wein.

Wisst ihr, was die Liebe ist? Ein kurzer Traum im Mai.
Wenn dein Mund sich satt geküsst, ist der Traum vorbei.
Nichts als die Erinnerung bleibt dir allein zurück,
Und du kannst nur träumen von vergang'nem Glück.

Du schwarzer Zigeuner, komm, spiel mir was vor.
Denn ich will vergessen heut', was ich verlor.
Du schwarzer Zigeuner, du kennst meinen Schmerz,
Und wenn deine Geige weint, weint auch mein Herz.

Spiel mir das süße Lied aus gold'ner Zeit.
Spiel mir das alte Lied von Lieb' und Leid.
Du schwarzer Zigeuner, komm, spiel mir ins Ohr.
Denn ich will vergessen ganz, was ich verlor.

Fritz Löhner-Beda

11 Write a short story based on the song.

Was hat der Sänger im Mai erlebt? Wen hat er verloren? Wie geht es ihm jetzt? Was macht er eines Abends? Was will er von dem Zigeuner?

12 Read the following text about Romanies in Switzerland.

Kemal

Kemal kommt aus der Dreiländerecke (Frühere Jugoslawische Republik) Makedonien / Bulgarien / Griechenland.

„Wir Zigeuner lebten hier seit Jahrhunderten Haus an Haus mit Nichtzigeunern." Seine Familie erhielt bei der Landverteilung unter Tito etwas Boden, der knapp für den Eigenbedarf reichte. Im Übrigen arbeiteten die Männer im Tabakanbau oder suchten sich einen Verdienst als kleine Händler. Unter Tito, dessen Regierungszeit viele Roma zur goldenen Ära erklären, konnte Kemal studieren; er entschied sich für Soziologie, weil er sich davon Aufschluss über die sozialen Verhältnisse erhoffte, die er als Roma trotz aller Gleichberechtigung als ungerecht empfand.

Als Jugoslawien auseinanderbrach und die Arbeitslosigkeit anstieg, folgte er seinen Verwandten, die als Saisonarbeiter in der Schweiz ein Auskommen gefunden hatten. Damals brauchte die Schweiz Arbeitskräfte. Bei der Privatschule Bénédict lernte Kemal schnell Deutsch.

Viele kamen wie er. Sie alle widersprechen den vorgefassten Bildern von Zigeunern. Sie haben nichts mit lustigem Zigeunerleben zu tun und nichts mit dem Zigeunerbild der Wiener Operetten. Sie spielen – von Ausnahmen abgesehen – keine Geigenmusik. Sie betreiben keine Wahrsagerei. Sie stehlen und lügen wohl nicht mehr als altansässige Schweizer auch. ...

Die osteuropäischen Roma fahren nicht, sie haben nie im Wohnwagen gelebt.

Sie sind nicht auf der Durchreise, es sei denn[1], dass im Verständnis der Roma vielleicht das ganze Leben eine Reise ist.

[1] es sei denn, dass: unless

aus: *Weltwoche*

13 In the song and the text "Kemal" mark the places where clichés and prejudices are mentioned.

In der Diskussion

14 Prepare a TV discussion on the topic of "Vorurteile, Stereotypen, Klischees" and then act it out.

a Write down some notes on your opinion and think about some arguments to support it.

b Select those expressions from the following table which you need for the discussion.

Participants in the discussion

expressing an opinion / setting out ideas: Ich bin der Meinung / der Ansicht, ... – Ich glaube / Ich denke / Ich meine ... Meiner Meinung nach ... – Ich möchte dazu Folgendes sagen: ... –

agreeing: Das sehe ich auch so. – Ich glaube / finde / meine auch, ... – Das ist auch meine Meinung.

expressing doubt: Das mag schon sein, aber ... – Das stimmt schon, aber ... – Man muss aber auch sehen, dass ... – ... einerseits ... andererseits ...

contradicting: Also, das glaube ich nicht. – Das finde ich nicht. – Ich bin da ganz anderer Meinung/ Ansicht. – Man kann das auch anders sehen. – Das stimmt nicht.

Presenter

introducing the discussion: Ich begrüße heute ... – Das Thema unserer heutigen Diskussion ist ... – Wir sprechen heute über ... –

guiding the discussion: Was meinen Sie dazu? – Was denken Sie darüber? – Wie ist Ihre Meinung? Können Sie das näher erklären? – Was meinen Sie damit? – Was wollen Sie damit sagen?

summarising the discussion, drawing to a close: Wir haben also verschiedene Meinungen gehört. Ich fasse nun zusammen: ... – Ich bedanke mich für ... – Bis zu unserer nächsten Sendung ... – Auf Wiedersehen!

Der Mann, der den Zufall verkaufte

Cultural information

A father of two daughters in the Swiss town of Biel had a problem. His phone bill was reaching astronomic heights. Instead of forbidding his daughters to continue with their constant phone calls, he went into 31-year-old Markus Mettler's shop and asked how he could reduce his bill. Markus passed the enquiry on to one of his 20 employees. Half an hour later, for twenty-five Swiss francs, he came up with three solutions: he could turn his private phone into a pay phone, b) the calls would be broadcast through the flat via loudspeaker if they went on for more than a minute, c) he could get friends and relatives to sponsor his phone bill instead of giving presents. The shop is called "Brainstore" and is a perfectly normal shop with assistants, a cash register and counter. You can buy or have tailored whatever you happen to need: a suggestion for a party, an election campaign for a local politician, an idea for a present.

The text

The text about the "Mann, der den Zufall verkaufte" is also about an idea for a present. Here the assistant just gives the customer an impulse to find an idea himself and become creative himself. Creativity is an attribute still very much needed in our modern industrialised society. The ability to get ideas to flow, to release them, to let one's imagination roam and not just think logically, not take anything for granted, question everything, all these are prerequisites for creativity.

Learning strategies

Imagination and creativity are also important aids when learning a foreign language. The famous "Nürnberger Trichter", applied to someone's head and through which the language is poured into your head – it doesn't exist of course. You only learn a foreign language by exposure to it and using it as often as you can. Try reading German newspapers regularly. Find a partner, someone who speaks German as their mother tongue and who is learning English. Spend half your time together using German, half English. Each of you will learn from the other. Keep a diary in German. Look for a German pen pal on the Internet. Maybe you're able to pick up a German TV or radio station. Record the odd programme and work through them.

Nürnberger Trichter

Der Mann, der den Zufall verkaufte

1 Clarify the concept "Agentur zur Herbeischaffung ersehnter Gegenstände" with the help of a dictionary, and guess what could be meant by it.

2 **a** Read lines 1–3. What might the following words mean? Note down the answers in English.

betrieb ....
lief sehr gut ....
beschaffen ....

b What terms are the key words in lines 4–14. Note them down.

c What concept is predominant in lines 15–26?

d What was the longed-for object? (lines 27–31)

Kapolto – der Name ist wahrscheinlich ein Pseudonym – betrieb eine Agentur zur Herbeischaffung ersehnter Gegenstände. Die Agentur lief sehr gut. Sie versprach, ersehnte Gegenstände zu beschaffen. Das wollten die Leute.
Ein solcher Fall war die Herbeiführung einer Geschenkidee. Ein Kunde wusste einfach
5 kein passendes Weihnachtsgeschenk für seinen Freund. Kleinigkeit. Kapolto sprach: „Geh hin und kauf einen Gartenschlauch."
Der Kunde war verwirrt. Ein Gartenschlauch? Sein Freund wohnte im Hochhaus, ohne Garten. Aber die Leute waren ja gerade auf dieses bisschen Geheimnistuerei scharf. Bestimmt ein Koan[1], wie es Zen-Meister[2] verwenden, dachte der Kunde, mal sehen, was
10 nun passiert. Er zahlte für die Beratung, ging und kaufte einen Gartenschlauch.
Am nächsten Morgen kam der Kunde wütend zurück und warf Kapolto den Schlauch vor die Füße: „Den können Sie sich ans Bein binden[3], rausgeschmissenes Geld! Kaum hatte ich den bezahlt, da sehe ich im selben Geschäft das ideale Geschenk, ein wunderschönes Blumengesteck, wie es mein Freund schon immer wollte."
15 Kapolto blieb in solchen Fällen sehr ruhig: „Sicher, das ist meine Methode."
„Was?"
„Wir mussten doch eine Idee herbeiführen. Nun? Wann haben wir Ideen?"
„Möchte ich auch mal gerne wissen."
„Wir haben Ideen, wenn wir sie nicht brauchen, und wir haben keine, wenn wir wel-
20 che brauchen."
„Ja, das stimmt, und?"
„Also, um eine Idee zu kriegen, muss ich sie erst nicht mehr brauchen, ich muss sie überflüssig machen, damit sie sich freisetzen kann."
„Aha."
25 „So musste erst der Schlauch gekauft werden."
Der Kunde war beeindruckt und zahlte die zusätzliche Audienz. Guter Rat ist teuer.
Wieder zu Hause, wollte der Kunde sein so bedeutungsvoll herbeigeführtes Geschenk, dieses Blumengesteck, nochmal fotografieren, mit dem Schlauch dezent im Hintergrund, ehe er das Geschenk aus der Hand geben wollte, so als Souvenir für sich selber.
30 Dabei fiel ihm ein, dass sein Freund sich schon immer eine Polaroid-Kamera gewünscht hatte. Genau. Das war das richtige Geschenk.

Bernhard Lassahn

[1] Koan: object for solving meditation problems in Zen Buddhism
[2] Zen-Meister: master of a Buddhist school of meditation
[3] Den können Sie sich ans Bein binden.(ugs): You can keep that.

3 Where did chance play a role? Mark the lines down the margin.

4 Which sentence expresses Herr Kapolto's philosophy best? Underline it.

5 a The following verbs and verbal expressions express moods, feelings and wishes. Find them again in the text and match them.

Verben/verbale Ausdrücke	Wer?
1 etwas ersehnen (line 2)	
2 etwas wollen (line 3)	
3 verwirrt sein (line 7)	
4 scharf sein auf etwas (line 8)	a Menschen im Allgemeinen
5 wütend sein (line 11)	b Kapolto
6 etwas wollen (line 14)	c der Kunde
7 ruhig bleiben (line 15)	d der Freund des Kunden
8 beeindruckt sein (line 26)	
9 etwas wollen (lines 27, 29)	
10 sich etwas wünschen (line 30)	

b Sort the verbs and verbal expressions into the table.

neutral	intense	very intense

Aussprache: Konsonantenverbindung *ng*

6 a Listen and repeat.

die Beratung die Zeitung die Hoffnung die Einladung am Anfang
der Junge der Hunger bringen anfangen ich singe er ist gegangen
unbedingt lange langweilig
Inge will unbedingt lange singen. Junge, bring das Ding, ich hab' Hunger!

b Note down other words in which *ng* is pronounced like this.

c Listen and compare, and repeat.

unglücklich ungefähr ungesund angenehm
das Angebot im Singular das Unglück

d Listen and repeat.

Ich langweile mich ungern. Ungefähr drei Stunden lang dauerte die Beratung.
Die Zeitung bringt unangenehme Meldungen. Entschuldigung, aber die Übung ist ungesund!

Partizip I und II (Übersicht)

7 **a** In A and B fill in examples from the text.
b Which participles are declined? Underline the endings.

	Examples from the text
A Participle as part of the verb phrase Sie ist **verliebt**. (*sein* + Partizip II) Das war **spannend**. (*sein* + Partizip I) Sie ist nicht **gekommen**. (Perfekt) Er hatte es **versprochen**. (Plusquamperfekt) Wir wurden **gefragt**. (Passiv)	Der Kunde war verwirrt.
B Present or past participle before a noun die von der Arbeit **kommenden** Väter der **betonierte** Parkplatz	rausgeschmissenes Geld
C Present or past participle as a noun die **Regierenden** wenn wir einen **Verletzten** aus dem Wrack schneiden	
D Present or past participle as an adverb Sie zogen **singend** durch die Stadt. Er blieb **unverletzt** liegen.	
E Past participle as an abbreviated sub-clause (wenn es) in Zahlen **ausgedrückt** (wird)	

Adjectives from participles:
bekannt, verrückt, spannend, befriedigend, aufregend, verliebt, verheiratet, befreundet

Nouns from participles:
der Reisende, die Hungernden, die Wartenden, die Studierten, die Gebildeten, die Angestellte, die Verliebte, die Verwandten, der Bekannte

8 Which groups in the overview do these examples from previous units belong to?
Fill in the letter from the overview.

1 Es war wie ausgedacht. E **2** Es ist ungerecht verteilt. ☐ **3** eine in Vergessenheit geratene Sache ☐
4 der Weitgereiste ☐ **5** eine gut aussehende Frau ☐ **6** Wir sind ausgebildet. ☐ **7** Alles gelogen. ☐
8 lachende Menschen ☐ **9** was Gestorbenes ☐ **10** bei Licht betrachtet ☐ **11** ..., die ich je erlebt hatte. ☐ **12** zum folgenden Fernsehabend ☐ **13** ein Paar handgestrickter Socken ☐
14 die Herrschenden ☐ **15** Er wurde von seiner Frau unterstützt. ☐ **16** Merkmal eines zivilisierten Menschen ☐ **17** 82 % der befragten Ostdeutschen ☐

9 Form similar sequences.

sich verletzen: Er hat sich verletzt. – Er ist verletzt. – Der verletzte Mann war im Auto. – Die Verletzten wurden ins Krankenhaus gebracht.

beleidigen ◆ sich verlieben ◆ verhaften

Aussprache: Konsonanten treffen aufeinander

Wolf Schneider schreibt in seinem Buch „Deutsch für Kenner“:

> Das Deutsche ist arm an Farben und reich an Konsonanten. In Wörtern wie „Schrank“ oder „schwarz“ wird ein einziger Vokal von vier gesprochenen Konsonanten eingerahmt. Das Verb „schrumpfen“ lässt sogar die Form „du schrumpfst“ zu, bei der sieben gesprochene Konsonanten den einsamen Vokal umzingeln, davon fünf hintereinander: m-p-f-s-t.

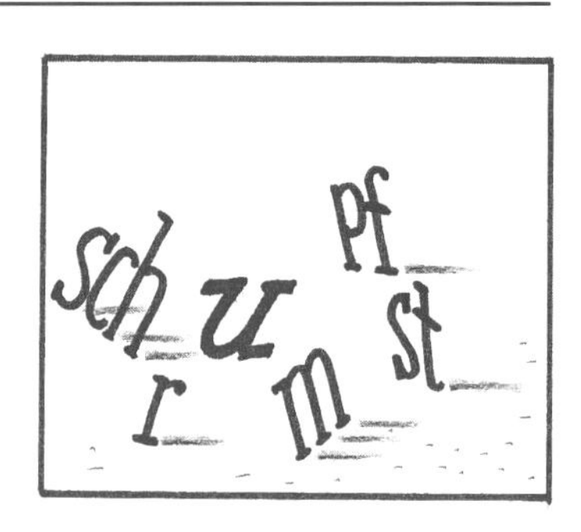

10 a Listen and read.

das Weihna**chtsg**eschenk ◆ der Gebu**rtst**a**gsbr**ief ◆ die Gebu**rtst**a**gsbl**ume ◆
die A**rb**eit**sz**eit ◆ die Beru**fs**au**sb**i**ld**ung ◆ der Si**tzpl**atz ◆ das Ho**chh**aus ◆
ei**nschl**afen ◆ **Entsch**eide dich! ◆ du**rchschn**ittlich ◆ der fü**nft**e Mai ◆ fu**rchtb**ar

b Listen again and repeat.

c Read the following sentences first with pauses, and then faster and faster without a pause.

Ich bin / meistens / müde.
Ein ganz / toller Film / war das!
Sein Freund / wohnte / in einem Hochhaus.
Er wird morgen / mein großes Geschenk / bekommen.
Der Kunde / wusste einfach / kein passendes Weihnachtsgeschenk / für seinen Freund.

Die kleinen Wörter

11 a Find one sentence in the text for each word and add the English translation.

einfach ....

ja gerade ....

bestimmt Bestimmt ein Koan, wie ..., dachte der Kunde.

schon immer ....

doch ....

auch mal ....

also ....

erst ....

b Complete the dialogue with words from a.

- Hallo, Margot. Wie siehst du denn heute aus? Du gehst ...bestimmt... auf die Party von Georg.
- ▲ Nein, ich arbeite .... (1) im Hotel Koblenzer Hof als Sekretärin.
- Und da musst du so elegant angezogen sein?
- ▲ Ich hatte .... (2) nichts anderes.
- So möchte ich .... (3) aussehen.
- ▲ Sag das nicht. Du hattest .... (4) .... die besseren Klamotten[1].
- Das ist es ....(5). Ich habe die besseren Klamotten, aber du siehst .... (6) besser aus.

[1] Klamotten (ugs.) = Kleidung

c Listen to the dialogue and repeat the sentences one by one.

12 a Listen and repeat.

- Guten Tag, womit kann ich dienen?
- ▲ Sie haben doch diese Agentur für Ideen.
- Ja, da sind Sie richtig, das Brainstore.
- ▲ Ich wollte schon immer mal ...
- Sie haben bestimmt ein Problem.
- ▲ Sehen Sie, meine Töchter telefonieren immer so viel.
- Das tun sie wohl alle, die Töchter.
- ▲ Ich habe einfach unheimlich hohe Telefonkosten. Da wollte ich Sie fragen, ...
- Also, ...

b Continue the dialogue.

Die Österreicher

Text

How do the Austrians think Germans and other foreigners see them? This question is the focus of the first text. In the second text an Austrian – the theatre and cultural critic Hans Weigel – talks about the Austrians. His views are almost certainly not shared by all Austrians. "The adjunct 'Austrian' has a negative touch to it for Austrians, and their favourite song 'Oh du, mein Österreich' doesn't sound like a fanfare, but is a heartfelt groan of resignation," Weigel claims. But this in fact, he says, speaks for Austria's strength and vitality. For a community that thinks so little of itself yet nevertheless enjoys a high standard of living must be especially healthy and robust.

As a result of the two World Wars, Austria has shrunk to a nation of not more than 8 million people. There are people who think Austria is just "Germany's backyard". Yet while Germany's history has been characterized by disintegration of purely Germanic tribes, it is one of Austria's notable achievements that it created under Habsburg rule a productive multi-ethnic state. Austria's often contradictory and self-critical culture is an expression of its links with the Balkans. An example of typical Austrian irony and not seldom black humour is the song "Taubenvergiften" (Poisoning doves) by the satirist Georg Kreisler.

The history of Austria

955	Battle of Lechfeld (near Augsburg) against Hungary; foundation of the Eastern March.
1282	Rudolf I of Habsburg, start of the Habsburg dynasty; "Alii bella gerant, tu felix Austria nube." (Others may wage war, you – blessed Austria – marry.)
1519	Emperor Charles V rules over Austria, Hungary, Bohemia, the Netherlands, Spain and its colonies; an empire "on which the sun never set".
1867	Dual monarchy of Austria-Hungary
1918	Fall of the monarchy, proclamation of the Republic; Hungary and Czechoslovakia become independent states.
1938	Anschluss with Nazi Germany
1945	Restoration of the Republic of Austria Like Germany, Austria and the capital Vienna is divided into four occupation zones.
1955	Treaty grants Austria full sovereignty in return for commitment to perpetual neutrality.
1995	Member of the European Union

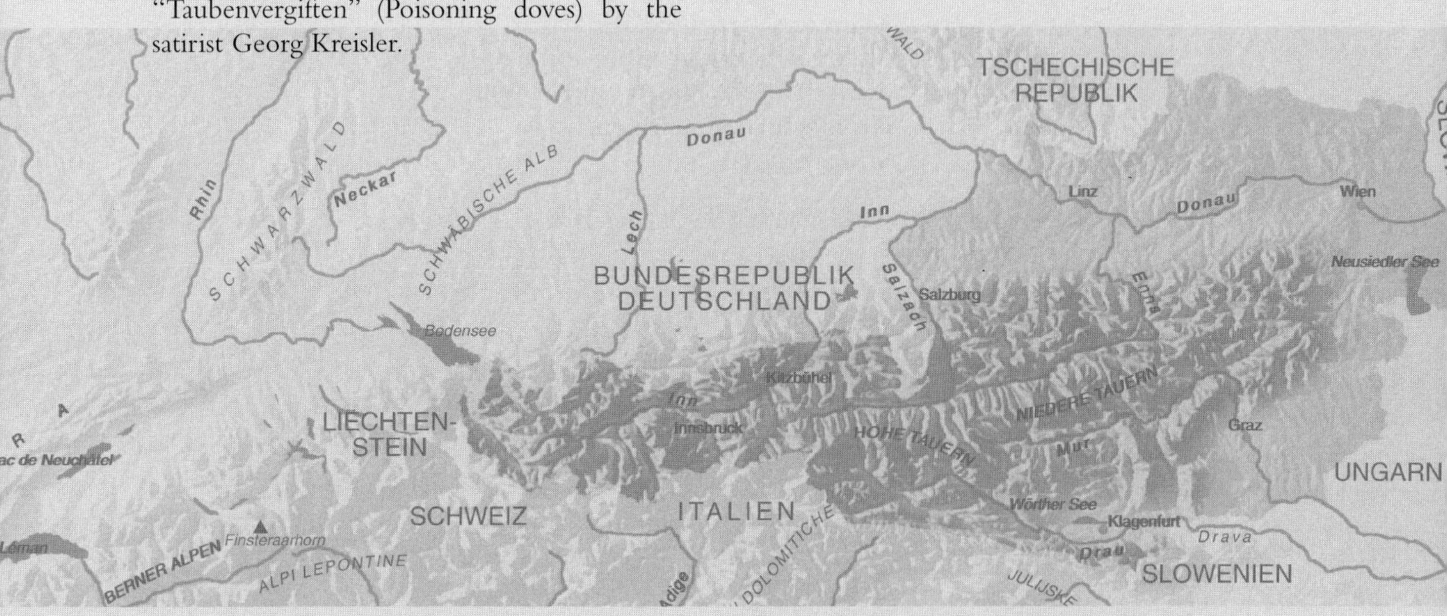

Stimmt das oder stimmt das nicht?

1 What do you associate with Austria? Complete the word-spider.

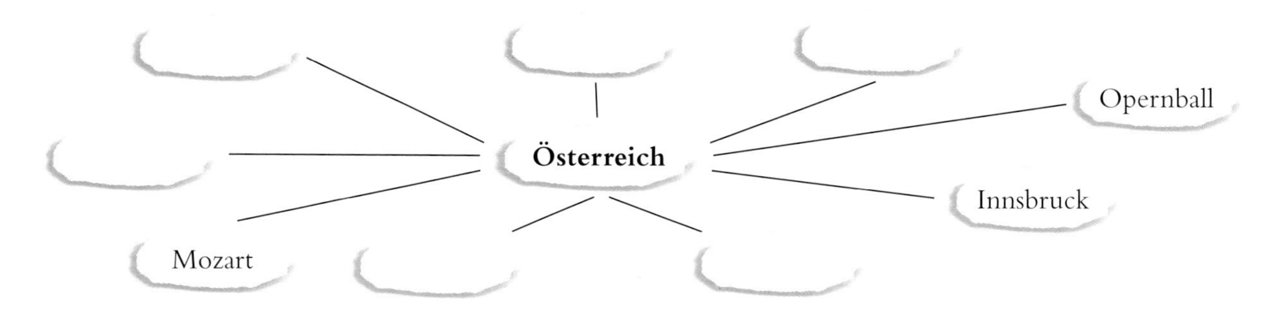

2 First read the four sentences in part A. Who might they have been written by?

3 Read sections B and C.

a Who is section B addressed to?

b Mark the key words in sections B and C.

A

Die Österreicher tragen Tiroler Hüte und jodeln[1].

Wenn die Wiener nichts zu nörgeln[2] haben, begehen sie Selbstmord.

[1] jodeln: yodel [2] nörgeln: grumble

Wenn die Österreicher keine Titel haben, machen sie sich einfach welche.

Die Österreicher haben in Wirklichkeit den Untergang des Habsburgerreiches immer noch nicht verkraftet.

B

Stimmt das oder stimmt das nicht? Mit den Vorurteilen ist das so eine Sache. Wäre doch schön, wenn die Vorurteile, die wir Österreicher gegenüber unseren deutschen Nachbarn haben, auch ein bisschen abnehmen. Stimmt doch!

Bild dir dein Urteil selbst über Deutschland!

C

Jodelnde Vorurteile

„Gegen Vorurteile ist kein Kraut gewachsen – außer Vorurteile." Ausgehend von dieser Prämisse stellen die Art-Direktorin Doris Forsthuber und der Texter Alexander Rabl ein Konzept vor, das verblüffend einfach wirkt, aber zugleich unendlich viele Möglichkeiten offen hält, gegen festgefahrene Vorurteile ins Feld zu ziehen.

„Wir zeigen den Österreichern, wie lächerlich und haltlos Vorurteile über andere eigentlich sind. Und zwar anhand von Vorurteilen, die die Deutschen gegenüber Österreichern haben (könnten) und von denen jeder in Österreich weiß, dass es eben Vorurteile sind", so die Urheber dieser Kampagne.

Texte A–C aus: *Marketing für Deutschland*

4 a What might these expressions mean? Note down your ideas in English.

Selbstmord begehen ⊛ etwas nicht verkraften ⊛ gegen etwas ist kein Kraut gewachsen ⊛ festgefahrene Vorurteile ⊛ gegen etwas ins Feld ziehen

b Match.

1 ☐ 2 ☐ 3 ☐ 4 ☐ 5 ☐ 6 ☐ 7 ☐ 8 ☐ 9 ☐ 10 ☐

1 die Wahrheit …
2 … Meinungen
3 gegen die Ideologie …
4 … Verhandlungen
5 eine Dummheit …
6 gegen den Tod …
7 gegen Intoleranz …
8 den Verlust …
9 gegen Vorurteile …
10 einen Mord …

a … verkraften
b … begehen
c … ins Feld ziehen
d … ist kein Kraut gewachsen
e festgefahrene …

5 What do people in your country know about Austria? Make some notes.

Wie alt ist Österreich?

6 Read the text.
a Mark all the geographical names.
b In which countries are the places mentioned?

Hans Weigel, Journalist und bissiger Theaterkritiker, über sein Land in dem Text „Das Land ohne Hymne" (1956)

Wie alt ist Österreich also? Sagen Sie irgendeine Zahl zwischen null und tausend, und sie hat etwas für sich. Im September 1946 gab es feierliche Staatsakte unter dem Motto „950 Jahre Österreich". Im Jahre 1955 feierte man Österreichs zehnjährigen Bestand und sprach zugleich von „Österreichs Jahr null". Ein tausendjähriges Reich[1] und ein eben erstandener Kleinstaat, ein würdiger Greis, ein dreißigjähriger Anfänger[2], ein Halbwüchsiger und ein Baby unter den Staaten, alles das zugleich und doch keines ganz – dazu eine Hauptstadt mit imperialem Zuschnitt[3] für ein Land von nicht ganz sieben Millionen Einwohnern – für die heute Fünfzigjährigen waren einst noch Prag, Triest, Agram[4], Krakau Inland, als die heute Zwanzigjährigen zur Schule gingen, waren Flensburg, Königsberg und Karlsruhe Inland, nicht nur die Gegenwart wechselte ihr Gesicht, auch die jeweils glorreiche Vergangenheit schwankte, und so hat der heutige Österreicher bestenfalls schon Gewissheit darüber, was er nicht ist, kaum jedoch darüber, was er ist.

1 tausendjähriges Reich: reference with a double meaning – Austria has been in existence over 1000 years, since 955; Hitler spoke of his regime as the 1000-year-Reich of the future.
2 The author is exaggerating here: it's 37 years since the abolition of the monarchy.
3 mit imperialem Zuschnitt: of imperial dimensions
4 Agram = Zagreb

7 a Fill in expressions from the text.

Alter eines Menschen	bis ein Jahr	von 12 bis 18 Jahre	mit 50	ab 75
Bezeichnung	....	....	Erwachsener	....

b What happened then? Take notes on the following dates from the text and the table on page 285.

996 ....
1946 ....
1955 ....

8 a Listen to the song about the poisoning of doves.
Where does the poisoning take place? At what time of year? Who is participating? What does the man suggest to his girlfriend?

b Underline all the passages where enthusiasm for nature is voiced.

c In which lines do you find black humour?

Taubenvergiften

Schatz, das Wetter ist wunderschön!
Da leid ich's nicht länger zu Haus.
Heute muss man ins Grüne gehn,
in den bunten Frühling hinaus.
5 Jeder Bursch und sein Mäderl
mit einem Fresspaketerl,
sitzen heute im grünen Klee.
Schatz, ich hab eine Idee:

Schau, die Sonne ist warm, und die Lüfte sind lau,
10 gehen wir Taubenvergiften im Park!
Die Bäume sind grün, und der Himmel ist blau,
gehen wir Taubenvergiften im Park!
Wir sitzen zusamm' in der Laube[1],
und a jeder vergiftet a Taube.
15 Der Frühling, der dringt bis ins innerste Mark[2]
beim Taubenvergiften im Park.

[1] Laube: summerhouse
[2] dringt bis ins innerste Mark: penetrates people to the quick
[3] Scherzl: crust

Schatz, geh, bring das Arsen g'schwind her!
Das tut sich am Besten bewährn.
Streu's auf ein Grahambrot kreuz über quer!
20 Nimm's Scherzl[3], das fressen s' so gern.
Erst verjagen wir die Spatzen,
denn die tun ei'm alles verpatzen.
So ein Spatz ist zu g'schwind,
der frisst's Gift auf im Nu,
25 und das arme Tauberl schaut zu.

Ja, der Frühling, der Frühling, der Frühling ist hier,
gehen wir Taubenvergiften im Park!
Kann's geben im Leben ein größ'res Pläsier,
als das Taubenvergiften im Park?
30 Der Hansl geht gern mit der Mali,
denn die Mali, die zahlt's Zyankali.
Die Herzen sind schwach, und die Liebe ist stark
beim Taubenvergiften im Park.
Nimm für uns was zum Naschen –
35 in der anderen Taschn.
Gehen wir Taubenvergiften im Park!

Georg Kreisler

Deutsch in Österreich

In the song there are some dialectal features typical of the Viennese region.

Wiener Varianten	**Hochdeutsch**
der Bursch	der Junge / der junge Mann
g'schwind	schnell
das Pläsier	das Vergnügen
da leid ich's nicht	da ertrage (ertrage) ich es nicht
das Tauberl, das Fresspaketerl, das Mäderl	die Taube, das Fresspaket, das Mädchen
a jeder, a Taube, fressen s'	ein jeder, eine Taube, fressen sie

Im Buchladen

Cultural information

"Why do you want to give him a book for his birthday, he's got one already!" is a joke in the German-speaking countries showing contempt for people who read little or not at all, who are uneducated. In some people's livingrooms the well-stocked bookcase is the focus of attention, while the TV is hidden shamefully away in the corner or an annex.
So books still play quite a role, both culturally and economically, in the country where the first books were printed by Johannes Gutenberg in Mainz in about the year 1450.
In Germany there is the "Börsenverein des Deutschen Buchhandels" (Association of the German Book Trade) which protects the interests of this important sector of the economy in the three countries. It is also one of the organizers of the "Frankfurter Buchmesse" (Frankfurt Book Fair), the largest book fair in the world. More than 360,000 books from over 100 countries are exhibited there annually in October. Each year there is a special focus on the book production of one country. This country is given the opportunity to present its literature in a number of special events.
The fact that books are not only read by the so-called educated classes, is a result of the early activities of the trade unions and so-called Worker Education Associations back in the 19th century. They ensured that people on low incomes were given access to world literature by means of cheap editions produced by the so-called book clubs. It is from one of these book clubs that the largest media conglomerate in Europe has grown, the "Bertelsmann AG", whose activities are of course no longer focussed solely on books. The "Stiftung Lesen", an association devoted to promoting reading in schools and families by means of grants, also ensures that reading is not neglected.

The text

In the text, the Bavarian satirist Gerhard Polt uses a number of features of dialect and the spoken language. As German dialects are generally only spoken, there is no fixed form in which they are written. Our transcription of the text is a high-German translation.

Language

Written German is governed (at present) by the rules of the Spelling Reform of 1.8.98. As there has been a good deal of argument about this reform, not all publications and publishers follow it. If in doubt, check things in the spelling "Bible", the "Duden, Die deutsche Rechtschreibung".

Im Buchladen

1 What can you see in the drawing? What sort of people are they? What is their relationship to one another?

2 a Listen to the dialogue. What does the customer want? Take notes.

b Listen to the dialogue again and read it at the same time.

Kunde: Grüß Gott[1], Fräulein! Ich hätte gern ein Buch!

Verkäuferin: Ja, guten Tag, was hätten Sie sich denn da gedacht?

Kunde: Ja, es ist so, wissen Sie, mein Cousin, der Alois, er hat Geburtstag, jetzt haben wir uns gedacht, mei[2], Sie verstehen? Ein Paperback, das ist halt doch – äh – zu dünn, nicht wahr? Das macht doch nicht viel her! Jetzt haben wir uns gedacht, halt doch irgendetwas, was etwas hermacht, verstehen Sie?

Verkäuferin: Ja, also haben Sie irgendeine Vorstellung von einem Inhalt?

Kunde: Ja, mei, es ist so, also der Alois hat ja die Zeit nicht, verstehen Sie, also wenn er reinschaut – ned – nachher sagen wir mal, er möchte gern lachen ... lachen, verstehen Sie?

Verkäuferin: Ja, also gut, da hätte ich eine Jubiläumsausgabe von Wilhelm Busch[3].

Kunde: Hähähä, ja na, hähä! Der Alois ist schon vierzig Jahre, wissen Sie! Nein, nein, kein Kinderbuch, hähä! Ja, der Struwwelpeter[4] und so ... ich kenne mich aus, hähä! Nein, nein, es soll etwas sein, sagen wir mal, verstehen Sie, etwas Repräsentatives. Der Alois ist altdeutsch eingerichtet. Jetzt, sagen wir mal so: Wenn man hereinkommt, man kommt beim Alois, von der Diele kommt man herein, jetzt wenn man ins Wohnzimmer kommt, dass man es vielleicht auf einen Tisch legen kann oder so, dass man halt dann gleich das sieht, und bevor man Kaffee trinkt oder so, dass man es halt auch sieht. Verstehen Sie, das wär's gewesen.

Verkäuferin: Ja, also, hier – hätten wir noch etwas anderes, das wäre eine Ausgabe von Immanuel Kant[5], das wären sozusagen dreizehnhundert Seiten, ein Buch, das durchaus zeigen würde ... das Niveau verbreitet, nicht wahr? Und das sofort demonstriert, in welcher Haushaltung man sich da befindet.

Kunde: Hä, ja, eh, ja, das klingt nicht schlecht, nicht? Immanuel Kant, ja jetzt, was sagt jetzt dieser, dieser, äh, Kant, dieser Immanuel Kant so?

Verkäuferin: Immanuel Kant[5] beschäftigt sich mit der hermeneutischen Fundamentalontologie als Analytik der Existenzialität des Denkens, des Wesens vom Sein, nur in etwas anderer Art als Heidegger[6]... aber ich würde doch sagen, in einer etwas spezifizierten Art und Weise.

Kunde: Hä, ja, hähä, ja, da wird, hä, da wird er schauen, der Alois! Ja, ob jetzt natürlich, äh, hm, vielleicht haben Sie doch was anderes, sagen wir mal ein Tierbuch, hähä, oder so was, wissen Sie schon, gell[7], Tierbuch oder so, äh. Aber wissen Sie, Fräulein, genau so schwer, ne? Also, und auch so grünen Einband!

Gerhard Polt / Christian Müller

1 Grüß Gott: usual form of greeting in southern Germany and Austria
2 mei, ja mei: Bavarian expression, here: embarrassment
3 Wilhelm Busch: popular 19th century author of picture stories
4 „Der Struwwelpeter": famous children's book
5 Immanuel Kant: German philosopher (1724–1804)
6 Martin Heidegger: German philosopher (1889–1976)
7 gell = nicht wahr: don't you (southern German, Austrian)

3 What do we find out about Cousin Alois? Takes notes.

4 With the help of your notes from sections 2a and 3 summarize what happens in the dialogue.

5 Mark all the formulations and expressions in the text that the people use to steer and structure the conversation but which don't have any special meaning.

Ja, es ist so, wissen Sie, ...; ... mei, Sie verstehen?; ... nicht wahr?

6 Rewrite the following dialogue adding the following expressions from the text at the appropriate points.

ja, also gut • verstehen Sie • wissen Sie • ja, es ist so • also • sagen wir mal • ja, also • ich würde sagen

- Guten Tag. Suchen Sie etwas Bestimmtes?
- .... (1), mein Sohn hat Geburtstag. Da hätte ich gern einen Computer.
- Ist er denn schon so groß?
- .... (2), er kam gerade aufs Gymnasium.
- .... (3) etwa 13 Jahre!
- Nein erst 11, aber .... (4), er ist interessiert und intelligent.
- .... (5), da hätte ich etwas Passendes von der Firma Intersoft.
- Die kennt doch niemand.
- Sie ist, ... (6), spezialisiert auf Geräte für Schulen.
- .... (7), ich möchte kein Spielzeug. Der Computer muss auch für Erwachsene sein, ... (8).
- .... (9), dieser Computer ist für Erwachsene.

Wenn du morgen ...

7 Look at the cartoon and read the sentences.
Which marks/grades are good (+), which are poor (–), which are moderate (∗)?

Note 1 ☐ Note 2 ☐ Note 3 ☐ Note 4 ☐ Note 5 ☐ Note 6 ☐

[1] Tagesschau: news [2] Sesamstraße: children's TV programme

Bedingung ausdrücken

Conditions are expressed by means of

- sub-clauses with the conjunctions *wenn*; *falls*; *im Falle, dass* or without a conjunction, e. g. *Schreibst du eine Eins, ... / Solltest du eine Eins schreiben, ...*
- prepositions + nouns, e. g. *bei einer Zwei ... ; mit einer guten Note*

8 Rewrite the following sentences.

Du schreibst eine Eins. Dann darfst du fernsehen. — wenn

Wenn du eine Eins schreibst, darfst du fernsehen.

1 Du hast keine Zeit. Dann lass es sein. — sollt-
2 Das Wetter ist schön. Wir machen einen Ausflug. — bei
3 Sie haben ein Problem. Sie sollten zum Chef gehen. — mit
4 Sie wollen ein spannendes Buch lesen. Hier ist ein Roman von Karl May. — falls
5 Ich bin früher fertig. Dann komme ich zu dir. — wenn
6 Sind Sie im Oktober in Frankfurt? Dann sollten Sie zur Buchmesse gehen. — im Falle, dass

9 a Read the text.
b Match the following headings to the relevant sections.

der Leseprozess (lines ☐ – ☐), der Erfolg (lines ☐ – ☐), ein Geschenk zu Weihnachten (lines ☐ – ☐), die Ziele der Eltern (lines ☐ – ☐)

Mein erstes Buch

Mein erstes Buch war Zwangslektüre, eine echte Qual. Ich bekam es von einer Tante geschenkt, die glaubte, höheren Geist in der Familie vertreten zu müssen, und sogar ein Modejournal abonniert hatte. 5 Es war ein Weihnachtsgeschenk, ich war neunjährig, und es war ein richtiges Buch, dick und ohne Bilder: „Christeli" von Elisabeth Müller, sehr, sehr traurig und sentimental, sehr, sehr brav und unspannend.
Ich begann einen Kampf mit diesem Buch. Ich hatte es 10 zu lesen – selbst meine Eltern beharrten darauf, vor allem, weil meine Schwäche in Orthographie sich bereits zeigte und die Hoffnung bestand, durch Lesen zu besseren Diktaten zu kommen, durch bessere Diktate zu besseren Noten, dadurch zu besseren Erfolgs- 15 chancen, zu einem besseren Lohn und einer schöneren Frau, zu einem größeren Haus und vielleicht einem Auto. Lesen war in diesem Zusammenhang immerhin noch karrierefreundlich. Zweitens hatte meine Mutter nicht die Absicht, sich von ihrer Schwester mit Mode- 20 journal blamieren zu lassen. Sie wollte zum mindesten einen Sohn haben, der auch liest, genau so liest wie der Sohn ihrer Schwester.
Das Buch war grauenhaft langweilig. Ich hatte zwei Lesezeichen darin: das erste zeigte an, wie weit ich schon war, das zweite zeigte mein selbstgestecktes Ziel, 25 bis da und da – bis auf Seite 48 – will ich heute durchhalten. Ich hielt nie durch und erreichte mein Tagesziel nicht. Immerhin war ich stolz darauf, daß mich die Tante für erwachsen genug hielt, ein Leser zu sein. Immerhin war ich einer mit einem Buch und fühlte 30 mich im geheimen allen Fußballern und Bäumekletterern ohne Buch überlegen. Ich hatte eine Ahnung davon, daß Bücher lesen etwas Besseres sei.
Ein Jahr später, am 23. Dezember, las ich die letzten zwei Seiten. Ich hatte ein ganzes Buch gelesen, ich hat- 35 te es geschafft, ich war stolz darauf und beschloß, ein Leser zu bleiben – einer, der richtige Bücher von der ersten bis zur letzten Seite liest. Als Fußballer war ich ohnehin schlecht.

Peter Bichsel

Aussprache und Intonation: laut lesen

10 a Listen and read. Pay attention to the pronunciation of the unstressed *e* and *er* at the end of a word.

Mein erstes, richtiges Buch bekam ich zu Weihnachten. Meine Eltern meinten, ich könne durch Lesen zu besseren Diktaten kommen, durch bessere Diktate zu besseren Noten, durch gute Noten zu besseren Chancen, zu einem besseren Lohn und einer schöneren Frau. Nach einem Jahr, am dreiundzwanzigsten Dezember, las ich die letzten zwei Seiten. Ich beschloss, ein Leser zu bleiben – einer, der richtige Bücher von der ersten bis zur letzten Seite liest.

b Listen again to the text in a and mark the sense units and stresses.

Mein érstes, / ríchtiges Buch / bekam ich zu Wéihnachten.
Meine Eltern méinten, / ich könne durch Lésen / zu besseren Diktáten kommen.

In speech, longer sentences are divided up into sense units sometimes marked by punctuation. Between them a short pause is taken, with a longer one at the end of the sentence. In each sense unit, the word which is the most important in meaning gets the main stress.

11 Choose a section from the text "Mein erstes Buch".

a Divide the longer sentences up into sense units and mark the stress.

b Read the section aloud.

Notwendigkeit / Zwang ausdrücken

Ich begann einen Kampf mit diesem Buch.
Ich hatte es zu lesen.

haben + *zu* + Infinitiv, *müssen*

Ich **hatte** das Buch **zu lesen**.	Ich **musste** das Buch **lesen**.
Das Formular **ist** genau **zu lesen**.	Das Formular **muss** genau **gelesen werden**.
	Das Formular **muss man** genau **lesen**.

haben + *zu* + infinitive = *müssen* + infinitive
sein + *zu* + infinitive = → *müssen* + passive infinitive (*werden* + past participle)
→ *muss man* + infinitive

12 Replace *müssen* with *haben* or *sein* + *zu* + infinitive.

1 Ich kann nicht kommen. Ich muss zur Zeit viel tun.
2 Das alles muss erledigt werden.
3 Die Kassetten müssen bald bestellt werden.
4 Du musst heute Abend noch Vokabeln lernen.
5 Hier sind die Personen, die angerufen werden müssen.
6 Wir müssen noch zwei Texte lesen.

nötig / notwendig sein

Ist es wirklich **notwendig**, dass wir alle neuen Wörter in Sätzen lernen?
Heute **ist** es **nötig/notwendig**, mehrere Fremdsprachen zu können.
Vor sechshundert Jahren **war** es **notwendig**, dass jedes Buch mit der Hand geschrieben wurde.

Nötig/notwendig sein can be used with an infinitive or *dass*-clause.
A *dass*-clause is used if you want to mention the subject.

13 Complete the sentences.

1 Ist es wirklich notwendig, ...	lernen – alle Regeln
2 Ist es nötig, ...	mitkommen – ich – zum Arzt
3 Es war nötig, ...	sprechen – sein Vater – mit ihm
4 Wird es nötig sein, ...	erklären – noch einmal – die Sache
5 Es war nicht notwendig, ...	mitbringen – du – mir – ein Geschenk

Die Schönheits-Tipps von Kaiserin Sissi

One of the interesting female figures of the 19th century was Empress Elizabeth, named Sissi. She grew up near Munich and was married to the Austrian Emperor Franz Joseph at the age of 16. After she had given birth to several children, and in particular a successor to the throne, she distanced herself more and more from the conventions of the Austrian Court and did what she pleased: she corresponded, she read a great deal, she philosophized, wrote poems and learned foreign languages, among them Hungarian and Greek. Like her role model, the French author George Sand, she generally preferred to wear trousers, at the time an exclusively male piece of clothing. She brought up her children in a liberal spirit and in opposition to the spirit of the Austrian court. Her great passion was physical culture. She was an outstanding horserider and was happiest out in the open air. For her period she was an emancipated woman.

A hundred years on, her fate became interwoven with that of another woman, the actress Romy Schneider. Her parents initiated her to the theatre at an early age, and by the age of 18 she had already become a star, thanks to her portrayal of the empress in the film "Sissi" (1957). This film was such a success that two further Sissi films were made. In each of these films, Romy Schneider had to play the young empress as an attractive, lively young woman who enlivened the stiff ceremonious court life with her cheerfulness and charm. The films were optimistic tearjerkers appealing to the masses, but far from the truth. For the public Romy was Sissi, and Sissi was Romy. The actress felt misinterpreted and went to France to shake off the image of the sweet little princess. And there she did indeed get to play other roles. She played alongside Alain Delon, Yves Montand, Michel Piccoli; she became one of the few Germans to make it as international filmstars. The periodical Paris Press wrote at the time: "40 years after Garbo (Greta) and Marlene (Dietrich), 15 years after Marilyn (Monroe) the screen once again has a great star." In 1999, in a survey carried out by the newspaper Le Parisien and a French TV station, she was named "Actress of the Century". Romy herself, however, had decreed that her gravestone should be inscribed with her real name, Rosemarie Albach. So great was her desire for another identity. Both women have in common their German-Austrian origins. Their breaking away from the conventions of a rigid society and their search for another identity is also something they share, and both women suffered a tragic blow from fate, when one of their children died young.

Die Schönheits-Tipps von Kaiserin Sissi

1 a What is the newspaper article: a bit of jounalistic research, a book review? First read the two headings.

b What information do you expect from the article? Make notes.

2 What sections do the headings go with? Skim through the text and write the line numbers next to the headings.

1 Neues auf dem Büchermarkt ☐ – ☐
2 Sissis Schönheits- und Fitnessprogramm ☐ – ☐
3 Wer und wie war Sissi? ☐ – ☐
4 Sissis Rezepte für die Frau von heute ☐ – ☐
5 Was der Haut gut tut ☐ – ☐

Die Schönheits-Tipps von Kaiserin Sissi

Eine Münchner Autorin verrät die Rezepturen Ihrer Hoheit

Von Juliane Becker

Sie war eine Landpomeranze[1], durch Heirat zur Kaiserin geworden, unerfahren in politischen Belangen, manisch-depressiv. Und doch wurde sie zum Mythos: Sissi – Kaiserin von Österreich-Ungarn. 1998 jährte sich ihr 100. Todestag. Berühmt wurde Sissi vor allem ihrer Schönheit wegen. Dass diese nicht nur ein Geschenk Gottes, sondern Ergebnis sehr harter Arbeit war, das demonstriert jetzt nachdrücklich und zum Nachmachen ein neues Buch.

„Sisis kaiserliches Schönheits- und Gesundheitsbuch", so der Titel des mit rotem Samt gebundenen 218-Seiten-Bandes von Jutta Wellmann. Sisi mit einem „s" in der Mitte, absichtlich, denn, so glaubt die Autorin, diese Schreibweise war die von Sissi selbst verwandte. Wellmanns Buch ist prächtig aufgemacht und reich illustriert, mit Bildmaterial, Zeichnungen, Skizzen und vielen, vielen Rezepten versehen. Das sieht ein bisschen aus wie ein Jungmädchen-Poesiealbum und ist zum Selber-Anrühren für daheim gedacht. Autorin Wellmann (47) hat en détail zusammengetragen, mit welchen Mixturen und Geheimtipps das Possenhofener[2] Landmädel[3] zum ersten Glamourstar der Neuzeit wurde.

Das ist historisch nicht immer sauber recherchiert und stellenweise spekulativ – aber sehr unterhaltsam. Denn Wellmann geht einer eigentlich sehr interessanten Frage nach: Was tat eine Frau vor 100 Jahren, wenn sie schön, schlank und fit sein wollte? Ohne Hightech und moderne Chemie, nur mit dem, was Haus, Hof und Garten bieten? Naturkosmetik hieß die Devise.

Leicht, das zur Warnung vorab, ist es freilich nicht, auf Sissis Schönheitsspuren zu wandern[4]. Eher ziemlich anstrengend. Denn die Kaiserin gab alles, alles, alles dafür, begehrenswert und schlank zu bleiben. Jeden Morgen um 6 Uhr war Sissis Nacht zu Ende. Dann ging es los: kalt baden, Ganzkörpermassage, drei Stunden cremen, kämmen und frisieren, vier Stunden joggen, zwei Stunden turnen und zeitig zu Bett gehen. Zu essen gab es auch wenig: ein Tässchen Tee am Morgen, ein Schlückchen Milch, ein bisschen Rinderbrühe und dann und wann ein Ei.

Billig im Unterhalt war die Kaiserin dennoch nicht, denn was Sissi an Lebensmitteln nicht aß, das schmierte sie auf Gesicht und Körper. Aus Erdbeeren und Gurken, Milch und Honig, Olivenöl und Mandelkleie, Eigelb und Quitten ließ Sissi ihre Appreturen mixen. Essenzen und Wässerchen, pflegende Öle und duftende Lotionen. Und ganz wichtig: Masken für Gesicht und Körper und jede Lebenslage, für müde Haut und für fahle, gegen Fältchen, für rosigen Teint. Sissis Favoriten: eine Erdbeermaske für strahlende Haut. Frisch pürierte Erdbeeren, zwei Esslöffel Quark und einen Teelöffel Honig verquirlen und auf das ganze Gesicht (Augenpartie aussparen) auftragen. Oder eine Gurkenkompresse zur Erfrischung aus dem Mix einer halben pürierten Salatgurke und einem Esslöffel Honig. Oder Sissis Tipp für straffe Haut, aus einer halben Tasse Haferflocken mit Milch gekocht und – abgekühlt – mit zwei Esslöffeln Rosenwasser verfeinert. Alles naturrein und ohne Konservierungsstoffe.

Jutta Wellmann hat Sissis Original-Rezepte – die im letzten Jahr im Dorotheum in Wien versteigert wurden – auf heutige Verhältnisse übertragen: Gesundheitsschädliches – die Kaiserin schwor zum Beispiel auf den Mineralstoff Borax, der keinem gut tut – eliminiert, und was an Zutaten zu teuer und/oder nicht mehr im Handel ist, auch. So wird Sissis Schönheitsbrevier zum Ratgeber für die Frau und zum Muss für alle Sissi-Fans.

aus: *Abendzeitung*

[1] Landpomeranze: country cousin
[2] Possenhofen: place near München
[3] Landmädel: country girl
[4] auf jds. Spuren wandern: follow in sb's footsteps

3 Read lines 1–27 and mark the passages that answer the following questions.

1 How is Sissi described?
2 What was the reason for the publication of a new book about Sissi?
3 What is the name of the book and the author?
4 Why is Sissi spelt with only one *s* in the book's title?
5 What does the journalist think of the book: content, design?

4 Does it say this in the text? Read from line 28 to the end and note down: R (right), F (falsch = wrong).

1 If you want to follow Sissi's beauty programme, you need a lot of time and discipline. ☐
2 Sissi only followed her beauty programme very reluctantly. ☐
3 Sissi didn't eat much, but her cosmetic products consisted of foods. ☐
4 The book passes on Sissi's beauty remedies in their original form. ☐

Das Adjektiv: ohne Artikel

Sissis Schönheit war das Ergebnis sehr **harter** Arbeit.
Ohne Hightech und **moderne** Chemie.
Sissis Favorit: eine Maske mit frisch **pürierten** Erdbeeren und **selbst gemachtem** Quark.

5 a Read lines 38–54 of the text and fill in the adjectives.

Was ließ Sissi mixen?

.... Öle und

.... Lotionen.

Wofür waren ihre Schönheitsrezepte gut?

Für ...., ...,

...., ... Haut,

für .... Teint.

b Fill in the missing endings.

	Singular			**Plural**
	maskulin	**neutral**	**feminin**	**m, n, f**
N	rosig**er** Teint	frisch**es** Obst	modern**e** Chemie	pflegend...... Öle
A	für rosig....... Teint	frisch**es** Obst	ohne modern...... Chemie	duftend...... Lotionen
D	mit frisch...... Quark	mit rein**em** Olivenöl	mit gekocht**er** Milch	mit püriert...... Erdbeeren
G	das Ergebnis intensiv**en** Sports	das Ergebnis täglich**en** Trainings	das Ergebnis hart...... Arbeit	die Wirkung pflegend**er** Öle

6 Fill in the adjective endings.

Rosenwasser

¼ Liter warm............ destilliert............ Wasser über 100 g frisch............ Rosenblätter gießen und mindestens drei Tage an einem warm............ Ort stehen lassen. Anschließend durch einen Filter gießen und die Rosenblätter gut auspressen. Den Extrakt in ein Flakon füllen und kühl aufbewahren.
Das Gleiche kann man auch mit frisch............ Orangenblüten machen.

Zimteiscreme

2 Esslöffel Honig
4 Esslöffel Wasser
3 Zimtstangen
0,2 l süß......... Sahne
1 Eigelb
⅓ Teelöffel Vanille
½ Teelöffel gemahlen......... Zimt

Zimtstangen im Honig und Wasser ca. 10 Minuten kochen, dann herausnehmen. Sahne erhitzen. Das Eigelb schlagen und einige Tropfen der heiß............ Sahne hinzufügen. Dann das Eigelb in die heiß.......... Sahne gießen. So lange kochen, bis die Sahne dick geworden ist. Die Masse kalt werden lassen und mit Honig-Wasser-Sirup, Vanille und gemahlen............ Zimt vermischen. In den Kühlschrank stellen.

7 Give away a secret recipe, for example for a medicinal compound, something to eat, something to drink, ... Describe what ingredients are needed and how it is made.

es

Jeden Morgen um 6 Uhr war Sissis Nacht zu Ende. Dann **ging es los**.
Zu essen **gab es** auch wenig.
Leicht ist es nicht, auf Sissis Schönheitsspuren zu wandern.

8 What do these expressions with es mean in English?

unpersönliches es

9 Read the following sentences and complete the rule.

Es war einmal ...
Es ist Frühling/Sommer.
Es ist nicht weit, es sind nur drei Kilometer.
Bleib da, jetzt wird es interessant.
Es waren genau sechshundert Leute.
Es regnet schon seit drei Tagen.
Es ist Freitag, der 13. April.
Es wird Abend. Es wird schon dunkel.
Es ist fünf Uhr.
Es ist nicht leicht, so viele neue Wörter zu lernen.
Es bleibt lange hell.

Es is used as an impersonal subject

- with the verbs ...., ..., ...
  + noun (seasons, times of day), numeral adjective;
- with the so-called "weather verbs": es regnet, es schneit, ...

10 a Translate the following fixed expressions into English.

Was gibt es (zu essen / im Kino / im Fernsehen ...)?

Wie gefällt es Ihnen (hier / im Sprachkurs / in Ihrer Firma ...)?

Es ist mir egal.

Es tut mir Leid.

Gibt es (etwas Neues / noch Karten ...)?

Wie war es (im Urlaub / auf der Party / im Theater ...)?

Ich habe es eilig.

Wie geht es dir/Ihnen?

Wie spät ist es?

Es geht los.

If *es* follows a verb, it can be abbreviated to *'s*.
Wie geht es dir? → Wie geht's dir? Ich habe es eilig. → Ich hab's eilig.

b Make little dialogues.

■ Wann fahren wir endlich? ▲ Moment noch, es geht gleich los!

es als Verweis

11 a Underline the word that es refers to.

Ich habe die Maske gemacht und finde das Rezept gut. Man kann es leicht nachmachen und teuer ist es auch nicht.

■ Er joggt jeden Tag zwei Stunden um fit zu werden.
▲ Er ist es doch schon.

es refers to a neuter noun in the nominative or accusative or an adjective.

es in the accusative can never be placed at the beginning of a sentence.

b Which es in a can be placed at the beginning of the sentence?

12 Underline the sentences that es refers to.

1 Du sagst, die Diät hilft sicher, aber ich glaube es nicht.

2 Habe ich es dir noch nicht gesagt? Ich mache wieder eine neue Diät.

3 Es ist nicht leicht, dich zu verstehen.

4 ■ Du wolltest mir doch die Rezepte geben.
▲ Tut mir Leid, ich habe es vergessen.

5 Es ist mir egal, wann du das machst.

es refers to a clause:
- to a preceding or following main clause.
- to a following sub-clause / infinitive clause with *zu*.

If the sub-clause/infinitive clause with *zu* is in front of the main clause, *es* is dropped:
Dich zu verstehen ist nicht leicht.
Wann du das machst, ist mir egal.

Sissi – historisch genauer betrachtet

Viel ist über Sissi geschrieben und veröffentlicht worden: die Rose aus dem Bayernland. Über ihren Körperkult, Schönheitstrip, Schönheitswahn kann man Ausführliches erfahren. Welche Bücher sie gelesen hat, ist dagegen kaum bekannt. Mehr über sie erfährt man aus ihren Tagebüchern, die das Leben der Kaiserin widerspiegeln und verständlicherweise zu ihren Lebzeiten nicht an die Öffentlichkeit kamen. Erst 1953 tauchten sie auf und Historiker konnten sich damit beschäftigen.

13 Read the excerpts from Sissi's diaries.
What picture of her do they give?

**Ich wollt', die Leute ließen mich
In Ruh' und ungeschoren,
Ich bin ja doch nur sicherlich
Ein Mensch, wie sie geboren.**

Die meisten Mädchen heiraten überhaupt nur aus Sehnsucht nach Freiheit. Übrigens hat die Liebe auch Flügel zum Fortfliegen.

Die Leute wissen nicht, was sie mit mir beginnen sollen[1], weil ich in keine ihrer Traditionen und längst anerkannten Begriffe hineinpasse. Sie wollen nicht, dass man ihre Schubladenordnung störe.

[1] nicht wissen, was man mit jdm. beginnen/anfangen soll: not know what to make of s.o.

Historisch betrachtet war Sissi wohl eine moderne Frau nach unseren Maßstäben. Wer Sissi als oberflächliche Schaufensterpuppe schildert, liegt falsch, meint die Historikerin Martha Schad, die mehrere Bücher zum Leben der Kaiserin herausgegeben hat.

14 a Listen to a conversation with the historian. In what order are the following points covered in the conversation? Number them.

her daughter's education ☐
Sissi's knowledge of languages ☐
Sissi and politics ☐
Sissi's character ☐

b Listen to the conversation again and take notes on the points in a.

Ihre letzten Jahre verbrachte Elisabeth mit ruhelosen Reisen und gefährlichen Hungerkuren. In Genf wurde sie am 10. September 1898 von einem italienischen Anarchisten erstochen, der alle Adligen hasste.

Warum?

Cultural information

A group of three very young women had a meteoric rise in the German pop charts in 1997/98, and then almost as quickly disappeared again. "Tic Tac Toe" they called themselves, and played cheeky, but also reflective songs like "Warum?".

The problem with German groups is that a lot of them only think they can make it if they sing their songs in English. But there's also a theory that the German language doesn't go with the syncopated rhythms of music that have evolved from jazz. In addition, some German rock groups' success was inhibited by the fact that they were often rather serious and politically involved, so that there was too little entertainment value in their music.

A lot of German groups evolved from school music. This is why early German rock was often too intellectual. Because, you see, music is promoted in all shapes and sizes at German grammar schools, to a far greater extent than in many other countries. Basic musical training often begins very early and is developed further later on, with practice rooms being provided for the pupils.

Although the conditions are actually quite favourable, only very few rock groups have been really successful. And in fact the groups that made a name for themselves internationally, were ones that used English texts, such as the "Scorpions". The group "Kraftwerk" became known all over the world with their title "Autobahn", which summoned the arrival of techno music. At the beginning of the 1980s, a genuinely original German style of pop music evolved that was marketed as Neue Deutsche Welle; it included Nena (99 Luftballons) and also the Austrian Falco. Among more recent groups, "Die Ärzte", "Die Toten Hosen" and "Die fantastischen Vier" have achieved international recognition.

Text

The text of "Tic Tac Toe's" song is written throughout in small letters. When the idea of a spelling reform began to surface, there were people, mainly among intellectuals, who were all for getting rid of capital letters within a sentence. Their arguments were not taken on board in the 1999 reform. And it's a fact that German texts would be more difficult to read if nouns did not stand out on account of their initial capital letters.

Learning strategies

When you listen to the song for the first time, it is a good idea to focus your concentration on what you can understand, to avoid being thrown off course by what you can't understand first time round – a rule that it's worth following in fact when reading, but especially listening to any foreign text.

Warum?

1 Listen to the song and concentrate on what you can understand.

2 a Read these lines from the song.

1 ________

wir kannten uns seit jahren ...
uns gehörte die welt und dafür brauchten wir kein geld
...
nur ein blick von dir und ich wusste genau
was du denkst was du fühlst
...

2 ________

keine party ohne uns ...
und wenn ich heute daran denke ...
tut es mir leid dass ich nicht härter zu dir war
... doch ich wollte nicht verstehn
... es ist zu spät

3 ________

und warum?
nur für den kick – für den augenblick?
und warum?
nur für ein stück – von dem falschen glück?
und warum?
du kommst nie mehr zurück – komm zurück

4 ________

ab und zu mal einen rauchen ...
das war ja noch o.k. was ich gut versteh
doch dann fing es an mit den sachen die warn weniger zum lachen
doch du musstest sie ja machen
ich stand nur daneben konnte nicht mehr mit dir reden
alles was du sagtest war das ist mein leben
mein leben das gehört mir ganz allein ...
lass es sein lass es sein ...

5 ________

ich sah dir in die augen sie warn tot sie warn leer
sie konnten nicht mehr lachen sie warn müde sie warn schwer
...
und warum?

b Who is *wir*? What do you think the song is about?

c Listen to the song again.
What is the theme from the fourth verse on. What words show this?

3 Now read the whole text.
The narrator describes what she now thinks and feels, what the friendship was like at the beginning and how it then developed. In which line does the change begin?
Mark the passages with different colours.

warum?

1
wir kannten uns seit jahren sind zusammen abgefahren
uns gehörte die welt und dafür brauchten wir kein geld
wir haben uns einfach treiben lassen wir wollten nichts verpassen
wir wollten nicht so werden wie die leute die wir hassen
nur ein blick von dir und ich wußte genau
was du denkst was du fühlst - dieses große vertrauen unter fraun
das hat mich umgehaun
es war völlig klar ich konnte immer auf dich bauen

2
keine party ohne uns immer mitten rein da zu sein
wo das leben tobt ohne jedes verbot
sie war geil diese zeit wir warn zu allem bereit
und wenn ich heute daran denke und es tief in mir schreit
tut es mir leid das ich nicht härter zu dir war
denn ich ahnte die gefahr sie war da sie war nah
sie war kaum zu übersehn doch ich wollte nicht verstehn
der wind hat sich gedreht es ist zu spät

3
und warum?
nur für den kick - für den augenblick?
und warum?
nur für ein stück - von dem falschen glück?
und warum?
nur für den kick - für den augenblick?
und warum?
du kommst nie mehr zurück—komm zurück....

4
ab und zu mal einen rauchen mal in andere welten tauchen
das war ja noch o.k. was ich gut versteh
doch dann fing es an mit den sachen die warn weniger zum lachen
doch du mußtest sie ja machen
ich stand nur daneben konnte nicht mehr mit dir reden
alles was du sagtes war das ist mein leben
mein leben das gehört mir ganz allein und da mischt sich keiner ein
laß es sein laß es sein - das schränkt mich ein

5
ich sah dir in die augen sie warn tot sie warn leer
sie konnten nicht mehr lachen sie warn müde sie warn schwer
du hattest nicht mehr viel zu geben denn in deinem neuen leben
hattest du dich voll und ganz an eine fremde macht ergeben

6
geld geld geld nur für geld hast du dich gequält
um es zu bekommen wie gewonnen - so zerronnen
dafür gingst aufn strich aber nicht für dich
sondern nur für deinen dealer mit dem lächeln im gesicht

und warum?

Tic Tac Toe

4 What does it mean? Match.

1 ☐ 2 ☐ 3 ☐ 4 ☐ 5 ☐

1 abfahren (auf jdn./etw. abfahren) *Jugendsprache*
2 etw. haut jdn. um *ugs.*
3 auf jdn./etw. bauen
4 Wie gewonnen – so zerronnen. *Redensart*
5 etw. ist geil *Jugendsprache*

a No sooner do you have something than you lose it again.
b sth. is great
c sth. has a great effect on s.o.
d be very enthusiastic (about s.o./sth.)
e rely on s.o./sth.

5 Rewrite verses 1 and 4 with big and small letters and add the punctuation (full stop, comma, colon and inverted commas for direct speech).

Hervorheben

6 a How is it expressed in the text?

Dieses große Vertrauen unter Frauen hat mich umgehauen.
Diese Zeit war geil.
Mein Leben gehört mir allein.

b Emphasize the nouns underlined by using the definite article or a personal pronoun.

1 Meine Freundin hat einen neuen Freund.

Dieser Typ ist schrecklich. Er ist schrecklich, der/dieser Typ.

2 Gestern habe ich meine Nachbarin getroffen.

Diese Person nervt mich ständig. ....

3 Dieser endlose Diaabend war ja furchtbar. ....

4 Mein Tagebuch darf niemand lesen. ....

7 For reasons of rhythm, a lot of sentences in the text are just placed one after another without linking words. What linking words (conjunctions, adverbs) would fit in the following sentences?

und (auch) ● (und) jetzt ● denn ● um ... zu ● dass ● nicht nur ..., sondern auch

1 Wir kannten uns seit Jahren, sind zusammen abgefahren. ....

2 Wir haben uns einfach treiben lassen, wir wollten nichts ....

verpassen, wir wollten nicht so werden wie ... .

3 Es war völlig klar, ich konnte auf dich bauen. ....

4 Sie war da, sie war nah, sie war kaum zu übersehn. ....

5 Der Wind hat sich gedreht, es ist zu spät. ....

6 Ab und zu mal einen rauchen, mal in andere Welten ....

tauchen, das war ja noch o.k., was ich gut versteh. ... und ich versteh das auch gut.

7 Lass es sein, lass es sein – das schränkt mich ein. ....

8 Summarize the text in your own words.

What are the narrator's feelings now?
How did she feel about the friendship at first?
How does she describe the change in her friend?

In dem Lied erzählt eine junge Frau von ihrer Freundschaft ...

RAMSTEIN

Cultural information

Ramstein is a small town in southwest Germany whose name means more to Americans than most Germans. In 1945, after the war, the Allies (France, Great Britain, the Soviet Union and the USA) divided up the cities of Berlin and Vienna and the states of Austria and Germany into four zones. While Austria regained its full freedom and unity in the treaty of 1955, Germany and its former capital Berlin remained divided. The Soviet zone became the GDR, the other zones the FRG. Despite its return to sovereignty, foreign troops remained on German soil in large numbers. The American troops, numbering at times as many as 200,000, were centred on the Rhine-Main area around Frankfurt. The village of Ramstein became the largest US air base, with thousands of US troops passing through. The Americans outnumbered the Germans, but there was little contact between them. The Americans did their shopping in American shops, paying in dollars, and the Germans in German shops with marks. The military police had jurisdiction for the Americans, the state police for the Germans. It was only in the occasional pub that Germans were to be found alongside Americans, who rarely spoke much German.

The text

In 1988, a year before the historic fall of the Berlin Wall that resulted in the gradual withdrawal of American troops from Germany, the well-known German writer Hans Magnus Enzensberger wrote a radio play with the title "Böhmen am Meer", set in the year 2006 and whose opening reminds us of Ramstein. Radio plays have a great tradition in the German-speaking countries, and are still very popular. The "Hörspielpreis der Kriegsblinden" is one of the most renowned literary awards.

Learning strategies

If you want to listen to something and understand it, you normally have to cope with the fact that what you hear quickly disappears and, in contrast to written text, cannot be retrieved. You don't have time to think about what you don't understand or what technique could help you. So make a habit of listening to longer texts so that you get used to applying the techniques faster and faster, eventually automatically. Always listen to the whole text first to get a general idea of what it's about. Concentrate on what you understand and use that to speculate about what you haven't yet registered. Then listen to the text in sections, if necessary listening to each section several times, because every time you listen you'll be able to understand more and correct or confirm your speculations. Regularly think over what helped you understand. In this unit there's a short checklist for reference.

Ramstein

1 Listen to the whole report and answer the questions.

a What medium is the report designed for?

b In which year and at what time of year was it to be heard?

c In which place is the first part spoken, in which place the second?

d How many people talk and who are they?

2 Listen to part 1 of the report again.

a What information were you given? Takes notes.

b Are the following statements true or false? Write down R (richtig = true), F (falsch = false).

1 Es ist Donnerstag, der 21. September. ☐

2 In New York ist es sehr warm. ☐

3 Die Börsenkurse sind nach oben gegangen. ☐

4 WNCQ ist die einzige Radiostation in den USA mit einem Korrespondenten in Europa. ☐

5 Timothy Tailor hat vor vielen Jahren einen Bericht über Europa gemacht. ☐

3 Listen to part 2 (Timothy Tailor's report) again.

a First read the following information.

Jeden Abend gab es im Golden Gate eine Schlägerei zwischen den amerikanischen Soldaten. ☐

Die Kneipe sieht aus wie vor zwölf Jahren. ☐

Vor zwölf Jahren war das Golden Gate jeden Abend voller Gäste. ☐

Die amerikanischen Soldaten fanden Ramstein schrecklich. ☐

Timothy Tailor war vor zwölf Jahren das letzte Mal in Ramstein. ☐

Damals war er ein schicker junger Offizier. ☐

Die Speisekarte im Golden Gate ist noch genau wie früher. ☐

b What order is the information given in? Note down the answers as you listen.

4 a Describe the photo.

b Check the meaning of the following words.

Schweinskotelett ● Plastikfolie ● Tischdecke ● Knie ● Gaststube ● Wirtin ● einarmiger Bandit ● Kartoffelsalat ● Tischplatte ● Mappe

c Listen to the description of the pub again and complete the text.

Das ist die ...Wirtin.................... vom Golden Gate. In ihrer .... (1) sieht es genauso aus wie vor zwölf Jahren. Der einarmige .... (2) an der Wand blinkt sinnlos vor sich hin, unverrückt thront das Senfglas auf der karierten .... (3) und unter der schweren .... (4) lauern die Querhölzer, an denen sich jeder, der die deutsche Gemütlichkeit nicht kennt, die .... (5) wund schlägt.

Auch die .... (6) ist unverändert, eine kunstlederne .... (7), schwer wie ein Messbuch, unter der vergilbten .... (8) wird das alte Menü angeboten: .... (9) mit Kartoffelpüree, Jägerschnitzel Hawaii, Würstchen mit Kartoffelpüree, Würstchen mit .... (10) und zum .... (11) gibt es Schoppenwein lieblich und Schoppenwein herb.

5 How does Frau Leininger express her surprise? How does she greet the guest? How does she speak about her memories? How does she issue an invitation? Sort sentences 1–10.

Überraschung ..2............ Begrüßung .... Erinnerungen .... Einladung ....

1. Na, was darf's denn sein? Ein kleines Schnäpschen zur Feier des Tages? Sie sind natürlich eingeladen, Herr Tail Ohr.
2. Herr Tail Ohr! Sind Sie es wirklich?
3. Sie sollen sich wie zu Hause fühlen.
4. Ja, ist es denn die Möglichkeit, Herr Tail Ohr!
5. Mein Gott, damals, als Sie hier waren in Ihrer schicken Offiziersuniform, Herr Tail Ohr.
6. Nein, nein, nein, wer hätte das gedacht, der Herr Tail Ohr!
7. Ein bisschen Musik, Herr Tail Ohr, bis Ihr Essen fertig ist?
8. Was machen Sie denn hier bei uns in Ramstein?
9. Willkommen, Herr Teil Ohr, in Ramstein!
10. Hach, das waren noch Zeiten, ach ja, das kommt nicht wieder, die schönsten Jahre unseres Lebens.

6 In the text we don't find out whether or how Timothy Tailor reacts to Frau Leininger's sentences in 5.

a Which sentences does Tailor not have to reply to without being impolite? Mark them.

1 ☐ 2 ☐ 3 ☐ 4 ☐ 5 ☐ 6 ☐ 7 ☐ 8 ☐ 9 ☐ 10 ☐

b Which sentences could you reply to with the following replies? Match them.

1 .... **2** .... **3** .... **4** .... **5** ....
6 .... **7** .... **8** .... **9** .... **10** ....

a Ach, das ist aber sehr aufmerksam.
b Na ja, die Zeiten ändern sich.
c Aber ja, bitte.
d Das ist doch nicht nötig.
e Danke, danke!
f Da haben Sie wohl Recht.
g Ich wollte mal sehen, wie es hier so geht.

7 Complete the sentences.

wie leer es hier ist ● dass ich nach Europa deportiert worden war ● bis in die neunziger Jahre der größte militärische Stützpunkt der USA auf dem europäischen Kontinent ● ich kann mich nicht erinnern ● warum man ihn in diese unwirtliche Gegend geschickt hatte ● laut, überfüllt und gewalttätig ● den Weihnachtsbaum mit Gin zu löschen

1 Wissen Sie noch, wie Sie versucht haben, ...
2 Nein, beim besten Willen, ich kann mich nicht erinnern.
3 Dafür fällt mir auf, ...
4 Ich habe das Golden Gate ganz anders in Erinnerung, nämlich ...
5 Ramstein, müssen Sie wissen, war ...
6 Keiner von den Soldaten hatte auch nur die geringste Ahnung, ...
7 Auch ich hatte das Gefühl, ...

Texte erschließen: Hörtexte

Concentrate on what you can understand easily and create in this way "islands of comprehension" which you can use as a base for working out the rest.

8 Which of the following decoding techniques did you use while working through "Ramstein"? Mark them.

1	Recognizing the text variety	
2	Making hypotheses on the basis of the title:	What do I know about the topic? What could the text be about?
3	Noting the context:	What can I hear? (sounds) What can I see? (gestures, facial expressions, surroundings)
4	Asking questions about the speakers:	How many speakers are there? Who talks to whom, when and where? What do they talk about and for what purpose?
5	Recognizing the atmosphere:	How do the people talk? (Are they excited, neutral, arguing, ...?)
6	Noting the intonation:	Which words are stressed and are therefore important? Does the intonation indicate a question or a statement? Where does the speaker make pauses?
	Noting the end of the sentence:	What is the core message of the sentence?
7	Noting the structure of the text:	Where does the speaker, the scene change? What structuring words do I hear, e.g. *zuerst, dann, schließlich?* Where is another aspect of the topic broached?
8	Recognizing names, internationalisms, numbers	
9	Recognizing key words	
10	Working out the meaning of unknown words from the context or word formation	
11	Paying attention to the meaning of conjunctions	
12	Recognizing text links:	What do words of reference refer to?

Die Zaubersprache

The text

Elias Canetti (1905-1994), the author of the text, is of particular interest to people learning German: because he wrote his books (novels, an autobiography) in German although he didn't learn this language – *die Zaubersprache* (the language of magic) of his parents – until he was 8 years old. He first grew up in a small town in Bulgaria, where seven different languages were spoken before the First World War. His parents were Sephardic Jews, his mother tongue Spaniolo, a language derived from Spanish. In 1981 Canetti was awarded the Nobel Prize for Literature.

Today, with so many people living in Germany whose mother tongue is not German, literature written by non-Germans has a special relevance. Recognition of this fact can be seen in the Adelbert-von-Chamisso Prize, awarded since 1984 to authors who have a mother tongue other than German.

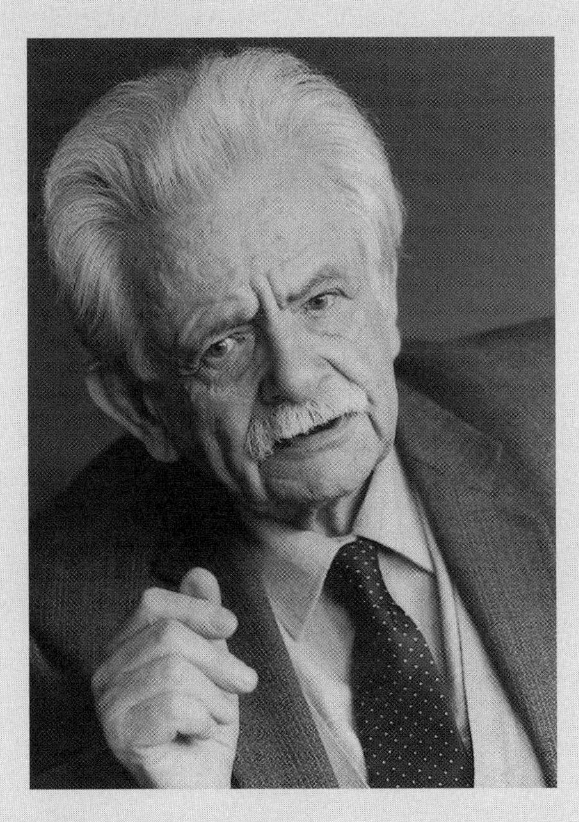

Learning strategies

It's always worthwhile taking a look at how other people learned a foreign language, without recourse to modern methods or simply because they had to learn on their own, like Elias Canetti. A particularly interesting case is that of the German archaeologist Heinrich Schliemann (1822-1890), who used his language skills to amass a huge fortune as a businessman, which he then used to finance archaeological excavations, the one that ensured his fame being the discovery of ancient Troy. In his school-leaving certificate Schliemann's French was described as "satisfactory", his English as "passable", and his Latin as "unsatisfactory". But then, by the time he was 35, he succeeded in learning 15 European languages, mastering them orally and in writing. Schliemann largely did without language teachers, rejected the learning of grammar rules, although he did use a dictionary and a grammar for reference. He usually learned by heart texts that he already knew in another language. He often went to church, for example, where he repeated the prayers or readings. As soon as he had mastered the basics, he worked with the great literature of the language in question. Thus he learned the whole of the Koran in Arabic, reciting it at night on the roof of his house in Athens. When he was learning a foreign language, he made all his diary entries in that language. This learning method enabled him to improve his memory to such an extent that towards the end of his life he was able to learn and remember 320 words a day.

Die Zaubersprache

1 What's it like when people speak a language in your presence that you don't understand? How do you react?

Ich fühle mich ausgeschlossen. ◆ Ich frage mich, warum sie das tun. ◆ Ich werde neugierig, möchte wissen, wovon sie sprechen. ◆ Ich versuche über ihr Verhalten und den Klang der Sprache zu erkennen, wovon sie sprechen. ◆ Wenn ich Bekannte eine andere Sprache sprechen höre, scheinen sie mir verwandelt. ◆ Ich höre angespannt und intensiv zu.

2 a Read the following excerpt.

Wenn der Vater vom Geschäft nach Hause kam, sprach er gleich mit der Mutter. Sie liebten sich sehr in dieser Zeit und hatten eine eigene Sprache unter sich, die ich nicht verstand, sie sprachen Deutsch, die Sprache ihrer glücklichen Schulzeit in Wien. ...

Ich hatte also guten Grund, mich ausgeschlossen zu fühlen, wenn die Eltern mit ihren Gesprächen anfingen. Sie wurden überaus lebhaft und lustig dabei und ich verband diese Verwandlung, die ich wohl bemerkte, mit dem Klang der deutschen Sprache. Ich hörte ihnen mit der größten Anspannung zu und fragte sie dann, was dies oder jenes bedeute. Sie lachten und sagten, es sei noch zu früh für mich, das seien Dinge, die ich erst später verstehen könne. Es war schon viel, dass sie mir das Wort „Wien" preisgaben[1], das einzige. Ich glaubte, dass es sich um wunderbare Dinge handeln müsse, die man nur in dieser Sprache sagen könne. Wenn ich lange vergeblich gebettelt hatte, lief ich zornig davon, in ein anderes Zimmer, das selten benutzt wurde, und sagte mir die Sätze, die ich von ihnen gehört hatte, her, im genauen Tonfall, wie Zauberformeln[2], ich übte sie oft für mich und sobald ich allein war, ließ ich die Sätze oder auch einzelne Wörter, die ich eingelernt hatte, hintereinander los, so rasch, dass mich sicher niemand verstanden hätte. Ich hütete mich aber davor, die Eltern das je merken zu lassen, und erwiderte ihr Geheimnis mit meinem.

... unter vielen heftigen[3] Wünschen dieser Zeit blieb es für mich der heftigste, ihre geheime Sprache zu verstehen. Ich kann nicht erklären, warum ich dem Vater nicht eigentlich dafür grollte[4]. Wohl aber bewahrte ich einen tiefen Groll gegen die Mutter und er verging erst, als sie mir Jahre später, nach seinem Tod, selber Deutsch beibrachte.

Elias Canetti

1 preisgeben: reveal
2 die Zauberfomel, -n: magic formula
3 heftig: powerful
4 jdm. grollen: bear sb a grudge

b What answers to these questions do you find in the text?

1. Warum meinte Canetti, dass es sich in den Gesprächen seiner Eltern auf Deutsch um wunderbare Dinge handeln musste?
2. Was machte er, wenn seine Eltern ihm nicht sagten, was sie auf Deutsch gesprochen hatten?
3. Was war wohl der Grund, dass seine Eltern unter sich Deutsch sprachen?

Das Verb: Konjunktiv II Vergangenheit

Wenn seine Eltern nicht so lebhaft und lustig **gewesen wären**, wenn sie Deutsch sprachen, **hätte** er sich wahrscheinlich nicht so ausgeschlossen **gefühlt**.

... und sobald ich allein war, ließ ich die Sätze oder auch einzelne Wörter, die ich eingelernt hatte, hintereinander los, so rasch, dass mich sicher niemand **verstanden hätte**.

3 Complete the rule.

> Subjunctive II past:
> Subjunctive II present of the verbs .... or .... + ...

4 Form sentences in the subjunctive II past.

1 Gut, dass du mich erinnert hast. (Verabredung sicher vergessen)
Ich hätte die Verabredung sicher vergessen.

2 Endlich kommt ihr. (nicht länger warten)
....

3 Danke, dass du uns geholfen hast. (es allein nicht schaffen)
....

4 Der Bus hatte Verspätung. (beinahe zu spät kommen)
....

Was wäre gewesen, wenn ...?

5 a Read the "circular story" on the right.
b Write a story like it yourself, e.g.:

Ein furchtbarer Tag
Sie haben gestern Abend zu lange gefeiert.
Sie sind heute zu spät aufgestanden.
Sie haben den Bus verpasst.
Sie sind zu spät zur Konferenz gekommen.
Sie haben die Geschäftspartner verärgert.
Sie haben den Auftrag nicht bekommen.
...
Und das alles, weil Sie gestern ihren alten Freund Oskar getroffen haben. Aber:
Was wäre gewesen, wenn ...?

Wenn ich gestern meinen alten
Freund Oskar nicht getroffen hätte,
hätte ich nicht so lange gefeiert.
Wenn ich nicht so lange ...

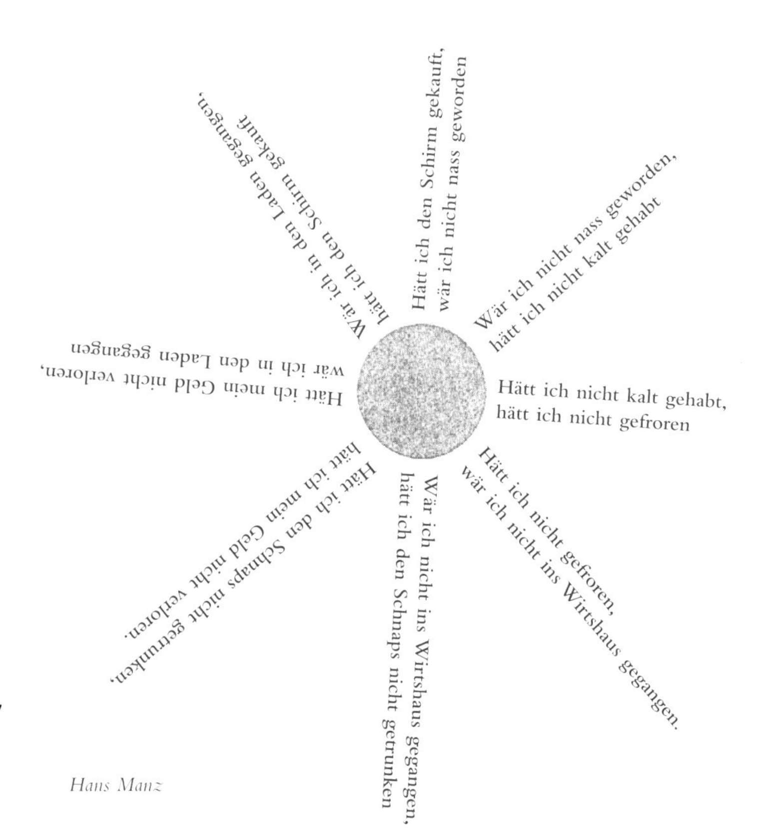

Hans Manz

Vermutung ausdrücken: von unsicher bis sicher

6 Which words express a supposition in these sentences?

1 Es muss sich um wunderbare Dinge handeln, die man nur in dieser Sprache sagen kann.
2 Es handelt sich wahrscheinlich um wunderbare Dinge, ...
3 Ich meine, dass es sich um wunderbare Dinge handelt, ...
4 Es wird sich wohl um wunderbare Dinge handeln, ...

There are various ways of expressing suppositions:

with words like

vielleicht [ ]   bestimmt [ ]   sicher [ ]   gewiss [ ]   wahrscheinlich [ ]
möglicherweise [ ]   vermutlich [ ]   wohl [ ]

with verbs/adjectives like

vermuten [ ]   denken [ ]   meinen [ ]   glauben [ ]   überzeugt sein [ ]
sicher sein [ ]

with modal verbs

müssen (muss [ ] / müsste [ ])   dürfen (dürfte) [ ]
können (kann [ ] / könnte [ ])
with the future [+] [1]

[1] By adding adverbs you can make the supposition more certain (e.g. *sicher*) or uncertain (e.g. *vielleicht*): Er wird sicher pünktlich sein. Ich werde vielleicht erst später kommen können.

7 Enter:

uncertain	almost certain	certain.
[?]	[+]	[++]

8 **a** Ask questions about the photographs.
Wo könnte das sein? Was macht die Person? Wer war hier und warum? ...

b Express suppositions and give reasons for them.

Sprache und Stil

geschriebene Sprache – gesprochene Sprache

9 Transform the sentences that are more written language into ones that are more spoken language.

	more written language	more spoken language
conjunctions/ tense	Er hörte genau zu, da er alles verstehen wollte.	Er hat genau zugehört, er wollte (nämlich) alles verstehen. ... weil er alles verstehen wollte. (1)
	Sie ging weg ohne noch ein einziges Wort zu sagen.	Sie ist weggegangen und .... (2)
	Anstatt immer gleich wütend zu werden, solltest du erst mal genau zuhören.	Du solltest erst mal genau zuhören und nicht .... (3)
	Canetti übte die Sätze genau ein, ebenso den Tonfall.	Canetti übte die Sätze und .... (4)
subjunctive II	„Wenn ich ein Vöglein wär', flög ich zu dir."	Wenn ich ein Vöglein wär', würde ich .... (5)
	Wenn er sie wirklich liebte, spräche er nicht im Konjunktiv.	Wenn .... (6)
passive	Es wurde noch bis weit nach Mitternacht gesungen und getanzt.	Die Gäste .... (7)
noun + preposition/ noun + genitive noun	Vor lauter Ärger konnte sie lange nicht einschlafen.	Sie hat sich total geärgert und .... (8)
	Die Bedeutung des Wortes war mir nicht klar.	Ich wusste nicht, was .... (9)
	Die Bewohner des Hauses Nummer 14 kennen einander kaum.	Die Leute in Nummer 14 .... (10)
	Er sagte mir nicht den Grund für seine so plötzliche Reise.	Er hat mir nicht gesagt, warum .... (11)
	Wegen der hohen Benzinpreise fahre ich jetzt mit dem Fahrrad.	Weil das Benzin .... (12)

how this nation,

10 Put the following love letter into a proper form.

Kurt Tucholsky wrote in his article "Newspaper German and letter style": It's baffling how this nation, which is supposed to suffer so much under its civil servants, is constantly trying to emulate them – for the worse, of course. I mean, isn't it possible to write politely? And yet every carrier sees it as a point of honour to send off letters that sound like decrees. ... I imagine a love letter from such a correspondent would go something like this:

Geheim! Tagebuch-Nr. 69/218

Hierorts, den heutigen

1. Meine Neigung zu dir ist unverändert.
2. Du stehst heute Abend, 7 1/2 Uhr, am zweiten Ausgang des Zoologischen Gartens, wie gehabt.
3. Anzug: Grünes Kleid, grüner Hut, braune Schuhe. Die Mitnahme eines Regenschirms empfiehlt sich.
4. Abendessen im Gambrinus, 8.10 Uhr.
5. Es wird nachher in meiner Wohnung voraussichtlich zu Zärtlichkeiten kommen.

(gez.) Bosch
Oberbuchhalter

Erfahrungen beim Fremdsprachenlernen

11 **a** Read the following text and note down key words.
b Compare the authors' experience with your own.

Eine Sprache an und für sich zu lernen und nur für sich selbst, das hat Ähnlichkeiten mit dem Sich-ins-Schlaraffenland[1]-Durchfressen[2]: ein langer, dunkler Tunnel, mit dem Licht der eigenen Sprache noch im Rücken, das Hirn übersättigt[3] mit Vokabeln wie der Magen der Schlaraffenländer mit Pflaumenmus. Zwischendurch das nicht nur unangenehme Gefühl des leicht Verrücktwerdens: verrückt, so wie man einen Stuhl verrückt, das heißt, in eine andere Welt geschoben werden, mit sich selbst sprechen, sich selbst sprechen hören und sich auch viel besser sprechen hören, als man es in Wirklichkeit tut. Es spielt keine Rolle, wie gut ich in Wirklichkeit bin, sondern nur, wie gut es mir tut.
Und plötzlich ist der Tunnel stockdunkel – eine panische Erinnerung an das Scheitern in der Schule. Was anfänglich so leicht war, taugt plötzlich gar nichts mehr. Man versteht kein Wort mehr und ist plötzlich wieder unfähig, auch nur einen Satz zu bilden. Die einfachsten Vokabeln für „Kommen", „Gehen" und „Haben" sind weg. ...
Ich bin erstens ein fauler Mensch und zweitens einer, der sich gerne langweilt. Trotzdem ertrage ich ab und zu selbst die Verbindung von Faulheit und Langeweile schlecht. Deshalb kam ich auf die Idee, mich mit Englischlernen zu beschäftigen. Hinten war dunkel und vorn war dunkel; aus Langeweile entschied ich mich trotzdem für den Weg nach vorn. Und nach wenigen Schritten begann es nun hell zu werden.
Ich verstand die ersten Wörter auf meinen alten Jazzplatten, zwei ganze Sätze aus den BBC-Nachrichten, einen ganzen Pornoroman und fast „Fiesta" von Hemingway. Seither gehe ich so langsam wie möglich – ich möchte den Sonnenaufgang verlängern. Es ist schön, wenn Sprache durch das Dunkel hervorbricht.

Peter Bichsel

1 das Schlaraffenland: land of milk and honey
2 sich durchfressen: plough your way through
3 übersättigt: surfeited

Es ist leicht, Millionär zu werden

Willkommen in **Peter's Stüberl !**
Das gemütliche Wiener Gasthaus im 9. Bezirk

Startseite
Stadtplan
Sparverein
Aktuelles

Aus unserer Speisekarte:
Suppen
kleine Speisen
vom Rind
vom Schwein
vom Huhn
vom Fisch

Email
Gästebuch

letzte Bearbeitung 16.04.2001, K. Köhler

Maria und Peter Keller
Spitalgasse 3 (Nähe "Altes AKH" und WIENSTROM GmbH)
A-1090 Wien
Tel.: +43 1 406 31 92
Montag bis Freitag 9 - 22 Uhr (Feiertags geschlossen)

Ganztägig Küchenbetrieb
beste Wiener Küche **und** Hausmannskost
zwei Mittagsmenus **um öS 65,-- bzw. 75,--**

gepflegte Weine aus der
Kellerei PITTNER (Drasenhofen/NÖ)

Stiegl und Hirter **Bier** vom **Faß**.

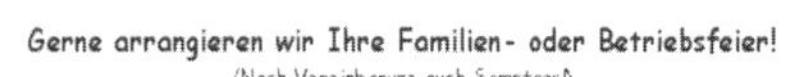

(Nach Vereinbarung auch Samstags!)

Cultural information

There is an old German saying, "You can learn how to save from the rich". The title of the text seems to promise a particular technique of *Sparen* (saving).

The people in the three German-speaking countries have always had a special relationship to saving, to collecting money on the one hand and being mean about spending it on the other. As early as the late 19th century, so-called *Sparkassen* (savings banks) were founded all over the place, the aim being to provide ordinary folk and those employed in industry with an opportunity to set a little aside. They were to be encouraged not to tuck their money away in the so-called "savings stocking" under their pillow, but to take it to a public institution which would pay interest on it and pass the money on into the economy for investments. Those who did this in Germany were out of luck. The inflation that raged after the two world wars meant any money deposited in banks and savings banks was lost. The result was that after the Second World War many people gave up saving this way and instead put their money in so-called *Bausparkassen* (building societies) with the aim of exchanging it as soon as possible for a house or flat. Various laws were passed by the state to promote this form of saving. This is why every town, and also the villages are now surrounded by new housing estates, where all the houses look alike. Many people's life motto is encased in the Swabian "Schaffen, schaffen, Häusle bauen, sterben". (Häusle: Swabian dialect form of "Haus").

Saving is even regarded as a sort of sport. So-called *Sparvereine* (savings clubs) often have their base in a pub, the members being regulars of the pub in question.

There are many families who day by day compare the offers of the big supermarkets and buy their Limburg cheese in a different place from their Emmentaler because it's cheaper there. It's also customary to buy fresh food only in quantities people are sure of being able to eat up. And if you go out for a cup of coffee with a German, be prepared for the fact that everybody will pay for his own, unless someone has said beforehand: "Ich lade dich ein."

Sparverein „Schwarzer Adler" Webseite
http://members.aon.at/peterstube/Sparverein.htm

Sparverein „Schwarzer Adler"

Vereinssitz	Gasthaus Peter's Stüberl, Spitalgasse 3
Obmann	Peter Keller
Kassierer	Ing. Kurt Köhler
Schriftführer	Rudolf Stöckl
Beisitzer	Uwe Hobisch
Bankverbindung	BAWAG, Zweigstelle Alserstraße
Mitgliederzahl	72 (Stand Juni 1999)
Zinssatz	2,5 % (Stand Juni 1999)

Neue Mitglieder jederzeit willkommen!
Auskunft in Peter's Stüberl

1 First read the text "Vom Schuldner zum Finanz-Fachmann" in the box right at the bottom.

a Work out the meaning of this from the context: Mit 26 Jahren steckte Bodo Schäfer (38) tief in den Miesen.

b How did Bodo Schäfer change his life? What was the result of this change?

2 Read the interview and mark all the sentences that offer advice.

Wege zum Sparen: Was ein Gewinner rät – Wo sich 10 Mark im Monat anlegen lassen

„Es ist leicht, Millionär zu werden"

Der Finanzberater Bodo Schäfer über die Kunst, Geld zu scheffeln

AZ: Sie behaupten, Millionär könne jeder werden. Glauben Sie an Wunder?

Schäfer: Es geht hier nicht um Wunder, sondern um die richtige Strategie.

Das hört sich gut an. Aber wie soll eine 23-jährige Verkäuferin mit 1000 Euro netto im Monat Millionärin werden?

Zuerst einmal muss sie ihre Einstellung ändern. Dazu sollte sie sich ein Heft anlegen, in das sie ihre täglichen Erfolge notiert: Zum Beispiel, wenn der Chef sie gelobt hat, oder sie jemanden zum Lachen gebracht hat. Wenn Sie das jeden Tag macht, garantiere ich ihr, dass sie in drei Monaten etwa 20 Prozent mehr verdient. Das Gehalt steigt nämlich immer parallel zum Selbstbewusstsein.

Hoffentlich spielt der Chef da mit. Was kann die Verkäuferin noch tun?

In 15 bis 20 Jahren wäre sie Millionärin, wenn sie ab sofort drei Dinge macht: Sie muss 10 Prozent ihres Lohns auf einem Sparkonto zur Seite legen, einen Teil jeder kommenden Gehaltserhöhung ebenfalls darauf überweisen und das Geld in Aktienfonds anlegen, die im Durchschnitt pro Jahr mindestens 12 Prozent Rendite abwerfen sollten.

Am Monatsbeginn mit dem Sparen anfangen

Das ist bei einem so geringen Gehalt alles andere als leicht.

Ich rate, das Geld bereits am Ersten jedes Monats auf das unantastbare Sparkonto zu tun. Die meisten machen den Fehler, das sparen zu wollen, was am Monatsende übrig bleibt. Erfahrungsgemäß klappt das aber nicht, weil wir grundsätzlich alles ausgeben, was da ist.

Viele Arbeitnehmer brauchen jede Mark fürs tägliche Leben. Wie sollen sie es schaffen, so viel Geld zur Seite zu legen?

Der Trick ist, das Sparen nicht als Last zu sehen: Sparen heißt nämlich nichts anderes, als sich selbst zu bezahlen. Wir entlohnen alle, den Bäcker, den Friseur – nur uns nicht.

Wie überzeugen Sie jemanden, der gar nicht ans Sparen denkt und sagt, ich will hier und jetzt leben und überziehe dafür gerne mal mein Konto?

Man soll hier und jetzt leben, das kann ich nur unterstreichen. Und genau deshalb ist es falsch, für Konsumzwecke Schulden zu machen. Das bringt nichts als Ärger: Magenschmerzen, Beziehungsprobleme, keine Konzentration mehr im Job. Es macht nur Spaß, Geld auszugeben, wenn man es auch hat. Deshalb empfehle ich, neben dem Sparkonto noch ein so genanntes Spaßkonto anzulegen. Auf das werden – ebenfalls am Monatsersten – vielleicht fünf Prozent des Nettogehalts überwiesen. So können wir uns Extras gönnen und bauen nebenbei Vermögen auf.

Aber ist es für jemand, der Schulden hat, überhaupt sinnvoll, noch Geld fürs Sparkonto abzuzwacken?

Das rate ich ihm sogar. Und zwar mit Hilfe der 50/50-Regel: Sie besagt, dass man das Geld für die Schulden-Rückzahlung in zwei gleiche Teile splitten soll. Mit dem einen Teil werden die Schulden abgestottert, der andere wird gespart. Der Grund für dieses Vorgehen liegt auf der Hand: Wenn das ganze Geld zum Abzahlen verwendet wird, ist man am Schluss im besten Fall auf Null. Null ist nichts, das heißt, man hat die ganze Zeit auf kein Ziel hingearbeitet. Mit der 50/50-Regel dauert das Abzahlen ein bisschen länger, gleichzeitig baut sich aber schon Kapital auf. So fühlt man sich gut und hat die Motivation weiter zu sparen.

Wenn es so einfach ist, zu Vermögen zu kommen, warum gibt es dann nicht mehr Millionäre in Deutschland?

Weil es zwar leicht ist, Millionär zu werden, aber bequemer ist, es nicht zu werden. So ist es wirklich kein Problem, täglich in fünf Minuten seine Erfolge zu notieren, wie ich es empfehle. Es ist aber einfacher, es bleiben zu lassen und dafür fünf Minuten länger zu schlafen. Die Summe vieler kleiner Schritte führt zu Vermögen. Dieser Weg ist den meisten zu anstrengend.

aus: *Abendzeitung*

Vom Schuldner zum Finanz-Fachmann

Mit 26 Jahren steckte Bodo Schäfer (38) noch tief in den Miesen. Bis ihm ein Freund die Leviten las[1] – und dem Kölner eine völlig neue Einstellung zum Thema Geld beibrachte. Schäfer erkannte: Weder der Chef noch das soziale Umfeld oder der Partner, sondern nur er selbst ist verantwortlich für seine finanzielle Situation. Daraufhin lebte der studierte Jurist einige Monate von nur fünf Mark am Tag, stotterte seine Schulden ab und begann, gleichzeitig schon Kapital aufzubauen. Mit Erfolg: Wenige Jahre später hatte er die erste Million.

[1] jdm. die Leviten lesen: read sb the riot act

3 Which of the advice do you find practicable, which not? Give reasons for your opinion.

Sätze/Satzteile verbinden: *weder ... noch*

Bodo Schäfer erkannte: **Weder** der Chef **noch** das soziale Umfeld oder der Partner, sondern nur er selbst ist verantwortlich für seine finanzielle Situation.

> *weder ... noch* usually links words and phrases, sometimes also two main clauses. The subject and verb cannot be omitted in the second main clause.
> Er hat **weder** Geld auf der Bank, **noch** versucht er eine Arbeit zu finden.
> **Weder** hat er Geld auf der Bank, **noch** versucht er eine Arbeit zu finden.
> *Weder ... noch* can be used as a short answer on its own:
> Hat er Geld, oder ist er intelligent? **Weder noch**!

4 Negate the sentences with *weder ... noch*.

1 Er will ein Sparkonto und ein Spaßkonto anlegen. Ich will weder ein Sparkonto noch ein Spaßkonto anlegen.
2 Er hat Zeit und Motivation, Vermögen aufzubauen. Ich ...
3 Er kann seine Schulden abzahlen und auch noch sparen. Ich ...
4 Er und auch seine Frau finden Sparen sehr wichtig. Weder ich ...
5 Er hat einen Finanzberater und besucht auch Seminare zu Finanzfragen. Ich ...
6 Ihn hat der Chef gelobt und er hat sein Gehalt erhöht. Mich ...

Ratschläge geben

5 How can you become a millionaire? Give advice using the following expressions.

Einstellung ändern • das Konto überziehen • Geld auf einem Sparkonto zur Seite legen • Geld in Aktienfonds anlegen • am Monatsbeginn mit dem Sparen anfangen • das sparen wollen, was am Monatsende übrig bleibt • das Sparen nicht als Last sehen • sich die täglichen Erfolge notieren • für Konsumzwecke Schulden machen • neben dem Sparkonto ein so genanntes Spaßkonto anlegen • auf das Spaßkonto fünf Prozent des Nettogehalts überweisen • hier und jetzt leben • nicht alles ausgeben, was da ist

+	–
Sie müssen / Du musst ...	Machen Sie / Mach nicht den Fehler, ...
Man soll/sollte ...	Es ist falsch, ...
Ich rate Ihnen/dir ...	Sie sollten / Du solltest nicht ...
Ich empfehle Ihnen/dir ...	Ich würde nicht ...
Es ist sinnvoll, ...	Ich warne Sie/dich davor, ...
Es ist besser, wenn ...	
Ich würde ...	

6 On the Internet there's a forum where you can get advice on learning German.

a Read these enquiries from five learners.

Kirki K., Istanbul

Wenn ich mit jemand Deutsch sprechen will, dann fallen mir immer nur einzelne Wörter und keine ganzen Sätze ein. Dabei bin ich in der Schule in Grammatik ganz gut.

Megan E., Houston/Texas

Ich habe Probleme mit der Aussprache. Wenn ich mit einem Deutschen spreche, habe ich den Eindruck, dass er mich gar nicht versteht, obwohl ich glaube, dass ich viele Wörter kenne und nicht viele Fehler mache.

Jeanette C., Le Mans

Ich habe Angst zu sprechen, weil ich noch viele Fehler mache. Und Fehler sollte man doch nie machen! Oder?

Boris G., Lipezk/Russland

Beim Lesen von Zeitungen gibt es immer so viele unbekannte Wörter, und ich muss ständig im Wörterbuch und in der Grammatik nachschlagen. Das nimmt viel Zeit und ist langweilig.

Olga B., Brno

Die deutsche Grammatik ist so kompliziert! Ich mache immer wieder Fehler, beim Schreiben und noch mehr beim Sprechen. Kann man sie überhaupt lernen?

b What advice could the five learners be given? Jot down ideas and notes making use of the advice in the following list.

- versuchen die Bedeutung von unbekannten Wörtern zu erraten, z.B. aus ihrer Umgebung, aus der Wortart
- Texte auf Kassette immer wieder anhören
- nicht versuchen, jedes Wort zu verstehen
- einen Brief- oder E-Mail-Partner in einem deutschsprachigen Land suchen (Internet)
- Möglichkeiten suchen, mit Menschen zu sprechen, deren Muttersprache Deutsch ist
- deutschsprachige Radiosender hören
- deutschsprachige Fernsehsender sehen
- Sätze nachsprechen und dabei auf Melodie und Rhythmus achten
- Verse, Gedichte und Lieder auswendig lernen und aufsagen oder singen
- Wortkarten mit Beispielsätzen anlegen
- Wörter notieren, die zu einem Thema gehören
- Nomen mit den dazu passenden Verben oder Adjektiven notieren
- Listen zur Grammatik anlegen (Nomen mit Artikel und Pluralform, Nomen mit Adjektiv, unregelmäßige Verben mit Präsens-, Perfekt- und Präteritumformen, Verben mit Präpositionen)
- die grammatischen Strukturen in Texten beobachten
- eine Liste mit Redewendungen anlegen und auswendig lernen

c You are the editor of the forum. Reply in writing to one of the enquiries and give precise advice on how to solve the problem.

Das Mädchen Sophie

Wenn so eine Welle des Aufruhrs
durch das Land geht,
wenn es in der Luft liegt,
wenn viele mitmachen,
dann kann in einer letzten,
gewaltigen Anstrengung
dieses System abgeschüttelt werden.

If such a wave of protest
goes through the land,
if there's something afoot,
if lots join in,
then in one last,
great effort
this system can be cast off.

from a pamphlet of the White Rose resistance movement

+++ Willi Graf, 25 Jahre - hingerichtet 12.10.1943 +++ Kurt Huber, 49 Jahre - hingerichtet 13.7.1943 +++ Christoph Probst, 23 Jahre - hingerichtet 22.2.1943 +++ Alexander Schmorell, 25 Jahre - hingerichtet 13.7.1943 +++ Hans Scholl, 24 Jahre - hingerichtet 22.2.1943 +++ Sophie Scholl, 21 Jahre - hingerichtet 22.2.1943

Graf, Huber, Probst, Schmorrel and the two Scholls were the core of the resistance movement *Weiße Rose* (white rose). With the help of sympathisers they wrote, printed and distributed pamphlets opposing the national-socialist government. This was not only very dangerous, but also very difficult to carry out practically; it was not for example possible to buy stamps in large numbers without arousing suspicion, paper was rationed because of the war, and how was a printing machine to be come by? So resistance required not only courage, but also resourcefulness. The members of the *Weiße Rose* also took care of internees in the concentration camps, for example by establishing contact with relatives or smuggling bread into the camps.
On 18.2.1943, at a time when it looked as though public opinion might slowly turn against the Nazi regime – in Munich, for example, in some circles the Nazi salute was looked down on – Hans and Sophie Scholl were arrested at the Ludwig-Maximilian University. The university caretaker had seen them putting out pamphlets outside the lecture halls. During their interrogations and their trial they both claimed right up to the end that they alone were responsible for the pamphlets. However, the members of the resistance group *Weiße Rose* were arrested one by one and executed.

... the uncertainty in which we constantly live our lives and which prohibits any happy plans for the morrow, casting its shadow on all the following days, preys on my mind day and night and does not really leave me for a minute ... Each word, before it is spoken, is examined from all sides to see if there is a shimmer of ambiguity cloying to it. Trust in others has to give way to mistrust and care ...

From one of Sophie Scholl's letters, 7.11.1942

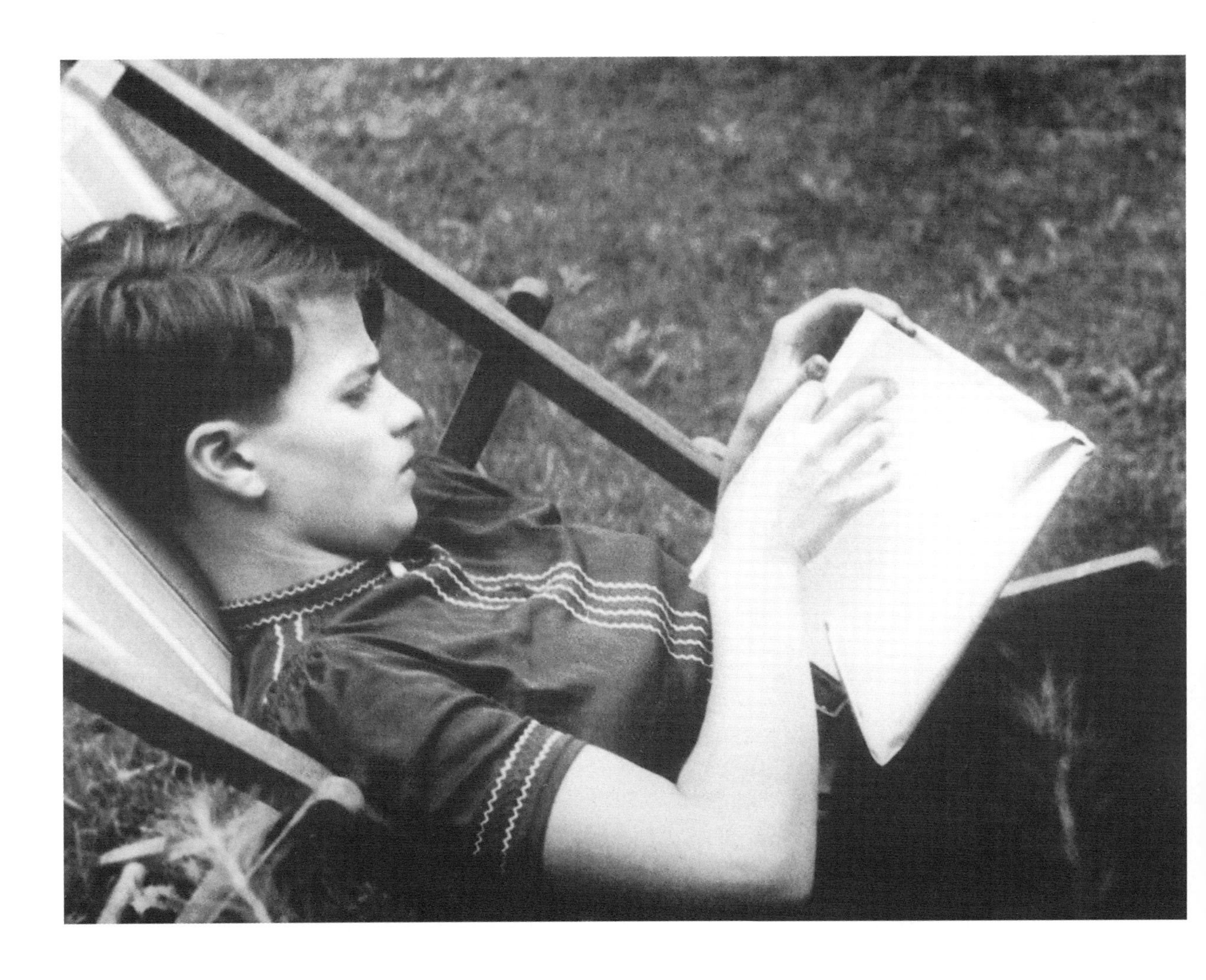

Ich liege ganz ruhig im Gras, mit ausgestreckten Armen und Beinen, und bin glücklich. Durch die blühenden Zweige eines Apfelbaumes sehe ich den blauen Vorsommerhimmel über mir, freundliche weiße Wolkengebilde schwimmen sachte durch mein Blickfeld. ...
Wenn ich meinen Kopf wende, berührt er den rauen Stamm des Apfelbaumes. ... Ich drücke mein Gesicht an seine dunkle warme Rinde und denke: Heimat, und bin so unsäglich dankbar in diesem Augenblick.

Sophie Scholl

Skim through the text and try to imagine the concrete situation:
Where is Sophie?
What season it is now?
What is she doing? What can she

Tip

- Deduce the meaning of un-known words from the cont e. g. Apfelbaum - Stamm.

Sophie Scholl

Geboren am 9. Mai 1921 in Forchtenberg, heutiges Bundesland Baden-Württemberg; später wohnhaft in Ulm an der Donau; drei Geschwister; Hobbys: Sport, vor allem Schwimmen, Wandern, Klavierspielen, Zeichnen, Töpfern, Lesen

Jugend im Dritten Reich

An einem Morgen hörte ich auf der Schultreppe eine Klassenkameradin zur andern sagen: „Jetzt ist Hitler an die Regierung gekommen." ... Zum ersten Mal trat die Politik in unser Leben. Hans war damals 15 Jahre alt, Sophie 12. Wir hörten viel von Vaterland reden, von Kameradschaft, Volksgemeinschaft und Heimatliebe. Das imponierte uns und wir horchten begeistert auf, wenn wir in der Schule oder auf der Straße davon sprechen hörten. ... Wir hatten den Geruch von Moos, von feuchter Erde und duftenden Äpfeln im Sinn, wenn wir an Heimat dachten. ...

Inge Scholl, Sophies ältere Schwester

„... wenn wir in der Schule oder auf der Straße davon sprechen hörten."

What is meant by *davon*?

Tips
- look for key words
- break down compounds

Die Geschwister Scholl traten gegen den Willen ihres Vaters, der liberal dachte und gegen Hitler war, in die Hitler-Jugend ein.

Hitler-Jugend (HJ): Jugendorganisation der Nationalsozialisten. Ziel: Erziehung der Kinder und Jugendlichen zu Anhängern Hitlers. Mittel: Organisierung der Freizeit, z. B. in Form von Paraden, Sport, Zeltlagern, Heimabenden mit Spielen, Singen, Lesen, kreativer Tätigkeit usw.; dabei dauernde Indoktrinierung. Mädchen waren im Bund Deutscher Mädel (BDM) organisiert, einer Untergruppe der Hitler-Jugend.

What do we find out about the Hitler Youth Movement? Who was the organization for? What aims did it have? What did people do there?

Tips
- look for internationalisms
- break down compounds

War es nicht großartig, mit jungen Menschen, denen man sonst vielleicht nie näher gekommen wäre, plötzlich etwas Gemeinsames zu haben? Wir trafen uns zu den Heimabenden, es wurde vorgelesen und gesungen oder wir machten Spiele oder Bastelarbeiten. Wir hörten, dass wir für eine große Sache leben sollten. Wir wurden ernst genommen und das gab uns einen besonderen Auftrieb. Wir glaubten, Mitglieder einer großen Organisation zu sein, die alle umfasste und jeden würdigte, vom Zehnjährigen bis zum Erwachsenen.

Inge Scholl

What did Inge Scholl feel about her membership of the BDM?

Eines Tages erzählte ein Mädchen Inge Scholl entsetzt von einer Besprechung, an der Sophie teilgenommen hatte. Eine hohe BDM-Führerin sei aus Stuttgart gekommen, um mit den Mädchen über die Lektüre an den Heimabenden zu sprechen. Sophie habe vorgeschlagen, Heinrich Heine zu lesen. Als sie gemerkt habe, wie die anderen ablehnend reagierten, weil Heine ein jüdischer Dichter war, habe sie fast flüsternd gesagt: „Wer Heine nicht kennt, kennt die deutsche Literatur nicht."

Which people are mentioned? Who is telling whom something? What is being told?

Tip
- activate previous knowledge (situation of Jews in the Third Reich)

Gefühle

Der Wind reißt den blauen Himmel auf, da kommt die Sonne heraus und küsst mich zärtlich. Ich möchte sie wieder küssen, doch gleich habe ich meinen Wunsch vergessen, weil der Wind mich jetzt anspringt. Ich spüre, wie herrlich hart ich bin, ich lache laut vor Freude, weil ich dem Wind ein solcher Widerstand bin. Alle Kräfte spüre ich in mir.

Sophie Scholl

What does the wind mean to Sophie?

Mein lieber Fritz, *Ulm, April 1940*

denke, wenn du dies Päckchen öffnest, ich wäre dabei. Nein, dann wäre ein Päckchen unnötig, ich würde einen Tee machen und Brote richten, es sollte so richtig gemütlich werden. Du müsstest sittsam mir gegenübersitzen, damit du den Tee nicht verschüttest, und nachher würden wir auf deinem Sofa (oder hast du keines?) sitzen und uns angucken, und auf einmal wäre das Heft oder Buch auf den Boden gefallen und wir würden es beide liegen lassen. Kindisch, gelt? Wärst du nicht so weit weg, dann würde ich dir Szilla, Anemonen, Huflattich, Kuckucksblumen und Veilchen schicken. Aber sie würden so nur verwelken. Such dir selbst mal welche. Ich will dir heute nicht viel schreiben, ich will auch nicht schreiben, wovon alle Welt spricht (in sehr verschiedener Weise). Am liebsten würde ich dir Frühlingsgeschichten erzählen. Über den Wald, die Wiese, das Wasser und uns beide. Und werde nur kein hochmütiger, gleichgültiger Leutnant. (Entschuldige!) Aber die Gefahr, gleichgültig zu werden, ist groß. Das wäre, glaube ich, schlimm.

Alles Gute, viele Grüße
deine Sophie

What picture do we get of Sophie?
What picture do we get of the relationship between Sophie and Fritz?

Tips
- deduce the meaning of unknown words from the context
- pay attention to links between sentences

... Wenn du eine Wut auf mich hast, dann hab sie ruhig, aber schrei sie dem Wind oder auch mir zu und drück sie nicht so in Dich hinein ...

... Nicht wahr, manchmal denkst du an mich? Du träumst dann manchmal von unseren Ferien. Aber denke nicht nur an mich, wie ich bin, sondern auch, wie ich sein möchte. Erst wenn du mich dann noch ebenso lieb hast, können wir uns ganz verstehen ...

Sophie Scholl

Krieg

1.9.1939: Deutschland überfällt Polen – Beginn des Zweiten Weltkriegs

Ulm, 29.5.1940

Mein lieber Fritz,
es ist ein ganz herrliches Vorsommerwetter, wenn ich Zeit hätte, würde ich mich an die Iller legen, baden, nichts tun und versuchen, nur an das zu denken, was ich um mich herum an Schönem sehe. Es ist nicht leicht, alle Gedanken an den Krieg zu verbannen. Wenn ich auch nicht viel von Politik verstehe und auch nicht den Ehrgeiz habe, es zu tun, so habe ich doch ein bisschen ein Gefühl dafür, was Recht und Unrecht ist, denn dies hat ja mit Politik und Nationalität nichts zu tun ...

... Du findest es sicher unweiblich, wie ich dir schreibe. Es wirkt lächerlich an einem Mädchen, wenn es sich um Politik kümmert. Sie soll ihre weiblichen Gefühle bestimmen lassen über ihr Denken. Vor allem das Mitleid. Ich aber finde, dass zuerst das Denken kommt ...

There are some contrasts in the text. Find them.

Tip
- also pay attention to words like: wenn auch ... so doch, aber

Fritz Hartnagel erzählt:

Im Winter 1941/42, die deutschen Soldaten standen vor Leningrad und Moskau, sollte die Bevölkerung warme Kleidung und Decken für die Soldaten spenden. Sophie jedoch wollte nichts geben. Als ich von Sophies harter Reaktion erfuhr, habe ich ihr vor Augen geführt, was eine solche Haltung für die Soldaten draußen bedeutete, die keine Handschuhe, keine Pullover und keine warmen Socken besaßen. Sie blieb jedoch bei ihrer unnachgiebigen Haltung und begründete sie mit den Worten: „Ob jetzt deutsche Soldaten erfrieren oder russische, das bleibt sich gleich und ist gleich schlimm. Aber wir müssen den Krieg verlieren. Wenn wir jetzt Wollsachen spenden, tragen wir dazu bei, den Krieg zu verlängern.“ Auf mich wirkte dieser Standpunkt schockierend. Wir diskutierten heftig. Mehr und mehr musste ich jedoch einsehen, dass ihre Haltung nur konsequent war.

Fritz Hartnagel talks about a difference of opinion with Sophie. What was it about? Why does Fritz want Sophie to donate something? Why doesn't Sophie want to?

Da fällt mir das Wort ein: Il faut avoir l'esprit dur et le cœur tendre.
(Man braucht einen harten Geist und ein weiches Herz.)

Sophie Scholl

Die Weiße Rose

Der Spielfilm „Die Weiße Rose" von Michael Verhoeven und Mario Krebs stellt die Geschichte der gleichnamigen Widerstandsbewegung dar.
In dem Drehbuchausschnitt geht es um eine Diskussion zwischen Sophie und Hans Scholl über das Für und Wider von Widerstand gegen eine Diktatur.

Skim through the text. What features does the text variety "film script" have?

Was vorher geschah

Im Mai 1942 beginnt Sophie in München an der Ludwig-Maximilians-Universität Biologie und Philosophie zu studieren.
Während einer Vorlesung findet sie unter ihrer Bank ein Flugblatt, das zum Widerstand gegen den Hitler-Staat aufruft. Sie merkt bald, dass ihr Bruder Hans, bei dem sie wohnt, etwas damit zu tun hat. Sophie bekommt Angst um ihn und um die ganze Familie, denn kurz vorher ist ihr Vater wegen seiner liberalen Ansichten verhaftet worden.

Wohnung Hans und Sophie
INNEN/NACHT

ZIMMER HANS
Hans, Sophie

SOPHIE: Was glaubst du, was die gesucht haben in seinem Büro? Die interessieren sich doch nicht für Steuerakten ...[1] Warum haben sie ihn verhaftet? Nur wegen seiner Äußerung? Hans! Ich will, dass du mit mir sprichst.

HANS: So eine Durchsuchung, das ist Routine. Was willst du eigentlich?

Er steht auf, geht in Richtung Bad.

ZIMMER SOPHIE
Sophie läuft hinter ihm her.

SOPHIE: Unsere Familie ist für die Gestapo kein unbeschriebenes Blatt. Begreifst du das nicht?

Hans reißt die Tür zum Bad auf. Licht an. Durchblick.

Hast du vergessen, wie schnell sie damals deine Jugendgruppe aufgerollt haben?[2]

HANS: Das war anders. Wir waren ständig auf Fahrt, das war viel riskanter ...

SOPHIE: Aber jetzt, wo sie den Vater haben, müssen wir doppelt vorsichtig sein. Und da stellst du Flugblätter her ...

Hans lehnt sich an den Türpfosten.

HANS: Man muss den Leuten doch sagen, was wirklich los ist.

Sophie kommt heran.

In Polen, wo sie 300 000 Juden ermordet haben, kaum dass die Wehrmacht[3] einmarschiert war.

Sie stehen sich gegenüber.

Und wer dem Adel angehörte ... alle in unserem Alter, ins Konzentrationslager.

Sophie schaut ihn zweifelnd an.

Verstehst du, wenn jemand unsere Flugblätter liest, vielleicht redet der offen mit anderen darüber ...

SOPHIE: Die Menschen sind doch inzwischen viel zu abgestumpft.

Hans läuft durchs Zimmer. Sophie hinter ihm her.

HANS: Es gibt Tausende, die nicht mehr einverstanden sind. Und keiner weiß vom anderen ...

SOPHIE: Wer hat denn den Mut, überhaupt etwas zu tun?

ZIMMER HANS

Hans nimmt seinen Schlafanzug, bleibt bei Sophie stehen.

HANS: Hast du vergessen, die geheimen Predigten von Bischof Galen, die damals verschickt wurden? Wie uns das aufgerüttelt hat. Wir haben doch immer schon darauf gewartet, dass wieder was im Briefkasten liegt.

SOPHIE: I weiß net[4].
Hans, ich hab's doch selbst g'sehn. Die meisten hab'n doch Angst, die Flugblätter überhaupt mitzunehmen oder zu lesen.

HANS: Ach, hör auf, außerdem ist des meine Sache.

Er geht ins Bad.

BADEZIMMER

Sophie steht neben Hans, der sich wäscht.

HANS: Einer muss doch mal den ersten Schritt machen. Wie sollen die Leute Mut finden, wie sollen sie sich wehren ...?
Immer haben sie das Gefühl, alleine dazustehn.
Schau – an der Front. Jeden Moment kann's mich da erwischen. Aber hier ... weiß ich wenigstens, wofür.
Schluss, aus! Ich mag nicht mehr.
Kümmere dich nicht um Sachen, von denen du nichts verstehst.

Sophie wendet sich erbost ab, geht hinaus. Sie wirft die Tür zu.

1 Steuerakten: tax files
2 Sie haben die Jugendgruppe aufgerollt. = Sie haben die Jugendgruppe verboten und Mitglieder verhaftet. Diese Jugendgruppe von Hans gab es schon vor dem Dritten Reich; ihr Merkmal war liberales und international ausgerichtetes Denken.
3 Wehrmacht = die deutsche Armee im Dritten Reich
4 I weiß net = Ich weiß nicht.

What do you think the following sentences in the text mean?

Unsere Familie ist für die Gestapo kein unbeschriebenes Blatt.
Man muss den Leuten doch sagen, was wirklich los ist.
Verstehst du, wenn jemand unsere Flugblätter liest, vielleicht redet der offen mit anderen darüber.
Die meisten hab'n doch Angst, die Flugblätter überhaupt mitzunehmen oder zu lesen.
Jeden Moment kann's mich da erwischen.

Resistance or not? What arguments does Hans have, and Sophie?

Hans	**Sophie**
Man muss sagen, was los ist.	Familie ist in Gefahr.

München, 17.2.1943

Liebe Lisa,

ich lasse mir gerade das Forellenquintett vom Grammophon vorspielen. Am liebsten möchte ich da selbst eine Forelle sein, wenn ich mir das Andantino anhöre. ...
O, ich freue mich wieder so sehr auf den Frühling. Man spürt und riecht in diesem Ding von Schubert förmlich die Lüfte und Düfte und vernimmt den ganzen Jubel der Vögel und der ganzen Kreatur. Die Wiederholung des Themas durch das Klavier – wie kaltes, klares, perlendes Wasser, oh, es kann einen entzücken.

Lass doch bald von dir hören.
Herzlichst

deine Sophie

aus dem letzten Brief von Sophie Scholl

Am nächsten Tag wurden Sophie und Hans Scholl in der Universität verhaftet.
Der Hausmeister hatte sie beobachtet, wie sie Flugblätter vor den Hörsälen auslegten.

Baummieter

Trees and forests have always been an important symbol for Germans. They give expression to both dreams and fears. "The Germans still like to seek out the forest where their ancestors once lived, and feel at one with the trees," wrote Elias Canetti. The Blaue Blume of the age of romanticism is also part of this tradition of the love of woods and nature.

After the Second World War, great tracts of forest were felled by the population and the Allies because firewood, and also wood for building, was in short supply. But the Germans founded the "Association for the Protection of the German Forest", and thus ensured re-forestation was achieved, faster in fact than the rebuilding of German towns and cities. Today Germany again has as much forest as it did 600 years ago. A quarter of the total area of the country is covered by forest.

In 1978, when first reports appeared in the German press about the poor state of the forests, the whole nation was confounded. The term *Waldsterben* (death of the forest) was created and was immediately in general use. The ecological movement in Germany developed more vigorously in Germany because of the threat to the forests.

Closely linked to this emotional realtionship to forest is the hiking movement, with its well-organized mountain walking and hiking clubs. In 1994, two million hikers were counted on 90,000 organized hikes, focussing mainly on wooded countryside.

In a place where forest plays such a key role, it's easy to politicize it. When the national socialists were preparing for World War II, they compared the army with the forests. A well-disciplined army was like a marching forest, in which the individual was nothing but a part of a larger whole and hence also ready to die for that larger whole.

This has changed substantially. After 1945, the military lost much of their status in society. There is hardly a country in the world where military symbolism is so poorly developed as in Germany.

Simultaneously the symbolic quality of woodland has changed. Parallels could only be drawn between the forest and the army because the forests were largely monocultures with the trees planted in orderly straight lines. Nowadays we know that such forests are much more susceptible to pollutants, disease and parasites than the original mixed forests. This is why environmentalists, forestry experts and lovers of forest nowadays advocate mixed forest, with lots of varieties of trees, a forest of individuals.

The Austrian artist Friedensreich Hundertwasser was also a passionate lover of "tree-people". He had the idea of adopting trees as tenants in flats and living together with them.

Learning strategies

We deliberately decided to do without explanations and exercises in this last unit of the book. It is up to you to find the Blaue Blume that points you on the right path to enriching your knowledge of German from the materials that are offered. However, with the listening text on Friedensreich Hundertwasser it is a good idea to read the text about the artist and to look closely at the illustrations and captions before you listen. They reflect the topics that are dealt with in the listening text.

Baummieter

Auckland, Neuseeland, 9. Juni 1973,
Winter

Caro Giulio Macchi,

endlich habe ich Zeit mich um die Triennale von Mailand zu kümmern.
Ich bin sehr geehrt, dass ich dran teilnehmen kann. Ich habe viele Ideen zu realisieren.
Erstes Projekt: Ein Baum oder mehrere Bäume sollen aus den Fenstern wachsen. Große Bäume aus dem dritten oder vierten Stock zum Beispiel.
In einem Haus in der Ausstellung oder nicht weit davon. Dies soll etwas Bleibendes sein, also nicht nur für die Ausstellung.

Um ein Beispiel zu geben: So viel Raum in der monotonen, sterilen Stadt ist nicht bewohnt. Also warum soll nicht ein Baum anstatt eines Menschen in einer Wohnung wohnen, wenn der Sauerstoff rar wird? Man braucht nur ein Fenster einer Wohnung und etwas Raum dahinter.

Dies ist etwas sehr Wichtiges und kann die Städte mehr revolutionieren, als wenn man nur die Dächer mit Wäldern bedeckt. Denn die Baummieter, die sich aus den Fenstern lehnen, die sieht man schon von weitem, an denen kann sich jeder freuen, die Dachgärten und Dachwälder sieht man meist von der Straße nicht. ...

Friedensreich Hundertwasser

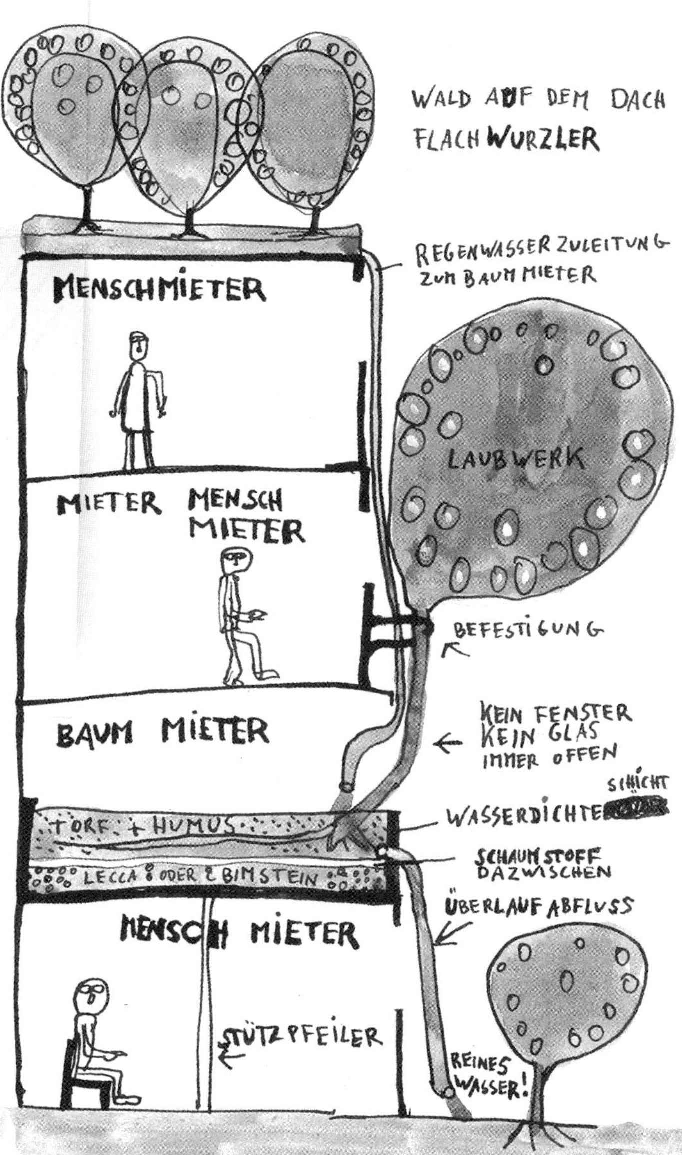

Liebe Hausbewohner!

Wir freuen uns einen Beitrag zur Verbesserung der Lebensqualität in Ihrem Bereich leisten zu können. In Ihrem Haus werden fünf Baummieter nach Entwürfen von Hundertwasser einziehen. Die Baummieter bewohnen einen zirka vier Quadratmeter großen loggiaartigen Wohnbereich, welcher vom menschlichen Wohnraum fachgerecht getrennt wird. Es werden drei Baummieter aus Fenstern im ersten Stock direkt über der Zentralsparkasse und zwei Baummieter zu ebener Erde direkt aus der Bank herauswachsen. Die Vorteile hauseigener Baummieter sind unbestritten und vielfältig. Da die Straße wegen des Verkehrs und der Untergrundeinrichtungen für Baumpflanzungen weitgehend ausfällt, Dachbepflanzungen jedoch meist Penthousecharakter annehmen und für den Mann auf der Straße unsichtbar bleiben und auch aus konstruktionellen Gründen oft unmöglich sind, bieten sich die senkrechten Hausfassaden zu einer Bewaldung der Stadt an.

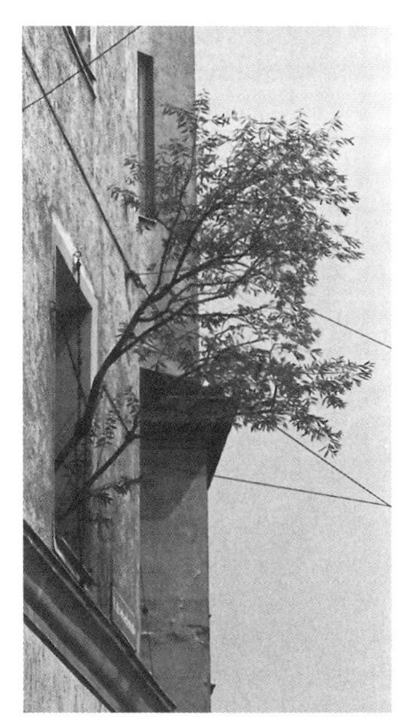

Baummieter Alserbachstraße, Wien 1983

Hier nur einige der Vorteile:

1. Baummieter, das heißt Bäume, die aus dem Fenster wachsen, sind weithin sichtbar und kommen vielen Menschen zugute.
2. Baummieter erzeugen Sauerstoff.
3. Baummieter verbessern das Stadt- und Wohnklima beträchtlich durch Milderung der Feucht-Trocken-Warm-Kalt-Gegensätze. Weniger Kopfweh – mehr Wohlbefinden.
4. Baummieter sind eine perfekte Staubschluck- und Staubfilteranlage. Besonders der feine, giftige Staub, den auch die Staubsauger nicht schlucken können, wird von den Baummietern in ihrem Bereich weitgehend neutralisiert und abgebaut. Die Hausfrau hat weniger Staub in der Wohnung.
5. Der Straßenlärm wird bedeutend gemildert, da die Echowirkung der senkrechten Häuserschluchten eingedämmt wird.
6. Baummieter bilden einen teilweisen Sichtschutz und erzeugen Geborgenheit.
7. Da die Baummieter mit wenigen Kubikmetern Erde auskommen müssen, können sie sich nicht zu großen Bäumen entwickeln. Daher wird die schattenspendende Eigenschaft sehr beschränkt bleiben. Sonne und Licht gelangen also gut auch an die Fenster, vor denen Baummieter wachsen, insbesondere im Winter, wenn die Blätter abgefallen sind.
8. Keine Belästigung durch Spinnen und Ameisen, da diese nicht in Bäumen wohnen. Hoffentlich kommen jedoch Schmetterlinge und Vögel.
9. So kommt die Schönheit und Lebensfreude wieder im Zusammenleben mit einem Stück hauseigener Natur.

Imagine you live in this building and have received this letter.

Which arguments sound convincing? What objections do you have?
What sort of questions do you ask yourself?

Write a text on one of the following topics.

Mit einem Baummieter leben – ein Menschmieter erzählt
Baummieter und Menschmieter im Gespräch miteinander

Gegen die gerade Linie – ein Künstlerleben

Er war ein kompromissloser Künstler gegen die gerade Linie: Friedrich Stowasser wurde 1928 in Wien als Sohn jüdischer Eltern geboren. Während der NS-Zeit besuchte er die Montessori-Schule. Er wurde wie durch ein Wunder nicht deportiert, musste aber mit ansehen, wie die meisten seiner Verwandten in Konzentrationslager abtransportiert wurden. Nach dem Krieg begann er ein Kunststudium. Doch schon nach drei Monaten brach er es ab und ging auf Reisen, nach Italien, Paris – wo er seinen Künstlernamen Friedensreich Hundertwasser annahm – Nordafrika. In den 50er und 60er Jahren entwickelte er seinen bunten, unverwechselbaren Stil. Anfang der 80er wurde Hundertwasser Leiter der Meisterschule für Malerei an der Akademie der Bildenden Künste Wien. In dieser Zeit wurde auch aus dem Maler der Architekt Hundertwasser. Am 19. Februar 2000 starb Friedensreich Hundertwasser auf dem Weg in seine zweite Heimat Neuseeland.

aus: Abendzeitung

Sein Lieblingsmotiv: die Spirale

Seine zweite Heimat Neuseeland

Friedensreich Hundertwasser

1983 bis 1985 schuf der Künstler sein erstes großes Bauwerk, das Hundertwasser-Haus in der Wiener Löwengasse.

Baum-Sprache

Ich könnte Bäume ausreißen!

den Wald vor Bäumen nicht sehen

Die Bäume wachsen nicht in den Himmel.

Wie der Baum, so die Früchte.

Der Apfel fällt nicht weit vom Stamm.

Alte Bäume lassen sich nicht mehr biegen.

Drunt' in der grünen Au
Steht a Birnbaum so blau, Juchhe
Drunt' in der grünen Au
Steht a Birnbaum so blau.
Was wächst auf dem Baum?
A wunderschöner Ast!
Ast auf dem Baum, Baum in der Au
Drunt' in der grünen Au
Steht a Birnbaum so blau.

Was wächst an dem Ast?
A wunderschöner Zweig!
Zweig an dem Ast, Ast auf dem Baum ...

Was ist auf dem Zweig?
A wunderschönes Nest!
Nest auf dem Zweig ...

Was ist in dem Nest?
A wunderschönes Ei!
Ei im Nest ...

Was ist in dem Ei?
A wunderschöner Vogel!
Vogel im Ei ...

Was hat denn der Vogel?
Gar wunderschöne Federn!
Federn.

Was wird aus den Federn?
A wunderschönes Bett!
Bett aus Federn ...

Wer liegt in dem Bett?
A wunderschönes Dirndl!
Dirndl im Bett ...

Volkslied

Der Pflaumenbaum

Im Hofe steht ein Pflaumenbaum
Der ist so klein, man glaubt es kaum.
Er hat ein Gitter drum
So tritt ihn keiner um.

Der Kleine kann nicht größer wer'n.
Ja, größer wer'n, das möcht er gern.
's ist keine Red davon
Er hat zu wenig Sonn.

Den Pflaumenbaum glaubt man ihm kaum
Weil er nie eine Pflaume hat
Doch er ist ein Pflaumenbaum
Man kennt es an dem Blatt.

Bertolt Brecht

Ein Fichtenbaum steht einsam
Im Norden auf kahler Höh.
Ihn schläfert; mit weißer Decke
Umhüllen ihn Eis und Schnee.

Er träumt von einer Palme
Die fern im Morgenland
Einsam und schweigend trauert
Auf brennender Felsenwand.

Heinrich Heine

Register

Register

Quellenverzeichnis

Titelfoto: Photonica, Hamburg (Meredith Heuer) **Seite 2:** Gedicht von Norbert Höchtlen aus: Hans-Joachim Gelberg (Hrsg.) Überall und neben dir. © 1986 Beltz Verlag, Weinheim und Basel, Programm Beltz & Gelberg, Weinheim **Seite 3:** Hörtext aus: Gerhard Polt/ Hanns Christian Müller, Da schau her, © 1984 by Haffmans Verlag AG, Zürich **Seite 4:** Bildgeschichte von Paul Maar aus: Dann wird es wohl das Nashorn sein. © 1988 Beltz Verlag, Weinheim und Basel, Programm Beltz & Gelberg, Weinheim **Seite 6:** Bahn-Card-Formular: Deutsche Bahn AG **Seite 7:** Original-Umschlag von Comenius „Orbis Pictus": Harenberg Edition, Die bibliophilen Taschenbücher Nr. 30, © 1978 Harenberg Kommunikation, Dortmund; Abbildung: AKG Berlin **Seite 8:** Abbildung Der Mensch aus: „Orbis Pictus" siehe oben Seite 7; Gedicht von Hans Jürgen Schumacher aus: Die letzte Umarmung, © 1997 Kinder- und Jugendbuch Verlag Mückenschwein, Stralsund * **Seite 9:** Wörterbuchauszüge aus: Langenscheidts Großwörterbuch Deutsch als Fremdsprache, Neubearbeitung 1998, Langenscheidt KG, München **Seite 10:** Abbildungen und Ausschnitt aus: „Orbis Pictus" siehe oben Seite 7 **Seite 11:** Abbildung: AKG Berlin; Text aus: Das neue Duden-Lexikon, © 1991 Bibliographisches Institut & F.A. Brockhaus AG, Mannheim **Seite 13/14:** Cartoons aus: Schreibsucht. Gasterzähler am Werk. Hrsg. Paul Portmann und Autorinnen, © Paul Portmann-Tselikas, Graz **Seite 16:** Inhaltsverzeichnis aus: Michael Winkler, Deutsche Literatur im Exil 1933-1945, © 1972 Philipp Reclam Verlag, Stuttgart **Seite 18:** Bild Agata und Semra aus: Helga Glantschnig (Hrsg.), Blume ist Kind von Wiese, © 1993 Luchterhand Literaturverlag, München; Foto: MHV-Archiv (Werner Bönzli) **Seite 22/23:** Bildunterschriften aus: Zeitmagazin Nr. 22 vom 24.05.96 (Synästhetiker sehen mehr als andere: Sie haben einen 6. Sinn); Bilder von Michael Dannenmann, Düsseldorf **Seite 27:** Foto: Hubert Eichheim **Seite 28:** B, F: du, Die Zeitschrift der Kultur, Zürich; C: AKG Berlin; D: Zürich Tourismus; E: Sonnenuhr des mittelalterlichen Bauern aus: Anton Lübke, Das große Uhrenbuch, © Wasmuth Verlag, Tübingen **Seite 30:** Nacht in der Wildnis von Josef Guggenmos aus: Sonne, Mond und Luftballon, © 1991 Beltz Verlag, Weinheim und Basel, Programm Beltz & Gelberg, Weinheim **Seite 33:** Foto: Süddeutscher Verlag, Bilderdienst (AP), DIZ München **Seite 34:** Zitat aus: Krämer/Trenkler, Lexikon der populären Irrtümer, © 1996 Eichborn Verlag, Frankfurt **Seite 40/41:** Bildgeschichte von Erich Rauschenbach/ Cartoon-Caricature-Contor München, www.c5.net **Seite 41:** Foto: Süddeutscher Verlag, Bilderdienst (Hipp-Photo), DIZ München **Seite 43:** Foto: Hubert Eichheim **Seite 44:** Foto A + C + Seite 46: Manfred Schwaiger-Rupp, Stuttgart; B + D: MHV-Archiv (Michael Sailer); E: AKG Berlin (Paul Almasy); F: MHV-Archiv (Dieter Reichler) **Seite 45:** Hör- und Lesetext „Guten Tag": M + T: Thommie Bayer/Bernhard Lassahn © by Neue Welt Musikverlag GmbH, München **Seite 48:** Fotos: MHV-Archiv (links: Michael Sailer, rechts: Dieter Reichler) **Seite 49:** Hörtext: Oh, wann kommst du (Miriam Frances) © Tabestry Music Ltd., Essex Musikvertrieb GmbH, Hamburg **Seite 50:** Zeichnung von Paul Maar aus: Onkel Florians Flohmarkt, © 1977 Verlag Friedrich Oetinger, Hamburg **Seite 51:** Globus-Infografik, Hamburg **Seite 52:** Bildgeschichte von Clothing Poth/CCC, www.c5.net; Wörterbuchauszug aus: Langenscheidts Großwörterbuch Deutsch als Fremdsprache, Neubearbeitung 1998, Langenscheidt KG, München **Seite 58:** Hör- und Lesetext: Heute hier, morgen dort. Text: Hannes Wader, Komponist: Gary Bolstadt, © Aktive Musik Verlagsgesellschaft mbH, Dortmund **Seite 61:** Bildgeschichte: Marie Marcks, Heidelberg **Seite 63:** Foto aus dem Film „Man spricht deutsch" © Deutsches Filminstitut, Frankfurt **Seite 64/65:** Gedicht von Roswitha Fröhlich aus: Hans-Joachim Gelberg (Hrsg.), Der fliegende Robert, © 1991 Beltz Verlag, Weinheim und Basel, Programm Beltz & Gelberg, Weinheim **Seite 69:** Abbildung und Text: Mark Twain, Illustration * **Seite 70:** Text von einem unbekannten Verfasser aus: ADAC motorwelt 5/96 © ADAC Verlag, München; Wörterbuchauszüge aus: Duden Universalwörterbuch © Bibliographisches Institut & F.A. Brockhaus AG, Mannheim **Seite 72/73:** Foto: Hubert Eichheim; Text von Hans Baumann aus: Hans-Joachim Gelberg (Hrsg.), Menschengeschichten, © 1975 Beltz Verlag, Weinheim und Basel, Programm Beltz & Gelberg, Weinheim **Seite 74:** Gedicht von Josef Guggenmos aus: Sieben kleine Bären, © 1971 Georg Bitter Verlag, Recklinghausen * **Seite 75:** Gedicht von Paul Maar aus: Dann wird es wohl das Nashorn sein, © 1988 Beltz Verlag, Weinheim und Basel, Programm Beltz & Gelberg, Weinheim **Seite 79:** Bildgeschichte von de Bosc © by Erika Lüning, Krummesse **Seite 82:** Bildgeschichte „Weibsbilder" © Amelie Holtfreter-Glienke, Berlin **Seite 87/88:** Fotos: Hubert Eichheim **Seite 89:** Foto: Gerd Pfeiffer, München **Seite 90:** Text von Gerhard Abele aus: Stehkneipen, Gespräche an der Theke © G. Abele, München **Seite 92:** Hör- und Lesetext: Der Mann am Klavier, Musik: Horst Heinz Henning, Text: Heinz Therningsohn/Chris Neuhausen, © 1954 by Melodie der Welt, J. Michel KG, Musikverlag, Frankfurt/Main. Abdruck erfolgt mit freundlicher Genehmigung von Melodie der Welt, J. Michel KG, Musikversand, Frankfurt am Main. **Seite 95:** Foto: AP-Photo/ Keystone/L. Ehmann **Seite 96:** Foto: Jutta Duhm-Heitzmann; Text aus: Mitten ins Herz, Edition Braus, © Bettina Flitner, Köln **Seite 97:** Fotos: MHV-Archiv (Michael Sailer) **Seite 100:** Hör- und Lesetext: Ich hab' mein Herz in Heidelberg verloren, Text: Beda und Ernst Neubach, Musik: Fred Raymond, Boheme Verlag, Berlin **Seite 101:** Diagramm der Bevölkerungspyramide vom Statistischen Bundesamt, Berlin **Seite 102:** Hör- und Lesetext: Halloh, Halloh, ich suche eine Frau von Joachim Neck-Schippel, © by Florida Musikverlag, A. Seith, München **Seite 104:** Foto von Elisabeth Ecknigk **Seite 106:** Phantomfoto © Polizeipräsidium München **Seite 107:** Hintergrundbild von Meinholf Neuhäuser * **Seite 112:** Bildgeschichte von Janosch aus: Hans-Joachim Gelberg (Hrsg.), Der fliegende Robert, © 1991 Beltz Verlag, Weinheim und Basel, Programm Beltz & Gelberg, Weinheim **Seite 113:** Foto: MHV-Archiv (Michael Sailer) **Seite 114/115:** Foto und Text aus SZ-Magazin vom 04.04.1999, Süddeutsche Zeitung Magazin, München **Seite 117:** Text von Hans Manz aus: Welt der Wörter, © 1991 Beltz Verlag, Weinheim und Basel, Programm Beltz & Gelberg, Weinheim **Seite 119:** Bild von Felix Nussbaum, Privatbesitz Osnabrück © VG Bild-Kunst Bonn 2001 (Christian Grovermann, Foto Strenger) **Seite 120/121:** Bildgeschichte von Angelika Kaufmann aus: Hans-Joachim Gelberg (Hrsg.) Der Fliegende Robert, ©1991 Beltz Verlag, Weinheim und Basel, Programm Beltz & Gelberg Weinheim **Seite 126:** Hör- und Lesetext von der Gruppe Clinch aus der LP „Gefühlsarm, Text: Wefel (Copyright unbekannt)* **Seite 127/128:** Fotos: Gerd Pfeiffer, München; Text „und" von Susanne Kilian, Eltville **Seite 132/153:** Bildgeschichte von Paul Maar aus: Onkel Florians Flohmarkt © Verlag Friedrich Oetinger, Hamburg **Seite 135/136:** Abbildungen und Text aus: Antoine de Saint-Exupéry, Der Kleine Prinz, © 1950 und 1998 Karl Rauch Verlag Düsseldorf **Seite 141:** Zeichnung von Karl Wächter © by Karl Wächter, Frankfurt/Main **Seite 142:** Text „Ich denke" von Hans Manz aus: Vorlesebuch Religion von Steinwede/Ruprecht, © Verlag Ernst Kaufmann, Lahr **Seite 143:** Bild und Text von Ulrich Engel aus: Deutsche Grammatik, Heidelberg, Groos, Tokyo, Sansya Publ. 1988, S. 705 (Bild) und 706 (Text) **Seite 145:** Foto: dpa (Baum) **Seite 146:** Text von Rudolf Otto Wiemer * **Seite 150:** Text von Thomas Brasch aus: Der schöne 27. September, © 1980 Suhrkamp Verlag, Frankfurt am Main **Seite 154:** Hörtext: „Theater" von Eduard von Jan und Claudia Hümmler-Hille aus: Hören Sie mal! 2 © Max Hueber Verlag, Ismaning **Seite 155:** Hintergrundbild: MHV-Archiv (Dieter Reichler) **Seite 156:** Fotos: Arbeitsgemeinschaft ‚Stadtteilmarketing Mümmelsmannsberg' Kommunikationsbüro Bettina Soltau, Hamburg; Hör- und Lesetext: Sie wohnt auf dem Mond von Hans Scheibner, Musik: Berry Sarluis © 1976 by Moorea Music Hamburg **Seite 158:** Text aus BISS 5/1997, München **Seite 161:** Foto: AP-Photo/B. Kammerer **Seite 162:** Foto: H. Rüffler, München **Seite 163:** Text aus: Brigitte 9/1996 (Blaulicht – Gespräch mit Michael Wüst, THW, Freising) © Picture Press, Hamburg **Seite 164/165:** Foto: Hubert Eichheim; Hör- und Lesetext: Rüstige Alte, Team 50plus – Die älteste Greenpeace-Aktivistin Deutschlands von Ursula Schwarzer aus: Hörfunksendung des Bayerischen Rundfunks (BR 2 Notizbuch vom 27.05.98) **Seite 169:** Zeichnung von Georg Grosz aus: Das neue Gesicht der herrschenden Klasse, © 1930 Malik Verlag, Berlin * **Seite 170:** Text von J. Ubaldo Ribeiro aus: Ein Brasilianer in Berlin © 1994 Suhrkamp Verlag, Frankfurt am Main **Seite 176:** Hör- und Lesetext: Deutschland ist... Text: Gunter Gabriel/Michael Kunze, Musik: Gunter Gabriel © 1990 by EDITION NAZ der EMI MUSIC PUBLISHING GERMANY GMBH & Co. KG, Hamburg **Seite 177:** Foto: Hubert Eichheim **Seite 178/179:** Text von Wolfdietrich Schnurre aus: Ich frag ja bloß © 1973 Paul List Verlag, München

Seite 185: Foto: Gerd Pfeiffer, München **Seite 186/187:** Text von Sabine Ehrentreich, Badische Zeitung vom 03.01.1998 **Seite 187:** Abbildung aus: Lutz Röhrich, Lexikon der sprichwörtlichen Redensarten. Band 3. Herder/Spektrum Bd. 4800 © 1999 Herder Verlag, Freiburg, 15. Auflage; Wörterbuchauszüge aus: Duden, Deutsches Universalwörterbuch, © 1996 Bibliographisches Institut & F.A. Brockhaus AG, Mannheim **Seite 190:** Zeichnung von Tomi Ungerer aus: Das Spiel ist aus. Werkschau 1956-1995, © 1995 Jonas Verlag, Marburg **Seite 191:** Abbildung und Text von Sabine Model, Heitersheim **Seite 193:** Abbildung aus: http://www.bio-chart.com **Seite 194:** Text von Elna Utermöhle und Ennio Flaiano zitiert aus: Bonus 12/96. Das Magazin der Volksbanken und Raiffeisenbanken **Seite 197:** Text von Max Frisch zitiert aus: Stich-Worte. Ausgesucht von Uwe Johnson, © 1975 Suhrkamp Verlag, Frankfurt/Main **Seite 199:** Foto: AP-Photo/R. Pfeil **Seite 200:** Text aus: DIE WELT vom 13.11.1995, Axel Springer Verlag, Hamburg; Foto: Ullstein Bilderdienst, Berlin **Seite 205/206:** Bildgeschichte von Kamagurka aus: Titanic 6/1997, © BVBA KZL Kamagurka, Gent (Belgien) **Seite 207:** Foto: Ullstein Bilderdienst, Berlin **Seite 208:** Karikatur von Ernst Hürlimann/CCC, www.c5.net **Seite 209:** Text von Petra Schmitt aus: Stern 14/81-19/81, Picture Press, Hamburg **Seite 213:** Foto: Ullstein Bilderdienst, Berlin **Seite 214/215:** Abbildung: Bundesarchiv, Koblenz; Interview von Ursula Lebert über „Was macht die Liebe aus?" aus: Brigitte 4/97, Picture Press, Hamburg **Seite 218:** Karikatur aus: Haarscharf hrsg. von Ernesto Clusellas/Klein, © 1985 Carusell-Verlag, Michelsneukirchen, Seite 30 * **Seite 219:** Abbildung: AKG Berlin **Seite 220:** Text aus: Krämer/Trenkler Lexikon der populären Irrtümer, Eichborn AG, Frankfurt/Main **Seite 222:** Globus Infografik, Hamburg **Seite 225:** Foto: AKG, Berlin **Seite 226:** Text von Heinrich Spoerl zitiert aus: Man kann ruhig darüber sprechen. Heitere Geschichten und Plaudereien. Aschehoug Dansk Forlag A/S, Copenhaben **Seite 229:** Hör- und Lesetext „Ganz Einfach" von Gerhard Schöne (Gesang und Text) aus der CD: Menschenskind © by Gerhard Schöne, Berlin **Seite 230:** Text von Karlheinz Geißler, München; Wirtschaftswoche-Grafik „Immer mehr Freizeit" vom 17.04.1997, © Verlagsgruppe Handelsblatt (Genios), Düsseldorf **Seite 231:** Hintergrundbild:

Quellenverzeichnis

Ullstein Bilderdienst, Berlin; Texte: Willy Brandt, Aus dem Bericht zur Lage der Nation am 14. Januar 1970; Willi Stoph, Aus der Grundsatzerklärung in Erfurt am 19. März 1979 **Seite 232:** Text von Freya Klier, Agentur für Autorenrechte Monica Böhme, Hamburg **Seite 233:** Gedicht von Rainer Kunze aus: ders., einundzwanzig variationen über das thema „die post". In: ders., Gespräch mit der Amsel, © 1984 S. Fischer Verlag GmbH, Frankfurt/Main; Abbildung aus: Vom Gestern zum Heute. 200 Jahre deutsche Geschichte in Texten und Dokumenten, Hrsg. Rosemarie Wildermuth © 1987 Ellermann Verlag, München; Text von Christa Wolf aus der Danksagung nach Empfang des Bremer Literaturpreises 1977, zitiert nach SZ vom 11./12.02.1978 **Seite 234:** Text von Regine Hildebrandt aus: Wer sich nicht bewegt hat schon verloren, © 1997 Verlag J.H.W. Dietz Nachfolger, Bonn; Foto: Ullstein Bilderdienst, Berlin **Seite 236:** Hör- und Lesetext „50 Jahre Deutschland – Jahrgang 49 – aufgewachsen in zwei deutschen Staaten" von Felix Kuballa, © WDR Köln **Seite 237:** Fotos: AP-Photo/H.J. Knipperitz/F. Rumpenhorst **Seite 238/239:** Bildgeschichte von Heidrun Petridel aus: Hans-Joachim Gelberg (Hrsg.) Geh und spiel mit dem Riesen, © 1972 Beltz Verlag, Weinheim und Basel, Programm Beltz & Gelberg, Weinheim; Fotos: Andreas Tomaszewski, Ismaning **Seite 241:** Hör- und Lesetext „Ein Dichter sieht Hände" von Bettina Weiz und Hildegard Fendt aus der Hörfunksendung „Die Geschichte der Hand" des Bayerischen Rundfunks (BR 2 Notizbuch vom 25.02.1997); Foto: Ullstein Bilderdienst, Berlin; Hörtext „Ich küsse Ihre Hand Madame" Komponist: Ralph Erwin, Text: Fritz Rotter, © August Seith Musikverlag, München **Seite 243:** Foto: Gerd Pfeiffer, München **Seite 245:** Text von Wolfdietrich Schnurre aus: Der Schattenfotograf, © 1994 Paul List Verlag, München **Seite 246:** Foto: WDR Köln; Text aus dem Buch: Jürgen Domian, Extreme Leben © 1198 vgs verlagsgesellschaft, Köln **Seite 247:** Hörtext „Zeit haben" von H. Troxler aus: Hörfunksendung des Bayerischen Rundfunks (BR 2 Notizbuch vom 24.12.1998)* **Seite 249:** Karte aus: Schweizer Brevier © Kümmerly + Frey AG, Zollikofen – Bern **Seite 251:** Text von Peter Bichsel aus: Des Schweizers Schweiz © 1997 Suhrkamp Verlag, Frankfurt/Main **Seite 254:** Text aus: BuchJournal Special. Schweiz Heft 3, Herbst 1998; Hrsg. Börsenverein des Deutschen Buchhandels, Frankfurt/Main; Abbildung von Wilhelm Tell aus der Zentral- und Hochschulbibliothek, Luzern; Foto von Baseler Fastnacht © Basel Tourismus; Bild von H. Nägeli aus: Mein Revoltieren, mein Sprayen, © 1983 Benteli Verlag, Bern **Seite 256:** Text 1 + 2 zitiert aus: Internationales Handbuch – Länder aktuell, Munzinger-Archiv, Ravensburg; Text 3 zitiert aus: Merian, Die Schweiz, S. 36, Reise durch Jura, Mittelland und Alpen; Text 4 zitiert aus: Merian, die Schweiz, S. 16, Me cha nöd chlage; Text 5 zitiert aus: Merian, Die Schweiz, S. 29, Behagen am Komfort. © Hoffmann und Campe Verlag vom 03.05.1998 **Seite 258:** Text von Waltraud Legros aus: Was die Wörter erzählen. Eine kleine etymologische Fundgrube © 1997 Deutscher Taschenbuch Verlag, München **Seite 262/263:** Text von Martin Wüst aus: Grosstalk, 9/1997, crossair, Basel **Seite 267:** Foto: Süddeutscher Verlag, Bilderdienst, DIZ München (Karlheinz Egginger) **Seite 268-272:** Hör- und Lesetext „Ein Weg zurück": Marion Hollerung **Seite 273:** Foto: Süddeutscher Verlag, Bilderdienst, DIZ München (Martin Fejer) **Seite 274:** Text von Jan Yoors aus: Die Zigeuner. Aus dem Englischen von Ursula Heilamnn © 1967 by Jan Yoors. Klett-Cotta, Stuttgart 1970. Abdruck der deutschen Übersetzung mit freundlicher Genehmigung des Verlages Klett-Cotta. **Seite 277:** Hör- und Lesetext „Schwarzer Zigeuner" Text: Fritz Löhner-Beda, Musik: Karel Vacek, © by Statni Tschechischer Staatsverlag, Prag, für Tschech. Republik. © by Dacapo Verlag, Eva Hein, Wien, für alle Länder der Welt. © by Wiener Arion Musikverlag Ges.m.b.H. Wien. Melodie der Welt, J. Michel KG, Musikverlag, Frankfurt/Main, für Deutschland. **Seite 278:** Text aus Weltwoche aktuell 16/98 © Weltwoche Zürich **Seite 279:** Abbildung: Ullstein Bilderdienst, Berlin **Seite 280:** Text von Bernhard Lasahn aus: Land mit lila Kühen, © Verlagsgruppe Random House, München **Seite 283:** Text von Wolf Schneider zitiert aus: Deutsch für Kenner © 1988 Bertelsmann Verlag, Gütersloh **Seite 286:** Texte A-C aus: Marketing für Deutschland, Hrsg. Wirtschaftsjunioren Deutschland, Berlin **Seite 287:** Text von Hans Weigel zitiert aus: Das Land ohne Hymnen, © 1954 Steingrüben Verlag, Stuttgart **Seite 288:** Hör- und Lesetext „Taubenvergiften" von Georg Kreisler, Basel **Seite 290/291:** Hör- und Lesetext „In der Buchhandlung" von Gerhard Polt/Hanns-Christian Müller aus: Da schau her © 1984 by Haffmans Verlag AG, Zürich **Seite 292:** Bildgeschichte von Erich Rauschenbach aus: Schüler-Sprüche Nr. 3, Hrsg. Christian Roman, © 1986 by Eichborn Verlag AG, Frankfurt/Main **Seite 293:** Text von Peter Bichsel aus: Der Leser. Das Erzählen, © 1997 by Suhrkamp Verlag Frankfurt am Main **Seite 295:** Foto: Ullstein Bilderdienst, Berlin; Text von Juliane Becker aus: AZ vom 28./29.03.1998, Verlag Die Abendzeitung, München **Seite 300:** Bild von Franz Xaver Winterthaler, Kunsthistorisches Museum, Wien; Hörtext „Kaiserin Elisabeth von Österreich" aus: Frauen der bayerischen Geschichte, Moderation: Angelika Schneiderat, Leitung der Sendereihe ‚Sonntags geöffnet': Christine Klumbies, Hörfunksendung des Bayerischen Rundfunks (BR 2 am 06.09.98) **Seite 301:** Foto: Musik + Show, Claus Lange, Hamburg (Namia Botsch) **Seite 302/303:** Hör- und Lesetext „Warum" Musik + Text: Thorsten Boerger © George Glueck Music GmbH c/o Sony/ATV Music Publishing (Germany) GmbH, Berlin **Seite 305/306:** Fotos: Ullstein Bilderdienst, Berlin **Seite 306/307:** Hör- und Lesetext „Ramstein"/Böhmen am Meer aus: Ach, Europa! von Hans Magnus Enzensberger © Suhrkamp Verlg, Frankfurt am Main, Originalton aus dem Hörspiel vom WDR am 02.06.1988 **Seite 309:** Foto von Isolde Ohlbaum, München **Seite 310:** Text von Elias Canetti aus: Die gerettete Zunge © 1978 Carl Hanser Verlag, München – Wien **Seite 311:** Kreislaufgeschichte von Hans Manz aus: Die Welt der Wörter, Sprachbuch für Kinder und Neugierige, © 1991 Beltz Verlag, Weinheim und Basel, Programm Beltz & Gelberg, Weinheim **Seite 312:** Fotos: Hubert Eichheim **Seite 314:** Text oben von Kurt Tucholsky zitiert aus: Zeitungsdeutsch und Briefstil. Gesammelte Werke, © 1960 Rowohlt Verlag, Reinbek; Text unten von Peter Bichsel aus: Schulmeistereien, © 1998 Suhrkamp Verlag, Frankfurt am Main **Seite 315:** Foto: Gasthaus Peter's Stüberl, © Peter Keller, Wien **Seite 316:** Interview mit Bodo Schäfer aus: AZ vom 15.09.1998, Verlag Die Abendzeitung, München **Seite 319-326:** Briefe von Sophie und Inge Scholl/Foto auf Seite 320 © by Manuel Aicher, Dietikon/Geschwister Scholl Archiv, Rotis **Seite 324/325:** Foto aus dem Film „Die Weisse Rose" © Deutsches Filminstitut, Frankfurt/Main; Text aus dem Drehbuch von Michael Verhoeven, © von Loeper Literaturverlag, Karlsruhe **Seite 327:** Hintergrundfoto: Andreas Tomaszewski, Ismaning **Seite 328:** Abbildung: Hundertwasser, Baummieter, Tusche und Aquarell, 1976 © 2001 J. Harel, Wien **Seite 329:** Foto: Hundertwasser, Baummieter Alsterbach-Strasse, Wien, 1980 © 2002 J. Harel, Wien **Seite 330:** Hundertwasser-Spirale: 443 Sonne für die Kolchosen, Mixed media, 1960, © 2001 J. Harel, Wien; Hundertwasser auf dem Moped aus: Hundertwasser, Taschenverlag, Köln; Hundertwasser auf dem Dach: © plus 49, Hamburg (Gerd Ludwig); Hundertwasser-Haus: © Wien Tourismus; Text aus: AZ vom 28.02.2000; Verlag Die Abendzeitung, München **Seite 328/329:** Hör- und Lesetext von Ferry Radax aus einer Sendung vom WDR (ausgestrahlt in ARTE am 19.11.99) unter dem Titel „Hundertwasser – Leben in Spiralen" **Seite 331:** Gedicht von Bertold Brecht aus: Werke. Große kommentierte Berliner und Frankfurter Ausgabe, Band 12, © 1988 Suhrkamp Verlag Frankfurt am Main

Wir haben uns bemüht alle Inhaber von Bild- und Textrechten ausfindig zu machen. Sollten Rechteinhaber hier nicht aufgeführt sein, so wäre der Verlag für entsprechende Hinweise dankbar. Insbesondere bei den Angaben mit *.